Funny Money Universe

James Bolden

FUNNY MONEY UNIVERSE:
FROM YOUR STREET TO WALL STREET
by James E. Bolden

Cover Concept, Book Design
and Layout by Ryan Burkhart, Firsthand Creative, Austin, Texas

Photography by Jim McGuire Studios, Charlotte, North Carolina

Disclaimer: The information provided in this manual is not financial, legal, or any other form of professional advice. It is general information on financial, legal, and other issues commonly encountered by the general public. This manual is not financial, legal, or other professional advice; and, is not a substitute for an advisor, financial, and/or legal firm. I am not an advisor, attorney, or a financial advisor; and, nothing herein should be construed as or relied upon as financial or legal advice in lieu of seeking professional financial or legal counsel.

For further information about this book, please contact

Funny Money Universe
P.O. Box 5747
Florence, SC 29502-5747
www.theFMU.com

ISBN 0-6153551-9-6
ISBN 978-0-615-35519-1

This book is dedicated to all of those
who have stood in someone else's shadow...

Table of Contents

Introduction*

Be Careful What you Wish For

*If you are anything like me or my banker, before you make any commitments you are going to read the first page and the last page... let me help you out. Turn to my forward, "*The Last Word,*" which incidentally, is at the very end of my book. Then come back here if you are ready to take a promising financial journey.

Finally, I had made it!

It was a dream come true and even though I was living it, I still dared not believe it.

I had spent the better part of the past five years working toward one goal and consumed with reaching that very moment. Not until now had that work become real to me.

During those years, I had cut back, downsized, right-sized, and basically turned into a hermit in order to reach my goal. I also had been brow beaten, beaten up, beat down, and kicked to the curb. My financial battle scars were very real.

Those were five of the absolute roughest financial years of my life. But I did not care, I now know it was worth every scar.

I had to give up my independence and move into a cramped studio apartment with a long-time friend where I was treated more like an imprisoned child than an adult. I had no privacy, no voice, and nowhere else to go.

Although it was beyond nerve-wracking, I am so grateful to my friend now because her unconventional help broke my pride but not my spirit. She backed me so far into a corner that I had to succeed. I was forced to succeed! There were no other options.

My weekends were spent walking the streets of Foggy Bottom, and being jealous of all the others who could financially enjoy the amenities, the shopping, and fine dining experiences in the area where we lived, while all I was able to barely afford was a dream of a better future.

I did not have a wallet during those years because I had no money. I carried my driver's license, my metro card, my door keys, and the *list*. Nothing more was necessary.

My wardrobe remained unchanged for those five years, and everything I owned was packed into one traveler's trunk.

As for meals, a few of them actually came from select trash cans of my neighbors.

And the kicker to all this was that I had a full-time job making more than $60,000.00 per year as a young urban professional. But the truth is that I was flat broke!

But nothing was more important to me than the *list*. It completely ruled my life and dictated my every move. However, my survival was not the only matter at stake here. Others were counting on me to succeed. In fact, others, who will remain nameless for now, needed me to succeed.

So for the first time in my adult life I was learning how to succeed by developing the ability to think in practical terms.

You see, I had made a record number of bad financial moves, and even though I did not know how to fix them all, I kept them on my *list* because I promised myself one day I would make good on my obligations.

I was consumed with being debt free and worry free, and no sacrifice was too great to achieve this collective goal.

Most importantly, I was happy because my *list* had served its purpose of forcing me to make real financial choices unlike those previous decisions that lead to my own wilderness experience.

So again when it finally mentally registered that all my hard work had brought me the financial success I had drooled over for so long, all I could do was sit down in my own new apartment and shed a few tears.

Why?

Because that was the first private moment I had had in more than five years. Think about that for a moment.

I had gone from being a pauper to owning the *very* first one of the hottest new luxury sedans to hit the market. But this was no overnight success story.

I was now on the A-list for the best of the best of all spots in town, and I had every credit card imaginable in my wallet with unimaginable limits.

As I look back, I can hear my mother saying, "be careful what you wish for because you just might get it."

I never really understood what that meant until a few days ago.

Translated, what my mother was really saying was are you prepared to manage this new found success, and all that comes with it?

I was immediately reminded of Joseph.

Joseph had great dreams of success that were thrust upon him from the ground up, literally.

Genesis 37–50 tells Joseph's tremendous story. Actually there are several stories within the story, but I am going to focus on one point.

Joseph believed his dreams so much that he told his family. His family believed his dreams even more than he did, and their belief drove them to do unthinkable things.

Now while you and I have the benefit of seeing the end result, Joseph could only live day by day in faith. And this he did consistently.

Despite the fact that he was deceived by his brothers, thrown into a pit, twice sold into slavery, scorned of a woman, falsely accused, thrown into prison, and became ruler over all, Joseph never changed! His character was obedient and intact no matter where he found himself geographically.

Now you ask, what is my point?

Very simply, the difficulty of Joseph's everyday life prepared him to be successful under any circumstances, even as the ruler over all of Egypt – as a Hebrew.

I, on the other hand, was not prepared. In all my getting, I failed to get understanding.

You see, I was so focused on becoming rich that I did not think about how that would change me, or what to do with my money once I had complete control over it.

For example, we have all seen the tragic stories of individuals winning the lottery and being broker than broke a few years later. The reason why is that if your character has flaws in it before you become rich, money will only heighten those flaws sooner than later.

Although it had taken me more than five years to reach that pinnacle, a fall happens before you ever have the chance to plant your feet on the ground. And since my character was not prepared for success, I fell just like those lottery winners.

Less than two years had passed before I awoke into a nightmare worse than my first financial disaster.

It was 1993, but this time I was locked in my room (apartment) as Otis Redding put it. This time I was pondering my future with far greater consequences than even I could have imagined.

Before, I was working from blind ignorance, this time I made sure it would be informed consent.

I know the word *ignorance* by itself implies some level of blindness. Blind ignorance means that despite all of my education, I was still so dumb that I did not even have enough street smarts to know I was dumb. Therefore, I was blindly ignorant.

However, my success was no fluke. It was genuine, but my ability to handle it was a different matter.

The Bible tells us to whom much is given, much is required (Luke 12:48).

So finally I realized that my success is attached to both my character and responsibility, not just my selfish indulgences.

There I was wallowing in the shattered indulgence I had created. My thoughts kept circling the same idea like a vulture.

Bankruptcy was the irrevocable final solution to my long line of big money mistakes.

I was finally ready to get off that financial rollercoaster and start over again the right way. But that was easier said than done.

Back then there was not the plethora of credit counselors, debt consolidation firms, or any other real debt relief assistance available for me to consult as exists today, including any self-help books that offered any useful options beyond what I already knew was available to me.

So there I was a working professional with a Bachelor of Science degree in Finance, and I was in the most serious financial trouble of my young life.

As I thought back to my college years and all the financial courses I had taken, I could not recall a course in Financial Recovery 101.

Then it hit me. I was completely alone!

I tried to put the matter off until I could get a handle on what I was up against, which would give me time to come up with a gameplan.

Remembering that I had a couple of important business dinners I was hosting that week, I rushed out to the grocery store for a rare weekly visit, but I was not prepared for what would happen next.

After spending two hours walking around that store making my selections, I finally got up to the register where the total rang up to be $204.32.

I swiped my Visa check card and had started to leave with my groceries when my card declined just as I picked up my bags. Then I swiped a different card and it declined also.

Meanwhile, the line behind me was growing, both in size and agitation. I then swiped a third and then a fourth card. I was struggling to be calm and not be embarrassed. Then I started all over again.

Finally, I accepted my fate and walked out of the store without any groceries and a bag full of shame that I had to carry all over my face.

I was a thirty–something who had fallen into a credit hole with no way out.

Now fast forward to today – there is a credit repair shop or sign on every street corner, or at least every other traffic light. In fact, there are so many options out there that, inadvertently, you are more susceptible to someone else's errors in their zealousness to make a quick dollar than I was to my own spendthrift thinking.

In the last 15+ years, the credit landscape has changed from one extreme to another. And I must admit I made a lot more mistakes during those years before things began to change.

But the straw that broke the proverbial camel's back, for me, was the day that a well-known consumer agency told me there was nothing they could do to help me.

That was it!

From that point forward I learned everything I could about the world of credit and finance. I did the only thing I could do as a broke individual, I learned how to fix my own mistakes because I could not afford to do anything else.

I learned how to do it ***because I was forced into a situation that made me acquire the necessary knowledge.***

Back to Joseph.

Joseph had the same three resources I had, but he learned how to apply his earlier than I did – an unshakeable faith, a willingness to learn, and the ability to impact his world. He applied the first one to the second one and together they changed the third one in a large way.

Despite my setbacks I have never doubted what I believed in or what I was fighting for – which has, in turn, driven me to learn. Together they have brought me to this point.

I have spent the last 15 years recovering from my own poor financial decisions and realizing there are countless individuals out there who are repeatedly living my previous nightmare. If this is you, then I believe you should also have the opportunity to create your own success and to do so without losing the shirt off your back.

It Starts at Home

Although my parents may not have directly taught me many things about money, they did teach me that you have to give back to your community no matter how difficult your personal circumstances.

When I was a child my parents did not believe in using credit; in truth, my parents probably did not use credit because they could not obtain any credit – so everything was cash or no carry. Needless to say, our family did not have access to many nice little pleasures that most people live for and, without which, consider life not worth living.

I did not know about any of those little things because I was content, and had no idea that my friends thought my life was missing anything.

In my parent's defense, I honestly did not know we were poor because we were a happy family. Although it may sound like a cliché, it is absolutely true. We ate our meals together, we played together, and we spent our weekends doing things as a family. I do not have one bad memory about my childhood.

In my parent's defense, I also did not know we were poor because we were happy.

And despite my best efforts, my parents were far better money managers with far less to manage than I could ever hope even with so much more money available to me!

But the strangest tidbit of all was that I never once heard my parents talk about money – period.

So I honestly do not know where I got the idea that I had to have so many "things" to be happy, especially after seeing so many of my friends' families with so many things live such unhappy lives.

It was not until I was much older and had finally left home that these things were made plain before me, so I thought.

That is also when I determined, to my own ignorance, "to have it all," and enjoy all those things I had supposedly missed. Little did I know this decision required good credit and money management skills, and I had neither. But that did not stop me or my materialistic dreams.

And then, literally, I laid down one night financially okay - and awoke the next morning to find myself drowning in debt. I had dug myself in so deeply that bankruptcy looked like the only way out. But I still yearned for the "good life," and was not smart enough to know that a bankruptcy could short-circuit my attempts to attain the very lifestyle I so desperately desired. Much to my surprise, neither stopped the other.

That is when I decided I would no longer be a passive consumer who just reacted to financial decisions others imposed on me. I learned everything I could about the little "secrets" that impact buying power, - my buying power not from theoretical books but from practical application.

I soon discovered that approximately 6% of the U. S. population ever achieved real financial security because only that 6% take the initiative to do two things – learn how their money can make money, and put their natural talents into moneymaking enterprises.

The remaining 94% choose to be uneducated about these matters and let others dictate their financial paths.

I used to be in the larger group. I am now in the smaller group and still working.

Do Not Chase Money

One of my first and most enduring lessons was that money forever moves. Intuitively, I should have known this from my undergraduate studies, but I did not know it then like I do now.

Money never stays in one place. For example, when you put your money in the bank, it continues to move. The bank pools your money together along with other people's money to purchase their investments and make loans, even if you do not personally qualify for a loan from your own bank. And the interest you earn is but a small piece of the banks larger earnings made from you lending them your money to use in the form of a savings or some sort of interest-bearing account.

When Bill Gates started Microsoft, he probably went to a few people and asked them to invest in his idea. Some probably agreed and some probably did not. Those who did are probably millionaires if not billionaires; those who did not are still kicking themselves today. The same is true of Walt Disney, Henry Ford, and countless others.

Now while the goal is to be in the pathway of money moving in a positive manner, you may also find yourself in the path of money moving in the negative. Such was the mortgage debacle across the United States and the world that actually started in 2000. That is when housing was fueled by low interest rates and excess liquidity (which really means people had ***Funny Money*** – money on paper only) tied up in their homes; and, people were more than willing to find ways to encourage them to spend it and get into much more debt.

Therefore, the trick to amassing wealth is not to see how many dollars you can get and keep. Rather, you must learn where the money is going, and position yourself to be there to let it pass through you on its way to its next moving target. The stock market is both the preeminent example of both money moving and *Funny Money.*

The two most well-known individuals I see doing this the best are Warren Buffett and Oprah Winfrey. The lesson here is the better you position yourself, the more money flows through you.

This is seen most often on the Oprah show by her frequently giving away gifts. And for Mr. Buffett, he makes more money just by giving free public advice about money.

Together they have become trusted voices for both companies and consumers, sort of like a bridge between the haves and have-nots.

A wealthy person is simply a conduit for money - a lot comes to them, and even more goes from them. Therefore, whether coming or going large amounts are constantly in their possession. You can start today being a conduit by saving, in a regular savings plan and a retirement account – but that is only a trickle of what you can do with your money.

Let's read a passage from The Bible that makes this point more eloquently then I ever could – Matthew 25:14–30 (NIV)

> 14 “Again, it will be like a man going on a journey, who
> called his servants and entrusted his property to them.
> 15 To one he gave five talents of money, to another two
> talents, and to another one talent, each according to
> his ability. Then he went on his journey. 16 The man
> who had received the five talents went at once and put
> his money to work and gained five more. 17 So also, the
> one with the two talents gained two more. 18 But the
> man who had received the one talent went off, dug a
> hole in the ground and hid his master's money.
> 19 After a long time the master of those servants re-
> turned and settled accounts with them. 20 The man who
> had received the five talents brought the other five.
> ‘Master,’ he said, ‘you entrusted me with five talents.
> See, I have gained five more.’
> 21 His master replied, ‘Well done, good and faithful
> servant! You have been faithful with a few things; I
> will put you in charge of many things. Come and share
> your master's happiness!’
> 22 The man with the two talents also came. ‘Master,’
> he said, ‘you entrusted me with two talents; see, I have
> gained two more.’
> 23 His master replied, ‘Well done, good and faithful
> servant! You have been faithful with a few things; I
> will put you in charge of many things. Come and share
> your master's happiness!’
> 24 Then the man who had received the one talent came.
> ‘Master,’ he said, ‘I knew that you are a hard man, har-
> vesting where you have not sown and gathering where
> you have not scattered seed. 25 So I was afraid and went
> out and hid your talent in the ground. See, here is what
> belongs to you.’
> 26 His master replied, ‘You wicked, lazy servant! So
> you knew that I harvest where I have not sown and
> gather where I have not scattered seed? 27 Well then,

you should have put my money on deposit with the bankers, so that when I returned I would have received it back with interest.
28 *'Take the talent from him and give it to the one who has the ten talents.* 29 *For everyone who has will be given more, and he will have an abundance. Whoever does not have, even what he has will be taken from him.* 30 *And throw that worthless servant outside, into the darkness, where there will be weeping and gnashing of teeth."*

The master in this parable is far better than many bosses today (personal experience). He knows the capabilities of each member of his staff and he assigns them tasks accordingly.

On this particular day, he tells his staff he is going on a trip and gives no indication when he is going to return.

In his absence he leaves three of his servants with money, according to their abilities, for them to keep while he is gone. Notice how he gave them no specific instructions on what to do with the money. He left it up to each servant on how to make the best use of his money.

Now the first servant doubled his money and so did the second servant. But the third servant was a little different.

His problem is less about the money and more about the reasons behind his lack of action. So when his boss returned he decided to tell him off - to give him a piece of his mind, sort of.

He said, "Master you are a hard man who harvests where you have not sown and gathers where you have not scattered seed."

He goes on to tell his master what he thinks of him, and to everyone's surprise his master agrees that the character description is absolutely on point.

Then the servant made the most important statement of all.

"I was afraid!"

Not only was the servant scared of his boss, but he was even more scared to dream.

Before I continue, let me make one other important point. There are some people who only spend their days dreaming and never put their hands to work. And then there are others who do the exact opposite. Both are equally dangerous.

Both the scared servant and the dreamer have missed the point of balance.

The servant has the money but no dream of how to make it grow. The dreamer has all dreams but no money because he refuses to work.

Both working and dreaming are talents to be used and, when combined appropriately, can bring you so much more wealth.

But most importantly, fear, in this instance was a character flaw that impacted this servant's financial future.

The Sower

I once had a very good friend who had an unbelievable eye for fashion. He could draw sketches of clothing lines years before they ever hit the market.

He did not have many resources so he would use whatever he had – paper bags, old pieces of wood, and even toilet tissue. You name it he could use it, which actually added more depth to the finished sketch.

All throughout high school his talent only got better.

Graduation came and went. It was time to either go to school or to work.

Paris refused to do either. He sat around waiting for people to give him money to feed his dream as if they owed him something, including me.

When everyone around him finally cut him off, he started going to fabric stores and eventually talked them into coming on board.

He was a smooth talker and even better marketer.

To this day I do not know how he did it.

Stop.

I do know how he did it. He believed in himself and his product, and he refused to take no for an answer. He would go back to the same individuals and places of business on numerous occasions.

As I was saying, he sold the fabric stores on his designs and how their support would bring them lots of dollars because of his advertising.

He also learned how to pitch his ideas to the wealthy, including wearing his own haute couture designs to A-list parties. Thus, he picked up several wealthy supporters along the way.

So Paris had all the necessary tools he required to succeed - talent, materials, financial resources, and an unshakeable belief in himself.

Unfortunately, he squandered the money. Against sound advice, he spent the money on everything else but fashion designing.

He used the materials to make clothes for himself because he believed he was his own best advertisement. But he just threw the clothes together instead of taking time to sew them correctly as his drawings depicted.

A wise person uses credit only when there is a profit to be made in using it. Credit is the most valuable financial tool in the world today.

Paris was so busy enjoying his own success that he quickly drained his resources and forgot about succeeding.

So he ended up penniless, although he once had the means to take care of himself and his family for the rest of his life.

Paris was a have who deliberately spent himself into a have-not.

My dear friend, like so many others, had the opportunity to get all the extra flavor in life that ordinary folks could never have. By doing for a few years what most people are unwilling to ever do, Paris, like so many others, had the ability to spend the rest of his life enjoying the things others desired but could never have.

But he fell prey to his own success.

Trading Days

Please understand that you cannot provide for tomorrow's security by spending tomorrow's income today, unless that income is invested! In short, a wise person uses credit only when there is a profit to be made in using it.

After all, if you are going to pay 18% interest to the bank, you really should be making more than 18% from the bank or some other type of investment.

When you use credit, you are selling your future income at a discount (because you pay interest for having the money now instead of waiting until you have actually earned the money). For example, if you borrow $100 today at 4% interest, then in one year you owe $104, but that makes the $100 only worth $96.15 today. This is of course without compounding. This is not the way to generate wealth because you are slowly depleting your own wealth for the opportunity to use the money before you actually earn it.

Credit is the most valuable tool in the world today. Cash does not even come in a close second - but knowledge does. With credit you can obtain just about anything, including investments that will create even greater wealth. Knowledge allows you to make wise choices or at least more informed ones.

For example, for just a few thousand dollars and in some cases with $0 you can take advantage of value appreciation and other advantages of owning a home.

Purchasing a home means you immediately gain control of over $100,000+ worth of real estate (and the ability to potentially profit from the entire dollar value of the property's value, regardless of the cost) while only investing a small portion of your own money.

Without the right knowledge, however, you can never hope to make the financial system work for you.

When 96% of the population fails to achieve financial security it is not due to a lack of money - again, money is only a tool.

Rather, they suffer from a shortage of knowledge that could have helped them to amass wealth.

Understand this important concept: achieving wealth has nothing to do with collecting dollars, nor is it connected to how much you earn. All that matters is how you use what you have.

Again, let us take another look at a text in Scripture, Luke 16 (NIV), that drives home the point.

> [1] *"Jesus told his disciples: "There was a rich man*
> *whose manager was accused of wasting his posses-*
> *sions.* [2] *So he called him in and asked him, 'What is this*

I hear about you? Give an account of your manage-
ment, because you cannot be manager any longer.'
3 *The manager said to himself, 'What shall I do now?*
My master is taking away my job. I'm not strong
enough to dig, and I'm ashamed to beg – 4 *I know*
what I'll do so that, when I lose my job here, people
will welcome me into their houses.'
5 *So he called in each one of his master's debtors. He*
asked the first, 'How much do you owe my master?'
6 *'Eight hundred gallons of olive oil,' he replied.*
"The manager told him, 'Take your bill, sit down
quickly, and make it four hundred.'
7 *Then he asked the second, 'And how much do you*
owe?'
'A thousand bushels of wheat,' he replied.
"He told him, 'Take your bill and make it eight hun-
dred.'
8 *The master commended the dishonest manager*
because he had acted shrewdly. For the people of this
world are more shrewd in dealing with their own kind
than are the people of the light. 9 *I tell you, use worldly*
wealth to gain friends for yourselves, so that when it is
gone, you will be welcomed into eternal dwellings.
10 *Whoever can be trusted with very little can also be*
trusted with much, and whoever is dishonest with very
little will also be dishonest with much. 11 *So if you have*
not been trustworthy in handling worldly wealth, who
will trust you with true riches? 12 *And if you have not*
been trustworthy with someone else's property, who
will give you property of your own?"

End Result

I know people who earn over $200,000 per year and still live from paycheck to paycheck. I also know people who earn less than $14,000 a year who regularly invest in their future and will someday have financial security.

So do not use the excuse that you do not make enough money. Fortunes can be built on very little seed money; and, if you really have what it takes to achieve wealth, you will find a way.

Financial independence is probably the single most important material goal for most individuals.

Most people believe the first step to securing financial independence is to secure a good job and the second is homeownership.

If both of these were true, we would not be in the middle of a housing credit crisis that is having crippling effects throughout our economy and the entire world. And the individuals losing their homes are mostly gainfully employed.

Therefore, clearly having a job and owning a house does not automatically lead to financial independence.

However, the opposite is also true that the possibility does exist for a job and a home to lead to financial independence, if the individual is willing to make those necessary and sometimes painful decisions that will influence their financial well being far into the future.

I believe the #1 reason people miss the opportunity to secure their financial futures is because they do not have the knowledge of what to do or not to do when it comes to matters of the wallet.

"My people are destroyed for lack of knowledge." (Hosea 4:6)

The have-nots have to learn to do what the haves do by putting their money to work so that it generates income and not debt.

Maya Angelou once said, "When you know better, you do better."

This book is intended to help you do all the above.

If you are willing...

Take the Credit Quiz

The hardest thing to do is to face the truth about ourselves.

The second hardest is to change those truths.

The following quiz is your mirror and if you are serious about changing, then the remainder of this book will teach you how to change those truths through knowledge.

Each question is worth 7 points. The quiz has a built in gift of 5 points. So if you have more than 6 negative answers, then you need to get to work on a gameplan.

	Yes	No
Are your credit cards charged to their limits?	☐	☐
Do you know your total debt load?	☐	☐
Do you know what is considered a reasonable debt load?	☐	☐
If you lost your job tomorrow, would your family be in a crisis situation?	☐	☐
Do you save?	☐	☐
Do you regularly spend more money than you can earn?	☐	☐
Are you borrowing money to pay for items you used to pay for with cash, like groceries?	☐	☐
Have you consolidated your debt, like transferring balances around on your credit cards or taken out home equity loans?	☐	☐
After consolidating your old debt are you now taking on new debt?	☐	☐
Do you regularly make only the minimum payment on your credit cards?	☐	☐
Are you regularly late in paying your bills?	☐	☐
Are you dodging collection calls from your creditors?	☐	☐
Have your card privileges been revoked or are you required to pay your utility bills in cash?	☐	☐
Are you currently under threat of legal action because of debt?	☐	☐
Do you know your score or do you check your credit report regularly?	☐	☐

My Score ______________

Chapter One

Change the Channel

Six out of ten Americans are in debt, and this phenomenon has been a perpetual cycle handed down from generation to generation, not including the fact that most Americans have grown up watching the U. S. government run up unchecked astronomical debts.

While the possibility forever exists that anyone's life can change in an instant, most enduring and sustainable changes happen incrementally as individuals become more knowledgeable and more diligent over time.

Most individuals are in debt because that is all they have ever been taught. Because of those teachings they are prisoners of the debtor's mindset, old-school, left-brain, or whatever you choose to call it.

Another reason, and maybe the main reason, people are debtors is because money talk is taboo.

Let me explain.

How many times have you been at a party and were told there are two subjects you never discuss in public gatherings – religion and politics.

The reason why these subjects are not discussed is because they make most partygoers uncomfortable.

They are uncomfortable discussion topics because they are emotionally charged and divisive subjects, not very good ideas for a party atmosphere.

Money is also an unmentionable, in part, for the same reason. But even more so, money discussions are distasteful because of the anxiety attached to it (money).

If you do not have enough, you are embarrassed.

If you have a lot people are going to ask you for some.

Therefore, in polite company, the subject is not discussed. This is also one reason why socio-economic levels do not mix very well.

Now, if no one talks about money, then how does one move from a poor man's mentality to a wealthy mindset?

Visualization.

You learned this in the first grade but then it was called drawing.

Draw me a picture of...

Since then you have reinforced this visualization lesson through reading books, and, most likely, television.

If people see themselves as poor, they remain poor.

Others see themselves wealthy, and they begin to do things that lead them to wealth.

If you want to be a millionaire you must develop a millionaire's mindset. That means you have to actually see yourself earning a million dollars per year.

This breaks down to be about $480.77 per hour for 40 hours of work for 1 year.

But to get to the million, you have to first believe in yourself and your ability to earn this money. You have to start thinking like a millionaire.

Remember Joseph? He believed he was a leader before he ever got the first leadership position. Betrayal by his own brothers, being sold into slavery, and cast into prison could not quench this fire. In fact, the opposite occurred. Those things only made him more driven to succeed. He still believed he was a leader; he just did not know when, where, or how it was going to happen.

Now let me also tell you this. You are right no matter what you believe.

If you believe you cannot make a million, then you are right. You cannot make a million.

But if you believe you can make a million, then you are also correct. You can make a million.

No one can tell you what to believe, but everyone can see by your actions exactly what you believe.

Whatever you believe, you are going to act on that belief and bring what you believe from your mind into full reality. But either way, you are correct, and any unmanaged debt will only add to your woes by slowing your dream down — almost to a screeching halt, or encourage you into greater action!

Let me tell you about two business partners I know.

The first partner came from a wealthy background. He hardly put any effort into the business, and he just sat around and waited for success to come to him and his partner. Although he was younger than his partner, he was also a grumpy, bitter person with a generally negative disposition.

Circumstances are temporal, that means they are subject to change.

Your faith should be unshakeable because everybody else is already doubting your success.

His partner on the other hand was a few years older and from a poor background. He had initiative, drive, and a positive outlook. He worked effortlessly every day toward making their business a success, and he put every ounce of money and brain power he had into that success.

Now these two partners always had a difference of opinion. The second partner never conferred with the first partner on any matters because he felt like the first partner never had anything constructive to add.

In truth, the first partner had made several bad financial decisions that had cost their firm quite a bit of money, and he showed absolutely no interest in the business.

Now the obvious first question would be why are they still in business together?

I asked them both that same question, individually and apart from the other. I was quite surprised at their responses.

The second partner said he owed it to his friend to make sure that he had every opportunity to succeed despite his own shortcomings.

It may sound corny but it is true — you can achieve what you believe. And the opposite is equally true, where there is no belief, there is no success. If you do not believe me go sit in any classroom in the country and you will see this in action every day.

The first partner said that he felt safe and secure with the other guy as his partner.

What was surprising was that their answers had nothing to do with money, directly anyway. It was all about their individual mindsets.

Those two partners are still in business today and quite successful. The reason why is they recognized their shortcomings and made the necessary changes for one to accommodate the other, which eventually exponentially increased their earning power.

So by now you are asking what does this have to do with debt?

Quite simply it is this: in order to become a millionaire you are going to have to change your way of thinking about money and about debt.

Millionaires adjust to change more rapidly than most non-millionaires, and this high tolerance for change helps them to earn money and decrease debt faster than their non-millionaire counterparts.

Now if you are not a millionaire and are in debt, do not despair. Read on!

I tell you this because no one cares more about your money than you do. But caring is not enough by itself. You also need knowledge to make better decisions than you have in the past and to develop a sense of direction for your financial future.

Some of this shifting mindset is going to come quickly for some and a little slower for others, but the only pace that is required is the one you set for yourself. The same is also true for your debt reduction plan. In other words, how quickly do you want to come out of debt? We will discuss this in more detail in subsequent chapters.

The only expectations are those that you put on yourself. Fast or slow, you are the drummer.

It is a fact that by the time most individuals leave high school, they have had little or no financial management training whatsoever up to and including college. I am living proof.

However, solid money management skills are an integral part of any quality life. This manual is designed to instill into every reader a culture of good credit, regular savings, investment shopping, and so much more. These are concepts to neither be feared nor shunned.

In my studies and travels, I have found one major difference between wealthy people and those not so wealthy. Wealthy individuals are teachable. In other words, they have a teachable spirit (a willingness to learn).

If anyone is unwilling to learn, then that is tantamount to giving the financial industry a license to steal from you as much as they can possibly get away with!

Friendly Advice

I have some of the most well meaning friends in the world and I love them all dearly. Yet this particular group all have one thing in common - - they are all broke. Those that are the most broke are also always the first in line to offer financial advice without the asking. So I did the only thing I could do - - I got me some new friends.

Okay, now that I have stopped laughing, I am only kidding. I still have the same friends, but new financial advisors. And guess what? Even after watching me succeed, my friends are still broke!

You Have To Want To Be Successful

Regardless of whether you are broke or not, people spend their money in many ways, sometimes by force, if you will. If you are like most Americans, the bulk of your income goes for day-to-day living expenses - - food, shelter, and clothing - - with little or no money left over to invest in the future or to pay down debt.

Now I ask you, if there is any money left over, what do you do with it? Go ahead say it out loud........

I am in no hurry, I can wait.

Or let me ask it another way; "Is your money working as hard for you as you are for it?"

If you are already struggling with debt why would you take the bait in the form of one of those free credit offers mailed out by the truckloads every day?

Again, if you are like the average American citizen you are more than $10,000 in debt and that does not even include a mortgage. I would also be willing to bet that your money is not working as hard for you as the consumer lending industry is working to get it from you.

Regardless of how you spend your money, you are either investing in your future or someone else's, i.e. debt. I, like you, would prefer you invest in your own future instead of lining someone else's pockets.

Invested savings lines your pocket, debt lines someone else. It is just that simple.

In order to improve your finances and your future, all the while gaining financial independence, you need to understand the tools available to you and to use those tools to your advantage.

If you remember my fashion designer friend Paris, he refused to tighten his financial belt and become more disciplined with the use of his resources. Think of it this way. He had an umbrella (his resources) so he thought he could stand in the rain infinitum and not ever get wet.

But his resources dried up, much like an umbrella getting overused, worn out and with holes in it, so the rain began to beat down on him. Instead of trying to conserve his resources, he decided to stay outside in the rain, longer than was prudent. The rain never stopped, but neither did the sun, the wind, and the snow.

"Laughter does the heart good like a medicine." Proverbs 17:22

You are going to make some mistakes along the way, so make sure you find time to laugh.

In other words, he did not have a teachable spirit. And you know the rest of the story.

Credit Can Change, So Can You

We are going to begin our discussion with the most vital (in my opinion) of all financial tools, credit.

The importance of good credit cannot be over-emphasized. In today's society credit is not a luxury. It is a necessary essential for personal financial growth and prosperity.

Here is another key fact to understand:

> ***Statistics show only five percent of the entire wealth of the world is ever printed as actual currency. The remaining 95 percent exists only in the form of credit.***
>
> ***Therefore, if your credit is poor, you do not have access to 95 percent of the world's wealth.***

This drastically limits any opportunities for financial security. Meanwhile, if you have any kind of debt, you are helping drive the windfall profits made by the consumer industry.

That old adage is true, the rich get richer and the poor get poorer. And the two are only separated by knowledge.

Hosea 4:6 states, "My people are destroyed for lack of knowledge."

But the Bible does not end it there. It goes on to tell the children of Israel why they are destroyed - - "because thou hast rejected knowledge." (KJV)

This is not some get rich quick scheme, so you are not going to buy this book and become rich over night. But you will start making better decisions a little at a time.

So today, you might start by saving a few pennies, but tomorrow you may be investing several thousand dollars.

This is about living a disciplined, balanced, and prosperous life not for just a few years, but for the fullness of life and on into the lives of your children.

As for the U. S., we are rapidly becoming a two-class society in which people without good credit (nearly 60 percent of the population) are treated as second-class citizens.

While it is true that if you want things in your life to change, you have to change the things in your life, but if your willingness to learn = 0, and your willingness to change = 100, then 0 X 100 = 0 (by the way, math is required).

Therefore, you will continue to get what you have always gotten because you will always do what you have always done!

But, there is still hope.

New Way of Thinking

There is an alternative training model that teaches that the success of anything does not mean that the contributors to that success are equal parts.

When it comes to financial success, there are two extremely important but unequal aspects to this type of success.

The first part of the model is based on your motivation. How you are motivated refers to your thoughts, and your dreams - those intangible things that drive you to aspire to greater heights financially. Why you do what you do is 90 percent of wealth creation!

The second part of this training model addresses your actions. These are the actual steps, techniques, and skills used in the work you do to create wealth. These actions represent the final 10 percent of effort in this model.

The problem is that most people focus on either one contributor or the other but both are actually needed. The ultimate goal for everyone is to learn how to focus on their actions without understanding.

Simply put, this means an individual may not always understand what they do or why they do what they do. Initially, this should not stop anyone from taking certain actions. But do not forget that an *individual's thought process is a powerful process and is the greater of the two contributors.*

So while your thought process may want to interfere with your initial actions do not let it. While many people fear this process the successful individual embraces that fear for their own good.

In 1998, Bobby McFerrin recorded a song entitled, *"Don't Worry, Be Happy."* Many people laughed when they heard this song although it won a Grammy Award. But the song is actually quite powerful. If you could learn just one thing from this chapter, it would be to stop worrying! Just do what you need to do and stop worrying about the how - - this one small change will yield unimaginable results.

For example, I do not know how this law works but it does. The Law of Reciprocity states whatever you give out will come back to you. So the more you give, the more comes back to you. Again, I do not know how this law works, but it does! But most people spend so much time trying to figure out how the law works they never give and therefore the cycle is stopped before it ever starts.

If there is any doubt that the Law of Reciprocity works go look up sowing and reaping in the Bible, and you will find that the Bible clearly teaches about giving and receiving, and, planting and harvesting.

Let me stop to make a quick point.

As I stated earlier in the book, do not chase money. Stated another way, do not give to get. If getting is your reward, then you have already earned you reward when you gave.

And since the Law of Reciprocity is a spiritual law that works in this natural world, it does not just work with money.

So if you are less than kind, you will get that in return and so on.

To this end, the following tools will also work in all aspects of your individual lives.

Now there are four phases of financial change.

Phase I is unconscious incompetence. This is when you do not know that you do not know.

Phase II is conscious incompetence. This is when you know that you do not know.

Phase III is conscious competence. This is actively thinking through processes, a conscious effort to apply new principles and develop new habits over time.

Phase IV is unconscious competence. This is when it happens automatically. Successful people just do it without thinking about it. It just happens. This is the ultimate goal of all who aspire to this training model.

Making wealth in the beginning is a process until you reach Phase IV.

Level IV is the Law of Reciprocity in perpetual motion.

4 Phases of Change

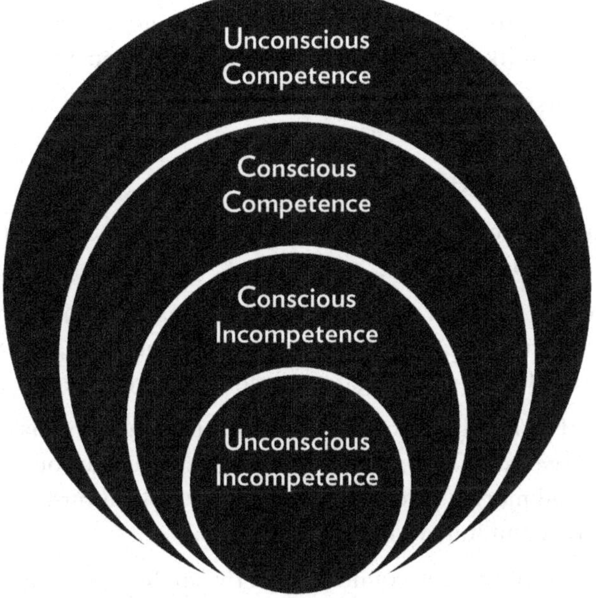

Don't Stop There

For future reading on creating and living a successful life, I recommend you review the reading list by the Napoleon Hill Foundation. This recommended reading list can be found at its website www.naphill.org.

During all of his research, Napoleon Hill identified a common denominator for success - a clear purpose and a burning desire for its achievement.

Napoleon Hill is probably most famous for his work with Andrew Carnegie over the course of a 20-year project where Hill identified 16 lessons in the law of success.

Although the concepts contained in *Think and Grow Rich* are too numerous to be presented in this work, I strongly suggest that each of you print this work from the internet and read it in detail.

Let me add one more skill to your new mind shift as stated above. Your wealth creation goals should have a definite purpose, a specific goal, and a clearly defined dream.

Do not try to do a lot of things at once and hope you hit the target.

Instead, focus on one specific objective at a time and then add new skills and knowledge as you grow. This kind of mental focusing will create forward progress, and most likely some positive income while you are growing.

Debt free is at first a mindset, then a habit, and finally a lifestyle.

What It All Means

Before we start the next chapter and the nuts and bolt work, let me give you some numbers to think about.

According to their public website in 2005, Fair Isaac Corporation described the credit use of the typical consumer that showed on average that most consumers had a total of eleven obligations held at the credit reporting agencies.

The majority of those obligations were credit cards (such as gas cards, department store charge cards, or bank cards) and installment accounts (such as student loans and mortgage loans). Of the eleven obligations, seven were likely to be credit cards and four were probably loans.

On average, most of those accounts held at the credit reporting agencies were paid on time. Fewer than four out of ten were ever more than 30 days late; only two out of ten were more than 60 days late; and 95 percent had never been more than 90+ days late.

That was then.

Today it is generally believed that most American consumers do not know their credit score held by the three major credit reporting agencies, are deeply in debt, and are late on one or more accounts.

Do not let these facts discourage you because some facts can change, despite the fact that U. S. consumer debt has reached pandemic levels.

But we all need to know where we are to help us understand where we are going.

Those who are in debt are unwilling participants of choices of ignorance. Therefore, you can also choose not to be a part of that problem, if you know how.

Not necessarily a pretty thought but a necessary point.

In order to move forward you have to understand where you came from. If there is any doubt let me make it plain.

We live in a society so governed by advertising that it controls our desires and the consumer finance industry helps to fuel those desires by forever dangling credit in our mailboxes and on television for all to see.

This is also were debt freedom begins - - in the mind.

The news and other media gives you facts all day long. But facts change, the truth does not. And the real truth is that you do not have to live in a cardboard box of facts.

Your mindset, dreams, thought processes, spending habits, and so on did not happen overnight. Therefore, they are not going to go away or change overnight.

One of my quirkiest friends from work sent me an email that I thought would help close out this chapter.

The Duck

There was a little boy visiting his grandparents on their farm. He was given a slingshot to play with out in the woods.
He practiced in the woods; but he could never hit the target. Getting a little discouraged, he headed back for dinner.
As he was walking back he saw Grandma's pet duck. Just out of impulse, he let the slingshot fly, hit the duck square in the head and killed it. He was shocked and grieved!
In a panic, he hid the dead duck in the wood pile; only to see his sister watching!
Sally had seen it all, but she said nothing.

After lunch the next day Grandma said, 'Sally, let's wash the dishes.'
But Sally said, 'Grandma, Johnny told me he wanted to help in the kitchen.'
Then she whispered to him, 'Remember the duck?'
So Johnny did the dishes.
Later that day, Grandpa asked if the children wanted to go fishing and Grandma said, 'I'm sorry but I need Sally to help make supper.'
Sally just smiled and said, 'Well that's all right because Johnny told me he wanted to help.'
She whispered again, 'Remember the duck?'
So Sally went fishing and Johnny stayed to help.
After several days of Johnny doing both his chores and Sally's; he finally could not stand it any longer.
He came to Grandma and confessed that he had killed the duck.
Grandma knelt down, gave him a hug and said, 'Sweetheart, I know. You see, I was standing at the window and I saw the whole thing, but because I love you, I forgave you. I was just wondering how long you would let Sally make a slave of you.'
Translated into financial terms - - when are you going to stop letting your past dictate your future. Everyone makes mistakes and the time has come to let your past mistakes go. This is your time and opportunity to write a new financial future.
Secondly, how long are you going to be a slave to bad debt or to the consumer finance industry?
As for me, I have been debt free many times before and after 1993, but it never lasted long because I was forever eyeing the next 'thing' I wanted which put me right back in the debt cycle.
This up and down cycle continued until I learned to put these same principles in action that I am sharing

with you today.
Anyone that has done anything of any importance has failed a few times along the way, except for one.
Go back and look at any individual in history you chose and you will find they made several mistakes along the way to their ultimate success.
The difference is they did not stop at their failures.

The *POWER* of 13

When an individual becomes a millionaire it is easy to get financial advice. However, getting there may be the proverbial horse of a different color.

It may be easy to pick out the millionaires at a country club. But if you were called into a police line up to pick out the millionaires, could you do it?

If you have any doubts that you would have some difficulty completing this task, I have listed below the 13 most powerful qualities that all millionaires possess.

1. Millionaires willingly adapt to change in order to achieve goals. This means that the mental change (intangible) is translated into real world action (tangibles) in a much shorter timeframe than most individuals. The only two required ingredients are ***you + a dedicated commitment.***

2. Visualization. This is the ability to see your intangible dreams in #1 above in the tangible world before they happen. (Take note that both the intangible and tangible worlds are very real, often times the former more than the latter.) The Bible calls this *faith.*

3. Develop positive habits. Swap your bad habits for millionaire habits. Millionaires do not waste time. Each day is carefully planned to achieve the most productivity. Tasks that do not add value are minimized near the end of each day's list.

4. Constant pressure. Consistently apply positive habits until they become an unconscious reaction like a second skin. I read somewhere that in order to form a new habit, an individual must do the same task for about 30 days. Think how many new habits you can form each year.

5. Let your imagination run wild. Think about the possibility of the impossible. You have to want to transition your thinking into a millionaire's mindset so bad that you can taste it. See yourself in a different set of clothes, a different car, and a MTV-type crib.

6. Be willing to work at becoming the new you every waking minute of every day.

7. Never accept failure as an option. Through a series of unfortunate events, Thomas Edison was completely deaf in his left ear and

almost 80% deaf in the right ear. But none of this stopped him from going on to invent some 1,093 different items we still use today including the first phonograph, the first incandescent electric light bulb, and his early lectures in Boston were the beginnings of the Massachusetts Institute of Technology (MIT). Beethoven produced the world's best symphonies although he too was deaf. Helen Keller told her own story although she was deaf, dumb, and blind. Therefore, you have no excuses not to succeed.

8. Put faith in you on automatic pilot. Your brain has two sides, a rational and irrational side. Your rational side works on whatever natural stimulation is received from its external environment. It is exactly as Luther Vandross sang – "A chair is still a chair." The other side of your mind, which rarely flourishes – again – because of external constraints, is the fun side, also the imaginative side that with a little prodding can believe the possibility of the impossible. The more you see yourself successful the easier it becomes to believe in yourself. This is a foundational lesson from Genesis. I personally know this to be true because I see it every day. I know a gentleman from an extremely wealthy family who has no faith in himself, and therefore he has no success to call his own. I also know another gentleman who was born beneath poverty but he believes in himself and everything he does, and despite what he is fed from his surroundings, he forever pushes his imaginative side of his brain and he wins!

9. While making money is important being happy is more important. And one of the best ways to be happy is to make money doing what pleases you most. This is true success. I know a lot of miserably rich lawyers and some very happy ones also. The difference between the two groups is their personal motivation. And of course, the ones who love, not their job, but their career choice are the ones who serve their clients the best. The others are just working in high priced jobs but with a minimum wage mentality. If a new job is part of your millionaire strategy, we will discuss this more in a later chapter.

10. So if you plan on being a millionaire that plan has to have goals embedded in it throughout the plan. Each goal has to have a concrete method to achieve that goal. Finally, this plan has to be worked every day. Remember the phrase, "Work your plan and plan your work."

S = D + P + W

Success is equal to a dream, plus a plan, and some sweat on your brow.

The plan to setting a plan is very simple.

a. It starts with a specific goal.
b. A specific timeframe to achieve that goal.
c. Write the goal and make it plain. *Then the LORD answered me and said, "Record the vision And inscribe it on tablets, That the one who reads it may run." (Habakkuk 2:2)*
d. Make your plan to reach your goal.
e. Decide how hard you are willing to work to achieve the goal.
f. Work your plan every day no matter the challenges.

Example of a Simplified Plan

Start with a specific dollar amount desired.

Decide what service/product of value you are going to trade for this money.

For example, if you desire $100,000 and you have a muffet that cost $100.00 (not including taxes or fees for simplicity sake), then you would have to sell 1,000 muffets for $100,000 and 10,000 muffets for $1,000,000 and so on.

What is your deadline date for the money?

How do you put this all together to get from 0 to $100,000 or $1,000,000.

Simple – write all of this in 1 simple sentence.

"I am going to acquire $100,00 over the next 90 days by calling on every customer in my address book to purchase a minimum of 5 new muffets at $100 per muffet until I have sold 1,000+ muffets, no matter what it takes."

Then you need to record your voice saying this exact statement on an iPod, cell phone, or even a compact disc so that you can play it over and over again.

"Faith cometh by hearing..." (Romans 10:17).

Your voice is the greatest motivator of all! And to hear yourself saying your dream out loud will motivate you into action. This will also increase your own faith to believe in your ability to gain this money and met this goal. And when this is in your spirit, it will come to pass!

Now there is clearly no reason to waste any more of your time. Each day you should wake up with a purpose and each night you should lie down with a feeling of accomplishment.

Your success will require no explanations.

Make up your mind this is what you want and be determined that nothing will stand in your way. This is called persistence, #11.

11. It is easy to be persistent when you are doing something you like to do. Think about some activity you like to do – play sports, play video games, or cook. Whatever your activity, I have no doubt that you pursue it with persistence. You should pursue your wealth with the same or greater persistence as you pursue your other activities. Most Americans do not remember President Calvin Coolidge. Coolidge was the 30th President of the United States. But what he is probably remembered the most for is his lesson on persistence.

> *"I have found it advisable not to give too much heed to what people say when I am trying to accomplish something of consequence. Invariably they proclaim it can't be done. I deem that the very best time to make the effort."*

Paul puts it another way in Philippians 3:14. *I press toward the mark for the prize of the high calling of God in Christ Jesus.*

12. Persistence will drive you to becoming responsible for your decisions. And responsibility will drive out your fears as your become more comfortable at making decisions. And since worry follows fear, drive out your fears and your worries will leave too. God did not give us a spirit of fear but of power and love and a sound mind. (2 Timothy 1:7) These are both primary components to a happy life.

Now we need to settle one more crucial factor. Millionarism has no age attached to it. So if you did not make your first million by your 25th birthday or 32nd birthday, never, never, never, never give up!

Abraham Lincoln, the 16th President of the United States always seemed to find himself in the mud. He failed at everything he tried, but he never stayed in the mud, meaning he never gave up. Although he fell down often, he did not wallow in self-pity or failure, he always got back up and tried again. This went on until he was well past 40-years-old.

His failure list includes 8 lost elections, 2 failed businesses, and 1 nervous breakdown.

Despite a 30-year failure history, he was elected President of the United States in 1860. Although I am sure he was expected to fail here also, under the threat of the country splitting apart at the seam, Abraham Lincoln became one of the most successful Presidents in our country's history.

That's real persistence pushing out fear of all kinds!

13. Finally, it all starts with you. Everything you desire begins in your mind. Wealth and poverty are the end results of your mental processes. These processes will call you to action or inaction. Exercise your mind in a systematic way so that you begin to think positively in all situations until you accomplish your goals. There is no defeat! Then start all over again with new plans and goals. By exercising your mind's imaginative side you will improve your self-esteem, purpose, and self-reliance. Ultimately, you will become so strong in yourself that you will no longer find time to try to win the approval of others.

Chapter Two

To Your Credit

When thinking of credit, many individuals envision being able to go on endless shopping sprees. However, credit is more than just plastic cards you use to purchase your latest list of wants.

Credit means that you are using money you have borrowed from someone else to pay for things you also want from someone else now.

It is your financial trustworthiness. In short, it is your word!

Good credit means that you have a history of repaying your financial obligations on-time which is the primary concern of your creditors. Combine this good payment history with consistent, stable employment, and a reasonable salary, then you are a prime marketing target for potential creditors, all other things being equal.

These creditors will willingly compete for your business because the criteria previously mentioned all suggest that you are both willing and able to repay the money (loan) to the company (lender) that extended you the loan without the lender exerting additional efforts to recover their funds.

Credit is a world of control or be controlled. The choice is yours but once you have made it, make sure you are prepared for the consequences.

For the lender, this is a win-win situation, because your positive actions will translate into lower costs and higher profits.

For you, this means lower carrying costs, i.e. interest rates, which will turn into lower payments. These lower payments will make your credit report look even stronger.

Bad credit is the exact opposite. Regularly paying your bills late or carrying a large debt load undoubtedly means that you will have problems getting any kind of credit. You may have problems ranging from seeking suitable employment to acquiring reasonable transportation, and everything in between.

Therefore, repaying debts on time is a crucial key in determining your credit potential.

The better your credit, the more willing companies and individuals will be to provide services to you and do so on favorable terms, i.e. lower carrying costs.

Regardless of what type of credit you may have, credit of any kind is a loan.

A loan has two components, the principal and its interest.

The principal is the amount of money you borrow and the interest is the additional money you repay the lender for the opportunity of using their money.

So, good credit determines: (a) if you are qualified to borrow the principal and (b) at what cost this money will be lent to you – (how much interest you will pay for this money.)

All lenders have various rates they charge their customers for the privilege of borrowing money.

The best customers get the lowest rates and the not so good customers get a higher rate. There are a number of factors that determine your "best" listing as a customer – how often you borrow money, if you repay your loans on time or early, and the length of your business relationship.

Also remember that unless you have a locked in rate, loans can have rates that change several times throughout the life of the loan, most often seen in housing loans and credit cards.

Locking in your interest rate means wherever your loan rate starts is where it will end.

A word to the wise.

If your interest rate is low continue to make your payments on time but do not rush to repay the money because the carrying costs have a miniscule impact on your budget.

However, if your interest rate is high, pay as much as you can on each payment– even doubling up on your payments whenever possible.

"It is better that you should not vow than that you should vow and not pay." Ecclesiastes 5:5 (NASB)

This will do 3 things.

It will a) pay your debt down faster, b) help lower your carrying costs because the interest will be calculated on a smaller balance, and finally c) help improve your credit score because early repayment will lower your debt to income ratio thus raising your credit score.

The Big Picture

The rules of credit are both few and simple, and many and complex.

In the simplest form, a lender extends you a line of credit. You agree to pay the lender back the amount you spend plus finance charges and perhaps additional service fees.

Many lenders, banks in particular, make most of their usual profits based on these extra fees they charge.

And they can charge as many fees as they desire and call them anything they like from activation fees to loan wrap up fees. The lower your credit score, the higher the fees and more types of fees that the lender will charge.

In general, a payment schedule is set up and you are required to make payments according to that schedule.

Once repaid, you are finished as long as any other contract terms have been met and the lender does not charge a loan close out fee.

There is nothing else required of you but to make sure you get a copy of your closed contract that shows the account was paid in full, for record keeping purposes.

This is the simple rule.

Good credit does not require a spotless payment history.

"The rich rules over the poor, and the borrower is servant to the lender." Proverbs 22:7 (AKJV)

But too many blemishes are indicative of a much deeper fundamental problem that will undoubtedly demand further investigation by any reputable lender.

Blemishes also leave financial scars long after the blemishes are gone, which makes it harder to get lenders (the same or a different lender) to see you differently after they have seen the blemishes.

When you apply for a credit card, personal loan, or any other type of credit, the lender has to first decide if you are a good credit risk.

The decision to lend or not to lend you money is in part decided by checking your credit record held at the credit reporting agency of the lender's choice.

Before we proceed any further let me make a controversial statement. If you are already in financial trouble with too many blemishes, a creditor is actually helping you by denying you additional credit.

If you have ever been denied credit, that decision should have forced you to get your financial house in order. But, if it did not, here is another opportunity to do so.

To determine if an applicant is a good credit risk, most lenders use some sort of scoring system.

Every lender has their own application and lending process but they all require the same basic information. The only difference may be the weight of certain pieces of specific information, i.e. the importance placed on items, for example salary or type of job.

Once upon a time, although it reads like a fairy tale, it is true that lenders

Controversy – If you are already in debt but continue to apply for more credit, a lender is doing you a favor by refusing to extend you any additional credit. This is going to save you years of heartache, problem telephone calls, credit collection threats, and ultimately save you money.

actually reviewed every single application by hand.

The process was slow and subjective but generally believed to have been favorable for those seeking credit.

Each reviewer assigned points to each part of the application such as the type of occupation, length of employment, and annual income.

Then, over time, application approvals moved from the human touch to the no-touch system, a computer generated review that has been preprogrammed with decision-making criteria.

The computer is programmed for three decisions: yes, no, and unable to compute. Door number three will require a human touch because of the ambiguity of answers in the application.

Therefore, the only way your application will be seen by anyone other than the clerk who logs it in is if it is kicked out by the computer for further review.

When reviewing an application for credit, generally, the greatest weight is given to the credit files held at the three major credit reporting agencies.

The credit bureau actually does two very important tasks for the lender. It verifies your application information by making sure to capture any changes in name, employment, and address. Secondly, it removes the creditor from the decision-making process.

A cumulative score is assigned by each credit reporting agency for everything within your credit profile when compared to the rest of the country.

So for example, an applicant may receive points or deductions for the number of previous or current creditors with deference to your payment.

Most creditors regularly do business with one if not all of the three major bureaus. So it is forever important to make sure that all three bureau reports are kept current.

You may never know in advance which bureau is going to influence your financial future. Fortunately, you have the right and privilege to keep a watchful eye on the bureau activities where your credit report is concerned.

You have a direct and critical role to play in your financial future.

If you are heavily laden with debt and continue to apply for more credit, a creditor will most likely deny your application because you are already overextended, even if you have never been late on any payments.

The thought process behind your denial would be that you may not be able to handle any additional payments based on your income and existing obligations. (Again, the lender may be correct, and thus doing you a favor).

Do you remember those grade school report cards, how hard you worked for those grades, and how proud you were when you got that report card that confirmed your good grades and hard work. The same principle applies now.

Each time you apply for credit, the creditor will access your credit report even if you are an existing customer. They want to ensure you still meet their qualification criteria with no surprises when it comes to repaying their money.

This credit file is your report card on your loan history.

Each inquiry by a creditor will be recorded in your report card. Some creditors automatically reject an applicant if their report shows an excessive number of inquiries over a short period.

When you were younger than you are now it probably felt that trouble seemed to follow you everywhere you went. So I was surprised when an elder member of my family waited until I was much older to wisely tell me, that "trouble is easy to get in, but hard to get out of."

Too many inquiries are a clear sign of : a) cash flow problems, b) too much credit, c) poor repayment history, or d) a combination of all the above.

So every time you think about applying for credit, look at

your inquiry section of your credit report for guidance because if you do not, your creditors will. These types of inquires will remain on your credit report for as long as two years.

On the other hand, if you are committed to relatively few creditors and have maintained a high credit rating with those creditors, new lenders will look at the length of those previous commitments most likely in a favorable manner.

If you are near the end of your current commitments, a new lender may consider extending you additional credit based on your debt-to-income ratio improving at the end of your current commitments.

Check your credit report at least three times per year. A good, no-cost way to do this is by staggering your free report from each bureau throughout the year. These reports will allow you to see how your payment history, account balances, and inquiries have all been reported.

It is good financial sense that credit problems are easier to prevent than cure; yet, even if you have serious credit problems, this manual can help you systematically repair those problems and improve your future financial decision-making and credit opportunities. I will give you even more concrete steps to take to deal with those problems in future chapters.

With access to easy and plentiful credit, it is understandable why so many people end up in debt.

Success in personal financial management requires both planning and perseverance.

While poorly managed credit can land you deeply in debt with a tough recovery road, the rewards for handling your credit well are equally great.

With good credit you may be able to improve your lifestyle through purchases that are only possible with good credit, utilize services that are only available if you have a credit card, and have the resources to pay for unexpected emergencies and make long-term investments.

Your Report Card

Your credit bureau reporting record contains four types of information.

The first section is the identification section.

This section includes your name and variations of the use of that same name, your Social Security Number, date of birth, current and previous addresses as reported by lenders, and your current and previous employers.

It is not uncommon to find some type of error in section one. Some are minor such as misspellings; others can be of a material matter.

Most of these errors have not been corrected because that is the way they were reported by previous lenders.

Errors relating to your name, date of birth, and Social Security number need to be addressed by you and corrected by the bureau.

The remaining three sections are your credit accounts information, public record information, and credit inquiries. We have briefly covered the inquiry sections and will continue the discussions in greater detail shortly.

Credit Reporting History

The history of credit reporting dates back to the 1950s when the first bureaus were small and community based.

In general, they only tracked consumer financial behaviors in specific areas and often only served one type of client, i.e. banks, finance companies, or regional retailers.

Together these bureaus represented a collaborative effort of a region to benefit its members by helping them to manage their credit portfolios for new and existing customers.[1]

Today, credit reporting agencies conduct a wide range of functions and offer a wide variety of fee-services.

By using the services of an agency, creditors, then and now, gain valuable information to add to their own records about consumers and, in the past at least, were encouraged to add their information to the agency's files to help their fellow members.

The three big houses of credit are now technically advanced firms compiling detailed reports that are, in part, supposed to be designed to protect the consumer.

As these agency systems have become more sophisticated, they have helped reduce both the costs of borrowing money and the amount of personal informa-

1 *An Overview and History of Credit Reporting*, Federal Reserve Bank of Philadelphia, June 2002

tion that has to be released in order to apply for a loan.

In this manner, the reporting agency has helped creditors accurately measure risk while also providing financial incentives for consumers to use their credit responsibly.

Those early agencies spent considerable amounts of time rummaging through local newspapers for notices of marriages, deaths, promotions, and even arrests. Any notices found would be clipped to the paper report and passed on through credit inquiries.

Remember the old adage, "no news is good news," it certainly has applications under these circumstances.

Those early credit reporting agencies were industry specific entities from the 1950's through the 60's.

What this meant was that finance companies-, banks-, and retailer-sponsored bureaus only shared information with like companies, i.e. banks with banks, retailers with retailers, and so on. The end result was that an individual's entire debt situation was never fully understood by any creditor, and how could it be.

During the 70's, the credit industry was under tremendous market pressure from both technological demands and political forces to improve their service and defend their value, which helped shape today's credit reporting agencies behemoth size, shrouds of secrecy, and market control that accepts no others but the 'Big Three.'

The passage of the Fair Credit Reporting Act (FCRA), was the first real stab at consumer relief.

FCRA protected the consumer by setting access standards and standards for accuracy of their credit reports.

After FCRA, the era of collecting newspaper clippings ended, and a new era of collecting verifiable credit-related information began.

Verifiable credit-related information included such items as a consumer's ability to consistently pay bills when due and the opposite, not paying bills when due.

Clearly the Big Three have transformed the way they conduct their business.

The time has now come for consumers to reform the way these businesses impact their individual lives.

Technologically speaking, the industry leaped forward in processing, organizing, and reporting information smarter and faster with the power of computers and databases, thus increasing its usefulness and functionality to attract more customers.

All of these changes forced consolidation of the industry so that smaller local operations eventually had to close and sell their information files to the larger agencies.

By the end of the 70's a few agencies emerged as leaders as the demand grew to reign in the unsecured lending market from banks, retailers, and finance companies.

By the start of the 1980's, TransUnion, Experian, and Equifax had clearly emerged as the Big Three we have come to know today by buying up smaller regional agencies.

This means that all of your personal, loan, and public record information along with any inquiries that were once read to customers over the telephone are now being stored electronically and transmitted the same way.[2]

To Teach or Be Taught

Most individuals spend a great deal of time thinking about money. Either they are worrying about there not being enough or they are worrying about how to get more of it.

In my opinion, worry is an excuse.

2 *An Overview and History of Credit Reporting*, Federal Reserve Bank of Philadelphia, June 2002

If you were not born wealthy, or with that automatic wealth building DNA, or did not have money management skills seared into your personality as a youth, do not give up so quickly.

It is possible to learn wealth building techniques later in life and to teach those same skills to your children.

There is no doubt that some individuals are born with the mindset and inner drive for wealth, but for the vast majority that are not born with this bent, learning money skills from the basics forward is the only way to achieve any kind of wealth. By all accounts, this second group does quite well at generating wealth from their learned skills.

Personally, although I truly believe I was born with a drive to succeed, I was not raised in an environment that encouraged the accumulation of wealth. I earned my wealth by being creative, taking calculated risks, and being persistent.

As an adult, if you are not learning wealth management skills, then you certainly are not teaching these skills to your children. Something seems inherently wrong with this concept because money is a necessary tool in today's world. As we think about teaching children how to survive, those lessons cannot ignore one of the most important tools -- money, and all that goes with it.

In actuality, by not teaching your children about money, you are, in fact, teaching your children a very negative lesson about money and thus increasing the difficulty of their adulthood and their earning potential.

Reflective of this fact is a report by the National Council on Economic Education that states only five states require some sort of financial education.

That makes a large economic education gap across the country that needs to be filled.

In order to teach a child or to be taught how to manage wealth, one should mimic the behaviors of those who have already succeeded.

These behaviors include budgeting not only money but time also, not spending every penny on unnecessary items, and treating debt like any other 4-letter word.

Other teaching requirements include priorities, risk, security, and philanthropy: "To whom much is given, much is required." (Luke 12:48a)

A prime example of ensuring the right lessons are reinforced is Christmas. Not nearly as many families go to church on Christmas morning as once did. Most wake up and start opening gifts.

However, reinforcing the lesson, in my opinion, means going to church first and then opening gifts afterwards or, as an alternative, going to church on Christmas Eve and then opening gifts the next morning.

A second way is to always be involved in some community project where each member of the family buys a gift for two individuals that are less fortunate, one for someone they each know and one for some they do not know.

This gives each the opportunity to – see how an unexpected gift positively impacts an individual's life and gives that individual hope for their own future.

Another way to reinforce the right priorities is to invest as a family so that your children will learn how to use their money to make money, not just spend everything they earn.

When people learn to be responsible with money, they automatically learn the consequences of the same.

Financial decisions have to be relevant to an individual's world for those lessons to stick.

Men love cars, girls love shopping, boys love tennis shoes, women love houses, shopping and so much more.

If a man wants a new car, show him how his spending is negatively impacting his ability to get that car and his spending habits will change, at least until he gets his new car. And the same follows for the remaining members of his household.

I would wager that each child would be willing to purchase less expensive items if they a) had to fork over part of the cost for the item, and b) had to forego something else they really desired more than the current purchase.

Learning consequences may help us all grow up to be better human beings without having to force our own desires on someone else, including our families.

Another positive consequence of money is that everyone has to work – to earn it (sort of). If you blow your earnings on every financial whim, your salary will always look too small to meet your true needs – shelter, food, clothing, and transportation.

But, if you are taught how to use your salary in a positive manner, then you will soon realize that it is not what you make, but how you use it.

This point was never made more abundantly clear to me than the lesson I recently learned from a dear friend.

His daughter had absolutely no desire to go to college. In fact, she was completely unsure of anything she wanted to do at all.

Her father only had one demand. She had to work.

As long as she worked, she could stay at home expense free but she had to save 25% of her weekly salary.

It was rough going initially.

Her friends were out buying all the hottest gadgets and clothes while she was lagging behind, so it seemed.

Then one day she realized how much money she had saved up, and she asked her daddy what to do with this money.

He suggested she make some sort of an investment.

She now owns her beauty shop, which is completely paid for, at the age of 25; now she is working on building her own home that she is designing herself, all without a college education but with a strong financial education.

By the way, she is the envy of all her friends not because of the money, but for having parents who cared enough to stay involved in her life.

To Choose or Not To Choose

If you are still having any doubts about your own financial success, I want to tell you a story about a young man I recently read about.

All this young man wanted to do since he was a kid was be a doctor. He was a phenomenal young man who could squat 455 pounds in sets of 10, and he was preparing for the Mr. North Carolina bodybuilding contest.

In early 2003, while in college, he went for a walk with his dogs and stopped to help a neighbor who was locked out of her apartment.

He climbed the balcony to reach her unlocked balcony door.

The railing he was hanging onto broke in his hands.

He fell backwards, was flipped upside down, and landed on the concrete sidewalk – on his head.

He was paralyzed in his arms and legs because of the spinal injury.

Ten weeks later he was back in school and graduated with the remainder of his class on time.

Although the paralysis changed his choice of a career in medicine, he is still a doctor.[3]

The Last Word

There are more than 2,000 passages in the Bible that address the topic of money.

While we may all individually struggle with what God wants from us, there are some things that are clear.

We are admonished to be good stewards and to give back because, according to Proverbs 11:25, "A generous person will be made rich, and whoever satisfies others will himself be satisfied."

This chapter has given you all the tools to start right where you are to begin being a good steward with your credit.

Do not settle for less than full success, dream the impossible, and live with expectancy.

---

3 The Charlotte Observer, July 27, 2008 , "For This Doctor, It's Personal"

Chapter Three

Ignorance of the Law

The accumulated summary of consumer credit law citations presented in this chapter were originally taken from the U.S. Department of Commerce's publication, **Credit and Financial Issues: Responsive Business Approaches to Consumer Needs.** This is not an exhaustive list nor is it intended to be a substitute for proper legal counsel. This list simply serves as a starting point for research purposes. Always consult professional legal help in matters of concern. Additional information may be found by contacting your local State Attorney General, your local chapter of the Better Business Bureau, or your chosen legal professional.

Consumer credit transactions are regulated both at the Federal and the State level. Therefore this list will help you become familiar with the laws that govern both you and those companies with whom you do business.

Federal Laws

- The Federal Consumer Credit Protection Act
- Truth in Lending Act
- Fair Credit Reporting Act
- Equal Credit Opportunity Act
- Fair Credit Billing Act
- Right to Financial Privacy Act
- Consumer Leasing Act
- Fair Debt Collection Practices Act
- Unsolicited Credit Card Act
- The Bankruptcy Reform Act of 1978

While State laws governing consumer transactions vary considerably, most State laws are based on Federal statutes that administrate several standard areas of consumer credit. Some of these laws include but are not limited to the following areas of individual State laws.

State Laws

- The Uniform Consumer Credit Code
- Usury or rate ceiling laws
- Consumer loan acts
- Mortgage lending acts
- Mortgage banker and broker acts
- Secondary mortgage acts

- Retail installment sales acts
- Seller and lender credit card acts
- Home solicitation sales acts
- Home improvement contracts acts
- Rental purchase agreement acts

Although these law title groups do not mean much to you at your first, second, or third read, however, as your credit knowledge grows, so too will your need to understand these laws.

Here is a brief list of some additional experts that can offer you more in depth explanations of the relevant jurisdictional laws in your area of business concern:

- Legal counsel
- State attorney general office
- State banking commission, consumer credit or financial institutions departments/commissions
- Trade associations

Federal Law Summaries

Most consumer credit businesses have a summary of the Federal laws summarized below either posted in their offices or available for review upon request. Once more, these summaries are provided for informational purposes only. However, these summaries are not intended to substitute for nor cannot be misconstrued as legal counsel.

Truth in Lending Act (TILA) (effective 1969; amended by Unsolicited Credit Card Act, effective 1970; amended by the Truth in Lending Simplification Act, effective 1982; amended by the Home Equity Loan Consumer Protection Act, effective 1989; amended by the Fair Credit and Charge Card Disclosure Act, effective 1989; amended by the Home Ownership and Equity Protection Act, effective October 1995). The basis of this federal law is to make sure that consumers are fully aware of the terms and cost of any consumer credit transaction. The law also gives consumers the right to cancel certain credit transactions that involve a lien on their principal dwelling. Further, TILA regulates certain credit card practices, and provides a means for fair and timely resolution of credit billing disputes. With the exception of certain high-cost mortgage loans, TILA does not regulate the charges that may be imposed on consumers for the access to credit.

This act and the subsequent laws that amended or added provisions were all enacted to prevent business abuses in consumer credit cost disclosures and to require disclosure uniformity across the credit industry.

Therefore, lenders are required to make all terms of credit known to consumers before they sign any loan documents. This disclosure ensures that each consumer will have complete knowledge of exactly what they are agreeing to before they sign.

Regulation Z is the specific provision of the Truth in Lending Act that implements the specifics of the credit cost disclosure statute. Regulation Z not only details who and what is covered by the regulation, but more importantly it details the specific disclosure and other requirements for open-end and closed-end credit transactions.

In their simplest form open-ended transactions allow a consumer to make repeated purchases or repeat loans. The guarantor (responsible party for repayment purposes) has the privilege of paying the balance in full, or the consumer may pay the balance in installments. Some common types of open-ended credit transactions include bank-issued credit cards, home equity lines of credit, department store cards, and overdraft privileges on checking accounts.

Closed-ended transactions, on the other hand, have a specific end date and a specific amount of credit. These kinds of transactions include but are not limited to vehicle loans, home appliances, and home furnishings.

Truth in Lending and Regulation Z also cover disclosures involving credit card offers received by mail or telephone, and applications distributed to the general public.

In addition to governing the advertising of such credit transactions, the act covers many other types of credit transactions as well as individual lenders. These individual lenders include any person who regularly extends credit for any reason that is subject to a finance charge or repayable by a written agreement in installments.

The law exempted credit transactions over $25,000 unless those transactions were secured by an equal amount in security interest such as real estate.

Specific and detailed disclosure requirements exist for all the various types of consumer transactions which fall under this disclosure's authority, including:

- Open-ended credit disclosures that cover credit cards, charge cards and other long term consumer credit transactions. Under these circumstances, the act requires certain specific disclosures be made before the consumer applies, agrees, or signs a credit or charge card application. These laws even require certain early disclosures and prohibits certain practices for home equity lines of credit. Additionally, all initial disclosure statements and monthly billing statement disclosures are required on open-ended transactions. There are also times in open-ended transactions when disclosure statements are required in addition to the initial and monthly disclosure statements. Further, each of these statements has its own mandated list of disclosures. Even before the current changes in credit card rules, there were provisions in Regulation Z that required a 15-day notice be given to cardholders before any changes were allowed in their credit terms. Most of you have seen this language before in one form or another, most likely as the insert in your credit card statement. Also, these disclosure statements are generally mailed to consumers just before card issuers raise their rates or change their terms.
- A miscellaneous provision that prohibits card issuers from issuing credit cards unless or in response to a verbal or written application, or as a card renewal. However, this provision does not prevent creditors from getting around its authority by distributing unsolicited applications for credit or from issuing renewals to consumers who previously accepted offers of credit.

- One other important provision that existed before current changes in the law were enacted. It provided that a cardholder was only required to repay a statutory $50 maximum to a card issuer for the unauthorized use of a card before the card issuer has been notified by the cardholder.

- Closed-end credit disclosures that are carefully defined and regulated under TILA and Regulation Z. In addition to ensuring that these disclosures were available for consumers to read prior to a loan closing, these same disclosures, if they are incorporated into the loan agreement, must be separate from all other loan documents or clearly delineated if incorporated within the loan documents. For example, on most car loans, there is a boxed section that has four areas clearly labeled for the buyer to see. Those four areas are: 1) the amount due at signing; 2) monthly payment amount and due date; 3) other charges, including end of loan charges; and, 4) the total amount of all payments due. This boxed section, generally separated by bold outside borders and bold print inside the box, has now become known as the Federal Box.

- Additional closed-ended transaction disclosures that were mandated in the Home Ownership and Equity Protection Act of 1994, which became effective October, 1995. Under this act, creditors were forced to make additional disclosures and were prohibited against other certain practices on specific types of closed-end home equity loans, namely those that had specific triggers relating to annual percentage rates, points, and/or fees. The act also has additional disclosure requirements based on advertisers' credit advertisements.

Note: The Truth in Lending Act and Regulation Z requirements are detailed and complex. Please make sure that you refer any questions of law to your chosen legal advisor who can best direct your actions appropriately to preserve all of your rights under the law.

Federal Trade Commission Credit Practices Rule, which became effective March 1, 1985, impacts all Americans who borrow money, purchase items on installment credit, or unfortunately cosign for someone else's debt. The rule was established by the Federal Trade Commission (FTC) basically to prohibit creditors from including certain provisions in consumer credit contracts that the FTC found to be unfair to consumers. The Credit Practices Rule does not apply to transactions involving the purchase of real estate; however, some of its prohibitions are listed below.

- Should you be sued for non-payment of a debt, the rule prohibits creditors from requiring you to agree in advance to give up your right to be notified of a court hearing. These kind of clauses were once known as "confessions of judgment."

- "Waivers of exemption" were also prohibited under this rule. These waivers were clauses that required consumers to give up their state-law protections that allowed consumers to keep certain personal belongings even if a debt was not paid as agreed. Customarily, state laws allow the consumer to keep their home, clothing, dishes, and other personal items of a fixed minimum value. An exclusion within the law does permit the creditor to repossess an item when that item is used as security for the same debt.

- The rule equally prohibits "wage assignment" clauses. These were contract clauses that required a buyer to agree in advance to wage deductions that would pay the creditor directly if they defaulted on a debt. However, a wage assignment clause is quite different from a payroll deduction plan. A payroll deduction plan is a plan setup through one's employer that a buyer uses to repay their loan.

- The final prohibition allowed consumers to keep their dishes and bed sheets. The "household goods security" clauses previously had required buyers to use certain household and personal belongings as collateral. This particular clause was perceived as a mean-spirited clause because creditors were requiring collateral of items they knew had little economic value, if any. The kinds of items collected could have included family photographs, the family Bible, household pets, wedding rings, and other uniquely personal items. In the lender's defense, the purpose was to exact leverage over the borrower to ensure repayment of the loan.

Finally, if any of you are unfortunate enough to be asked to be the cosigner on another's debt, please remember this rule requires you be given a notice that explains your responsibility for such a huge undertaking.

The notice must say:

"You are being asked to guarantee this debt. Think carefully before you do. If the borrower doesn't pay the debt you will have to. Be sure you can afford to pay if you have to, and that you want to accept this responsibility.

You may have to pay up to the full amount of the debt if the borrower does not pay. You may also have to pay late fees or collection costs, which increase this amount.

The creditor can collect this debt from you without first trying to collect from the borrower.*

The creditor can use the same collection methods against you that can be used against the borrower such as suing you, garnishing your wages, etc. If this debt is ever in default, that fact may become a part of your credit record.

This notice is not the contract that makes you liable for the debt."

**Note:* Depending on your state, this statement may not apply. If your state requires a creditor to first make all attempts to collect from the primary debtor before attempting to collect from the cosigner, this statement may be crossed out of a cosigner's notice.

One final note: Creditors are also prohibited from charging multiple late fees for one late payment.

Equal Credit Opportunity Act (ECOA) The act and all its amendments prohibit credit discrimination on the basis of race, color, religion, national origin, sex, marital status, age, or because an individual receives public assistance. However, creditors may gather all or some of this information in certain circumstances, but they may not use this information when deciding whether or not to extend a consumer credit or when setting credit terms. Income, expenses, debts, and credit history are factors that lenders may use to determine creditworthiness. One of the most important factors to remember under ECOA is that if you are denied credit, ask for an explanation. It may be something simple (like not being employed or living long enough in your community), or it may be that you have too many outstanding debts. But the key is to find out why your application was denied so that you know what to do in the future to overcome this obstacle. More detailed instructions are delineated also in later chapters in this handbook.

Here is a brief list of the other basic provisions of the ECOA.

- Creditors may not impose different terms or conditions, such as a higher interest rate or higher fees, on a loan based on race, color, religion, national origin, sex, marital status, age, or because an individual receives public assistance.
- A creditor may not ask if an applicant is widowed or divorced. The only formal terms a creditor may use are married, unmarried, or separated.
- Creditors may not ask questions about an applicant's marital status, one's spouse, plans for children, or alimony. However spousal questions are allowed in "community property" states, when a spouse will be allowed to use an account, and a few other limited circumstances. A creditor may also ask questions about dependent expenses, and if an applicant has to pay alimony or a similar payment.
- The ECOA also addresses other remedies including creditors beyond 62 years of age, income determinations, and other specific remedies to prevent discrimination.

Note: The ECOA and its amendments are detailed and complex. Please make sure that you refer any questions of law to your chosen legal advisor who can best direct your actions appropriately to preserve all of your rights under the law.

Fair Credit Billing Act (FCBA) (effective 1975) applies only to open-end credit transactions, such as credit cards, department store cards, and other similar accounts. Among other things, the act specifies a step-by step procedure for billing error resolutions only. The simplified process is as follows:

- The consumer must give written notice of a billing error within 60 days of receiving the bill in question. The notice must be sent to the address given for "billing inquiries," and not the address for sending payments. You must also include your name, address, account number, and a description of the billing error. It is suggested that you send your letter by certified mail, return receipt requested, so that you have proof of your dispute. Make sure you keep a copy of your entire package; and, make sure you include copies of your sales slips and other supporting documentation.

- Unless the problem is resolved, the creditor must respond within 30 days. The dispute must be resolved within two billing cycles, but not longer than 90 days after receiving your letter.

- During this resolution period no legal or other collection activity is permitted on the disputed and related charges. Although the consumer must pay all undisputed charges, the disputed charges may not be reported as delinquent, nor can the account be closed or restricted because of the consumer's dispute.

- If the consumer still believes the billing to be in dispute after the resolution period, the consumer must again notify the creditor in writing. Depending on the creditor's response to the consumer's second inquiry, there are a number of other options available under the law that are fully delineated at the Federal Trade Commission's website, www.ftc.gov.

Right to Financial Privacy Act (RFPA) (1979) provides privacy protection to customers of financial institutions when the Federal government is seeking financial record information about an institution's customers. The act defines a financial institution as any office of a bank, savings bank, other type of regulated financial institution, or bankcard issuers (retailers included).

Below are the methods by which governmental authorities may gain access to information contained in the financial records of any customer of a financial institution or card-issuer under the provisions of the act.

- The customer can authorize access to their records in writing.

- The financial records may be disclosed in response to an administrative subpoena. The customer must be mailed a copy of the subpoena. Within 10 days of receiving the notice, the customer has the right to file a motion to prevent disclosure.

- The financial records may be disclosed in response to a search warrant.

- The financial records may be disclosed in response to a judicial subpoena. A copy of the subpoena must have been served on the customer on or before the date on which the financial institution was served.

- In the absence of a subpoena, the financial records may be disclosed in response to a formal written request. However, government authorities may gain access to a consumer's financial records without a consumer's consent if the agency is investigating the financial institution, and not the consumer.

Consumer Leasing Act (CLA) (1976) dictates the disclosures for consumer leases. Leasing companies are required to do the following in writing:

- Give a brief description of the leased property.

- Disclose the total amount of the security deposit (if required), initial payment required, number of payments, amount of each payment, additional charges, due dates and total amount of payments, including penalties for late payments or delinquencies, customer appraisal and other rights. The other terms and conditions of the transaction, including guarantees, required insurance and any consumer liability at the end of the lease must also be disclosed. This includes:

- Identify any express warranty and the party responsible for the product's maintenance and service.

- State whether the customer has the option to purchase the leased property and provide information related to the purchase.

- Disclose early termination rights, if any.

- Disclose the customer's liability for the difference between the estimated value of the property and its realized value to the lessor at early termination or lease-end.

Fair Debt Collection Practices Act (FDCPA) (effective 1978, amended) applies to anyone who collects consumer debts on behalf of someone else. FDCPA also applies to attorneys who collect consumer debts. While FDCPA regulates the practices of debt collection agencies, and prohibits them from using unfair practices to collect overdue bills or calling debtors at unreasonable hours of the day and/or night, it generally applies only to third party debt collectors (companies other than the original owner that is paid to collect a debt for the owner) mentioned above. FDCPA generally does not apply to banks or other businesses collecting their own accounts. However, most states have similar laws that apply to these businesses as well. FDCPA prohibits all of the following:

- Threatening or using violence.
- Using obscene or profane language.
- Publishing a list of consumers who allegedly refuse to pay their debts.

The following restrictions are also placed on contacts made by debt collectors.

- Contacts must be limited to between 8:00 a.m. and 9:00 p.m.
- A debtor may be contacted at work unless the collector knows or has reason to know that the employer prohibits an employee from receiving such calls. There are some other restrictions placed on debt collectors that consumers should get to know.
- If a debtor is represented by an attorney, a collector cannot communicate directly with the debtor unless the attorney grants permission (which would be never) or under some other limited circumstances.
- FDCPA also identifies which third-parties can be contacted about a debtor for debt collection; how and when these contacts can be made; and, what acts are considered to be false, misleading or unfair.

A complete and updated copy of the FDCPA can be found by copying the website http://www.ftc.gov/bcp/edu/pubs/consumer/credit/cre27.pdf into your browser.

Electronic Fund Transfer Act (EFTA) (effective 1979) applies to all manner of electronic fund transfers (EFTs) involving asset accounts, including those transactions made at automatic teller machines (ATMs), telephone transfer systems, direct deposits, and automatic preauthorized payments to third parties. Some of EFTA's provisions include:

- Prohibiting issuance of unsolicited access devices such as ATM cards until they are validated by the financial institution at the consumer's request.
- Limiting consumer liability to $50 for unauthorized transfers involving an access device or card, with a few restrictions attached.
- Limiting consumer liability for unauthorized transfers involving an access device or card to $500 if the financial institution is notified more than two days after the loss of a card. If the consumer fails to notify the financial institution within two days, their liability could be unlimited if 60 days passes and the financial institution is still not notified even after the consumer's receipt of a periodic statement, unless there are mitigating circumstances.
- Allowing financial institutions to correct or re-credit an account after oral or written notice of errors is received.
- Allowing financial institutions 45 calendar days to resolve an error appearing on a periodic statement after being notified by a consumer. If the error cannot be resolved within ten business days, the account must be provisionally re-credited until the investigation is completed.
- Prohibiting creditors from requiring the use of EFTs to repay loans as a condition of credit. Employers and providers of government benefits may require the use of EFTs, but must give consumers the choice of financial institutions to be used.

The Bankruptcy Reform Act (effective 1979; amended) This act is known as the Bankruptcy Code and replaces the Bankruptcy Act of 1898. Different types of bankruptcy are named after chapters of the Bankruptcy Code. Here are the most common types of bankruptcy.

- Chapter 7 is the most common type of bankruptcy. It is known as a "straight" bankruptcy because for the most part it is a straight-forward process. Simply put all assets are liquidated in order to pay creditors.
- Chapter 11 provides primarily for a business bankruptcy. Chapter 11 allows a business to reorganize through a court approved plan to pay all or part of its business' debts to its creditors.

- Chapter 13 bankruptcy is for consumers with a regular income. Under Chapter 13 consumers develop a court approved plan to pay all or part of their debts to their creditors over a specified time period.

Upon the filing of a bankruptcy petition, an automatic stay is executed under the law. Just as the title states, the Bankruptcy Code automatically stops all efforts by creditors to collect a debt, take possession of collateral, enforce a lien, set off a debt or collect receivables of a debtor. Any relief from automatic stay restrictions must be requested of the bankruptcy court by the creditor and approved by the judge. Additional questions on bankruptcy should be directed to your chosen legal professional.

If a creditor wins a lawsuit against a debtor and awarded monetary judgment relief by the court, each state has set a specific time limit by which those judgments may be collected. Notwithstanding these limits, some states allow judgments to be renewed several times, which essentially could make some judgments enforceable throughout one's lifetime.

Accordingly, I have listed the basic statute of limitations for each state in the table on page 50.

The Fair Credit Reporting Act

The Fair Credit Reporting Act (FCRA) is a complex piece of federal legislation that contains a myriad number of provisions to regulate how credit reporting agencies use your information. FCRA imposes obligations on 1) credit bureaus (and similar agencies) that maintain consumer credit histories, 2) lenders and other businesses that buy reports from credit bureaus, and 3) parties who furnish consumer information to credit bureaus. Among other provisions, the FCRA limits the sale of credit reports by credit bureaus. This is done by 1) requiring the purchaser to have a permissible purpose to obtain the information, 2) allowing consumers to learn the information contained in their credit bureau files (including one annual free credit report from each of the three largest credit reporting agencies), and 3) specifying procedures for challenging errors in the data contained within their files.

Since there are many types of consumer reporting agencies, including credit bureaus and specialty agencies (such as agencies that sell information about check writing histories, medical records, and rental history records) the FCRA promotes the accuracy, fairness, and privacy of your individual information maintained by all credit reporting agencies.

If a creditor wins a lawsuit against a debtor and awarded monetary judgment relief by the court, each state has set a specific time limit by which those judgments may be collected. Notwithstanding these limits, some states allow judgments to be renewed several times, which essentially could make some judgments enforceable throughout one's lifetime.

Accordingly, I have listed the basic statute of limitations for each state in the table on page 51.

FCRA also restricts who has access to your sensitive credit information and how that information can be used. Thus, it is the primary law that governs what credit reporting agencies can and cannot do with your personal information, and it defines what is and is not a proper business purpose.

Below are several important features of how FCRA is designed to help consumers (for the complete text, visit the Federal Trade Commission's website at www.ftc.gov).

The 2003 amendment of the law was actually a third law, "The Fair and Accurate Credit Transactions Act of 2003." This law came with numerous improvements including the all important free annual credit report from the three largest credit reporting agencies. This provision not only helps to protect the privacy of consumer's information by allowing them to know who has accessed their information, but it also helps to guarantee that your information will be accurate as possible whenever and wherever supplied.

The 1996 amendment strengthened these guarantees by making credit reporting agencies liable for knowingly reporting misinformation. It also provided consumers with legal recourse against individuals who obtain their report without a permissible purpose. Finally, this amendment also requires the credit bureaus to investigate errors within a set period of time.

One of the biggest benefits of the 1996 amendment was that it helped to bring some uniformity to the individual reports maintained by the three largest credit reporting agencies. If your information is entered correctly and is properly verified, regardless of who examines your credit record from either of the three major credit reporting agencies, it should all look about the same.

Statute of Limitations for Judgments *SOL for each state indicated in years*			
Alabama	20	Montana	10
Alaska	5	Nebraska	20
Arizona	10	Nevada	10
Arkansas	10	New Hampshire	20
California	10	New Jersey	14
Colorado	20	New Mexico	20
Connecticut	20	New York	10
Delaware	No Limit	North Carolina	5
Florida	20	North Dakota	6
Georgia	7	Ohio	21
Hawaii	10	Oklahoma	5
Idaho	20	Oregon	10
Illinois	20	Pennsylvania	4
Indiana	20	Rhode Island	20
Iowa	6	South Carolina	10
Kansas	5	South Dakota	20
Kentucky	15	Tennessee	10
Louisiana	10	Texas	10
Maine	20	Utah	8
Maryland	12	Vermont	20
Massachusetts	20	Virginia	8
Michigan	10	Washington	10
Minnesota	10	Washington, D.C.	3
Mississippi	7	West Virginia	20
Missouri	10	Wisconsin	10
		Wyoming	5

The above information-matrix is for reference only. This information is believed to be accurate at the time of publication. Please verify the accuracy of this information for the latest updates with your chosen attorney, your State Attorney General, or your local Better Business Bureau.

Summary of Key Rights

The following is a summation of consumer rights established by the FCRA.

- Consumers must be able to find out what is in their file, and the credit reporting agencies must disclose this information to you once you have provided the agency with proper identification.

- Consumers have the right to dispute inaccurate information and to have that inaccurate information corrected or deleted. If you tell a credit reporting company, in writing, that your file contains inaccurate information, the agency is obligated to investigate the matter with the source that provided the information. If the investigation fails to resolve the dispute, you may add a brief statement to your credit file that explains the matter.

- Outdated information cannot be reported. A credit reporting company must correct or, as the case may be, delete from your credit file the information that is found to be inaccurate or can no longer be verified. However, the credit reporting agency has no obligation to remove accurate data from your file unless it is outdated or can no longer be verified. In general, negative information that is more than 7 years old (10 years for bankruptcies) must be removed from your file.

- Consumer consent is required for reports provided to employers. You must give your signed consent for reports to be provided to employers. A consumer reporting agency may not give out information about you to your employer, or a potential employer, without your specific written consent.

- Consumers must be told if information in their file is used against them. Anyone who uses your credit report or another type of consumer report against you, to deny you credit, insurance, or employment, or to take some other adverse action against you, must tell you. They must also give you the name, address, and phone number of the agency that provided the information.

Consumers can request their names be excluded from lists from unsolicited credit offers of any kind. Creditors and insurers may share information in your credit file with marketers who send you unsolicited offers. If you do not wish to be a part of such offers, and would like to request your name be removed, please call 888-567-8688.

Defined permissible purposes included in FCRA are:

- Providing your credit report to an employer with your signed consent.
- Court orders.
- Allowing credit reporting agencies to refuse requests for your information to anyone that lacks a permissible purpose, such as the evaluation of an application for a loan, credit, service, or employment.

Other permissible purposes include:

- Insurance underwriting purposes;
- Determining eligibility for a government benefit;
- Reviewing existing credit obligations for value and assessing risks; and,
- Responding to child-support inquiries.

To Receive Your Credit Report

Under the FACT Act amendment to the Fair Credit Reporting Act you are now entitled to one free credit report every year from each of the three major credit reporting agencies. You have three ways to access this free credit report. You can (1) request this free annual disclosure by calling toll free 1-877 – FACTACT, (2) or by using the mail request form available in this book, (3) or the quickest way is by going to the website www.annualcreditreport.com. By choosing option (3), you will have instant access to your credit reports once you verify a few pieces of information that only you should know.

Here are some other circumstances under which you may receive a free copy of your credit report.

- If you are unemployed and intend to apply for employment within the next 60 days.
- If you are on public welfare assistance.
- If you believe your file contains inaccurate information due to fraud.
- You are also entitled to a free report if you have received notice of an adverse decision (such as denial of credit, insurance, or employment) within the past 60 days.

When requesting a credit report by mail, be sure to include your full name, current address, Social Security Number, and most recent former address for file-matching purposes. You will also need to include any evidentiary support to bolster you request for a free copy in some cases. If you do not qualify for a free copy, you must include a personal check or money order made payable to the appropriate credit reporting agency based on the rate for the state where you live.

A more exhaustive list and other helpful information such as things to consider before buying a home, investing wisely, how to make a formal complaint, some sample complaint letters, seeking legal help, and a consumer assistance directory can be found in *The Consumer Action Handbook* annually produced by the U. S. General Services Administration Federal Consumer Information Center (FCIC).

You can either place your order for the handbook directly at the FCIC website www.pueblo.gsa.gov or by writing the Federal Consumer Information Center, Pueblo, CO 81009, or by calling 1-800-688-9889.

In addition, there are more in depth discussions on these topics found in later chapters of this manual.

Here is an abbreviated list of two other important consumer protection laws.

Fair Housing Act: A federal law that prohibits mortgage lenders from discriminating against applicants on the basis of race, color, religion, sex, handicap, familial status or national origin. The Equal Housing Opportunity symbol represents the commitment by lenders to doing business in accordance with the Fair Housing Act.

Real Estate Settlement Procedures Act (RESPA): Federal law that requires lenders to provide home mortgage borrowers with information about settlement costs prior to closing and prohibits lenders, realtors, and others involved in the mortgage industry from paying kickbacks and unearned fees. In addition, if an escrow account is established, RESPA regulates the amount of money homebuyers are required to place in the escrow account for property taxes and insurance and requires disclosures during the life of the loan regarding the escrow account. Finally, RESPA regulates the transfers of servicing between mortgage lenders

Below is a list of federal and state regulatory agencies that may be of some assistance should a dispute arise in your business relationships.

Consumer reporting agencies, creditors

Federal Trade Commission
Consumer Response Center – FCRA
Washington, DC 20580
1-877-382-4357

National banks, federal branches/agencies of foreign banks (word "National" or initials "N.A." appear in or after bank's name)

Office of the Comptroller of the Currency
Compliance Management, Mail Stop 6-6
Washington, DC 20219
800-613-6743

Federal Reserve System member banks (except national banks, and federal branches/agencies of foreign banks)

Federal Reserve Board
Division of Consumer & Community Affairs
Washington, DC 20551
202-452-3693

Savings associations and federally chartered savings banks (word "Federal" or initials "F.S.B." appear in federal institution's name)

Office of Thrift Supervision
Consumer Complaints
Washington, DC 20552
800-842-6929

Federal credit unions (words "Federal Credit Union" appear in institution's name)

National Credit Union Administration
1775 Duke Street
Alexandria, VA 22314
703-519-4600

State-chartered banks that are not members of the Federal Reserve System

Federal Deposit Insurance Corporation
Consumer Response Center
2345 Grand Avenue, Suite 100
Kansas City, Missouri 64108-2638
1-877-275-3342

Practical Application of the Law

Because the law does not necessarily keep up with the most current behavioral patterns of society, nor was it designed to do so, here are some brief observations for a few particular cases to help individuals decide whether or not they need to seek legal advice.

Again, please remember, these observations are in no way intended to be misconstrued as formal or informal legal advice, nor are they meant to replace the help that can only be received from your professional legal advisor.

If you happen to be in a non-traditional relationship, here are a few legal observations that may help you survive financially.

Although more than 40% of Fortune 500 companies provide health insurance, long-term care, and other benefits to domestic partners, these benefits are considered additional income by the Internal Revenue Service (IRS), and thus are taxable income under current law. So before adding your partner to your company's benefits plan, consult with your human resources department and your own legal advisor about your options to minimize this potential tax impact.

If you are the legal beneficiary of your partner's estate and vice versa, most states have an inheritance that is imposed on beneficiaries who are not family, legally that is. Depending on the size of your estate, you and your partner may want to consider relocating to a state that currently does not impose such a tax.

One other very large fact needs to be taken into consideration about your final estate(s). Same-sex couples, as well as unmarried couples, can be taxed up to 45% if their assets exceed the Federal exemption of $2 million (at the time of publication, this was the most up to date exemption information). It is very easy to exceed this exemption when assets are defined to include not only your primary residence, but life insurance, investments, retirement funds, and any business assets. Make sure you get some good legal advice to help you structure the transfer and minimize the IRS's take.

Domestic partners can also not expect to receive any Social Security benefits or Federal pensions from their departed partners. Make sure you investigate life insurance options to replace this lost income.

There is one more observation to consider. There are no unlimited gifts allowed by the Federal government between unmarried partners. For example, if you and your partner were to purchase a new car that cost $30,000, and one of you pays $10,000 and the other pays $20,000, then anything above $12,000 is considered taxable by the IRS.

Since the current Federal exemption is only $12,000 for such gifts, then the remaining $8,000 is considered a taxable gift by the IRS. To try and avoid this kind of potential tax bit, try to maintain an equal balance of expenses and payments for such items, and again talk to some professionals to discuss other possible ways to legally avoid such a tax trigger.

While we are on the subject of legal documentation, there are a few legal documents that you should always have and keep updated on a regular basis.

There are four legal documents that we all should have regardless of our financial situations.

The first one is a durable power of attorney for health care. Regardless of whether you have any medical conditions or not, you should always have an up-to-date advanced directive or health care proxy so that you decide who will make medical decisions for you as opposed to such personal decisions being made by a stranger, before or if you should ever become incapacitated.

The second is a durable power of attorney for finances. This document directs who and how your designee will handle your finances. This may or may not be the same person designated for your health care.

The third is a living will, which tells the doctors how your medical care is to be directed if you are unable to tell them yourself. We have all heard the terribly painful stories of families fighting over putting in and removing feeding tubes, blood transfusions, and breathing machines. This prevents all of those arguments that no one ever really wins. But more importantly, the living will keeps your voice alive when you may need it most.

The fourth and final document is a simple will. This will tell your surviving relatives who gets everything from the Apple computer to your annual passes to the zoo, and everything in between including the kids.

The only consideration I would offer all my readers is to make sure that your chosen parties will not make decisions that would offend your conscience if you were making these decisions; and, to make sure you choose individuals who are tough enough to withstand the considerable pressure they will have to bear.

To Declare or Not Declare

In the midst of the worst financial crisis that the world has ever experienced collectively, the question whether or not to file bankruptcy continues to weigh heavy on the minds of many. Here are some guidelines for consideration when confronted with this kind of decision from someone who has firsthand experience. Again, this advice does not replace that of professional legal counsel.

Educate yourself about the bankruptcy process and the applicable laws. Although you will no doubt have the advice of counsel, make sure you clearly understand what you are getting into. Bankruptcy is a long process, so you need to do your homework early. The problem is that most of us do not actually realize that we have to file bankruptcy until it is too late for us to consider other options.

When I was considering bankruptcy, I made a chart of all of the legal options available under the different types of bankruptcy chapters (Chapter 7, 11, 13). I also made three lists to go along with each option. I made a list of all of 1) my assets and my obligations; 2) my alternatives to bankruptcy; and 3) ways to recover from the bankruptcy impacts for the next 10 years.

After reviewing all of my information, I then made another appointment with a bankruptcy attorney to help me sort through all of this information to make a final decision. Once that decision was made, I started gathering all of my paperwork for 90 days. This included 90 days worth of pay stubs, retirement account balances, bank statements, all bills, any contracts, collection letters, tax appraisals, and any other paperwork requested by my attorney.

Since I had not saved enough money to pay my attorney's legal fees, I negotiated a payment plan (although my attorney could not legally file the paperwork until all my fees were paid) to pay my attorney as quickly as possible. I actually paid the agreed amount early by trimming all my expenses except for the bare essentials.

I did not have to worry about buying anything or giving any money away, things that could derail the judge approving my bankruptcy, because I did not have the financial means to do either of those things. I also stopped using my credit cards, before my credit lines were cut off.

But the hardest part of all was actually waiting for the judge to approve my bankruptcy petition.

So if you are considering bankruptcy, here are a few questions to ask yourself.

1. *Do you have few assets and little income?*
2. *Do you have a high debt load that does not include student loans, taxes, or child support?*
3. *Have you cosigned a loan that you cannot repay?*
4. *Have you previously filed bankruptcy within the last eight years?*
5. *Have your assets depreciated far beneath what you still owe on them?*

If you have answered yes to any of these questions, here is a really good bankruptcy quiz that I believe may help many of you:

http://moneycentral.msn.com/quiz/bankruptcy-quiz/home.aspx

As we close this chapter, let me leave you with a quote from Aristotle. "The law is reason free from passion." However, I assure you, if you get into a situation where you need the law, this is reason enough to passionately seek a solution or relief.

Chapter Four

What's in a Name?

I am a huge movie buff and I can recall the lines from hundreds of movies, but one in particular has always stuck in my mind.

The scene where Angela Bassett, as Tina Turner, giving up everything in divorce court but keeping her name has always been important to me from the first time that I saw it.

A good name for you or any individual starting out is as important as is the name of a new developer trying to sell a new construction project to skeptical buyers and the bank at the same time. If it is a condominium project, the developer must sell anywhere from 50% to 90% of all the units before any bank will lend them the money for construction.

For the individual it is the same concept. You have to prove yourself before any bank will lend you any money.

In a odd sort of way, you have to prove you do not need some money before you can borrow any money.

Usually, establishing your good name happens when you're young and often not accustomed to financial responsibilities. It is not uncommon for 20 – and even 30 – something adults to move back home once, twice, maybe even three times before they are finally financially strong enough to be out on their own. How you decide to manage your fun, finances and freedom will affect you today, tomorrow, and well into your future. It establishes your name. It is a marriage made for better or worse.

Most of us are all aware of the companies (credit reporting agencies) that keep track of our collective efforts to pay our bills on time or not pay them on time. The big three are Equifax, TransUnion, and Experian.

These same companies, in turn, sell this information to our potential creditors in the form of a credit report, all the while scoring our bill paying efforts in the process.

While maintaining good credit may seem difficult at first, understanding how the process works will make your personal financial management job much easier.

In today's marketplace a good credit history could determine whether or not you get a job, if you can get insurance with the insurer of your choice, and the price you pay for that insurance.

But one thing you may not know is that approximately 25% of all credit reports are believed to contain one or more errors. Errors that directly impact your purchasing power.

One of the reasons this book was written was to help every customer achieve a positive report that is free from errors.

A good payment history will help you reach this goal and solidify your financial future, just as a bad payment history will dampen your efforts and delay your fun for as long as seven years or more.

The Score Card

As previously discussed, 99% of all creditors use some type of scoring system to evaluate requests for credit.

This fact alone makes it vitally important for you to check your credit report from all three credit reporting agencies approximately once every four months.

By staggering the reports every four months, getting one from a different reporting agency every four months, this will help you stay abreast of any changes or unusual activity on your report that was not authorized or initiated by you.

This is important because your credit score used by a lender may be different from the credit score calculated by the credit bureau.

The final credit score computed by your lender will be determined by all of the following: your credit application information which generally includes your annual income, your employer's information, the type of position you hold, references provided at the creditor's request, and banking information, to name just a few.

The Big Three always have your three digits in sight, but how well do your know your own number?

The other part of the lender's credit score will include two items received from one of the three credit reporting agencies.

Those two items are your credit report and your credit score.

The credit report received from one of the big three lists all of your personal information, your outstanding debt load, the different types of accounts you own, how long you have owned those accounts, and your bill repayment history.

The credit score is the numerical equivalent of your cumulative report based on a non-disclosed pre-defined formula.

Together all of these factors make up your lender's detailed credit file, which when all this information is combined makes up your lender's score.

All of these particulars about your financial behavior and singularly identifying information are documented in your personal credit file that will determine your proportionate risk for a loan.

If everything in your credit profile indicates you are a good risk based on the lender's preset standards, you may not only get a loan, but you may also get that loan at a reasonable cost.

As your risk quotient rises, you may still get a loan but at a much higher cost (higher interest rate and extra fees).

Now if your risk quotient is too high, your loan request will be denied.

In its simplest form, the loan process looks like the diagram below.

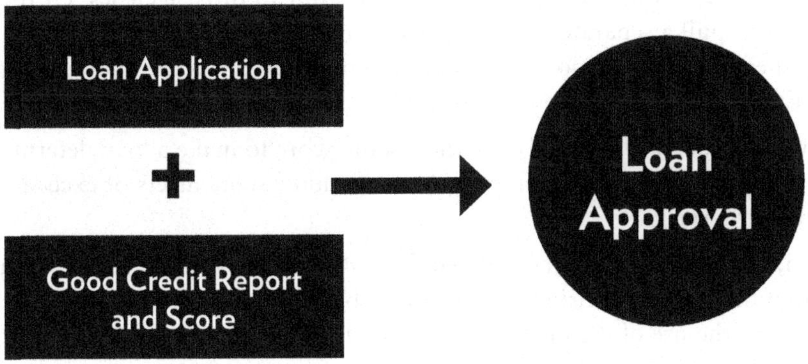

So it is easy to see exactly why a lender is interested in your information and why you should be too.

This gives you the opportunity to see how the lender sees you when reviewing your credit history even before your loan is denied or approved.

If you are a credit novice you may be a high-risk to a lender because you have no history for them to review; and, therefore the lenders have no way of knowing how responsible you are when it comes to financial obligations.

If you are one of those individuals with little or no credit history, you are known in the industry as a "thin file."

But there is a way to build both a good credit file and a positive credit history in a responsible manner.

Similar Is Not the Same

Although the big three collect the exact same information, there is a tremendous difference in the way it is scored. The weight of each item or the importance the credit bureau places on each item is considered proprietary information by each agency that is not revealed. While each credit reporting agency formats the exact information in a slightly different manner, all credit files contain the same categories of information.

For example, some transactions such as buying a house will require the lenders to do one of two things.

The lender will either pull a combined score from all three agencies. Or the lender will pull a separate score from each credit reporting agency. Historically speaking Trans Union is the highest score, Equifax is the middle score, and Experian will be the lowest of the three.

Then the lender will generally use the middle score to make a loan determination, other things being equal, provided the middle score meets or exceeds the lender's criteria.

Again, the middle score is considered the preferred the score of choice, meaning that most credit decisions will be made based on this middle score. The reason for the use of the median score is that it most closely resembles your true credit score.

So it is critical that the information in your report is accurate and up to date.

Each consumer's credit report includes five types of information — public record information, tradeline accounts information, creditor inquiry information, your personal information, and the fifth section is the inquiry section.

To see how your information is formatted, you may go to www.equifax.com, www.transunion.com, and www.experian.com to view an example of how each agency formats their credit files.

***Personal Note:** In today's market place and the concern for medical evidence being released inappropriately, I recommend that any outstanding medical bill be satisfied prior to that bill being reported to the credit reporting agencies. Otherwise you may open yourself up to further scrutiny than you would like by future lenders, employers, or others who have a legitimate reason to review your credit report.*

If this is not possible, I recommend making a reasonable payment plan and sticking to it. The goal is simply to prevent the medical information from being reported to the credit bureau for long as possible, and never is the true end result.

Off the Record

By law, credit reporting agencies cannot disclose certain medical information (relating to physical, mental, or behavioral health conditions).

Now, there is a caveat to that statement.

If a third party reports your payment history to any credit bureau and that information happens to include the name of a medical provider, the name(s) of that medical provider will be included in reports provided to you at your request.

However, in reports provided to others those names will simply be displayed only as medical payment data. However, there are times when this rule is not as tightly adhered to as it supposed to be.

Public record information is just as the name states, information that is gathered from public records.

Public records are open for all to see, not just your creditors, and maybe by your employers and others also.

This data can include overdue child support payments, bankruptcy filings which can remain on your report for up to 10 years, unpaid tax liens which can remain on your report for up to 15 years, and other public information that can remain as long as 7 years.

Other information not contained in your credit report includes checking or savings account data, bankruptcies more than 10 years old, and debts more than 7 years old (though you may have to work a little to get those removed).

On the Record

Tradeline accounts refer to active credit accounts and the historical data of other accounts from companies that are currently doing or have done business with you.

This section includes specific information such as the date opened, the loan amount or credit limit, the account balance, monthly payment amount, and probably most importantly your payment pattern.

The reporting agency also records whether there is a joint account holder or cosigner on any account who is also responsible for paying the account (note, word to the wise do not be surety (cosigner for another's debt) for anyone – this makes you doubly vulnerable).

While active positive credit information may remain on your report indefinitely, most negative information will stay on the report for up to 7 years.

Again remember, trouble is easy to get into but hard to get out of.

Credit Is

The types of credit that are extended to you may be part of the determining factors when evaluating your credit risk.

The two basic types of credit are secured and unsecured.

The most often thought of secured loans are an automobile and a home, and in that order.

Secured means that your loan is based on or attached to a tangible piece of real or personal property.

Real property cannot be moved, i.e. a house or any permanent structure.

Personal property can be moved, i.e. a car, mobile home, or jewelry.

If you fail to make a payment or a series of payments on either type of loan, the lender has the right to repossess the property from your possession.

An unsecured loan also known as a signature loan does not require any collateral or security, either personal or real property.

It is nothing more than your signature on documents that you promise to repay the debt as agreed.

Your name is on the line. But then again your good name has earned you good credit and the privilege of not having to tie up your property as collateral on a loan.

Now, an inquiry on your report is any request by other potential creditors or existing creditors to review your credit history, as allowed by law.

As previously covered, the Fair Credit Reporting Act allows legitimate credit grantors, those with an allowable purpose to inquire about your credit information without your consent.

All credit inquiries are not equal in the eyes of creditors.

Included in this section is the date of the inquiry and how long the inquiry will remain on your report.

Some of the reporting agencies will include the address of the inquiring party and sometimes a contact number.

Inquirers can be potential bank lenders, government agencies, insurance companies, landlords, and anyone you have given written permission to review your file, such as a new employer.

These inquiries are revealed to other creditors and will be included in your credit report, but not your credit score.

The only inquiry that counts toward your credit score is when you actually make an application for credit and authorize the lender to request a copy of your credit report.

While there may be a number of different types of inquiries on your credit report, it bears repeating that not all inquiries are counted toward your credit score.

Your own requests, credit checks by businesses wishing to offer you services (promotional inquiries), and inquires made by those whom you already have credit do not count against your score.

Your credit report also contains personal information and at a minimum includes your name, Social Security Number or just the last four digits, possibly previous and current addresses, maybe a telephone number, date of birth, and previous and current employers. This report may also include any variations on all the above.

The four R's are still important today - -reading, writing, arithmetic, and (financial) resources.

If you are married, your spouse's name may also appear on your copy of the report, but it will not appear on those copies provided to other requestors.

All of this information comes in whole or in part from credit applications, so accuracy and legibility when filling out these forms is critical, as well as consistency of information.

(Remember taking hand writing in grade school...never thought it would be of any importance did you?)

To This End

While it is true credit reporting agencies cannot collect or report any data about medical history, criminal records, race, political or religious preferences, personal lifestyle, or any other information unrelated to credit, there is still enough verifiable credit information available to give lenders a fairly accurate picture of your level of financial responsibility.

Just because a bankruptcy is no longer on your credit file does not mean you are out of the woods yet.

Some creditors ask for this information on their credit application along with the details.

That all encompassing question from which you cannot hide is 'have you ever filed for bankruptcy' – operative word ever.

Now if there are some unusual circumstances that have negatively impacted your ability to repay your bills like a prolonged illness, or loss of a spouse or child, then you have a right to add a statement that may or may not influence the credit grantor's decision.

But, as a general rule, these statements are only found when bad credit needs detailed explanations that only the credit holder can provide. In the end they may do little to change a decision, but never turn down an opportunity to improve how you are perceived by creditors.

If you are unfortunate enough to have bad credit but are fortunate enough to get a loan, you will be charged historically higher fees with a corresponding higher interest rate because although the lender extended you the loan, they still expect you to default.

The best revenge is to prove them wrong, and never use their services again.

Take that bad experience to your next lender and show them how well you did. That would turn your real negative into a positive.

The idea from the lenders' point of view is to make as much money as they can on each payment so that if (when) you default they may have gotten very close to the breakeven point before you completely stop making payments.

By the way, the lender is still going to sue you for the remainder of their money so you will be looking at additional charges including attorney fees and other similar charges.

Now if your credit is so bad that you cannot get a loan under any circumstances, then that means you are back in chapter one where everything is cash and carry, which can be a really tough life. But not impossible, I did it for several years.

Finally, while all three of your credit bureau reports should look about the same, you need to be reminded that not all lenders report to all three bureaus.

Even though the three bureaus share information, within certain parameters, with lenders and in some cases with each other, that still does not guarantee that the information will always be the same by the time you get your copy of the report.

Remember, credit reporting agencies gather information on an ongoing basis from many sources including you.

Lenders, employers, landlords, and other credit providers buy this information in the form of your credit report to help them decide whether to approve your consumer finance request or not, whatever that may be.

Because your credit file changes constantly, it is important that you review your information regularly.

One Last Word

According to the U. S. Public Interest Research Groups (USPIRG), 1 in 4 credit reports contains errors serious enough to cause consumers to be denied credit, an apartment, or even a job.

While Equifax, Experian, and TransUnion are methodical in collecting and compiling information about consumer creditworthiness from banks, creditors, and public records in order to build their files, they are not nearly as careful in ensuring that their practices do not result in avoidable errors.

A recent report by USPIRG collected 200 surveys from adults in 30 states.

There were four major findings according to the survey results.

1) 79% of the credit reports contained mistakes.

2) 30% of the credit reports contained accounts that had been closed by the consumer but were still listed incorrectly as open.

3) 25% of the credit reports contained errors serious enough to cause a consumer to be denied credit.

4) 54% of the credit reports contained personal demographic identifying information that was misspelled, long-since outdated, belonged to a stranger, or was simply incorrect.

In response to consumer demands for help, in December 2003, Congress passed the Fair and Accurate Credit Transactions Act (FACT), which included the monumental right to a free annual credit report from each of the big three bureaus on request, in addition to a number of other provisions designed to improve the accuracy of credit reports.

Although as a nation, consumers have had the free right to their credit reports since the later part of 2005, in the last five years, the big three bureaus have been fined millions of dollars for not cleaning up known errors. Clearly the job is not yet complete.

Even more needs to be done to give consumers the opportunity for redress through the courts.

Congress and state legislatures need to finish the job by strengthening consumers private right of action when a credit bureau or a creditor fails to protect personal information or to comply with an investigation, limit or prohibit the use of a consumer's Social Security Number, and give consumers more control over who has access to their credit reports and when.

One way to help give consumers back their control, as suggested by my banker, is to give every U. S. consumer a personal identification number(s) for each or all of their credit reports, which would guarantee their reports would not be accessed without their permission.

Every time their report is accessed without their PIN, the next time they did access their individual report, they would first get an alert giving them a list of who recently accessed their reports without their permission.

We will end this chapter just as we started it. How important is your name to you?

How prepared are you to manage this responsibility for good or bad. Either way what you do will either open or close doors. The doors are completely left to your choosing.

Chapter Five

You Are In Control

The cyclical U. S. economy is driven in large part by consumer confidence which is tracked monthly by the national Consumer Confidence Index that began in 1981.

During periods of high consumer confidence and economic optimism there is high activity on credit reports because consumers spending is up.

Simply put, consumers increase their spending by using credit to make major purchases, and use their credit cards more frequently (i.e., carry higher credit card balances). Therefore consumer spending drives consumers to put in more applications for credit, which in turn drives up consumer reporting activity.

The reverse is also true, which helps drive the U. S. economy in a downturn. During periods of lower optimism and low consumer confidence there is less activity on credit reports because consumers spending either drops off dramatically or becomes stagnant.

When the economy and consumer spending drop off, businesses go into a survivor mode and increase their pre-collection activity to make sure they minimize their losses.

For example, even if you are a consistent paying customer, if you have had just one late payment, or a few on-time, but smaller than usual payments, then a creditor may start calling you to make sure you are going to be able to make your monthly payments. This is done to protect the creditor from losing as few dollars as possible. Even though you may not see yourself as in trouble, the creditors see your account as a red flag that they need to resolve. So they try to collect as much money from you as they can before another creditor beats them

My mother always told me that somebody is always watching what you are doing, and what is done in the dark will always come to the light. Never has this been more true than where consumer credit files are concerned.

to it.

Credit already extended to customers that shows up on the consumer credit report as a loan also shows up on businesses' accounting records as accounts receivables.

Therefore, during times of low consumer confidence and decreased spending, businesses increase their pre-collection and proactive collection activities in order to minimize their losses on their accounts receivables before any late payment activity begins.

Because your credit report is clearly important to businesses no matter the level of consumer confidence, their need to know your financial situation reinforces the need for every consumer to be in control over their individual credit report.

This control starts by you requesting copies of your credit report for review.

As I have previously stated, the way to do this is to get your free copy of your credit report from each of the nationwide consumer reporting agencies, and to use the staggering process to get a report approximately every four months.

This free access is possible because of the FACTACT of 2003 (Chapter 3).

As discussed in previous chapters, the FCRA and the 2003 Act both promote the accuracy and privacy of an individual's information files held by the nation's big three consumer reporting agencies, and any smaller regionals, where those few may exist.

The nation's consumer protection agency, the Federal Trade Commission (FTC), is charged with enforcing both laws on behalf of all consumers.

However, I have found there is no one more interested in your credit report than you. And rightfully so.

Your credit report contains some of the most pertinent, personal, and powerful information about you, all housed in one report.

It is easy to see why identity theft is such a powerful, high impact crime that has to be aggressively prosecuted.

If an individual has a copy of your credit report and your police record (even if it is an empty report), they can practically tell your entire life's history.

These three bureaus (Equifax, Experian, and TransUnion) make millions of dollars each year selling your credit file information to employers, insurers, creditors, and other businesses that have a legitimate need.

Most smaller local credit bureaus are affiliated with one if not all of "The Big Three."

If you have ever used or even applied for credit, these companies will most likely have a file on you.

They compete with each other, and mostly do not share information, so the contents of each bureau's file may be somewhat different.

It is important to get copies of all three for the sake of accuracy.

Some outside companies offer a "merged" report showing all of the information held by all of the bureaus in one easy to read report.

1. Identification – This will include your name, address, Social Security Number, and date of birth. There may also be variations on your name (such as maiden names for married women) and possibly a phone number. For men this may also include Jr., Sr., and lineages (i.e., I, II, III, IV, etc.). This information generally comes from credit applications that you have previously submitted to creditors, and from your requests for copies of your credit reports. Also included in this

You + your credit report = time

The question is how much time are we talking?

Several good years of history

7 years of bad history, charged-off accounts, and slow payments

10 years for public records like bankruptcies, child support

2 years for credit inquiries

section may be previous addresses, and employers. Your report should not contain any data that does not have a direct impact on your financial history, such as race, national origin, or any other prejudicial preferences.

2. Accounts – These may also be called "tradelines," and may include credit cards, loans, checking overdraft credits, to name a few. Each item will specify what type of account it is, when it was opened, the date of the most recent activity, and information on your payment history as far back as three years or more. This section will also include any problems with the account, ranging from a late payment to a charge-off to settlements.

3. Public Filings – This includes bankruptcies, lawsuit judgments against you, tax liens, fines, child support recoveries, and other government-related negative items.

4. Inquiries – A list of companies that have ordered copies of your credit report including credit checks. These checks are related to applications which you have submitted to creditors, along with periodic monitoring by companies where you already have accounts, and promotional sweeps for "pre-approved" offers.

5. Warnings – If the credit bureau considers any of the information in your file to be suspicious, there may be a notation such as, "Multiple Social Securi-

ty Numbers Reported," or, "This address has been previously associated with fraud," or whatever it is that they are concerned about, including credit blocks and fraud alerts placed there by you. Your address can even be red-flagged as a result of the misbehavior of a previous occupant, or even a neighbor in a multi-unit apartment building.

This information is so important because together these groupings help determine your credit score, which may range from 300 to the low 900s depending on the calculation model used by the agency.

The matrix below is designed to show you the relationship between you and your credit report.

Also, it helps you breakdown the categories that impact your credit report so you can make a plan of attack on how to focus on each area until you achieve that perfect target score for you.

There Is One Born Every Minute

"Congratulations. You have been pre-approved for a credit card."

"Low interest rate."

"Credit limit of up to $100,000."

Attached to each of these offer letters will be a short application with some fine print on the front and back, which is actually the most important part of all these types of letters.

But what does it really mean?

Credit card issuers are forever seeking out new customers, which is the only way to sustain growth and profitability.

Establishing new accounts is an expensive business venture. Two of the highest costs are advertising and application processing.

The total cost for gaining a new customer known as the "acquisition cost" can reach as high as $200 or more per new account opened.

Part of the reason why new customer acquisitions are so expensive is that response rates for direct mail campaigns are very low. It is generally believed that the highest rate is about 3% or maybe less.

Banks try to target their mailings towards consumers who are most likely to respond, qualify, and become profitable customers as opposed to mailing credit card offers to everyone with an address.

This is where the fine print plays an important role. There are a lot of reasons not to accept these fixed (against you) offers.

But one of the primary reasons not to accept these offers is that if the minimum amount that you can qualify for is less than the smallest card you already hold, do not waste your time with the application.

The preponderance of customers are predetermined to be eligible for the minimum offer, which will be exactly what the offer says. The problem is that most individuals do not read the fine print, including me, that is until I learned better.

In preparation for a mail solicitation campaign, card issuers start by sending a set of minimum standards to one or all of the credit bureaus (Equifax, Experian, or Trans Union), to request a list of consumers whose credit reports meet their criteria checklist.

The bank may have acquired their consumer list from somewhere else, like a marketing database company, and then ask the reporting agency to return a subgroup that matches their criteria.

"Pre-approved" offers are then sent to everyone on the list approximately two months after the initial credit bureau screening. This means that your credit score could have changed several times by the time you actually receive the offer in your mailbox.

To be or not to be credit, that is the question. The answer may or may not belong to you.

If you have a copy of your credit report, you may see inquiries that are designated "promotional."

This means that your information file was reviewed for a "pre-approved" list as part of this pre-described process, although it does not mean that you will actually receive a credit card.

Since this type of inquiry was not initiated by you, it will not be seen by other prospective creditors and will not reduce your credit score.

But if you return the application, then you have caused an inquiry on your credit report that will be seen by all those reviewing your report.

Some sub-prime issuers actually use this type of screening to specifically target customers with moderately damaged credit, who are desperate enough to pay the high interest, extra fees, and a possible deposit in order to secure a credit card. Such as some of those cards that have a very low available balance that was significantly reduced by the deductions of all the fees before you ever get the card.

In truth this is a very smart move on the credit card company's part because they start collecting money before you ever start using the card, thus increasing their profit and lowering their risk in case you default.

If a consumer completes the application and returns it, it goes to a processing center (which may or may not be owned by a separate company from the issuer) where the data is entered into a computer system which then does the actual credit check that will become a visible inquiry on the credit report.

The primary goal is to determine if anything in the consumer's credit report has changed for the worse since the process started two months or more ago. By the way, the qualification criteria may have also changed since the initial offer was mailed to you.

This credit check is the official review that will be used for final approval or rejection of the application. Sometimes the slightest subtle changes in the consumer information (like total available credit or balance-to-limit ratio) can result in a rejection.

Oddly, sometimes "pre-approved" mailing lists from high-standard "prime" issuers include people who have no credit history at all. If these applications are returned, they will definitely be declined.

Again, a "pre-approved" credit card offer does not mean you will receive a card. Neither does it mean you will not receive a card. It only means you made the card issuers first cut.

Neither is there a guaranteed interest rate or credit limit.

If you meet the final qualifications, all of these promises most likely will change. As an added tidbit the average starting limits for gold and platinum cards are well under $10,000. Believe it or not, some of these starting limits are as low as $300.

There are some individuals who do not wish to receive pre-approved credit card offers. They object to direct mail (junk mail) campaigns, lack interest in obtaining more debt, and have serious privacy or security concerns.

If this is you, then you can call the following number to request that the credit bureaus do not include your file in any future pre-approved promotional campaigns – 1 (888) 567-8688.

In order to complete this request, the automated system will require certain types of identifying information.

Once approved, a two-year block can be added to your file over the phone, or you can obtain instructions for a permanent block. Either the temporary or permanent block can be reversed any time at your choosing.

How Free Is Free

In recognition of some of the challenges faced by consumers in acquiring their credit reports, as stated at the beginning of the chapter, the 2003 Act phased in free reports over a nine-month period from the West Coast to the East Coast starting December 1, 2004. By September 1, 2005, free credit reports were available to all U. S. citizens.

This plentiful availability has also opened up several ways to acquire copies of your credit report.

One centralized way is to log onto www.annualcreditreport.com.

If access to a computer is an issue, then you may call 1-877-322-8228 to request your report.

Finally, the third option is to complete the Annual Credit Report Request Form (a copy is enclosed for reproduction and your use) and mail it in to get your free report.

If you choose to complete the paper form, you will mail it to Annual Credit Report Request Service, P.O. Box 105281, Atlanta, GA 30348-5281.

Regardless of whether you (1) go to the website, (2) call the toll free number, or (3) complete the paper form, you will need to provide your name, address, Social Security Number, date of birth, previous address, and a few additional questions, like if you have moved within the past two years.

To protect your information and maintain the integrity of your file, each consumer reporting agency may ask you some questions about information in your file that only you should know.

For example, they may ask you how much your monthly mortgage payment is and who holds that mortgage, or a similar type question for another account. You may even be asked information that is completely false to make sure you are who you say you are.

Each agency may also ask a different question because their information and their sources of information about you may be slightly different.

There is one other unpleasant circumstance under which you may request a free copy of your credit report.

Although my hope is that none of my readers will experience this unpleasantness after reading this book, if you should experience this you will be better prepared than ever before.

Be prepared to defend your freedom to help lower your costs to $0 and save your dollars.

If you are denied credit for any reasons, the law requires you be notified in writing and the information supplier must be identified.

If you are denied employment based on your credit report, the law requires that you must first receive a copy of the report and a statement of your rights.

You are also entitled to review the credit report and to dispute any information believed to be inaccurate or incomplete. You have this right even if the potential employer had additional reasons not to hire you, even if you have excellent credit.

However, even if you have a high credit score, something on your credit report such as a high debt ratio may be of concern to a potential employer.

Of course the review of your credit report is only allowed after you have given written authorization to the employer candidate.

Under the Federal Fair Credit Reporting Act (FCRA), you may also have a series of additional rights. Consult your legal representative for further assistance.

Buyer Beware

Sometimes when consumers are interested in making a large purchase they go on line to one of the three credit reporting agencies where they may purchase a credit score, and end up getting a whole lot more than they bargained for.

We are all familiar with the freecreditreport.com singing commercials. Catchy lyrics, good tunes, and a decent singer all combine to get your attention.

But the fine print of the commercial that is not contained in the lyrics is that if you go to the website and sign up for a free credit report, you will automatically be enrolled in a Triple Advantage membership.

This new unexpected relationship with Experian will cost you $14.95 per month unless you cancel your trial membership within the 7-day trial period.

Most individuals are not going to take the time to read all of this fine print within 7-days, so Experian will probably collect two or three months worth of membership dues before their unsuspecting customers see the charge on their credit cards and cancel.

This means millions of dollars in pure revenue for Experian.

As for the credit score, one credit score does not tell the entire story. To get an accurate picture, an individual has to get a credit score from all three bureaus, and the median score of the three is the one that would be used in most credit-making decisions.

Another option for the credit score is to go directly to www.fico.com to get your score.

While Experian may own the commercial, the Big Three share the same kinds of marketing tactics.

Do not pay for a credit report before you get your government-mandated free report at www.AnnualCreditReport.com.

The normal pitch is that you can get a free credit report and score, but only if you subscribe to some sort of credit monitoring package. Again, this is generally in the fine print that most consumers never read.

The fact remains that regardless of which website is making you the 'free' offer, they are only repackaging the credit information found in the files of the three bureaus.

Equifax sells its information at www.Equifax.com.

Experian sells its information at www.Experian.com and at least six more sites controlled by Experian. One of those six is www.Consumerinfo.com.

TransUnion peddles its information at numerous sites including www.TrueCredit.com, www.speedycreditreports.com, www.free-credit-reports.com, www.SpendonLife.com, www.PrivacyMatters.com, www.FreeCreditReports-Instantly.com, www.Credit.com, and www.Free3BureauCreditReport.com.

These sites help keep the Chicago billionaire Pritzker family wealthy, and in total control as wholly and complete private owners of TransUnion.

Credit scores are bigger business than credit reports, and the three credit-reporting agencies are not about to give up their cash cows any time in the near future.

The Big Three are shopping for big dollars, make sure you know what you are buying.

At last count, these scores have turned into big business to the tune of $500 million annually between the three.

Recommendation: **If you are considering purchasing a credit score, do not shop online for that score where you may end up buying more than you intended. Use the contact information listed below to contact the agencies directly to make your request for a credit score.**

What consumers do not know is that they are the pawns in the middle of a turf war between the big three and the Fair Isaac Corporation, the owners of the FICO Score.

So in response to the FICO score, the three agencies have come together to offer the VantageScore, not to necessarily benefit the consumer but to maintain their profitability.

Do not be naïve: business firms only offer products that will make them money at little or no cost.

The VantageScore is an alternative based on an algorithm contrived by the big three.

The agencies pool all their information to come up with the VantageScore, which they are now selling as a more accurate picture than the FICO.

The biggest selling point for the VantageScore is that they are generally 30 to 40 points higher than the FICO score. But the question remains has the marketplace embraced the VantageScore or do they still prefer the FICO score?

TransUnion and Experian are simultaneously delivering VantageScores as well as their own individual proprietary scores.

However the downfall is that consumers may not know they are not buying FICO scores, let alone how their VantageScores are derived.

Consumers may actually be purchasing TransUnion's TransRisk score or Experian's Plus score without full disclosure. And it has not been definitively answered whether these scores are artificially inflated.

The only two places where consumers can purchase FICO scores on line is at www.myFICO.com and at www.Equifax.com.

One fact is undeniable, credit scoring is all over the place and a consumer may have to purchase several different scores to stay abreast of their own information. But do not rush to the checkout counter so fast.

As for the credit reports, these reports used to cost $9 each.

Then all you had to do was write a letter to each of the bureaus and request a copy of your report (sample letter enclosed Chapter 7).

Although this is no longer required, you may purchase a copy of your credit report anytime you like by using the information listed below.

If you choose to purchase your reports, I recommend you stagger your request so that you can keep a watchful eye on the accuracy of your information throughout the year, since you are already entitled to three free reports annually. The contact information is listed below.

Equifax Credit Information Services LLC
P. O. Box 740241
Atlanta, GA 30374
www.equifax.com

1-800-997-2493 – Order report by phone
1-800-685-1111 – General Information
1-888-909-7304 – Discuss report with credit specialist

Experian Information Solutions, Inc.
P. O. Box 2104
Allen, TX 75013-2104
www.experian.com
1-888-397-3742 – Order report by phone

Trans Union Corporation
P. O. Box 390
Springfield, PA 19064-0390
www.transunion.com
1-800-916-8800 / 1-800-888-4213 – Order report by phone
1-714-738-5072 – Customer Support

Let me reiterate the three primary reasons you should regularly check your credit report.

1. The information contained in your report directly effects how much you pay in borrowing costs.

2. To ensure the information in your credit file is truthful and accurate.

3. To protect yourself against identity theft.

Generally speaking, you should receive your credit report within 30 days after your request is received by the credit reporting agency regardless of the method you choose to make your request.

No Thank You

To opt out of pre-approved screening offers or those promotional advertisements we discussed earlier in the chapter, contact each credit bureau directly at either the address or telephone number listed below specifically set up for opting out of pre-approved screenings.

Equifax Options
P.O. Box 7401243
Atlanta, GA 30374-012
1 (800) 556-4711

Experian
P.O. Box 919
Allen, TX 75013
1 (800) 682-7654

or

Experian Consumer Opt Out
701 Experian Parkway
Allen, TX 75013
1 (800) 353 0809

TransUnion
Attn: Marketing Opt-Out
P.O. Box 97328
Jackson, MS 39288-7328
1 (800) 680-7293

The bureaus supposedly share opt-out requests because this saves them money without cutting into their profits and without the bureaus having to share any direct information from their files, so theoretically you only have to contact one. Opt-out requests are consumer requests to no longer be included in any advertising or marketing campaigns. So as a consumer you have the authority to close your credit report for review for any future such campaigns.

But I tend to be cautious, so if I were inclined to opt-out, I would send written requests to all three bureaus.

Made From Scratch

Now that we have talked extensively about repairing and preventing problems, let us turn out attention to building a solid credit portfolio.

I am sure we can unanimously agree that it is much easier to start with good habits rather than repair bad ones later on.

There has never been a more crucial time to establish good credit history than exist today. So if you are just starting out, this is a true once-in-a-lifetime opportunity – to build a strong credit history the right way.

If you have never had any credit, it still would not hurt to see if one of the Big Three has a file on you. It is quite possible that someone else's bad information has made its way onto your file by mistake or because of identity theft.

Either way, if there is bogus information on your file, you may want to deal with that first.

If the problem is associated with identity theft, the Federal Trade Commission has an identity theft site specifically designed to address this issue.

One of the quickest and easiest ways to make your introduction into the world of credit is to establish both a checking and savings account. This shows stability on your part to anyone who might be looking.

Second, if you already own a credit card, do not max it or any of them out, if you happen to have more than one.

Do your very best to keep 70% of your card available at all times. Or to put it another way, keep your spending down to under 30% of your card's total available balance. This shows that you are responsible, and if you should apply for any additional credit you will be a much better candidate.

If at all possible, the best thing to do is to pay your balance in full

Building good credit is like being a good hunter – learn to kill two birds with one stone. Or expend as little energy but get maximum impact from your efforts.

every month. This will ensure you do not drown in debt or get in over your head.

Both of these are important because the two most important factors in credit scores are how much available credit you have, and whether or not you pay your bills on time.

If you can manage to set up your credit card and other bill payments on automatic payment plans so that you will never miss a single payment, you will be completely in the driver's seat if you ever have need for further credit.

Third, if you are in college, and with some prudence, this may be the best time to apply for your first credit card because lenders are willing to risk a little money on you at the beginning of your career. Again, with some prudence, this may turn out to be a profitable, long-term relationship for both of you.

Shop around for a card that has a low annual fee and a low interest rate. An even better card would be one with no annual fee. It pays to shop around.

If all else fails and you cannot secure a regular card, then join a credit union to take advantage of their secure card programs. They are usually better than most others on the market.

To recap, a good card will have no application fee and a low annual fee. It may be converted to a regular, unsecured credit card after 12 to 18 months with on-time payments, and your good history will be reported to all three credit bureaus.

Now if you cannot secure a credit card or are not interested in a credit card (because you are authorized on your parents card), then here is a second option for getting your own credit.

Apply for either a gas card or a local department store card. These cards do not build your credit as quickly, but they are generally easier to get.

Remember do not over do it. One or two of these cards is enough.

Now, if you are beyond your college years, the best credit scores are held by individuals that have a good mix of responsible credit use. This mix includes installment accounts like auto loans and mortgages, and revolving accounts like credit cards and other lines of credit.

So a small installment loan from your credit union just might do the trick. And if you do not actually need the money, it works even more in your favor because then you can take the money and invest it so that you are earning money not just creating debt. This is one way to gain wealth.

Now that you have some real tools and a plan, believe in yourself and give it 100% every day.

Your efforts will pay huge dividends one day, possibly sooner than you think.

Chapter Six

What's Your Number?

Inevitably when we as individuals begin to look at our own situations, we do it through the eyes of others.

Our personal situations are never judged on their own merits, but are, instead, judged in comparison to other-'s' predicaments. But what we forget and others never know is that they are not aware of all of the facts – unless you are one of those unfortunate individuals that tells everything to everybody. The old cartoon called this "Blabbermouth."

Whether the emotional response is the envy of the Joneses that drives us into debt, the relief of knowing our situation is not as bad as our neighbors down the street, or the despair of knowing our situation is more serious than originally thought, one fact is clear: our personal situations are never a singular event.

But there is some good news in the midst all of this bad news, if you can consider it good news.

According to a report released by MSNBC.com in July, 2010, one in four consumers are now considered a poor risk for lenders. That means more than 25.5% of all Americans have a credit score of 599 or less.

The U. S. population is currently 310, 230,087 according to the U. S. Census Bureau and the 2010 Census. Therefore, 79,108,672 million Americans have a credit score of 599 or less.

This is a double-edged sword for the U. S. economy. These same poor credit risks were the same individuals that helped the economy grow, before the current recession-recovery the country is currently experiencing.

Now, the U. S. economy's recovery is stagnant because 25.5% of the country is strapped with so much debt that they cannot spend any money, which drives the economy down because businesses cannot add new jobs.

The lesson for both the U. S. and its citizens should be clear – you cannot increase your standard of living through debt because eventually you are going to have to pay the bills.

Proverbs 23 addresses these and other conditions of the human heart in much better prose than I ever could. The Bible teaches daily lessons to whosoever will; and, one of the greatest lessons it teaches is to not wear yourself out trying to get rich.

Having the wisdom to show some restraint in the pursuit of wealth may be more important than the wealth itself, in that you do not lose yourself and be completely consumed by wealth and wealth only.

Yes, I do believe in people being wealthy, but there is a way to do anything; it is just a matter of finding the right way that works for your situation without "selling your soul."

I personally know a gentleman who was so intent on climbing the corporate ladder that he stepped on, mistreated, abused, and used all his friends and his family to get to the top.

When he finally got there, the senior partner, the one he had done every favor for died two months after his arrival into the inner circle.

What my acquaintance did not know is that his "mentor" was not well received by the other partners, so his death was the perfect excuse to shake up the firm, and dismiss all those closely associated with the newly deceased.

So, there are times in our zest for riches when we forget all the mistakes we made in our quest, but others are not as forgetful or as forgiving.

Tennessee Williams made this poignant and memorable point in a beautiful way when he wrote, "life is all memory except for the one present moment that goes by so quick you can hardly catch it going."

Nevertheless, with a convenient memory and your deposit money you have saved for more than a year, you head to the dealership to purchase that car you picked out the day you started saving your deposit.

In all your getting, you failed to get one crucial piece that is vitally connected to your new car purchase.

Any way, out the door you go with your bankbook in hand. So you arrive at the dealership and the salesman tells you they must run your credit. You try to remain calm all the while you are freaking out inside like in the cartoons when something unexpected happens.

There are no small errors when it comes to your credit report.

Then the salesman breaks out in uncontrollable laughter. The laughter is so infectious that before you know it, you are surrounded by an office full of suits in laughter. You are even tempted to join in the laughter because of the jovial atmosphere until you realize they are laughing at you, not with you.

What a relief to find out it was all an error.

Do It Yourself Repair

When an individual is in a financial hole, it is hard to even consider the idea of looking at your credit information maintained in your credit files. But you should force yourself to do it!

Believe me when I tell you that I know firsthand the temptation of credit-repair companies. Many companies offer these services. That is they will help you find and supposedly repair any errors in your credit report.

Yet, as many individuals recommend not using these companies as there are repair companies on the market. Add my voice to this group of no's!

Those clients with whom I have spoken do not recommend using those firms because most are expensive and do very little to actually repair your credit.

The truth is that no one can eliminate negative information from your credit report, if that information is true.

You can do the work in disputing inaccuracies without paying someone to do it for you, if you know how.

Generally speaking, if you do find an error in your report, the reporting agency must investigate and respond to you within 30 days.

If you are in the process of applying for a loan, the reporting agency must immediately notify the lender of any incorrect information in your file maintained at their agency, and provide the lender with a corrected credit report at no cost to you.

The easiest way to approach the cleanup process is to start with the source, which, in most instances, is already listed on your credit report.

But before we get into actually repairing your credit, we need to talk about the credit score.

How To Score

Each item on your credit report is worth points. The total of the credit score points is basically a mathematical equation of the information listed in your credit report.

By comparing your information to the patterns of hundreds of thousands of past credit information files, FICO corporation calculates your credit score which identifies your level of future credit risk.

This is the driving force behind the FICO corporation (www.myfico.com).

As previously stated, the typical credit report contains four groups of information: your personal identifying information; credit information; public record information; and inquiries, (sometimes warnings).

These four groups of information are scored through the credit reporting system that has been in existence for approximately 45 years.

Today, the three-digit credit score is the number most Americans are now concerned about.

While the system has made tremendous strides through the years and has dramatically improved the efficiency of credit markets, there are still too many Americans whose reports contain substantive errors.

It has even been suggested that the credit reporting agencies are sharing consumer's information without their consent.

Whether this idea is or is not true may be more or less important than the need for consumers to stay abreast of their information more so than ever before.

To err is human – and there are a lot of opportunities for humanity inside any corporation.

How do these errors become a part of consumer credit reports?

Each month creditors and financial institutions send electronic files to one or all three credit reporting agencies. These files include consumer account numbers, types of credit, outstanding balances, collection actions, and bill-payment histories.

This includes international creditors who are also registered members of the three credit reporting agencies. These international creditors also add information to your credit file if you happen to be one who conducts multinational business.

So then the errors are either part of the files sent to the credit reporting agencies or they occur when the information is inputted into the agencies' system.

Either way, these errors become a permanent part of consumer files until they are discovered, and, as such, are part of the FICO score's computation.

There are two basic requirements for your FICO score to be calculated.

Your credit report must contain a minimum of one account that has been open for six months or longer. The second requirement is that it must also contain at least one account that has been updated within the last six months.

If these two requirements are met, then you have a credit score.

FICO in its duality, is both the name and identifier of the corporation that produces credit scores on behalf of the credit reporting agencies.

This Minneapolis-based Fair Isaac Corporation developed the credit score software in 1989.

While all of us have been deluged with all kinds of numbers and that deluge is growing, there is 1 number that most of us in the middle of the deluge do not know. Our FICO score!

The three-digit standard used to measure credit risk, the FICO score, was in actuality a joint project by Equifax and the Minneapolis firm. But today Fair Isaac Corporation supplies financial services to the world's largest banks and companies across more than 60 countries.[1]

FICO scores range from 300 to 900. The best interest rates are given to people with scores above 770, but a 700 score out of possible 900 is a good score.

Thus, your credit score provides the best guide to your future credit risk to a potential lender. The higher the score, the lower the risk, and vice versa.

Although your credit score is both a personal and emotional piece of information, it is not an indicator of whether or not you will be a "bad" or "good" customer.

---

1 Frontline: Secret History of the Credit Card – What You Should Know About Your Own, M. Wozniacka and S. Sen., Nov 23, 2004.

It is however one part, a rather large part, of most lenders' strategy in lending decisions.

FICO cutoff scores to get a loan are as varied as the potential lender, but usually there are other factors included in making a final decision whether to extend or not extend a loan offer to you.

It is important to dispel the fallacy that individuals with a high score are never declined for a loan.

If you have a good FICO score but you also have an excessively high debt to income ratio or have developed a pattern of slow payments due to your indebtedness, a lender may decline your application for credit.

It is generally recommended that your debt to income ratio should not exceed 15% of your take home pay. This 15% does not include your mortgage.

For example, if you make $3,500.00 per month after taxes, then your total expenses not including your mortgage should not exceed $525.00 per month.

FICO scores are often called BEACON scores by some consumers and lenders, and may also be known as the Fair Isaac Risk Model by Experian customers.

But these scores are not the same scores as the specialty scores of TransUnion and Experian we discussed earlier.

By purchasing your credit score from FICO you are purchasing the opportunity to see how creditors are judging you as a credit risk.

As of this print, the current prices for credit scores are: Equifax – $15.95, Experian – $15.00, and Trans Union – $11.95.

Please note, FICO scores are not the only scores used by lenders, nor are they the only credit bureau scores (as stated above) although they are the most popular today.

Because of this, your credit score will be different at each of the three credit reporting agencies at any given time and are almost guaranteed to change daily.

So your FICO score is used to predict how likely you are to repay a loan based on experience with millions of consumers, and there are numerous computer models that can be used to calculate this one score.

The current financial crisis in the U.S. has made your credit score the latest hot commodity. It also means that if there was ever such an animal as "easy credit," that animal is now extinct.

Now the mechanics of the score have become a primary focus for nearly everyone.

There are positive points for information in the report such as paying your bills on time, and there are also negative points on the report for example maxing out your credit card. The positive and negative numbers are added together and the end result is your credit score (in an overly simplified example).

As I have told you before, credit scores range from 300 to 900, and the higher the first digit the better. In addition, it is up to each creditor to determine what is considered an acceptable score for their line of business.

As such, it is up to the individual creditor to tell you why your score does or does not meet their business criteria to extend you credit.

Credit scoring is the fastest and most objective way to evaluate any credit report in a non-discriminatory manner. Your credit score is the blood pressure of your financial health.

It is non-discriminatory because it does not include your income, marital status, age, race, gender, religion, national origin, and employment, which can all be subjective factors depending on the reviewer.

The credit score contains five calculating factors used to calculate a FICO score at any given point in time. Each piece of information counts as a percentage of your total FICO score.

- Payment History = 35%
- Amounts Owed = 30%
- Length of Credit History = 5%
- New Credit = 10%
- Types of Credit In Use = 10%

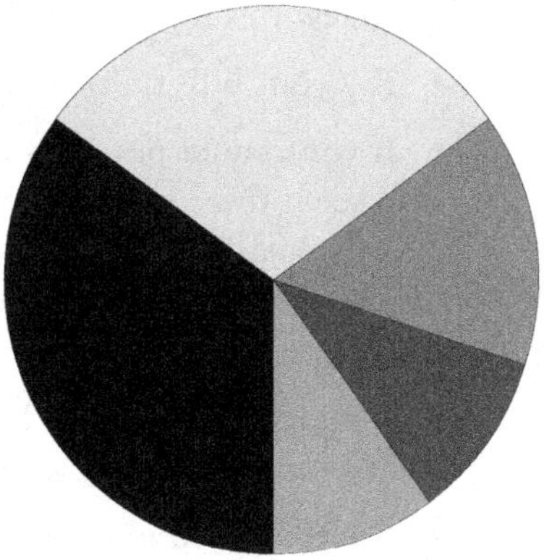

This information is derived from the Fair Isaac Corporation which, in turn, gets its information from each of the three credit reporting agencies based on the importance of the five categories for the general population.

The three credit reporting agencies are able to provide Fair Isaac with this information because they track most individuals every financial move better than they track it themselves.

Let us break these categories down further for your understanding.

1) **Payment History**

This category includes the number of accounts paid as agreed (the more the better), the number of past due obligations in your file, the length of time that obligation has been past due, and the amount past due.

A past due credit action is defined as delinquent and the length of that past due item is defined by the severity of that delinquency.

Accounts included in this category are automobile loans, credit cards, gas cards, and mortgages to name a few. Also included in this category are public records, i.e. lawsuits, judgments, liens, bankruptcies, wage attachments, and in some states child support.

The good news, for some, is that this category does not include utility bills unless those bills go into collection.

Here are a few tips to help you improve your payment history.

- Pay your bills on time.
- If you cannot pay your bills on time, contact your creditor immediately to see if there are some options available, such as delaying payments, making smaller payments for a limited period of time, paying interest only payments, skipping one payment, or having a payment moved to the end of the loan.
- If none of the options listed above work, considering seeking help from a reputable agency, such as Consumer Credit Counseling.
- Another good idea is to make sure that your good payment history is showing up at all three credit reporting agencies. If it is not reported automatically by your creditor, you can ask your creditor to report it for

you or you can write the agencies directly and ask them to add the account to your file.

2) **Amounts Owed**

This category is used to determine how much debt you have, or how much of your paycheck you are having to pay to others. It focuses on the number of accounts with balances, the amount owed on each account, and the amount of remaining credit.

For example if you have a credit card that has a $5,000 credit limit and you owe $2,500 on the card, your remaining credit is $2,500.

Percentage wise, half of your credit is used up on your card until you pay the balance down: $2,500/$5,000 = 50%.

If a lender were to review your file for a new loan, the entire $5,000 would be counted against you as debt because even though you have not used the remaining $2,500 on the card, you have the potential to do so and therefore you have $5,000 worth of debt.

Here are a few tips to help keep your balances low.

- If the dollar amounts you owe include an old collection account, if you pay it off it will look better on the credit report but that collection will still remain on the report for seven years (unless you negotiate for its removal). If the payment date was the last date of activity on that particular item, then the item will remain seven years from the last activity date.

- A good rule of thumb is to try and keep your credit card balances to under 25% of your total available credit on each card. This will also lower your debt to income ratio and improve your overall credit position. If your limit is $3,000, you should keep your balance below $750.00.

- Pay off as much debt as absolutely possible and close any unnecessary accounts. Now there are some who suggest that by closing accounts, you will actually lower your score. Personally, I believe that is only a temporary lowering while you are moving to a stronger financial position. If you decide to close your accounts, do not close all of your accounts at once. Stagger your closings so your credit score does not take a bit hit all at once.

- Also double check to make sure your creditors are reporting all of your information regarding your account to the credit reporting agency. Withheld information may be vital in helping to raise your credit score.

3) **Length of Credit History**

This category looks at how long you have had credit. When were the accounts opened and how long since the last activity on those accounts?

This is one reason why some recommend against closing accounts. This section of FICO scoring looks overall at how long you have had credit in years. So when you start closing accounts, you are shutting down years of credit history, which lowers your credit score.

Again, if you decide to start closing accounts, start by closing the cards you have had the least amount of time up to those you have had the longest. This helps ease the impact against your credit score.

If you have relatively few accounts, do not rush out to open several new accounts or credit cards because this may make you look desperate and may also have the reverse effect of what you intended.

Very little credit can be as detrimental as bad credit but if you have paid the bad credit off, again, leave those accounts open to show you are on the road to improvement. But the lesser of the two evils is to have very little positive credit rather than to have bad credit even if it is paid off.

Accurate negative information – this is the stuff that is from your own doing, such as late payments, which generally stay on your report for seven years, with a few exceptions.

According to the Federal Consumer Information Center:

- Information about criminal convictions may be reported without any time limitation.
- Bankruptcy information can follow you around for 10 years, or a lifetime.
- Credit information reported in response to an application for a job with a salary of more than $75,000 has no time limit.
- When you apply for credit or life insurance in the amount of $150,000 or more, any credit information reported at that time has no time limit. This is considered negative information only if you are denied the credit or life insurance.
- Information about a lawsuit or an unpaid judgment against you can

be reported for seven years or until the statute of limitations runs out, whichever is longer.

4) **Types of Credit Used**

How many different types of accounts are found in your credit file?

Is all of your debt to different finance companies or do you actually have other credit that can be looked on more favorably.

A reasonable adult's credit report should include a mortgage, auto loan, one or two credit cards, and maybe one or two other types of cards.

Now, if you have one or two accounts that are not reporting favorably, do not close those accounts. Instead, keep those accounts open and up to date to get the pay off down the road.

What I mean is that those slow accounts would look better if they remained open because then it looks like you and the creditor have come to some kind of agreement.

5) **New Credit**

This final category looks at the number of recently opened accounts, their total proportion to your debt load, the time since any new account openings, and the type of account opened.

It also looks at the re-establishment of positive credit history following past payment problems, the number of recent credit inquires, and the time since those credit inquires.

Finally, do not open any credit accounts unless absolutely necessary. And if you must open any new accounts be very diligent about making sure those accounts are paid on time and are strictly managed.

Credit inquiries are factored into the new credit category, which accounts for 10% of the overall information in your credit report.

When it comes to helping individuals with many of the today's financial decisions, the Internet can be worth its weight in gold, if one knows where to look. One website that I particular like in the area of debt management is www.bankrate.com. This website has several calculators that can help consumers make better financial decisions, one of which, is the Credit Risk Assessment calculator under the Debt Management tab.

You Against the World

For a small portion of the U. S. public, one additional credit inquiry would only take 5 points off their FICO score.

However, for the vast majority of Americans, one additional credit inquiry is enough to cause them to be denied additional credit by a lender.

The exception to this rule is if you apply for several credit cards within a short period of time (typically a 10-day window). This will not negatively impact your credit score because these are typically counted as a single inquiry and without a major impact.

It is also important to remember that when shopping for an auto loan or mortgage, the reporting agencies compensate for this by ignoring all mortgage and auto inquiries made in the 30 days prior to scoring, and only consider any inquiries made within the most recent 14-day period.

Important Rule: If you are going to shop for a loan, do your rate shopping within a focused time period, 30 days is probably most reasonable. Any longer than that may result in negative impacts to your credit score.

If you choose to buy a credit score, wait a minimum of six months before you purchase another one to give your information time to be updated at the bureau (including correcting any errors).

There are some concrete steps anyone can take to improve their credit score.

However, ultimately it is the lender's decision to extend or not extend credit, and the use of the credit score is at the lender's discretion.

Depending on the type of loan being requested, the lender may also look at your income, type of job, and other factors to arrive at their final decision.

Therefore, the lender's decision takes all these factors into account when your credit is being calculated, and no one piece of information alone will determine whether or not you get that loan, although there are influencing factors that weigh more heavily than others.

Your FICO score considers both the positive and the negative information in your report; therefore, the importance of any factor depends on the overall strength of your information.

For example, late payments will lower your score; but having only two accounts with a good track record will raise your score.

As we discussed earlier in Chapter 3, by law your credit score does not include your race, religion, color, sex, national origin, or marital status. It also does not include your age or where you live. This is known as redlining – a previously outlawed practice of discrimination by lenders based on where certain customers lived.

Several major financial institutions in today's market or their predecessors have been sued for redlining or reverse redlining. Reverse redlining is the practice of forcing less credit worthy families (white, black, Hispanics, and others) into mortgages that they cannot afford.

Finally, your credit report does not include inquires that are initiated by you, known as, "consumer-initiated" inquiries, nor does it include "promotional-inquiries," those requests lenders make to check your credit for a new credit offer which is similar to "pre-approved" offers. None of these inquiries are included in your credit score.

Below is a quick look at how a higher FICO score saves you money. These numbers are not set in stone by any one creditor. Instead they should be used as guidelines to measure your credit score against the national average.

FICO SCORE	APR*
780 – 900+ (Best Score)	5.897%
700 –779 (Better Score)	6.022%
675 – 699 (Good Score)	6.559%
620 – 674 (Poor Score)	7.709%
560 – 619 (Poorer Score)	8.531%
500 – 559 (Poorest Score)	9.289%
≤ 499 Do not submit any applications for credit.	

*Annual Percentage Rate

Despite some correctable drawbacks, credit scoring has dramatically improved commerce across the U.S. marketplace.

Probably the best thing that credit reporting does exceptionally well is that it removes numerous discriminatory factors that would otherwise cloud risk assessment decisions if left to the human imagination.

Credit scoring is supposed to help in the investment market by giving potential investors a much more accurate assessment of the underlying risk of securities. However, the current U.S. and worldwide financial cycle has thrown this once-upon-a-time-benefit into a freefall.

Although John Donne, the 17th century poet, may not have had credit in mind when he wrote, "no man is an island unto himself," it certainly makes a clear point that we are all in this credit market together, like it or not.

Buying securities or securitization is the process of bundling large pools of consumer loans and selling them as a form of surety to investors.

The most common types of securities are mortgage bundles followed by credit card loans, and then automobile loans.

The securitization process does two things. It allows the lenders to remove the loans from their books to help shift the risks and defray costs from potential defaults. And it also allows outside investors to share in the stream of revenue that flows as these loans are repaid.

Additionally, it also helps consumers seeking credit because these investments make large quantities of additional funds available to lenders. These funds are then passed through the credit markets back to new lenders, which also lowers the price (interest rate) of loans made to consumers.

Credit scoring has also increased the number of households involved in the credit market that would have never been considered 10 years ago. This has also made society as a whole more mobile because people can be tracked throughout the world now, which ultimately lowers prices and encourages economic development.

Credit scores change gradually in response to your better handling of your credit.

Past credit problems will impact your score less as time passes, and the more you can do to keep your current obligations current, the less those past mistakes will impact your overall credit score.

Again, let me also make one more quick comment about credit scoring and minorities.

The Equal Credit Opportunity Act prohibits lenders from considering non-verifiable, subjective factors when issuing credit to people of any color.

In fact, the credit scoring system is the least discriminatory practice used in the credit market today.

If a lender wanted to discriminate, they would have to find a much more subtle way to do so, such as the issue of redlining by banks approximately 10 years ago.

Today, a minor ding by an individual with a high credit score can negatively impact their ability to secure the lowest interest rates when shopping for a loan. Because so many lenders are faced with rising delinquencies and defaults, they are raising the bar for what is considered their best customers.

In order to stay abreast and improve your credit score, the general process is to get your free copy of each credit report from the reporting agencies.

Review those reports immediately for errors and respond within 30 days to any errors found.

Whether you stagger your requests from the three bureaus or order them all at once depends on what type of purchase you are considering.

If you are considering a mortgage, then you should get all the reports at once. This is also one of those times when purchasing your credit scores may be beneficial and money well spent.

My recommendation is to go to www.myfico.com to purchase all three reports and scores.

If you are considering changing banks, then you should stagger any requests for your credit reports.

Then make a conscious effort to pay your bills on time because this counts for 35% of your total score and late payments can kill any deal quickly.

Also, reduce the amount of outstanding debt held by you and your family. This is another 30% of your credit score.

Then you should lower your credit utilization. This simply means do not have open credit all over town with several small vendors.

These few steps will solidify your credit improvement plan and your credit score for years to come.

Experts say you have to perform an act the exact same way for 30 days before it becomes a habit. This is one habit that will forever pay dividends well into the future.

Learn From Other's Mistakes

I recently read about a lady who owned her own home in the Washington D.C. area with no mortgage who paid off her credit card accounts monthly.

She was shocked when a large "good hands" homeowner's insurance policy was offered to her at its second-best rating.

Although she knew insurance companies used credit histories and credit scores to underwrite policies and set premiums, she still could not believe that her squeaky clean credit did not equate to the company's best rate, including the fact she had no past insurance claims.

It turned out that good hands would not give her their best rating because she had a number of credit cards for short periods rather than a few cards for a long period.

The culprit was those new credit-card promotions that offer low interest rates or rebates that she just could not resist, which raises additional concerns for credit grantors.

If an individual has several credit cards, then that can be construed as bad because it looks like the individual is trying to run up debt.

On the other hand, it may be an unfair penalization of those individuals who are simply trying to take advantage of special offers as another way to better manage their money.

Unfortunately, credit raters do not look closely enough to make that distinction.

Although insurance companies use their own formula to predict insurance claims risks, credit-based insurance scores are confidential numerical rankings similar to the credit scores used by the Big Three. The only exception is that the insurance scores use about 30 factors from a consumer's credit history and current accounts.

Actuarial studies are those studies conducted by insurance companies to compute premium rates, dividends, and risks according to probabilities based on statistical records. These studies show how a person manages his or her financial affairs, which is what an insurance score indicates as a good predictor of insurance claims.

This is according to the Insurance Information Institute, the D.C.-based industry group.

The same statistics also show people who have a poor insurance score are more likely to file an insurance claim.

But insurance scoring always has been and continues to be controversial.

While insurers say two-thirds of policyholders have a lower premium because of good credit, many consumers and lawmakers are wary.

Forty-eight states now restrict credit scoring in insurance underwriting.

The prohibited actions include preventing insurance companies from denying coverage or canceling policies based solely on credit information.

Insurers are also required to disclose primary factors on which any adverse action is based.

Also, the Federal Trade Commission is studying the impact of credit scores and credit-based insurance scores on price and availability of policies.

For the customer I was reading about, the difference only amounted to about $16. However, in her opinion this amounted to a $16 penalty for being a smart consumer.

Which one is right?

But her chief complaint was that the good hands institute would not give her a straight answer about how she could get the best deal.

Nor would they tell her how close her score was to their cutoff for the next higher or lower rating.

In the insurance company's defense, the scoring method is proprietary information, that if revealed, would severely hamper their business in a very tight and competitive marketplace.

The insurance company had argued that there were too many factors involved to translate into a simple answer. But that makes no sense because those same factors help form an insurance score that determines each customer's premium.

If a company can determine a premium score, then all they need to do is explain how they arrived at that decision.

But the company has been silent on this point.

Instead what they suggest is that the customer can request that her credit score be reviewed at any time. The caveat is that the new score will then change her premium — for better or worse.

For the customer, this is not enough specific information to enable her to make an intelligent decision on this matter.

In support of the insurance company, one of the Big Three's vice president of consumer education agrees that insurance companies cannot distinguish how much a single factor weighs in calculating a score.

While it may be true that no one can tell how changing one item on a credit report will precisely affect a score, there has to be a reasonable balance somewhere for the customer and the insurance firm even if changing one item cannot bring a pre-determined specific increase by a known amount.

Now if the firms who are supposed to be considered experts in these matters recommend their customers contact a "professional or a financial adviser," who can give them some honest, solid advice, then that is the time to be really concerned.

Tougher laws may be part of the answer so that insurance companies will be forced to disclose enough information for consumers to make smart choices, without revealing any proprietary information.

But as long as the calculations are secret, there will forever be a cloud of perceived deception over the insurance industry.

Be Your Own Debt Doctor

With so much of your financial life riding on your credit record, and believe me when I tell you that so much can go wrong, it is not surprising that a number of people want to help you "fix" your credit.

Consumers get scammed out of millions of dollars a year by so-called credit repair clinics.

There are only two ways to clean up your credit report -- time, and the responsible use of credit.

Nothing else is going to do it.

However, you can manipulate both time and responsibility to your advantage.

But when someone tells you they can wipe your credit record clean, they are about to create even more problems for you than they can ever solve.

Those lofty promises generally come with less than noble or downright illegal methods to deliver on the promise.

Those methods can and oftentimes do include creating fraudulent identities, and producing false documents.

It may sound dull, but to heal your past credit abuses, simply pay your bills on time and demonstrate responsible credit management. The good news is that you have as much leverage with the credit bureaus as anyone out there. And there's no safer and more effective option than helping yourself get on the road to good credit.

Here Is Your Prescription

1. **Start with the source.** Since the three major credit bureaus (Equifax, Experian, and TransUnion) all have slightly different information about you, you need to order your credit report from all three bureaus.

2. **Determine what you owe and to whom.** This is easy to do once you have your credit reports, and your completed budget. Yes, you are going to need a budget, and I will give you some suggestions to help you. Most of your creditors will be listed on your report. For those that are not, they should already be listed on your budget.

3. **Catch up on payments.** If you are behind on any accounts, contact the

creditor directly and start working on a plan to catch up and then get out of this debt completely. One of the quickest ways to move your credit score upward is to pay down your debt. A sure fire way to raise your score is to take a credit card (one you already have) with a high limit and low interest rate, and use that card to pay off all your other debt. Once paid, leave those accounts open, and then start making large payments on the existing credit card debt. If this is not an option, then your second option is to pay as much as you can on each card until you get each card below half of the total available balance on each card. Then concentrate on paying the balances off in full from the lowest to the highest.

4. **Set a good example for lenders to see.** If lack of credit is one of the reasons your score is low, apply for a small loan from your bank, *and make regular, on-time payments until the loan is paid off in full.* If you cannot get a loan, *consider applying for a secured credit card, or a 1 or 2-year installment loan from a finance company.* If it is a credit card, pay the bill in full and on time every month. Two good places to look for a credit card on the internet are www.bankrate.com and www.creditcardassist.com. If it is an installment loan, *pay more than your required monthly payment before the due date every month.* To take your efforts one step further, set all of these accounts or as many as you can possibly manage on automatic payment, and then make additional payments along the way.

Now if you need to challenge or dispute incorrect or inaccurate information all you need to do is contact the credit reporting company; they will investigate the dispute and, if applicable, issue you a revised credit report for free.

Then start over again and dispute the next error until they have all been challenged and corrected,

A. Start a record. Be sure to keep good records of all of your phone conversations and copies of each letter you send every step of the way. Send all letters via certified mail, return receipt requested. Make sure you include copies of any pertinent documentation that supports your claim (such as an account statement that shows an account paid in full). Most important of all, tell the credit bureau exactly what you want them to do — whether it is to delete a false item completely or update an old entry.

B. Tell the credit reporting agencies exactly what information you believe is inaccurate. See the Federal Consumer Information Center (FCIC) sample dispute letter at their website or information manual you ordered based on information in Chapter 4. The FCIC suggests that you enclose a copy of your report with the items in question circled or marked in red.

Generally speaking, within 30 days, the credit reporting agency will reinvestigate the items in question and respond to you in writing with one of two answers. The item has either been deleted or the information has been updated, corrected, and will remain until a specific date. In general:

- Disputed information that cannot be verified, by law, must be deleted.
- If your report contains erroneous or incomplete information, the credit reporting agency must correct it or update it.

The best part is if any disputed information turns out to be inaccurate, the creditor must notify all nationwide credit reporting agencies, so they all can correct the information in your file.

Note: There are sometimes when inaccurate information is set to drop off automatically, such as within two or three months. If that is the case, do not dispute the information. Just let it drop off of your report on its own. Depending on where you go, from the many options listed in this manual to get your free credit report or to purchase a report, if you choose, some of those reports will have the date that a negative item is set to drop off your report. Please pay close attention to these dates, because if you dispute the items that are already set to drop off, you will be giving the creditor the opportunity to extend this negative data on your report for a much longer period, maybe as much as another seven years.

Re-dating data allows negative information to stay on your credit report longer by changing the "date reported" from an older date to a current date.

C. Inform the business that sent the erroneous information of your dispute. This step is not normally recommended until after you have heard back from the credit reporting agency. When you contact the business, be sure to include communications with the credit bureau as part of your documentation trail, and make sure you use any leverage you might have to force your resolution in your favor.

D. Do not forget the good stuff. If you have ever been told you were denied credit because of a thin file, then contact all your creditors and ask to have your accounts added to your credit bureau files. Companies are not compelled to comply with your request but most will if you ask. But some may do so with a small fee. It is up to you to determine if it is worth the fee.

E. Applaud your good works. If your disputes result in positive changes to your credit report, the credit bureau will give you the written results and a free copy of your report. While this marks the end of most disputes, be aware that the information can show up again. (*See Note discussion above.*)

F. The last word. If you are unsuccessful in removing information from your credit file, you always have the legal right to attach a letter of explanation to your credit file. Be sure to send your letter to all three of the major credit bureaus as well as the feuding business. The business is obligated to include your letter in any future input to the credit bureaus, and it is up to you to make sure they do. Be brief, and tell only facts that caused you to have a problem repaying your debt.

Chapter Seven

Come From Behind

Most individuals never have a need for credit until they leave the nest for the very first time.

Whether you choose to go to college or straight to work, if you have no credit, then any credit you may be able to obtain will most likely cost you more.

The way around this road block used to be having someone with good credit, like a parent or grandparent, add the individual to their best credit card account as an authorized user.

Once an individual became an authorized user they would immediately share the excellent history built up by the account owner as if it was their own.

Therefore, the true owner of the history is boosting the credit score of a relative by allowing that individual to piggyback on their success.

This makes the recipient of the boost look better to potential lenders than they might really be.

But this exemption may soon be coming to an end.

On the Horizon

At the time this book went to publication, Fair Isaac Corporation was working on a new scoring formula that would no longer recognize credit that does not belong to the name holder.

This means any authorized user's account information will not be recognized under the new scoring formula under review.

These changes are designed to prevent credit repairers from exploiting authorized user accounts for temporary credit bumps.

This new scoring system was expected to be in place at all three major credit reporting agencies by the second quarter 2009.*[1]

Once in place, the expectation is that millions of authorized users will see a decline in their credit scores.

If you are an authorized user without any credit of your own, your credit score will completely disappear.

Research shows that the authorized user accounts was the unwritten exemption to the rule of spending several years repairing credit reports and scores,

* As this book goes to print, the issue of piggybacking is still as yet unresolved.

The confidence in the mortgage loan process, although cumbersome, used to be a balanced look at all factors in the process to ensure that even during difficult times a customer could repay their mortgage.

The question has now been raised that with so many mortgage failures, is the mortgage process flawed? Or is there a better way to verify incomes, assets, etc. to account for repayment in tough times?

sometimes due to circumstances not of their own making (those who need to piggyback on other's credit).

Although the credit score can be marred by problems not created by the owner, such as identity theft, users were still denied credit without the ability to piggyback on another's credit. However, this practice is soon-to-be-banned.

Since the new FICO formula is designed to not include any user accounts, spenders that are not responsible for paying the bill each month, this new scoring system is billed to be a better predictor of actual consumer payment behavior.

The new formula will also require minimal changes to lenders' operating systems. This fix is also in response to industry mistakes and concerns because some lenders have been forced to take on unknown risk without foreknowledge. This is called truth in lending.

Truth in lending not only applies to the lender but also applies to the consumer; otherwise, without open, honest, and transparent lending, it becomes fraud.

Piggybacking, as the practice is known, also forced the nondiscriminatory FICO system to become discriminatory, because the system ignored an individual's bad credit in favor of someone else's good credit. If you were unfortunate enough not to be able to afford to piggyback on someone's account, then you had no choice but to accept the system's decision making process. This practice also allowed credit riders to threaten the entire integrity of the credit scoring system and cost all creditors higher carrying costs.

The mortgage industry started raising flags about this practice a few years ago because an increasing number of clients were starting to look creditworthy for houses that were otherwise questionable without the authorized user.

Although these concerns were largely ignored, in the opinion of many, these artificially inflated scores have been, in one way or another, a partial driver in the housing downturn that has swept the nation. They have also forced, in part, the before unheard of government bailout of Fannie Mae, Freddie Mac, and Wall Street in general.

Because of these and other developments, it was necessary for piggybacking to be eliminated because too many banks were too heavily leveraged in the mortgage market, and those that were paid to pay attention to these housing loans stopped paying attention until it was too late.

It is widely believed that approximately 90% of all lending institutions base their credit decisions on FICO scores. Piggybacking pushed FICO scores into the acceptable range for lending purposes.

Banks, mortgage firms, and other lending institutions are not the only ones interested in piggybacking. Federal regulators are also reviewing this practice, along with numerous other lending practices.

Numerous companies have made huge profits in fees from $800 to $2000+ by perfecting the piggybacking process. These firms specialized in capitalizing on this little-known practice to help individuals qualify. This is/was done for individuals who otherwise could not qualify by riding on the coattails of an authorized user with excellent pay history.

A portion, a small portion, of this fee went to authorized users for allowing strangers to "piggyback" on their good name. The remainder went to the matchmaker firm for bringing the two parties of need together.

Basically, the matchmaker helped their credit shopper to scam the computer system into believing they had a better repayment history than was actually true as a result of piggybacking. The practice worked as planned and did just as it was designed to do by lifting the score of the piggybacker.

Once the matchmaker filed an updated credit report to the three major bureaus on behalf of their credit shopper, as expected, the FICO score increased.

Almost as quickly as the authorized user was added, they were removed even faster from the primary account holder's account. However, the payment history remained on the credit seeker's report as their own indefinitely.

Every Action Has Consequences

Some unintended consequences of this new credit formula will be a negative impact on legitimate authorized users who have done nothing wrong, but instead, have simply built a strong credit history and used it responsibly. The most impacted groups will be young adults, primarily college students, and married couples.

To avoid this reverse impact on legitimate users, there are a few options available to minimize the rule change.

Option one may be to simply have those cards parents share with their college-aged children converted into joint ownership cards. A second option may be to open one card account with a reasonably large limit in the student's name.

As for married couples, the same two options apply. However, option two may be preferred because women tend to be authorized users on their husband's accounts, and the second option affords them some independence if they should become divorced or widowed.

Down to the Nitty Gritty

If you are planning any major purchases, I suggest you start reviewing your credit report and financial situation 12 months before your intended purchase date. This will give you ample time for all the updates and corrections to be correctly recorded in your credit record.

In truth, your first step in dealing with bad credit is to honestly self-examine the real reason(s) for your financial troubles. Each individual must address the underlying cause(s) first or any effort to reestablish their credit is a waste of time.

Banks, other lenders, and credit reporting agencies are extremely organized in conducting their business, and you must be equally organized in dealing with them as well.

While there exist some concrete fixes to these challenges, they are not necessarily quick.

One credit repair fix is to apply for a charge card. Generally speaking, these cards are offered through department stores or smaller local retailers. Unfortunately, they normally have very high interest rates and lower charge limits. The good news is that these cards are easier to get than those issued by larger commercial institutions.

A second option may be to apply for a secured credit card. Secured cards are easier to get than their unsecured counterparts. The bad news is that you will have to come up with a deposit to place with the lender before the card is released. Under a secure card lender your credit limit will be maximized at some percentage of your deposit. But the good news is that some secured cards will turn into unsecured cards with a certain number of timely payments.

Finally, a third option that requires no outside intervention or cooperation is to pay your card balances down to $0 or as close to $0 as possible, and then learn how to maintain a low balance owed on any outstanding credit cards. This will make a positive impact toward improving your credit score.

Before we close the door on piggybacking, there may yet be some good that comes out of the new scoring model of FICO.

Even the best of us makes a mistake every now and then, such as missing a utility bill, or maybe you forgot that library book until you received a collection letter about your late fees. Do not be concerned, yet.

Although the new FICO scoring system does address the piggybacking issue specifically, the new scoring formula may actually help others boost their scores by ignoring these minor, occasional slip-ups when determining an individual's creditworthiness.

The updated scoring system, called FICO 08, will no longer damage your score if the original amount that is in collections is less than $100. Further, if a consumer had a mistake more than two years ago, without any other blemishes, than there will be no negative impact to the credit score under FICO 08.

However, if you are a consumer that habitually pays their accounts late, then you are more likely to be penalized under FICO 08.

Additionally, if you, as a consumer, have a high usage rate, which means you are at or near your credit limits on your credit cards, even if you do pay on time every month, then you are going to continue to have a low score under FICO 08 as you did under the previous scoring model.

Finally, FICO 08 has been available at all three major credit reporting agencies – Equifax, Experian, and TransUnion since August, 2009. The whole purpose for all of these changes by FICO was/is to give lenders a better risk assessment of all borrowers; and, while many lenders have adopted the new FICO 08 model, as many more have yet to adopt the new model. So while credit-scoring is still a murky situation for the most important person in the entire process, the consumer, each of us must take the necessary steps to help ourselves regardless of the scoring model used by our creditors.

Set the Record Straight

While all consumers agree the need to correct credit reporting errors is vitally important to any strong financial position, many more do not know how to follow through on ensuring those errors are actually corrected.

There are three ways to dispute your credit report. You may use the universal dispute form included in this manual, you may write a letter, and thirdly you may dispute your report online.

Like any project of importance, you must be organized and prepare your work or office space with writing utensils, notepads, folders, stamps, and financial records for verification purposes.

Make several copies of the included universal dispute form so they will be available should they be needed.

Also attached is a chart that you should make copies of to track your errors with each credit reporting agency as a quick reference guide to see how you are progressing.

Now that you have ordered free copies of your credit agency reports, it is time to review every single item on the report for full and complete accuracy.

If you have not ordered your report as recommended, then your credit repair work starts now.

Here is the information again for you to order your credit report.

First, if you have not ordered a credit report within the past 12 months then you need to contact www.annualcreditreport.com to get your free annual report.

Do not order a report from the credit reporting agency's directly listed below without first making sure you have ordered your free copy first.

As a reminder, if you have been denied credit within the last 60 days, are unemployed and plan to look for a job within the next 60 days, are on welfare, or have been a victim of fraud, then you are also entitled to a free copy of your credit report.

Equifax	**Experian**	**TransUnion**
P. O. Box 740241	P. O. Box 2104	P. O. Box 390
Atlanta, GA 30374-0241	Allen, TX 75013-2104	Springfield, PA 19064-0390
www.equifax.com	www.experian.com	www.transunion.com
1-800-997-2493	1-888-397-3742	1-800-888-4213

So to start the process, once you have received the copies of your credit report, you start reviewing them one at a time.

If you find an error, using the chart below, first find the agency where the error was found, then go to the far left column and write down either the name of the company that caused the error or the section of the report where the error was found. Then on that same row, go over to the corresponding block underneath the particular reporting agency whose report has the error.

Some of the most common errors are accounts listed more than once, and/or charge-offs and good standing accounts not being listed or listed correctly. Charge-offs are accounts creditors no longer believe they are going to be able to collect what is due on the account. So they charge-off these accounts from their books as bad debt. By doing so, the companies can legally claim a tax exemption for a bad debt, even if they eventually get their money later, based on the specific collection efforts made to collect the debt prior to the debt being charged-off.

Errors one and three should be fairly easy to resolve -- ask for the duplicates to be removed in the case of error number one. Error number three requires either a quick phone call or short letter requesting the lender to report your good paying account to all three credit reporting agencies.

Error number two may be a little more challenging because a charge-off means that your creditor has stopped sending you bills and has written your account off for tax credit purposes.

However, they are still reporting your repayment problems to the credit bureau with the full balance owed, that you never paid.

You can either call them, write them, or refer to one of those letters you no doubt received from that creditor telling you they will accept a one-time payment of less than the original price if you respond in the next few days. Now, you may have some sort of reference point to begin your discussions.

But if you still find errors, detail the specifics about the error, including the date you mailed your dispute to the reporting agency, and any other information you believe is pertinent to this error.

Some examples of errors could be too old, fraud, unfamiliar, theft, mistake, wrong balance, paid off in full, never late, not mine, duplicate, incorrect dates, included in bankruptcy or divorce decree.

Again, include documentation with your mailed disputes such as copies of any negotiations, investigations or receipts. If you have no documentation, then dispute the error without documentation if you cannot recognize or contact the creditor.

Once you have reviewed all your reports and have listed all errors, then you should make a copy of your error report.

Mail a copy of your error report to each of the three major credit reporting agencies at the addresses listed previously certified return receipt. One other idea, that will cost you a little more in postage, is to mail your disputes with delivery confirmation and to do so by next day air. While this will get your dispute to the agency faster, it will not speed their response to you. However, it is another option that is available to you.

For now, your work is done until you get your responses back from the reporting agencies.

After the credit reporting agencies receive your list of errors, each of them will send you a letter stating they have received your disputed information claims.

Then they will start by their respective investigations and may or may not periodically update you on their progress.

The agencies will simultaneously contact the individual creditors to verify the accuracy of your complaint(s).

Each creditor will respond back to each of the agencies. The agencies, in turn, will respond back to you in writing to inform you of the final results of their fact finding investigation.

If the information has been changed, the agency will provide you with a corrected report at no cost. The creditor is also required to notify all national credit reporting agencies that the information is incorrect and provide updated corrected data.

However, if the information has not been changed, then the agency will not provide you with a new report free of charge.

Any information that cannot be verified must be deleted from your file. So then, incorrect or incomplete information must be corrected, completed, or deleted if it cannot be verified.

This entire process should take about 15-45 days, but normally happens in 30 days or less, unless your dispute is deemed frivolous.

Although the credit reporting agency has made no request for additional documents, it is always a good idea to send in a copy of your driver's license and any supporting documentation that supports your dispute.

Do not mail your original documents!

You only want to send copies of any documents you may possess that support your claim.

It may not hurt to include a copy of your actual credit report with the item in dispute circled in red ink.

Make sure your envelope is tightly sealed (taped if necessary) and personally delivered to the post office by you. Mail the letter certified return receipt so that you can prove your letter was sent and received by the reporting agency.

Deleted information may find its way back onto your credit report in the form of a new company that purchased the old debt from a previous lender. If this happens, it may be time to negotiate. But hold on for a moment.

Now as you are reviewing your other reports, if you find the same error on the remaining reports, you must follow these exact procedures for each successive report until you have marked every error on each of your three credit reports and completed your error dispute form in triplicate.

If you chose not to use the credit bureau error dispute matrix from Appendix A, you may do

the same thing on the universal dispute form, which can be dowloaded from www.equifax.com, www.experian.com, or www.transunion.com.

Under the Fair Credit Reporting Act, both the reporting agency and the creditor that provided the information to the agency are responsible for correcting any errors found on your credit report.

This ensures that any future reports containing information from that particular creditor will be accurate as well.

In addition, the reporting agency will also report your information to existing creditors accurately.

Now, if you choose not to use the universal dispute form above, you may write a letter to each of the credit reporting agencies.

This letter should include your complete name and mailing address, and it should clearly explain why you believe there is an error listed on your credit report.

A sample letter is included in Appendix A for your use.

However, I have personally found that the universal dispute form works as well if not better than the letter for several reasons. But the most important reason of all is that it saves time and makes identification of any problem areas easy for the reporting agency to research.

The biggest roadblock to credit repair is letter writing because sometimes you have to write several letters to a number of different parties in order to get your issue resolved.

If letter writing is not your forte, then I suggest you use the universal credit dispute form.

This is probably the number one reason why many individuals' give up and pay a "credit repair" service unfortunate amounts of high money to do this tedious job. And the job is either half done or not done at all.

Truth be known, if credit repairers do not get it right, and they usually do not, you are out of money that you could have used to pay down your debt, and your credit is still "funny," not in a laughing way.

If you forget to sign your letter, no action will be taken because without your signature your request is either considered frivolous or incomplete without your signature.

Regardless of whether you send a letter, universal dispute form, or some other type of documentation, make sure you keep a copy of everything you send to the reporting agency.

One final word, if you have disputed information and the information is verified and found correct according to the credit reporting agency, then you have the option of writing a 100-word statement to add to your credit file.

Be careful in your choice of words because this statement will be provided to every creditor each time you apply for new credit from this point forward.

Although this statement will not change your credit score, it is the best opportunity to explain why you have been repeatedly late, for example, because your child has a serious illness; you have been caring for an elderly parent along with your own household; the death of a loved one that was unfortunately uninsured and you had to pay the funeral expenses.

These kinds of statements speak both to the late payment situation and to your character. Both are big pluses in the eyes of the next credit reviewer.

> *To Whom It May Concern:*
>
> *I am writing this letter to be attached to my credit file so that any current and/or future creditors may fully understand the circumstances behind the reasons for my low credit score.*
>
> *My credit score was fine until my employer went bankrupt and refused to honor the agreements of our retirement plans. Although the case is still pending in court, I am struggling to continue meeting all of my obligations on unemployment compensation. I am being paid the maximum amount allowed in South Carolina, which is $300 per week.*
>
> *In addition, my son has been stricken with a rare disease that has created some large medical bills because my bankrupt company also bankrupted our health care plan.*

Note: The purpose of the sample letter above is to show you how to state only the facts that are involved in your case. Since you are only limited to 100-words or less, choose your words very carefully. Do not spend your time talking about your feelings or perceptions, because these personal thoughts do not matter to creditors. Creditors want to know if you – 1) can get back on track; 2) were a good customer before whatever happened that caused your credit to get derailed; and most of all, 3) are going to repay their money back. Anything you state that does not address these factors will be ignored as extraneous material.

Now if it gets to the point where you may need an attorney, get a reputable one either through the National Center for Consumer Advocates, www.naca.net or the National Consumer Law Center, www.nclc.org.

When it comes to writing your dispute letters, here are a few other things not to do.

- Do not insult the credit reporting agency employees by calling them degrading names out of anger.
- Do not ramble.
- Do not make statements that cannot be independently verified.
- Do not list all your complaints in one long run-on paragraph and expect the credit reporting agency to understand the problem.
- Do not make threats of any kind.
- Do not write the agency and start telling them all the things that have happened to you and your family that caused you to fall behind. Examples are my wife lost her job. I have been sick. We had a fire in our home. Our dog died. This is better left for your 100-word statement and it needs to be better organized.
- Explanations of why a debt was not paid does not constitute a dispute. As a matter of fact if you start telling the agency that kind of information it would seem to suggest that the report is already correct and no additional action need be taken.

Frivolous, unfounded, and unsubstantiated attacks may be a violation of federal law, and you can be held liable under the law. Therefore, please ensure you are aware of the tremendous importance of this undertaking.

Here are some additional points of consideration when working to correct your credit report.

1. To get a creditor's address when all else fails, mark an item, "Not my account," fill in dates, dollar amounts, even if $0, and creditor's name. The entry will: (a) either be removed or (b) you will receive a letter saying the account was verified with the necessary contact information listed. Because creditors are constantly moving, being sold, or going under, if it takes the credit bureau a long time to respond, then your chances are good these ac-

counts will drop off fairly quickly. However, if not, at least you now know how to address that situation as well.

2. Use the universal dispute form to remove errors or have improper credit entries like, fraud alerts, credit freezes, stolen identity tags, files more than 7 years old, duplicates, or just plain errors corrected.

3. If you are at a point where you need to negotiate with a creditor to get information changed, use the credit dispute form as a starting point. Then either write or call the creditor to try and make arrangements. When thinking about negotiations start from the bottom and work your way up. First, offer as little money (25-35% of the debt depending on the age) as possible to settle the account and remove the bad repayment history. Since older debts are easier to negotiate than newer ones, gradually increase your offer amounts to pay off older debt. If the creditor refuses to settle the account, then offer to pay it in full on the written agreement that the account will be re-opened with a positive updated payment history. This should be easier to accomplish because most credit card companies only report the previous 24 months. Collection agencies are a little harder to negotiate with because they are all about money. So if the account has been transferred to a collection agency, the best thing you can do is make sure you get a written agreement to remove all entries that refer to their agency and the original debt collected for, if you pay them off in full including fees. Car loans, home loans, and primary utilities are difficult if not impossible to get changed.

4. List as many substantive disputes as possible. And keep disputing until true errors are corrected. Include copies of as much verifiable information as possible such as your driver's license, Social Security card, phone bill, and/or your insurance policy cover sheet, to name a few.

5. When disputing unknown or vague accounts include only basic personal information. In this case less is better. Make the creditor verify the information or delete it.

6. Always remember you have the right to add up to a 100-word or less statement to any account on your report or to your report in general. If you have a specific disagreement with a creditor, write a letter about that specific account with pertinent details that speak directly to the disagreement. Mail this letter, as all correspondence, certified return receipt to each of the impacted bureaus (because the problem account may or may not be listed on your report held at each of the three major bureaus). This statement, in truth, will probably not

help your credit score, but at least it gives future creditors your perspective on the matter, which may help sway future borderline credit decisions in your favor.

7. Finally, make sure if you are married that both spouses submit separate dispute forms even if the information is duplicated. If there was a bankruptcy in either or both of your pasts, make sure all your accounts that were included in the final bankruptcy discharge from the court show included in bankruptcy with $0 balance.

Expert Advice

Here are some additional instructions provided by the Federal Trade Commission at their website www.ftc.gov for correcting credit reporting errors, along with other useful information about how to build a better credit report.

1) Under the FCRA, both the agency and the organization that provided the information, such as a bank or credit card company, have the separate responsibility for correcting inaccurate or incomplete information in any report.

2) To protect all your rights under the law, contact both the agency and the credit information provider.

3) Tell the credit reporting agency in writing exactly what information you believe is inaccurate.

4) Include copies of documents that support your belief.

5) In addition to providing your identifying information, the letter should plainly state each disputed account listed in your report.

6) Keep it simple. State the facts and clearly explain why the disputed items should be disputed. Then request that the disputed account be deleted or corrected.

7) Enclose a copy of your original report with the questionable items circled in bold red ink.

8) Finally, mail your letter certified mail, return receipt requested, and keep copies of all documents and attachments for quick retrieval should it be necessary.

9) By law, the credit reporting agency is required to investigate or reinvestigate any claim that is not deemed frivolous usually within 30 days.

10) The credit bureau also acts as an information broker by passing all the relevant data you provided (attachments or enclosures) over to the business in question, in addition to your dispute form.

11) After the business receives the disputed file information, the clock starts ticking at the credit bureau. The business must review, investigate, and respond back to the credit bureau within 30 days or the information must be deleted. This updated file correction must also be passed on to the remaining nationwide credit bureaus.

12) One caveat: If the information is later verified as accurate, then the account and its history can be added back to your file. The credit bureau is also required to give you a written notice of such a change that includes the name, address, and phone number of the information provider.

13) When all is said and done, the credit bureau will provide the consumer with the written results and a free copy of their report, if the dispute resulted in any changes.

14) At the consumer's request, the credit bureau must send correction notices to anyone who received their report in the previous six months.

15) Job applicants even have a better option. They can have a corrected copy of their report sent to anyone who received a copy during the past two years for employment purposes, all at no cost.

16) If a dispute still remains after a reinvestigation then the consumer may add a personal statement addressing the specifics of the dispute in their file.

17) Now, if the disputed information is inaccurate, the credit provider may not attempt to reuse the information again.

18) Complete and correct negative information may remain on a credit report for as long as 7 years.

19) There are few important exceptions worth mentioning:

> A. Criminal conviction information may be reported without any time limitation.
>
> B. Lawsuit or unpaid judgment information against an individual can be reported for 7 years or until the statute of limitations runs out, whichever is longer.
>
> C. Bankruptcy information may be reported for 10 years, officially.

However, it could plague you for a lifetime with one simple question on any application.

D. Credit information attached to job prospects with a salary greater than $75,000 have no time limit.

E. Credit information attached to credit or life insurance in excess of $150,000 also has no time limit.

Breaking the Code

Removing bad credit does not have to be a cost-prohibitive venture. In fact, the entire purpose of this book is to teach every consumer how to take care of their own credit and credit problems without having to spend thousands of dollars for a service that will never measure up to their price.

Just because something does not show up on a credit report from one bureau does not mean it is not on report at another.

The easiest way to get a copy of your credit report from each of the three bureaus listed above is to get your free reports through www.annualcreditreport.com.

Once you have received your free credit reports (either by mail or you printed them out directly from the website), the first required step is to verify all of your personal information is correct.

Since any errors are grounds for credit denial because of an ill-fated perception of fraud or deception, it is important to verify your name is spelled correctly, current and previous addresses are complete, and employment is correct with a contact telephone number.

Now it is equally important to learn how to read credit bureau code that is used in reporting credit activity.

Account Ownership/Responsible Party

J = Joint Account
I = Individual
T = Terminated
M = Maker(signer)
C = Co-Maker
U = Undesignated

A = Authorized User
B = On behalf of another
S = Shared

Account Definition

O = Open account (30+ days)
R = Revolving or option account (open-ended accounts, ex. Visa, MasterCard, Discover, or an open line of credit with no dollar limit)
I = Installment Account (fixed number of payments, ex. mortgage and auto)

Payment History Rating

O = Approved, but too new to rate (account open less than 30 days)

1 = Pays account as agreed

2 = Pays (or paid) after due date, more than 30 days but less than 60 days; 1 payment past due

3 = Pays after 60 days past due, but less than 90 days; 2 payments past due

4 = Pays after 90 days past due, but less than 120 days; 3 payments past due

5 = Regularly pays after 120 days past due; several payments past due

7 = Making payments under a previously negotiated payment plan arrangement

8 = Repossession

9 = Bad debt, placed for collection; written off/charged off account; skip tracing

Oftentimes, individual rating categories are combined, such as **I-1**, which means it is an installment loan that is paid as agreed.

Normally every payment is reported to the credit bureaus whether it be on time, late and, if late, how late.

Then they rate your actual payment(s) made during the most recent credit reporting period. Was the payment more than enough, just enough, or was it short and if so by how much.

The goal is to get all **R-1's** or **I-1's. O-1's** are not considered because most account scoring does not generally start until after the third billing cycle.

Although the credit bureaus are not directly responsible for what is on your report, they are completely responsible for the accuracy of the information contained in their reports.

Unfortunately, the real work and responsibility of ensuring your credit report is accurate falls squarely on your shoulders. The only positive aspect of being responsible is that your hard work will pay multiple benefits later on.

Credit bureaus conduct their business in such a way that makes one believe their primary function is to provide your credit information to interested parties with a legitimate need, for a fee of course.

Again, it has been estimated that at least 25% of all credit reports contain inaccurate information.

Therefore, credit reporting, or more importantly correct credit reporting is serious business.

Now that you know what is on your report, and how to read it, the next step is to mark every derogatory account on your report.

And then use the credit correction techniques of this and previous chapters to notify each bureau of the errors found.

Second, list all the incorrect account information and why they are wrong. Then make sure that you let the credit bureaus know the account information listed on your report does not agree with your records, and that you want these highly injurious accounts investigated for substantiation or removal.

One of your best strategic weapons is to send your disputed request during a busy season, like the holidays, inventory, or tax seasons.

Many business will be too busy to respond to the credit bureau's inquiries. Therefore, you stand a much better opportunity of having the account removed simply because the company ignored or overlooked the inquiry.

When you mail your request, be sure to send it registered mail, return receipt requested, and always keep a complete copy of your correspondence for your records.

Generally, once the bureau receives your request, they are required by law to contact the owner of the contested information for verification or re-verification.

The real beauty is that some creditors will simply not respond.

Either they no longer have the record, consider the matter too insignificant to warrant their attention because it does not impact their bottom line, or are just too busy to respond.

One of your best strategic weapons is to send your disputed request during a busy season, like the holidays, inventory, or tax seasons.

Whatever the reason, if at the end of 30 days they have not responded with updated information, the credit bureau must remove the item from the report.

If at the end of 45 days, you still have not received an updated copy of your credit report, mail a second registered letter, return receipt requested, requesting a status up-date on your original dispute investigation request. Be sure to include the date of your original request with a clear statement that more than 45 days have passed since your initial request.

If your first request did not elicit a response from the credit bureau, your second request surely will.

Once you receive your update, check it against the original in your files and note the differences.

You should be pleasantly pleased at your new report.

However, if there are still derogatory items listed on your report, then repeat the steps above.

When the credit bureau contacts the information provider this time, the creditor may be completely unwilling to respond a second time..

Another possibility may be that the creditor has mistakenly read the second request as a duplicate.

Again, no response works in your favor and the information will be removed.

If after your second round of disputes bad items still remain on your report, then here are some other options.

1. Offer the creditor a cash settlement provided the account information is removed from your report, or is marked "paid in full." Your first cash offer should be between 35-45% of the disputed report amount.

2. Offer to pay the amount in full, in monthly payments you can afford. The written agreement should clearly state that after 3 on-time payments, the creditor will re-write the account and mark the old account "paid as agreed" on your report.

3. If necessary, and if you can afford it, offer to pay the debt in full, provided the creditor immediately notifies the reporting agency that the account has been paid in full, and agrees to remove all derogatory history.

4. If you cannot get the creditor to negotiate with you, do not despair. Those certified return receipt letters are now going to come in handy. You have the legal right to enter a 100 – word or less statement describing your detailed good faith efforts to resolve the dispute, but the creditor refused. If you do not own the debt, the statement clearly explains this fact. But if you do own the account, then the statement shows your responsible efforts to rectify past problems. The statement will be permanently attached to your report for all future creditors to see. You may also request that a copy be sent to every creditor your report was sent to in the previous 90 days.

Building Good On Top of Bad

By now you may have realized that several of your smaller credit accounts have not shown up on your credit report.

The reason why is that if many of your good accounts are with smaller, local retailers, and most of these creditors do not report to the big three credit bureaus. The primary reason is they are not members of those bureaus or pay those member filing fees.

However, if you can document these accounts and your subsequent payment history, then you can write a letter to the bureaus requesting these files be added to your credit report.

Now, while these accounts, once added may not get updated, at least there will be no negative information attached to them, which is the ultimate goal.

Here is an additional idea that may have worked in years past but is going to be coolly received by most banks in today's market.

Although it may not work for all and at every bank, it may be worth exploring. But if it works, it would be a tremendous coup in your favor.

You will need to go to three different banks and request a savings account with restricted access by your request.

Next, go to each bank and ask for the smallest loan possible. Make sure the bank knows that you do not need the money. Instead, you are only attempting to build a better credit rating than you currently have.

Now the banks will each hold your savings as collateral for the loan and therefore make the loan 100% secured.

For this to work, you must visit all three banks on the same exact day so that you can honestly say you do not have any other loan obligations.

In about two weeks, make your first payment on each loan. Within 30 days make your second payment on each loan.

By now you have freed up enough money on each loan to make a small withdrawal, a withdrawal small enough to be used as payment number three on each of the loans.

Make these payments within the next 30 days.

Before another 30 days passes, go to each of the banks and withdraw the balance of the savings accounts.

Now use that money to make the fourth and final payment on each of your loans.

In about 90 days, you will have repaid three loans and improved your credit.

In your quest to rebuild your credit, if you are denied credit for any reason, ask the credit grantor to give you the specific reason for the denial. Perhaps the salary is not high enough or you have resided at your current residence for too short a period. Whatever the reason, you need to know so you know exactly what you need to work on.

If you have not been able to rebuild your credit in the traditional manner, then here is another option.

PRBC has not yet reached the status of being equal to the Big Three. But, they are the first real entrant into this credit repository turf war that has proven it has some viability, and its influence is growing.

Payment Reporting Builds Credit is what PRBC does for its customers, but the acronym actually stands for "Pay Rent Build Credit." This is the first real alternative credit bureau that is providing a tremendous service to a growing underserved credit population.

Conventionally, on-time payments for such things as rent, electric, gas, phone, cable, daycare, car insurance, and cell phones never get reported to the Big Three until and unless they go into collection.

PRBC has changed that conventional plan or at least has started to challenge it. Those who do pay some type of bill, and do so in a positive fashion, have a voice in the credit market.

If you are an on-time monthly bill payer, PRBC can help you build credit with bills you have already paid, and help you build credit while you pay your bills online. These efforts can lead to potential mortgage qualification and maybe better interest rates.

For further information go to their website, www.prbc.com.

Now that you have worked hard to reestablish your credit, here are a few simple guidelines on how to keep your credit.

1. Do not use your credit to purchase perishable items such as gas, food, airline tickets, or meals out, unless you are absolutely certain you will pay the bill in full before your statement arrives. This will help you avoid any unnecessary finance charges or late payment fees. An excellent idea would be to deduct the money from your checking account at the time of purchase. Now when the statement arrives there will be no surprises and you should have enough money to pay the bill in full.

2. Credit should be used sparingly for depreciable tangibles, such as cars, boats, or furniture. Always make the largest down payment possible and finance the balance for the shortest period of time to reduce excessive finance charges and possible late fees.

3. If you are using your credit cards frequently, keep all card balances under 25-30% of your total available credit limit. This gives you some breathing room for emergencies and goes an even longer way to improving your credit score.

4. Credit should be used as often as possible for the purchase of constructive debt or tangible items that increase in value. The best examples would be a

reasonable mortgage, gold, or silver coins. We will discuss other wealth building options in Chapter 11.

5. Since credit card debt is the most expensive kind of debt due to high interest rates and annual fees, call your creditors and ask them to lower your interest. Not only will this reduce your debt but it will help you pay the bill off quicker.

6. At no time should your consumer debt (excluding mortgage) exceed 20% of your income. If it does, start by calling all your creditors and ask them to remove any late fees, over limit fees, and any other fees to try and reduce the amount owed. Other techniques are covered later in the chapter.

To help you keep your credit in perspective, consider this: – $5,000 cash can leverage a $100,000 investment, such as a house. Even in a depressed market, if that house earns 5%, that is $5,000 a year. But only $250 of that is being earned by your $5,000 cash investment (5%). The rest, $4,750, is being earned by your $95,000 worth of credit.

It may also help if you avoid spending future unearned income for microwavable desires – wanting everything right now. Remember to plan for the unexpected, such as lay-offs, and short or long-term disabilities.

The sooner you start protecting your credit score the better.

If 800, is your minimum goal, then here are two things you can start doing right now to raise your score. Pay your bills on time and pay down your debt from the smallest to the largest.

Now, if you are in a position that neither of these options works for you, do not be discouraged.

If it is hard enough to make your minimum monthly payments, then let me give you a few ways to cut your monthly spending, which can give you extra money to apply towards your debt.

To begin, we will start at the bank. Stop paying those ATM, monthly, and overdraft fees – period.

If you need cash, use the no fee cash-back option when you are checking out at the store.

Start keeping track of all your checks, withdrawals, and any other debits from your account. In fact, a dear friend used to add $1 to every deduction she entered into her checkbook so at the end of each month she had a surplus instead of a budget deficit.

Since you are already at the store, you might as well start right now learning how to save on groceries.

Instead of buying all of those brand name items, buy the store brand that is probably made by the same manufacturer but packaged so as not to be a direct competitor.

Also spend more time on the outer aisles of the store. This will cut fat from both your budget and your diet.

Finally, plan your grocery shopping around the weekly sales ads at your local store, including shopping at lower-cost stores.

Your food budget can be slashed by another 30% simply by cutting your family's eating out in half.

There are two other budget-cutting measures that can bring you some big gains — shop for cheaper communication devices (i.e., cell phones, pages, and phone cards...look for family plans); and, shop for new auto insurance. A few websites that might help are www.insweb.com, www.insurance.com, and www.insure.com.

Together these few strategies may net you as much as $300 savings at the end of each month.

Over Your Head, But Not Out of Reach

If you feel that you are in over your head, it might be time to seek assistance. There is real help still available, but not necessarily in the form that you may think.

Be wary of credit repair clinics that offer to remove harmful but true information from your credit report. This $7 billion industry has no real governing rules, thus the quality of service offered by the providers is vastly different.

Many of these agencies are generally predators who bilk vulnerable customers out of lots of money, and leave them in a worse state of disrepair than when they started.

One of the originals in the consumer counseling business is Consumer Credit Counseling Service (CCCS). CCCS is a non-profit organization that offers free or low-cost financial counseling to families and individuals that are in need by serving as the mediator between the consumer and their creditor(s).

What sets CCCS apart from newcomers in the business is that they are still a non-profit organization, and their fees are designed to be just enough to cover their costs of doing business, i.e. offering you the services that you need. That is a rarity in the consumer financial services industry.

In contrast to CCCS, many other entrants in the industry require consumers to pay all of the associated contract fees before they actually set up a repayment plan for the individual or family to begin repaying their creditors.

More importantly, that delay means that your creditors are not aware that you have sought credit counseling resolution; and, therefore, they continue making their collection calls, and pressing forward with collection activities up to and including suing you in court.

For example, many of the for-profit firms will take your first six payments, or maybe more, and apply them to your "new" debt to the firm. Financially, this means pure profit for the company. Notwithstanding this fact, numerous individuals still sign up for these types of contracts only to find themselves still in trouble after the firm has taken their money.

Let me emphatically state that you cannot get out of debt by taking on more debt!

The general rule of business is: if a business requires you to pay the entire cost of a transaction upfront, that is a business deal that you should not take. There is no better summation for this crucial point than caveat emptor, which is the Latin phrase that means "let the buyer beware." That simple statement, in this specific instance, means that reputable counseling should either come free or at a low cost.

A reputable credit counselor should work with you and your unsecured creditors to come up with a comprehensive repayment plan for you to get out of debt. The details of any plan should: (1) eliminate any additional finance charges immediately; (2) eliminate any future late fees; (3) immediately stop all collection calls and collection activity; and, most importantly, (4) give you an exact date that you will be out of debt with your unsecured creditors only.

Unsecured debts generally include credit cards, charge cards, medical bills, collection accounts, and any other debt that is not backed or secured by some sort of tangible asset. However, unsecured debt does not include tax liens, back taxes of any kind, nor does it include student loans.

Reputable counseling agencies will tell you up front that they do not normally work with secured debt, such as house payments, car payments, or any other debt that is otherwise secured by an asset, including personal loans, if those loans are backed by some sort of collateral.

So, if you are needing help with secured debt, you will have to seek help someplace else besides a credit counseling service.

Before you seek the help of a credit counselor there is one other important factor you need to consider. While your debt counselor will generally not report your activity to the credit bureau, your creditors will most certainly report the fact that you had to turn to credit counseling for help.

Now, if you have sought counseling before your credit report has taken any negative hits, this is a considerably tough decision to make because your credit report is going to take a few very large hits, and all at once.

If you have an A credit rating, 901+ score or higher, you may see your credit rating drop to a C credit rating, 701 – 800 score, or even lower depending on how many of your creditors report this new information. However, under the new credit-scoring rule, FICO 08, if there is just a reference of credit counseling in your file, your score will not be impacted, either positive or negative.

Some major creditors require that you make a minimum number of payments before they stop collection activities, and before they will report your credit in a positive manner. The minimum number of payments vary from anywhere to two up to four payments.

But, if your credit is already messed up, then credit counseling can be a double-edged sword. For some reviewers, it may look like you are in even deeper trouble than you were before. However, some credit reviewers may see this as you taking a positive step to take responsibility for your debt, even if you have to take a few setbacks to get on the right track.

The way CCCS works, or did in the past when I sought their professional services, is that you call their office and explain that you need financial help. They then mail you a budget form along with some other forms that you are supposed to complete in time enough to bring the completed forms, in their entirety, to your initial consultation.

If you come to your initial visit with incomplete documentation, they will reschedule your consultation to give you time to complete your documentation. If your documentation is still not complete by your rescheduled visit, then

CCCS reserves the right to refuse you as a client.

But, if your forms are complete, then you can expect to have a long, detailed discussion about every aspect of your financial life. The counselor will review your budget with a fine-tooth-comb. Things that you would not normally include in your budget, such as bath and beauty products, will be added into the budget. The whole idea is to get an accurate picture of your monthly expenditures. So no expenditure will be overlooked in this process.

Then you will have the same sort of discussion about your individual debts. After that comes the hard part. Your counselor will make sure that you have enough money to cover your mortgage, primary utilities, and your debt payments. If there is anything left over, they will then look at your car payment, insurance, and other remaining bills. If you have any back taxes and/or student loans, they will be considered in your primary group of bills first.

If there is any shortage, then they will start slashing items out of your budget until your are spending less money than you are making, every single month. If you get any bonuses, they will take your bonuses as well to pay down your debt. By the time you are finished, you will be exhausted because you will have really worked to bring your financial house in order.

As for the actual debt repayment plan, you will make either regular monthly or bi-weekly payments to your counselor for a set dollar amount, and your counselor in turn will pay your bills for you (those unsecured bills included in your debt repayment plan). As for your other bills, they will want to see your receipts every month for proof that you are paying your other bills.

Before you leave the meeting, there are two more things required. You will not be allowed to write any checks, except to pay your bills, with the exception of your debt payments to the counselor. That payment has to be made in certified funds or a money order. The last and most brutal step is that you must surrender all of your charge cards and credit cards at that very moment.

Currently, there are more than 1,000 CCCS offices across the United States. All reputable counselors or credit repair services are affiliated with the National Foundation for Credit Counseling or the Association of Independent Consumer Credit Counseling Agencies.

Call 1-800-388-2227 for the phone number of the office nearest you, or visit the CCCS website at www.cccsatl.org.

I have used CCCS on several occasions during my tumultuous financial past. I failed the program once, had success on two separate occasions, and after my last experience, I refused to go back. That last experience was when I decided that I would learn how to do what CCCS does, on my own, and was also one of the driving forces behind me writing this book.

My last experience with CCCS made me so angry that I decided I would never put myself in the position to need their help ever again.

The counselor was less than professional, and she made no attempts to even offer any solutions to my situation. But the straw that broke the proverbial camel's back was when she said, without even reviewing all of my documents, "I can't help you with this! You don't have enough income. You just need to file bankruptcy." I have never needed or used a counseling service since that day!

Notwithstanding my one negative experience, there may come a time when you or someone you know may need credit counseling. But, do not be fooled by one of those predators that seek you out before you ever fall behind in your payments. If you can pay your bills, and are not being hounded by creditors, then you do not need credit counseling, not yet anyway.

On the other hand, if you cannot pay the minimum on your credit cards; you are paying one or more of your bills late on a regular basis; you are receiving more collection calls than any other calls; and, your efforts to negotiate your own debt reduction plan with your creditors has failed; then, you may be a candidate for credit counseling.

There are some limits to what a reputable credit counselor can do. If you are in so much debt that your monthly payments will stretch out beyond five years, most counselors will not be able to help you, only because most creditors will not allow payments to extend that far out.

In the end, whether you use or do not use a credit counseling service, your payment history prior to that point will remain a permanent part of your credit record for the allowable time period allotted by law, unless your creditor decides to do otherwise. But one thing is sure, you will never know unless you ask.

Not to discourage anyone from seeking professional counseling service, if there is a need, but according to the statistics, about 40% of all people who sign up for debt repayment plans dropout. About the same number drops out of Chapter 13 bankruptcy repayment plans as well.

So I am reminded of something my great aunt continues to tell me during each of our weekly lunches, “Trouble is easy to get into, but hard to get out of.”

From the Rubble

Although bad credit may make you feel like a bad person, do not despair. Bad credit happens to good people.

But there are ways to get your credit back on track.

Once you start working, keep working hard to show potential creditors that you are serious about getting your credit back in order. Doing so will improve your credit score and result in better credit offers and substantial savings.

First Things First

You can play the waiting game for 7 years for everything to come off your credit report or you can take a more proactive approach.

1. *Start small.* Rebuilding your credit is just like starting over from scratch. To do so smartly requires that you start small as the easiest and best option. The easiest option is to seek credit cards from local department stores or credit union.

2. *Consider a secured credit card.* These cards are guaranteed by your matching deposit made with the credit grantor. They offer the same purchasing power as their major unsecured counterparts. Just make sure the creditor reports your complete payment history to each of the three major credit bureaus so that your rebuilding efforts are not for naught. Of course the major drawback is that you have to put a deposit up front that is tied to a savings account to get this line of credit. But there are also some advantages. After you have added the initial deposit, you can add to that deposit anytime you like and as much as you like until you reach the maximum. This accomplishes two things – it will increase your credit line and build up a savings you otherwise would not have. At the same time, you have to charge in small amounts, make sure you pay the balance off in full every month, and after a year or 18 months your card will convert to an unsecured card with a large credit line. Yes, this requires discipline, but your efforts will be rewarded when you get your entire deposit back with interest. Then you can either take that same deposit money and get a second card, although I would not personally recommend having more than two major credit cards, and/or you can take that money and start

investing. This will work whether you have bad credit or not. Make sure you shop around for a strong secured card because some of them come with some pretty hefty fees for the privilege.

3. *Open new accounts and pay them off.* If you have the ability to repay a variety of different types of accounts, this would be a key step in rebuilding your credit. This would save time and be better than adding more debt to an already existing credit card. Opening new accounts and paying down old balances may make it easier to get more credit. With patience and timely repayments, you will be able to build a new credit history that creditors will look favorably upon when making decisions about your ability to handle even more credit.

4. *Use your new accounts responsibly.* Make sure you use your new accounts in moderation and make payments that are more than the minimum. Keep a small balance so that your positive payment history will continue to show up on your credit report.

5. *Keep your card balances low.* Make every possible effort to keep your card balance at 30% or less of your credit limit, 20% is even better. Pay more than the required minimum amount each month, and as previously stated start with your smallest balance first. This will keep you from becoming discouraged in the process. Once that card is paid, use all of that money to pay on the next card in addition to whatever else you have already been paying on that card. Keep repeating these efforts over and over again until all your cards are paid.

6. *Consider asking for help.* As an absolute last possibility, ask a friend or family member to cosign for a small loan. If you can stay current on a small loan, this will speed up the entire re-establishment process.

It takes time for new credit history to gain momentum. Meanwhile, you are demonstrating that you are not dependant on credit cards and loans for your financial survival.

Summarize the Big Picture

As we have already established, it is possible for incorrect, incomplete or outdated information to appear on your credit report. Since this can cost you valuable time and money, not to mention lower your chances of getting a loan, you need to take every possible precaution to correct those errors as soon as possible.

Here are those summary steps again. Now short of an error, if you see any evidence of fraud, immediately contact the credit reporting companies and have a fraud alert placed in your file. Also report the fraud to the police and your creditors. Fraud alert information will be covered in greater detail in a later chapter.

1. Contact the credit reporting company

Contact the credit bureau that is reporting the disputed information on your credit report. Send written documentation of the inaccuracy for their review. They will then investigate and provide you notification of your dispute. The account holder will then review the information, conduct their own investigation and report back. The credit bureau will then make all the appropriate changes to your credit file based on the investigation, and notify you of the update.

2. Contact the creditor regarding the problem

In some rare cases, you should contact the appropriate creditor or lender before contacting a credit reporting company, especially if you are a victim of fraud. You should also contact a creditor if you continue to have a dispute with them after they have verified information to the credit bureau. If you have proof that an item in question is incorrect, it should be resolved quickly, and reported to all three national credit bureaus. However, some small creditors that are not members of the credit bureau and do not regularly report information to them are still not required to notify the credit bureaus of this corrected information. These are all instances in which you will need to contact the agency directly. If your initial contact was by telephone, follow up your phone call in writing. List each disputed item, state how it is inaccurate, and attach copies of all supporting documentation. Be concise.

3. Contact the other credit reporting companies

If you find a disputed account with one credit bureau, it is only prudent that you contact the other credit bureaus to see if their reports contain the same error. This will promote prompt correction.

4. Ensure the error is fixed

You should have a written reply within 30 days (45 days if based upon your annual free credit file). If changes were made based on your dispute, you will be afforded an updated credit report at no cost to you. If no changes are made, then you will be notified of this in writing also, but without the additional free credit report.

5. If you cannot resolve a disputed item

When all else fails, you have the right to file a 100-word or less statement, free of charge, explaining the nature of your dispute. Your statement will become part of your credit file at the credit bureau, and will be included each time your credit file is accessed, for as long as the disputed item remains in your credit file.

A Few Extra Tips (One Size Does Not Fit All)

1. Negotiation is not always a bad deal. Negotiating with your creditors can help buy you some time to settle a debt when the money is not available. Although you need to be honest and explain your situation to your creditors, do not give up so much information that you give your creditors even more leverage over you. But since most creditors would rather negotiate than spend their money trying to collect and possible get nothing, you may end up with more time to pay, get some fees dropped, and maybe even settle for less than the full amount owed. But remember two things. Negotiated debt can show up on your credit report. Secondly, if you do get a debt reduction, this is now taxable income that you will have to pay income tax on (consult your tax accountant). If you have the money to negotiate with a small creditor, call them and explain that you are working to reestablish your credit, and that you want to take care of an old bill. Tell them you will pay the entire balance in full including a 90% down payment if the remaining balance can be paid over the next 12 months with equal payments, and if they will remove all the bad payment history from your credit reports.

2. If you have an old medical bill, for example, that has been turned over to a collection agency, call the collection agency and ask them if the bill is paid in full, would they remove the bad account information from your credit report. They may tell you that the original medical creditor is the only one who can authorize that. If so, call the original creditor to get their approval. Generally,

they are most agreeable in these matters. Most collections remain on your credit report for 7 years but have a diminished impact after 2 years, so negotiate after 1 year but before the 2nd year. After the 2nd year, the credit score will be negligible.

3. Remember that most collection accounts are utility bills, rent, insurance, doctor bills, or similar type bills, including some old credit card accounts. Although these show up as negative items on your report, they are not rated lines of credit.

4. The same technique above sometimes works on charge off accounts. Just remember to spread the payments out far enough that you can actually afford to make them as agreed. Make sure your negotiations include any duplicate or second party debts also. As always, get any agreement in writing.

5. Remember business is black and white, dollars and sense, so try to keep your emotions to a minimum. Do not take a "no" personally, but instead move to another account and come back to this one later when you have a better option for the creditor.

6. If you get into trouble with any account, call before the problem goes too far. This will help you help yourself more than you can initially realize.

7. You may have to work your way out of debt. Sometimes the only solution is to put away your credit cards, cut back on spending, and use your savings to reduce debt. If the situation is serious enough, you may even have to take on a part-time job.

8. If you are unable to work your way out of debt, talk to your lenders. Many lenders will help you rearrange your debt payments by extending your payment period, helping you consolidate your debts, or refinancing your debt. In some cases, repaying your debt may actually earn you some cash bonuses and other perks for paying on time.

9. Finally, remember, if none of these options work, consider getting professional counseling from a reputable consumer counseling service with an established debt management program. You can also contact the National Foundation for Credit Counseling at (800) 388-2227 or the Association of Independent Credit Counseling Agencies at (800) 450-1794 to begin the search for a reputable counselor, whether that counseling service is CCCS or a different provider

Debt Validation Attempt

Under the Federal Debt Collection Practices Act, you are allowed to challenge the validity of any debt that a collection agency states you owe. A sample letter that can be modified to fit your needs is included in Appendix A.

Section 809(b) of the Act provides that if the consumer disputes the debt or requests identification of the original creditor in writing, the collector must cease collection efforts until he verifies the debt, or identifies the original creditor and mails a response to the consumer. If the consumer's request for verification of the debt was made in accordance with Section 809(b) of the Act; the collector need not supply the documentation but only so long as collection efforts are not resumed. Section 809(b) requires that "the collector cease collection of the debt, or any disputed portion thereof, until the debt collector obtains verification of the debt . . . and a copy of such verification . . . is mailed to the consumer by the debt collector." In situations contemplated by Section 809(b), the Act imposes the obligation to furnish verification before the collector resumes collection efforts. In the event the collector decides not to pursue the collection efforts, there is no requirement to furnish the documentation of the indebtedness to the consumer. In the event that collection efforts are resumed, the requirement to furnish verification to the consumer prior to resumption of collection remains.

Your Name
Your Street Address
Your City, State, Zip Code

Collection Company
Company Address
City, State, Zip Code

Date:

Re: Acct # XXXX-XXXX-XXXX-XXXX

To Whom It May Concern:

This letter is being sent to you in response to a notice sent to me on (specific date). Be advised that this is not a refusal to pay, but a notice sent pursuant to the Fair Debt Collection Practices Act, 15 USC 1692g Sec. 809 (b) that your claim is disputed and validation is requested.

This is not a request for "verification" or proof of my mailing address, but a request for VALIDATION made pursuant to the above named Title and Section. I respectfully request that your office provide me with complete evidence that I have any legal obligation to pay you.

Specifically, please provide me with the following:

- an explanation of why the money is owed;
- a complete breakdown of all charges along with copies of any papers showing where I agreed to pay this debt; and,
- a verification or copy of any judgment, if applicable, that identifies the original creditor, and proves that the Statute of Limitations has not expired on this account.

If your offices are able to provide the proper documentation as requested, I will require at least 30 days to investigate this information and during such time all collection activity must cease and desist.

If your offices fail to respond to this validation request within 30 days from the date of your receipt, all references to this account must be deleted and completely removed from my credit file and a copy of such deletion request shall be sent to me immediately.

I would also like to request, in writing, that no telephone contact be made by your offices to my home or to my place of employment. If your offices attempt telephone communication with me, including but not limited to computer generated calls and calls or correspondence sent to or with any third parties, it will be considered harassment and I will have no choice but to file suit. All future communications with me must be done in writing and sent to the address noted in this letter above.

This is an attempt to correct your records voluntarily before I am forced to take legal action. Any information obtained shall be used to help that purpose.

Your Signature
Your Typed Name

It is important to note here that when you are disputing, validating, or negotiating with second party collectors or the original creditors to make sure you get everything in writing before you make any payments!

A couple of other important strategies are:

1) to maintain at least 3 open credit lines that report to the bureaus. These credit lines must be open for twelve months minimum and show no more than 75% of your available high credit limit borrowed.

2) to make sure, no payments, are even one date late. If you need help, then set these three accounts up on automatic bank draft. If you have been late, see if you can negotiate with the creditor to have these late entries removed.

3) to get a better credit score (720+)do the following –

a) have no more than one to two addresses in the last seven years. Make sure you have been at the last address for at least two years.

b) have no more than one to four job listings in the last seven years. Make sure you have been at the last job for at least two years.

c) maintain three to four lines of open credit that have been on the books for seven years with less than 75% owed and no late payments. These should include:

i.) one home loan with seven years of perfect payments.
ii.) one open car loan with two years on the books and no late payments.
iii.) one gas card, seven years on the books.
iv.) one major credit card, seven years on the books.
v.) a few other paid off loans, including old car loans that are closed; and,
vi.) zero to four inquiries you initiated for loans within the last two *years.*

Final Thought: Your credit may be 720 and still show some late payments, or even a bankruptcy if the bad credit is older than 2 years and you have since built new good credit. So always get and keep good credit lines open, current and active.

While a stable income and budgeting are the best cures for credit problems, if you cannot pay your bills through no fault of your own or because of situations you cannot control, realize you are not your bank account. So hold your head high, call and tell your creditors why you cannot pay. Meanwhile, keep cracking at it till something good happens.

Final Chapter Review List

Step 1. Order a copy of your credit report from each of the three main credit reporting agencies. You need to have a recent copy of your report, meaning a report that is less than 90 days ol d to start your dispute process. Start a communications log so that you can log every time you do something with a specific bureau. Make three files for Equifax, Experian, and TransUnion so that you can keep accurate records of all you do.

Step 2. Review your personal information. Make sure that your names and aliases, all addresses including zip codes, Social Security number, date of birth, spousal information, any ID numbers (government, student, drivers license), and employers' information are correct.

Step 3. If any of your personal information is incorrect, get this information corrected.

Step 4. Dispute any errors in your personal information with each of the three primary credit reporting agencies. Again you can use the universal dispute form or you can write a letter. Either way, make sure you take the time to explain in detail each individual error, what the correction should be, and any documentation to support your request.

Step 5. Go ahead and begin to look at your questionable items and make a list of what is most important. Or you can simply start going down the list of errors and attack each as you get to it on the report. In my mind a ranking would go from bankruptcy, liens, foreclosures, and so on until you get to credit inquiries.

Step 6. Make sure you dispute one item at a time. Now one at a time means two things. You can either list each item individually on your universal dispute form or you can literally dispute one item, get a response from the credit bureau, and then go on to the next item, and so on, and so on, until all your disputes have been addressed.

Step 7. Again, regardless of which method you use to dispute your reports, make sure you use specific words such as outdated, erroneous, and unverifiable to describe items that need to be disputed so that the agency will not view your disputes as frivolous.

Step 8. If the need arises, write a 2nd dispute letter to address any particular matter that has not been addressed in your initial letter for any dispute.

Step 9. If after a reasonable time has passed, 60+ days, and you have not heard from the credit reporting agency, you may file a formal complaint with the Federal Trade Commission (FTC). While the FTC does not resolve individual consumer disputes, it does gather complaint information to spot patterns of violations so they can institute legal action.

Federal Trade Commission
Consumer Response Center
Washington, DC 20580
Phone: 1 – 877-382-4357

Step 10. Now that all your personal information is corrected, it is time to dispute the questionable items on your list.

Step 11. If the agency mails you any stall letters to try and deter you from getting your information corrected, keep pushing until the report is corrected and free from errors, regardless of whether it has to be removed or updated.

Step 12. Continue disputing all items until you have completed your entire list of questionable items. Now that you have disputed all items on your credit report and gotten everything that can be removed taken off the report, now it is time for the next step.

Step 13. Anything that cannot be removed, get an address and a phone number. Write the company and very humbly explain your situation and try to negotiate a reasonable settlement, which includes a request to show the account as current and paid if you hold fast to the terms agreed to in your letter. A sample letter is in Appendix A.

Step 14. Make a personal commitment to never default or be late on any payments ever again. Either pay the bill before 30 days has elapsed, and if you cannot pay the bill, pick up the phone immediately and call the creditor to make arrangements to pay the bill. Make sure you call the creditor before the creditor calls you. Humility is the key.

Step 15. If there is any bad credit remaining, start building new credit. This may include you sending in $300 with an application and asking an old creditor to reopen an old account or starting a new account. Once opened, commit to making twelve months of consistent payments. Pay more than the minimum due each month. If you still have any old credit cards, pay down those balances to under 85% of the credit card and leave it at that point.

Step 16. DO NOT BECOME DISCOURAGED and let some company bilk you out of your money with false promises. If in doubt, call someone for advice.

If It Looks Like a Rat

You hear these advertisements on the radio, see them in newspapers, on TV, and on the Internet. You even get fliers in the mail and a few phone calls from telemarketers offering to repair your credit.

They all make the same claims:

> *"Credit problems? No problem!"*
>
> *"We can erase your bad credit — 100% guaranteed."*
>
> *"Create a new credit identity — legally."*
>
> *"We can remove bankruptcies, judgments, liens, and bad loans from your credit file forever!"*

Do yourself a favor and save your money, "don't believe the hype!"

Everyday these companies prey on consumers with poor credit histories.

After you pay them hundreds and in some cases thousands of dollars, they promise to clean up your credit report so you can get a car loan, a home mortgage, insurance, or even a job.

But the only thing that disappears is your money.

If you decide to respond to a credit repair offer, look for these tell-tale signs of a scam:

1. Does the company want you to pay for credit repair services before they provide any services?

2. Do they tell you your legal rights and what you can do for yourself for free before you pay them any money?

3. Do they try to get you to apply for an Employer Identification Number to use instead of your Social Security number under false pretenses, or try another illegal method to create a credit identity? Remember: if you too follow

illegal advice and commit mail or wire fraud, you may be subject to prosecution.

4. If you tell the company that under the Credit Repair Organizations Act, credit repair companies cannot require you to pay until they have completed the services they have promised, and if they still insist on money up front then you are being scammed. By law, under the Credit Repair Organizations Act, you must be given a copy of the "Consumer Credit File Rights Under State and Federal Law" before you sign a contract. They also must give you a written contract that spells out your rights and obligations, the payment terms for services, including their total cost and detailed description of the services to be performed, and how long it will take to achieve the results. Once you have received a copy of the contract, you have a three-day waiting period during which time you can cancel the contract without paying any fees.

5. Make sure you read these documents completely before you sign anything.

Bankruptcy Option?

For some individuals, bankruptcy is their only option to rebound from past credit problems. This is a decision that each individual must make in consultation with their legal representative.

Now while by far the most preferred option instead of bankruptcy is to pay off all debt, even if it takes years to do so, that does not preclude the fact that many individuals still opt for bankruptcy.

If you believe that bankruptcy is the best option for your situation, then let me give you a few reminders.

Although a bankruptcy stays on your credit report for up to ten years, the bankruptcy will actually remain with you for the rest of your financial life.

It is not uncommon for lenders to ask if you have ever filed for bankruptcy on their lending applications. So it may be necessary for you to answer this question in some detail for years to come.

Again, if you believe bankruptcy is the best option for your situation, there is nothing wrong with this decision. Remember: Henry Ford went bankrupt five times before his sixth company was a success.

If you do have to answer the question in the future, be prepared to show how your current situation differs from the situation that caused you to file for bankruptcy.

Also remember the bankruptcy laws have recently changed dramatically. So make sure you understand what you are agreeing to before you sign any documents.

This is completely your decision, so do not be rushed into it by anyone.

Before you make that final decision, start calling all of your creditors and tell them what you are planning to do. Generally, this will prompt most creditors to decide now is the time to start negotiating when previously they would not have considered negotiating.

This puts you in the driver's seat. The door is wide open. Here are some things to ask for in consideration:

- lower interest rate
- waiver of all fees for the past six months or one year
- specific payment plan (make sure you can afford the payments)
- after six months of on-time payments, report as positive to all three major credit reporting agencies, include removing all bad previous marks

This is just a starting list for negotiation ideas. If there is something else you need or believe is important to your financial future, then make sure you include that item in your list also.

The company is not going to offer you any freebies, so ask for anything you want. In my experience, nothing hurts me more than knowing I could have gained something if I had only had the courage to ask.

You also need to remember that the bankruptcy laws have changed, which may have some impact on your negotiations.

As of October 17, 2005, some of the new requirements include requiring each individual to *receive credit counseling within six months before your actual filing.*

A state-by-state list of government-approved organizations can be found at the U. S. Department of Justice, Trustee Program website, www.usdoj.gov/ust, which is the office that supervises bankruptcy cases and trustees.

The new law also requires that some debtors repay at least a portion of their debts based on what they can afford, which will be determined by the court in the form of a "means" test.

This is a change from Chapter 7 in previous bankruptcy laws that allowed individuals to erase all of their debts or Chapter 13, which required a portion of those debts to be repaid.

The means test is designed to require those who are financially able to help pay some part of their debt by comparing income to expenses, which cannot by law include such items as cell phones, restaurant meals, and similar luxury items.

However, remember Chapter 7 protections may still be available to those who can prove they would have difficulty adhering to a repayment plan because of a personal medical situation, a family situation, or some other similar situation with dire consequences.

Now that you have some idea of the law, you need to remember that not all creditors look at your credit report the same way.

Every creditor sets their own credit-granting standards and they are as different as the companies themselves.

Just as one company may look at your most recent history when considering you for new credit, and another may look at your debt to income ratio, so in the same way there is no way to determine how these companies will respond to your request to negotiate before bankruptcy. But it is worth a try.

To Budget or Not to Budget

Whether you get one creditor or none to negotiate with you, whether or not you file bankruptcy or not, the reality is that you are going to need a budget.

Whether or not you set your own budget or the court sets it for you, a budget is a "must have" if you are going to survive your own financial mistakes.

Although creating a budget can be a challenge, having the discipline to stick to it is the greatest challenge.

But if the whole idea of budgeting and keeping track of bills is over your head, right now, consider contacting a non-profit, reputable consumer credit counselor.

This service can be offered by your credit union, the United Way, colleges or universities, and some local governments.

Reputable means the counselor you choose to use does not charge exorbitant fees or pressures you into giving a "voluntary" donation that you obviously cannot afford.

Reputable counselors are also certified and trained in the areas of consumer credit, money and debt management, and budgeting. They will discuss your entire financial situation, and help you develop a personalized plan that is tailored to your money problems with one goal in mind – – to get you debt free as quickly and as painlessly as possible.

To give you some perspective on how important budgeting is, every business has to have a budget and operate within certain limits if it is going to survive.

When we see organizations downsizing, it is because their budgets are lopsided, i.e., they are spending more money than they are making.

Therefore, reigning in your household's spending is equally important to your financial survival, and budgeting can help you to do this in an orderly and systematic way.

Whether you develop your budget alone or with the help of a counselor, the steps are the same.

If you are still not sure you need to talk with a counselor, let me refer you to a website where I read a very good article about budgeting during a tough situation. Although, the title does not apply to all, the lessons within may be more helpful than any might imagine. The website is www.womansdivorce.com, look for tips on budgeting.

Know this: credit repair is serious business, and it is both possible and necessary to dig your way out of debt because the majority of Americans rely on some form of credit to buy homes, cars, and educate their children.

While even the most conscientious bill payer can encounter unexpected unemployment, medical emergencies, and other unforeseen circumstances, it is imperative to convince the financial world that you are a dependable, debt-paying customer.

In today's business world, a negative credit report can also cost you your job, so it becomes even more important that you do not just sit back and let your credit report or lack of financial discipline destroy your life.

If you cannot build a positive traditional credit report, then build a nontraditional history by keeping copies of ***all*** bills you pay, and copies of all the canceled checks used to pay these bills or the receipts if paid by cash.

You may even consider asking your creditors to write letters stating how long you have been a customer and how well you have paid your bills every month.

Show these records to any lenders or employers on demand to show you deserve their trust.

These efforts may not only help you take control of your credit; in addition, they may help you keep your job and start your budget.

Basically, there are four steps to making a budget.

Income (a recent bank statement can help you here)

Expenses (use that same bank statement here also)

Comparing 1 and 2

Setting priorities and making adjustments so that your income exceeds your expenses. This means if you are going to start saving money you need to have some goals. You need some short-term goals and some long-term goals.

So while you are working on your budget, have an additional sheet(s) handy to write down both your short-range and long-term goals. Examples include take my family on a real vacation (short-range), and long-term include purchasing our first piece of real estate investment.

For any budget to work, it must be accurate and reflect your actual expenditures by month, by quarter, bi-annually, and yearly.

Some individuals like the 60% rule of budgeting. The basic idea here is that all of your essentials comes out of the first 60% of your after-tax income (because taxes are taken out before you ever see it), and then the remaining priorities are basically funded on an as available basis.

I do not subscribe to that rule of budgeting.

Although we will cover more of this in Chapter 11, I believe you should pay your tithes, pay yourself, set aside investment money, then your essentials. This will ensure your priorities will not be overcome by frivolous living for the moment expenditures (remember my friend and his daughter with the beauty salon).

You must capture all of your expenses for the budget to work. So if you are not sure what you are spending your money on, then you need to write down every single expenditure until you have a strong sense of where your money goes, and where you can cut back.

Now when you get to the end of the budget process, do not make cuts so deep it lowers your standard of living, instead increase your income — by any legal means necessary.

Find ways to broaden your marketable skills to those who need what you have to offer. Work the phones, work the internet, use your network of friends, business associates, and family to bring in new income opportunities. This is the time to say, "If you got it, then flaunt it!"

Appendix A includes a sample budget sheet for your review, use, or adaptation.

Whether or not you chose to use that form, find one that works for you — one that you are comfortable with, and one that you will use every day, week, month, and year.

You can copy this worksheet into any kind of spreadsheet software and add more lines or categories, and you can delete the same or simply ignore those areas that do not apply to you and your household.

Also, if you are an Excel user, as with other software faithful, you may go online and find a budget more to your liking that is compatible with your software.

Again, it does not matter what tool you use as long as you use it!

Now while you are looking at your budget, you should also be looking at cutting expenses. To that end, here are some options to cutting your expenses and increasing your income.

- Make a distinction between your wants and needs. Buy only what is a necessity.
- Cut your eating out budget to the absolute minimum or as close to $0 as possible. If you do have to go out and eat, set a budget and do not exceed it, including taxes and tips.
- Start carrying your lunch to work.
- Start making a shopping list before you go out to the grocery store. Whenever we go to the mall for clothing or other large items, we know exactly what we are looking for and the price we are willing to pay for that item. Do the same thing for your groceries, and one way to do this is to plan your meals before you go to the grocery store.
- Start using coupons whenever and wherever possible.

- When you buy other items, comparison shop on line and by phone, then buy only when your item of choice is on sale.
- Combine your driving trips to save gas and use public transportation as much as possible.
- If you have never shopped at a thrift store, garage sale, or flea market, no better time to start than now.
- Consider canceling non-essential services or cutting back to the minimum. Cut your cable and start watching videos checked out from the library. Turn off your home phone and cut back your cell phone to the bare essential. Now if you need a home phone for a security system for example, then only have the basics and no long distance because you get free long distance with your mobile phone. Watch those minutes.
- Avoid pay day loans, rent-to-own stores, pawnbrokers, and check-cashing stores, period.
- Stop paying extra fees to your creditors. If you are going to be late, call them and ask them to waive all fees possible.
- Now that you have cut your expenses, increase your income by getting a part-time job, working overtime, and/or throwing your own garage sale.

A Longing To Be Free

While getting out of debt can be an uphill battle generally because of the lack of knowledge, it still strikes me as strange that individuals have to spend so much effort and time to get a separate "financial education" from all the other education and job training that exists in today's world.

Most people do not decide to get out of debt until something catastrophic happens or they just simply get fed up!

I know of several individuals that had to educate themselves out of debt after they were struck by financial tragedy.

It generally starts with a seminar that gives them some formal money management ideas, like consistent investing, debt elimination, and deferring taxes, legally. Then it progresses to self-education, i.e., spending time in the library reading books by experts and monthly magazines on the subject until they graduate to a professional relationship with a financial advisor.

This book is the beginning financial education for some and additional training for others. Either way, you are on the road to financial freedom.

To get there, individuals have created debt clubs, made debt contests, and even reverted back to the frugality of their college days to finish the race.

While those are all viable options for some, here are some more cost-cutting measures to consider.

After locking away your credit cards and not using them without canceling them:

- discuss with your family ways of cutting expenses;
- set goals that help to keep your family focused; and,
- consider using some of your savings to eliminate some of your high interest debt only if the numbers work in your family's favor.

I recently read about a former employee that worked at the same company where I once worked and how she and her family decided to become debt free.

My understanding is that this young lady was such a determined woman that when she decided she was ready to get married, she moved to another city and took a second job at a men's clothing store so she could meet her husband.

After three years together, they were more than $170,000 in debt and stressed out. To make ends meet, one month they would skip their light bill, the next month the water, and so on until they had cycled through all of their utility bills, and then it started over.

Even though it was stressful, notice they skipped bills that did not report to the three major credit reporting agencies.

With the same kind of determination and zeal, they approached becoming debt free.

Here are some of the things they did along with some others I have added:

Step 1. They took stock of what they owed, and they decided to downsize as a family. They sold her car first and replaced it with an inexpensive, completely paid for smaller vehicle.

Step 2. With the leftover money, they paid off the first debt and put the remainder to the next debt instead of paying minimum monthly balances. If you cannot do this right now, then here is a simple guide to help you pay off debt.

If your debt load is:

- $5,000 or less: Pay at least an extra $50 every month.
- Between $5,000 and $10,000: Pay at least an extra $100 every month.
- More than $10,000: Pay at least an extra $150 every month.

Step 3. They each increased their income potential by either taking on a second job or by having garage sales and selling items at the local flea market. This young lady even stretched her talents by using her current skills as a private contractor for a different employer on her own time, in addition to her second job.

Step 4. As a family, they clipped coupons, ate out less, and sold their big house to rent a smaller house, temporarily. At the end of 29 months they were debt free and no longer argued over money.

When last I heard, they had saved enough for a down-payment on a new home they built themselves by becoming the general contractor, and with plans they had purchased on the internet at a huge discount. They closed on the house with a mortgage they could afford on one salary if it came down to it.

They have a plan in place for the future should a job loss occur, they learned how to delay certain purchases despite what others think, and maybe most importantly they instituted a 24-hour rule. Before purchasing anything over $30 they wait 24-hours to decide if they really need it. Finally all purchases have to fit within the family budget, and even though they have credit cards they use cash more often than not.

Some other steps include:

Step 5. Contribute to your employer-sponsored retirement savings plan up to the maximum point of your employer's match. This is free money going in, so do all you can to take advantage of it.

Step 6. Start building up your emergency fund. Start with $2,000 because according to a study by The Consumer Federation of America, this is the average amount of "unexpected" expenses an individual faces in a given year. Once you have started, then grow that fund to three or six months of your expenses, and the best way to do this is to put this on some sort of automatic transfer from your paycheck to your savings. You do not miss what you cannot see.

Step 7. If you are ready to buy a home, it's time to save for a down payment. Your home down payment is one of the largest "big-ticket" items you'll ever make, so you'll need to make it a savings priority. (Other options are covered in Chapter 9.)

I will be the first one to tell you that when you make a resolve to change your life, that resolve will be tested immediately. The dog gets sick and needs emergency surgery, the furnace quits, the car breaks down, or something else happens.

Stand your ground!

If you have a small emergency fund set aside, use it and move on, that is why you saved it in the first place.

If you do not have the funds, rework the emergency into your new plan and keep moving. Your goals and numbers may change a little, but the end strategy will still be the same.

Some extra savings may be found in the following areas.

- Opting for basic TV service – no premium channels and renting movies free from the library.
- Chooses a dial-up Internet connection over high-speed service.
- Buy food in bulk to last for a couple of months.
- Carry your lunch to work.
- Make a budget for the holidays, birthdays, etc., and stick to it.
- Apply "extra" paychecks to debt (a biweekly pay schedule will provide a third check two months each year).
- Apply any bonuses toward debt.
- Find a comfortable thermostat setting for your family for both the winter and summer to save on the electric bill. Maybe 67 in the winter and 75 in the summer to start.
- Take out a preset amount of walking cash each week and when it is gone, it is gone.
- Keep the credit cards at home.
- Shop with a list and buy only what is on the list. Avoid window-shopping, even for sale items.
- Keep your car tuned up to avoid bigger expenses.
- Do not stop at any fast food restaurants and stay away from vending machines at work. Instead, make sure to carry fresh fruits and nuts for

in-between meal snacks.

- Shop for discounted items, discontinued items, or slightly damaged items when a need arises.
- Budget vacations and look for coupons wherever possible.

Statute Of Limitations For Debts

The statute of limitations (SOL) for a delinquent debt is the time limit for the creditor to file a lawsuit. This period starts when the debtor becomes delinquent. The fact that the SOL has "run" (expired) on a particular debt will not necessarily prevent a lawsuit from being filed (via a Summons And Complaint), but the defendant can have the suit dismissed on this basis.

There are two things that you should know about debt: the statute of limitations for reporting debt and the statue of limitations for collecting debt. These are two completely different things. Now the Federal statute for reporting debt is seven years. The statute of limitations for collecting debt is somewhat different. These vary from state to state.

Having this knowledge can actually help you negotiate payments to get items removed from your report for far less than it would any other time. This suggestion is NOT 100% foolproof. But, if done properly it can and will work.

A couple of tips:

1) when you contact the collector, write them, do not use the phone.

2) in the letter DO NOT admit to owing the debt. Admission of debt can re-start the statute of limitations, and may enable the creditor to sue you. You are also less likely to be able to negotiate a letter of deletion if you admit that this debt is yours. Simply state, "I am writing about account number 1234567," instead of writing "I am writing about my past due debt."

The Statute Of Limitations(SOL) *only* covers lawsuits. SOL expiration does *not* affect other types of collection action or reporting of the account to credit bureaus. The creditor or collection agency may theoretically continue with letters and telephone calls forever. However, third-party collectors are subject to the "cease and desist" provision of the Fair Debt Collection Practices Act. But, they will generally put much less effort into collecting "Out-Of-Statute" debts. However, do not expect them to give up as easily as in the past, only because creditors are carrying too much debt to ignore any potential income.

Out-Of-Statute debts can still be reported to credit bureaus for the time limits specified in the Fair Credit Reporting Act, which may work as an incentive to bring consumers to the negotiating table.

Credit cards are normally considered open accounts. Auto loans and other installment agreements are written contracts. If there has already been a lawsuit resulting in a judgment, that judgment has a separate SOL. These are important distinctions as far as SOL are concerned, as evidenced by the following table on pages 166-167.

After a creditor wins a lawsuit against a debtor and is awarded a judgment by the court, there is a time limit for collecting that judgment. However, many states allow judgments to be renewed one or more times, which could substantially extend the enforceability of a judgment, if the creditor is vigilant about the renewals. This can potentially result in a permanent legal obligation until it is paid.

If a lawsuit has not been filed yet, there is a separate time limit for doing so, which you can find by contacting your State's Attorney General. See Chapter 3 discussion on the law and statutes of limitations. Also, remember that each state has a calculated method of computing interest on these debts. Again, your State Attorney General can assist you with this information.

State	Oral Agreements	Written Contracts	Promissory Notes	Open Accounts
Alabama	6	6	6	3
Alaska	6	6	6	6
Arizona	3	6	5	3
Arkansas	3	5	6	3
California	2	4	4	4
Colorado	6	6	6	6
Connecticut	3	6	6	6
Delaware	3	3	6	3
District of Columbia	3	3	3	3
Florida	4	5	5	4
Georgia	4	6	6	4
Hawaii	6	6	6	6
Idaho	4	5	10	4
Illinois	5	10	6	5
Indiana	6	10	10	6
Iowa	5	10	5	5
Kansas	3	5	5	3
Kentucky	5	15	15	5
Louisiana	10	10	10	3
Maine	6	6	6	6
Maryland	3	3	6	3
Massachusetts	6	6	6	6
Michigan	6	6	6	6
Minnesota	6	6	6	6
Mississippi	3	3	3	3

Numbers on this chart indicate years.

State	Oral Agreements	Written Contracts	Promissory Notes	Open Accounts
Missouri	5	10	10	5
Montana	5	8	8	5
Nebraska	4	5	6	4
Nevada	4	6	3	4
New Hampshire	3	3	6	3
New Jersey	6	6	6	6
New Mexico	4	6	6	4
New York	6	6	6	6
North Carolina	3	3	5	3
North Dakota	6	6	6	6
Ohio	6	15	15	?
Oklahoma	3	5	5	3
Oregon	6	6	6	6
Pennsylvania	4	6	4	6
Rhode Island	15	15	10	10
South Carolina	10	10	3	3
South Dakota	6	6	6	6
Tennessee	6	6	6	6
Texas	4	4	4	4
Utah	4	6	6	4
Vermont	6	6	5	6
Virginia	3	5	6	3
Washington	3	6	6	3
West Virginia	5	10	6	5
Wisconsin	6	6	10	6
Wyoming	8	10	10	8

The information above is believed to be accurate at the time of publication, and is for informational purposes only. I am not an attorney, and nothing here should be construed as or relied upon as legal advice in lieu of seeking professional legal counsel .

Terms To Know

Collections Action – A creditor or third-party collection agency can legally demand or request payment on a debt, via letters and phone calls, as long as the debt remains unpaid. A debtor can order a third-party collector to cease communication, as per the Fair Debt Collection Practices Act, which should stop routine demands. Generally speaking, the older a debt is, the less vigorous the collection efforts will be, and the more likely the creditor or collector will give up easier, unless the debt is secured by some type of property which can be enforced for payment by a lawsuit.

Lawsuits – When a creditor has exhausted all options for collecting on a debt that is seriously delinquent and that debt is for a significant dollar amount, there exists the possibility that the creditor may file a lawsuit. The time limit for doing so is known as the statute of limitations, which is individually set by the states, respectively. The prevailing statute is the one for the state in which the debtor resided at the time of the delinquency. While an expired statute of limitations does not automatically prevent a lawsuit, it does however provide an absolute defense, whereby the debtor is simply required to file a response with the court that shows the statute of limitations for that debt has expired, and that lawsuit should be easily dismissed.

Judgments – If a lawsuit has already been filed and was won by a creditor, there is a separate statute of limitations for enforcing (collecting) on that judgment.

Federal Taxes – Ten years from the date of the assessment for delinquent amounts, unless a lien has been filed. Tax liens on, for example, real estate, remain until the back taxes have been paid.

Student Loans – There is no statute of limitations or other time limit for lawsuits or other enforcement action on defaulted federal student loans.

Credit Reporting Time Limits

As previously stated, there are various time limits set by law on various types of information that appear on consumer credit reports. Making payments or partial payments on bad debts will not impact credit reporting time limits, except in the case of tax liens and federal student loans. The 1996 amendments to the FCRA, set a specific starting date related to the original delinquency date to make sure collection agencies are not artificially resetting debt dates to negatively impact consumers longer than allowed by law (see FCRA Section 605 (c) (1).)

Inquiries – Remain on credit reports for two years.

Late Payments – These payments will remain seven years from the month in which the original late payment was due. If there are multiple late payments on one account, then they will each have a different expiration date based on their original due date.

Charge-Offs – These accounts also have a seven year window. The time runs from the date of the original delinquency, plus 180 days. If a payment was due on an account on January 1, 2008, but the debtor defaulted, and never caught up to become current again, and the account is eventually declared a charge-off by the creditor, then the seven year reporting time limit starts running on July 1, 2008, with the item scheduled to expire from the credit report on July 1, 2015.

Collection Accounts – Again, here is another seven year window. The time limit runs the same as that of charge-offs. This prevents collection agencies from improperly "re-setting the clock."

Lawsuits And Judgments – Seven years or until the governing statute of limitations has expired, whichever is longer.

Bankruptcy (Chapter 7) – Ten years from the date of entry of the order for relief, or the date of adjudication.

Bankruptcy (Chapter 13) – Seven years.

Paid Tax Liens – Seven years from the date of payment.

Unpaid Tax Liens – Forever (unless paid).

Unpaid Federal Student Loans – Forever (unless paid, after which they can appear for seven years).

Remember, there are three situations in which credit bureaus can legally disclose older information.

- A credit application involving a loan amount of $150,000 or more.
- An application for a life insurance policy in excess of $150,000 or more.
- An application for employment in a position paying $75,000 per year or more.

Collection Agency Inner Workings

There are two types of collection agencies. The first one is when the same creditor uses a separate company name, address, and phone number for their internal collections department. The creditor is trying to trick the consumer by providing the allusion of an outside agency on the premise that the debtors will take the repayment more seriously. This strategy is generally only used when the debt is recent or less than six months old in most cases.

The second type is when these collection activities are performed by third-party collection agencies. These are completely separate companies that have been hired by the original creditor to collect a debt. Their fee is generally some percentage of the money they collect, or they may have already paid the debtor some fee for the right to collect this debt. Most of these agencies are not very willing to negotiate because it cuts directly into their profit margin.

The individual collectors are often paid a low base wage plus commissions based on their personal performance (i.e., their ability to collect on debts owed).

Some agencies also purchase large groups of charged-off bad debts for a small percentage of the "face value" (amount owed.) After a debt is sold, the debtor now owes the full amount to the purchaser. Since the chances of recovery decrease substantially with time, an agency might only pay 1% – 5% of face value. The agencies' profits come from the difference between the purchase price and the amounts that are eventually collected.

Regardless of who is collecting the debt, the agencies use the same two collecting techniques – – letters and telephone calls. Both methods are employed simultaneously, but the letters are impersonal, and the telephone calls are extremely personal and will catch you off guard. The point of both techniques is to make that particular debt a point of urgency so you can respond, i.e., pay the debt sooner than later.

They can and do report to the credit bureaus on a regular basis. They can also recommend a lawsuit, or sue outright, although chances of this are often significantly less than they try to make them out to be. But do not be mistaken: if the debt is large enough, a creditor can and oftentimes does pursue consumers in court to recover these large account receivables.

Collection agencies cannot:

1) legally seize a debtor's assets, bank accounts, or paycheck unless there has already been a successful lawsuit with a judgment awarded to them.

2) legally make any kind of public announcements or disclosures concerning the debt, except to the credit bureaus.

3) legally get a debtor fired from his/her job.

4) legally engage in any type of physical violence or threats of any kind.

The third party collection activities are regulated by the *Fair Debt Collection Practices Act (FDCPA)*, which places many restrictions on their collection activities. However, the FDCPA only covers third-party collection agencies, not the original creditors.

The Federal Trade Commission (FTC) oversees the collections industry and has the authority to impose fines or other penalties for violations. However, the FTC does not get involved with individual consumers' complaints. Instead, the FTC looks for patterns of violations among the complaints they receive which could lead to action against a particular collection agency.

Even though a third-party collector may purchase a debt, it is still covered under the Fair Debt Collection Practices Act as a "third-party debt collector." And this purchase of debt does not change the time limit that the item can be reported on the credit report.

However, the statute of limitations *may* possibly be reset if the debtor makes a specific promise to pay or a partial payment.

Sometimes these agencies will purposely purchase a bundle of "out-of-statute" debts (where the SOL has already expired) hoping that they will dupe debtors into paying a debt they are no longer legally obligated to pay.

Finally these creditors may call your place of employment; however, they cannot legally tell your employer about the debt, or try to have you fired.

Fighting Back

The one best way to stop these collection activities is to use (section 805 of the) Fair Debt Collection Practices Act, which states:

"(c) CEASING COMMUNICATION. If a consumer notifies a debt collector in writing that the consumer refuses to pay a debt or that the consumer wishes the debt collector to cease further communication with the consumer,

the debt collector shall not communicate further with the consumer with respect to such debt, except –

(1) to advise the consumer that the debt collector's further efforts are being terminated;

(2) to notify the consumer that the debt collector or creditor may invoke specified remedies which are ordinarily invoked by such debt collector or creditor; or

(3) where applicable, to notify the consumer that the debt collector or creditor intends to invoke a specified remedy.

If such notice from the consumer is made by mail, notification shall be complete upon receipt."

The consumer can also send a "cease and desist" letter to the third-party collection agency making sure to cite the FDCPA, ordering them to stop the collection letters and calls. The agencies are legally obligated to comply. The only permissible contact thereafter is to notify the debtor of specific "remedies," the debtor is going to seek, like legal action.

After a "cease and desist" notice from the consumer, the debt may then be returned to the original creditor, passed on to another third-party agency, or simply filed away, depending on the circumstances. However, the agency may still report the account to the credit bureaus.

If you have the slightest concern about possible lawsuits, you may want to confirm this information with your local better business bureau, your state's attorney general, and/or a qualified attorney.

Chapter Eight

What About Your Friends?

According to the most recent statistics from CreditCards.com, as of March 2010, the total U. S. consumer debt, which includes credit card debt and noncredit-card debt, now stands at $2.45 trillion. However, this $2.45 trillion does not include any mortgage debt.

This is a dramatic change from 2007, when the Federal Reserve Board reported that the majority of U. S. households had no credit card debt.

Upon further examination of this $2.45 trillion, approximately $852.6 billion is credit card debt. This means that as U. S. credit card holders, we own more debt than ten of the largest economies in the world produce on an annual basis. Our credit card debt would make us the 16th largest producing economy in the world.

Rank	**Country**	**GDP (B$US)**	**Rank**	**Country**	**GDP (B$US)**
1	United States	13,780	14	South Korea	1,206
2	China	7,099	15	Turkey	854
3	Japan	4,272	16	**U.S. Consumer Debt**	**852.6**
4	India	2,966	17	Indonesia	844
5	Germany	2,807	18	Australia	773
6	United Kingdom	2,130	19	Iran	763
7	Russia	2,097	20	Taiwan	699
8	France	2,075	21	Netherlands	646
9	Brazil	1,849	22	Poland	623
10	Italy	1,800	23	Saudi Arabia	546
11	Spain	1,361	24	Argentina	526
12	Mexico	1,353	25	Thailand	522
13	Canada	1,271		South Africa	468

If that news does not bother you, I am not finished just yet. According to FinAid.org, a website that provides student loan information, our national student loan debt is now $850 billion, and rising.

Whether we admit it or not, these numbers are staggering! But more importantly, these numbers are having a negative impact on our ability to move forward as individuals and as a country.

Without even counting individual consumer mortgage debt, we are looking at roughly $3.5 trillion in consumer debt. This debt coupled with our national debt, which is almost $13 trillion, brings our total debt as a country (government debt + consumer debt), to almost $17 trillion worth of debt!

While I am clearly not passing judgment on the financial instrument – credit cards, this level of debt is not sustainable into the future on any level.

Credit cards play a large role in the overall U. S. economy because of the high cumulative dollar value attached to these generally small but numerous consumer transactions. The second reason credit cards are so important is because the U. S. economy is primarily built upon consumption and not production. So here is the real problem. How do we divest ourselves from this debt without toppling the very thing we are trying to save – our country's economy?

Most individuals think of credit cards as their friend because they (credit cards) can add some convenience to the rat race of everyday living. Having a credit card limits or eliminates trips to the bank for cash, and may actually add an element of safety to an individual's life by decreasing the amount of cash they carry on their person.

These same cards may even help out when an individual is short on cash or is in between pay days. Therefore, these cards do some things or act in ways that may be considered friendly.

These may be good enough reasons to carry a credit card until an unexpected expense or a poorly planned expense has pushed the credit card to its maximum spending limit or beyond.

However, this sounds more like credit cards are being used as additional earned income that can be spent whenever and wherever, without repercussion.

This is one of the basic definitions of *Funny Money* – spending money that you do not really have. Make no mistake, credit cards are *Funny Money*, if one cannot afford to pay the bill when it comes due.

Now if that seems not possible, consider these statistics:

1. As of January 2010, the Federal Reserve Bank of Boston reported that 609.8 million credit cards are held by U. S. consumers.

2. As of April 2009, the National Foundation for Credit Counseling reported that nearly 34 million Americans have been late making at least one credit card payment; and, another 18 million have skipped at least one payment in its entirety.

3. Further, 58 million Americans admit to not paying their bills on time, as of April 2009. This works out to be roughly 26% of Americans. Among African Americans, the number is 51% that admit to not paying their bills on time.

4. Finally, consider one more statistic. The credit card industry earned more than $21 billion in 2009 from penalty (late fees, over limit fees, etc.) fees alone.

These statistics demonstrate how the *Funny Money* of consumers has become real profit for credit card companies and banks, and a problem for the individual consumer and the U. S. economy, as a whole.

Now consider another set of statistics. According to the Census Bureau, for the first time ever, senior citizens, 65 and older, are now out-earning every other age group by roughly 5.8%, and this during the worst recession this country has ever experienced.

Here is one more statistic to consider. As of December 2009, three in four credit card holders age 60 or over always paid their credit card bills in full during the past 12 months.

This information suggests that senior citizens are better equipped to handle debt and cash better than younger adults. So, let us see what can be learned from the wisdom of age.

Contrary to popular belief, paying off credit debt is possible, but it is not a single stroke solution. This is evident from the statistics above. However, to achieve debt payoff will require more than minimum monthly payments, and will require these sustained payments over a period of time, normally two to three years, or maybe longer depending on the debt load.

But, before the financial dilemma I posed at the beginning of this chapter can be resolved, the delicacy of the situation needs to be more fully understand.

Most individuals turn to credit cards as a means of last resort because of other factors beyond their control.

Sometimes the decision to use credit cards boils down to a simple need to survive, and the credit cards are the last thread of life support that is pulled so tight it is about to snap, because of such factors as unemployment or a major medical crisis, for example. Roughly, 29% of low and middle income households were forced (in one opinion) to use credit card debt to pay for medical expenses.

However, when credit cards are no longer convenient and, instead, become necessary, this can be a very expensive way to borrow small amounts of money that can turn into very large debts.

In case you did not know it, when you do not pay your credit card balance in full every month, you are borrowing the bank's money and at a very robust price.

This may be your first sign of financial trouble, notwithstanding the fact that 40% of Americans spend more than they earn, primarily through the use of credit cards.

While there are those obvious signs of credit card problems, there are also those signs that are so obvious that they are not seen, i.e. like not being able to see the forest for the trees.

These trees, to use a metaphor, include such things as using credit cards to pay for necessities like groceries and trips to the nearest golden arches.

Without forewarning or maybe warning that was ignored, the credit card debt has taken on a life of its own and, when added to existing debt, becomes the driving force in the household for good or bad.

Sure enough, after this rise in debt, the rise in debt related phone calls from the credit card company's collections department will follow.

Then, here is the first piece to the financial riddle. When we were being taught how to use credit cards, we should have also demanded that our teachers teach us how to manage those cards. As Maya Angelou says, when you know better, you do better.

But since they did not, for whatever reason, including the possibility that our teachers may not have been taught how to manage the cards either, then we will start right where we are. First, we must insist that the next generation of card users are more prepared than we may have been (without accusing anyone, trying to place blame, or making excuses for our own mistakes).

Although unwelcomed, these phone calls may actually prove to be very useful as an introductory lesson to debt management.

Part of learning to manage debt is that we must also learn how to manage our attitudes toward debt, like a survey I recently read that stated 72% of Americans believe debt is an acceptable part of our lives.

But if that were true, then why does 64% of debt owners spend so much time worrying about their debt?

This tells me that debt is not a natural part of our lives, and that we are all, individually, seeking ways to solve our debt problems.

So when the calls are first initiated, if the consumer takes the time to try and put emotions and pride aside to explain why payments are regularly delinquent, the card carrier may be willing to help by authorizing new payment plans, moving due dates, and providing other guidance that could help save the credit history.

Therefore, the foundational tool to solving all current and future credit problems is discipline. The discipline to listen to a complete stranger lecture them about credit card debt (discipline of the past), discipline for the present, and future discipline.

Discipline for the past means owning one's mistakes, and making a commitment to gain the necessary knowledge to not repeat those mistakes, ever. Discipline for the present means changing the way one decides to make purchases and financial decisions overall.

For example, if anyone in your

Most friendships are easy until one or the other starts to take a different path. Then things can get rocky.

Never fear. Some friends are only meant to be in your life for a season. So learn to know when it is time to let go.

family wants to make a purchase that is more than, say $25, present discipline is making an agreement to wait a full 24 hours before making that purchase. This way, the purchase can be discussed with the entire family, and other factors can be considered, such as is this item really necessary, is it possible to wait for the item to go on sale, and/or if the item is a want or a need. But for the agreement to have meaning, there must be some sort of consequence for breaking the agreement, from mom and dad on down.

If spending money is an emotional crutch, then, as a consumer, one must find another way to build self-esteem, which can be anything from joining a club, to getting an extra job that keeps them so busy that they do not have time to shop because they are too busy working, or anything in between, as long as it is positive.

Discipline for the present also means being able to make a firm decision about the difference between wants and needs, which leads to the future, because present discipline will enable one to have the discipline of choice in the future.

Another recommendation a reader should take from this discussion is as soon as the financial difficulty is recognized, take the initiative to contact the creditor to make them aware of any hardship.

This shows the card company how serious a matter this is to you, and that you truly want this matter resolved. The sooner one can notify the credit card company the better it is for the consumer because it will increase their solution options, and ease the burden of the hardship by attacking the problem early.

However, the longer one waits, the opposite is true. The longer one waits, the harder it becomes to resolve the issue, the options are greatly decreased, and so too will be a decrease in the company's willingness to work together on this issue.

If your credit cards have turned against you, so to speak, as they have in approximately 60% of all U. S. households, do not despair. There are some concrete steps that may be taken to help eliminate the debt, improve your present financial situation, and increase your future financial security.

While it is vitally important for any delinquent consumer to initiate contact with their credit card company as soon as a problem arises, it is equally surprising that these same customers do not understand basic credit card finance.

What is so puzzling is that despite the fact that, as a nation, we are privy to the best educational system in the world, why are most individuals still being forced to get their best and hardest financial lessons in the "school of hard knocks."

I personally know countless individuals that have advanced degrees, and throughout all their years in school, they did not once have a true financial management course nor was there ever an offering for such a course, despite the obvious need to learn how to control spending up front.

Our colleges and universities will teach you how to track the expenditures of big business, how to calculate the hypotenuse of a right triangle, and they might even try to steer you in the direction of a high paying career.

But no one teaches you how to manage all that money you are supposed to be making, at least not that I am currently aware.

And what if your big money making career starts off a little slow; again, there is no one standing by to teach you how to maintain your financial stability on a smaller income until you get to that larger paycheck.

I know this to be so because I was one of those individuals, with an advanced degree, who had to get his financial knowledge from the hard knock school. To make matters even worse, before I received not one, but two advanced degrees, I had already gained a bachelor of science degree with a concentration in finance, and I was still unprepared for what I call, "Finance Anatomy 101."

Even after all of that learned education, I still received numerous phone calls saying my credit cards were all maxed out and the only money I had to live on was my regular paycheck.

So here are three dramatic steps to help those who have already tried the methods presented in Chapter 7 and are still having difficulties regaining control.

1) Eliminate debt by sitting down with someone you trust, with all of your bills, to help show you how to get back on track. **Do not** give anyone access to your bank account information, nor are you to allow anyone to sign any checks in your name, under any circumstances. This includes not surrendering your bank card (debit card) or any other cards to anyone, no matter how much you trust them. All you are looking for is guidance from a trusted voice. This may seem impossible, but if anyone can listen to a stranger lecture them on their credit card debt, then anyone certainly can listen to a friend or family member give them some real help (particularly if they are already on the

right track financially in their life). Be prepared, the conversation may become heated at times, but if it accomplishes the stated goal, then it may well be worth the intense discussions and the potential embarrassment.

2) The second alternative to eliminate debt is to register for a free or low cost budget course, generally offered by junior or community colleges around the country, when interest is great enough to support the cost of offering the course.

3) In order to improve your current financial situation, your money needs to work for you, instead of you working for your money. Therefore, you need to find ways to do this by investing your money. Most low to middle income families, particularly in the African-American community, do not invest because they do not know how, and because they believe they do not have enough money to invest. However, if you have enough money to own a credit card, then you have enough money to invest. (Luke 20:45 – 21:4) You can read more on investing in Chapter 11.

4) To ensure financial security for the future, everyone needs to develop their own individual development plan.

An Individual Development Plan

Banking on the financial life means that you have to start making a plan for your life right where you are. This includes repairing your credit (Chapter 5), setting up a realistic budget and paying off your debts (Chapter 7), and getting rid of those noose-like credit cards that keep you in financial limbo every month (Chapter 8).

But it does not end there. You must also look to your own future. This means you must be able to provide a safe and affordable environment for your family (Chapter 9), maintain inexpensive and reliable transportation (Chapter 10), and invest in your financial future (Chapter 11).

Banking on your financial future means you have to ask yourself some hard poignant questions, so no better time like the present.

1) Do you have enough life insurance for your family to live just as if you were alive after your death? What about braces, mortgage, groceries, college, and general every day expenses?

2) What if you are hurt in an accident and cannot work, are you protected?

3) Sure, there are lawyers, workmen's compensation, and maybe you even have some type of limited payment disability policy at your place of employment. But, all those things take time – the one luxury you cannot afford when you are in this situation.

4) While you should pursue every legal recourse available to you, with prudence and patience, there is another option that will allow you to do just this – take care of your family while you recuperate from an accident.

There are now insurance plans on the market that will pay all of your bills and daily expenditures while you are out of work, due to no fault of your own. Many will continue paying notwithstanding any other monies you receive from your legal options.

While there is one plan in particular that comes to mind, you should always start by contacting your current insurance agent because this should be the individual who you trust and are most comfortable with.

If not, then start by doing your own research on the internet, and then canvass a few companies about your ideas.

While it would be preferable to find one insurer to handle your life, home, and auto policies, it may mean that you have to change to a new agent to find all that you need, or a couple of good agents to make a total package for your familial situation.

Remember, this is business, and business relationships sometimes have to change for your financial future to be secure, so do not let your emotions get in the way of your business decisions.

Insurance consolidation will not only simplify your life, but it will make your insurance needs easier to manage.

You will need enough insurance to pay your debts and replace your current income plus lost future earnings. If you are unsure of what this amount should be, there are some wonderful websites on the internet that will help you, just Google – insurance calculator.

"The plans of the diligent lead to profit, as surely as haste leads to poverty." (Proverbs 21:5)

Any good insurance calculator will help you figure out your insurance needs so you do not pay for any more than you need or can afford. If any calculator requires you to put in your truly personal information such as your Social Security Number, do not use that calculator!

As you are talking to your current or potential insurance carriers, make sure you are getting all discounts possible – safety devices, good driving records, fire safety, home security discounts, educational discounts, neighborhood discounts, and so on.

Maybe you have quit smoking and lost weight, see if you can get a better rate on your whole life policy and, while you are at it, pick up a term life policy as well. Compare all this information with three carriers to make sure you are truly getting your best deal possible.

Any savings you find, put towards the purchase of the income replacement insurance we spoke of earlier by adding a disability and unemployment rider, if necessary, to beef up your policy.

Fast forward to retirement. Are you saving for retirement, regardless of when you expect to retire?

Conventional wisdom is that you should be investing approximately 20-22% of your current income towards that retirement. While I realize this is a lot of money, do not attempt to do it all at once, slowly keep increasing your retirement investment until you reach the maximum goal of 22% or the maximum allowed by your employer's plan, if that is the only plan you have. *Note: If your company's investment plan is all that you have, I can say without reservation, more is needed. You are clearly under-invested in the market.*

Also look into picking up your own private investment account at your bank, one that is insured by the Federal Deposit Insurance Corporation.

If you earn 8% interest and your savings are tax-deferred, meaning that you pay taxes later, then only saving $100 per month for 30 years will give you about $150,129.

That is a lot of money for doing nothing but what you always do!

Although I enjoy consolidations because they generally make financial planning easier, I am not necessarily in favor of consolidating your investment accounts into one company.

If this is something you are thinking about, think long and hard to make sure this decision does not come back to bite you later. Take a lesson from the Fall Financial Surprise of 2008.

After you retire, you should expect to withdraw approximately 4% of your retirement money every year. If this is not enough to afford you the kind of lifestyle you are accustomed to, then you either need to save more or find supplemental income, i.e. a part-time job or some other income-generating venture.

One of the best things you can do to plan for your future is to pay off your debt!

For example, if you were to get an unexpected cash windfall, you should pay yourself first and then put the rest toward paying off your debt. I recommend investing 40% and using the remaining 60% to pay down bad debt.

When paying off debt, remember to start with the smallest debts and then move on to larger debts. This will do two things, build momentum and excitement.

When your debt is paid off, if you do not already have one then you should start an emergency fund.

This fund is to help you get through potential short periods of difficult cash flow. A reasonable amount to have in your emergency savings account is three months gross salary or enough to pay your bills for more than six months comfortably.

One way to build this fund is to save one full paycheck every quarter for every year you work. It does not matter if you save it all at once or in pieces, just as long as you save! Another way to help you with this kind of Individual Development Account (IDA) is to visit the website, http://www.idanetwork.org.

Do not trust yourself to be disciplined enough to make these deposits on a regular basis. Set it all up to happen automatically and put the money away in accounts that cannot be easily raided by you.

These accounts will help your budgeting and your spending or overspending. So make sure you include putting money in your Christmas club account, vacation account, and special gifts account for other occasions throughout the year.

So if it is not in your account, then you cannot spend it!

If you feel safe and comfortable with the computer, learn to pay your bills online. It will save you time and money, and it may even help improve your credit score by helping you to pay your bills on time on a regular basis.

For more help in this area, you may want to consider talking with your insurance agent to see if they can provide you with a free financial analysis.

There are two ways to do this. You may simply get a form to take home and fill in at your leisure; or, you may have to make an appointment with your agent, that could take from one to three hours to complete, depending on your financial situation.

A third option is to look for event budgets in Excel or online that can help provide you with some additional guidance. However, in my opinion, these individual event budgets, while they do serve a need at the appropriate time, will not serve you as well, in this instance, as an overall financial needs analysis.

At first glance it may seem absurd to go from discussing credit card debt to investing for the future; however, the purpose is to begin thinking about how it feels to be out of debt, and to begin thinking about positive expenditures as opposed to more temporary expenditures – going from bad debt to good debt.

Good debt is debt that makes money – such as borrowing money to pay for a home, or using a small personal loan to purchase an IRA or a CD (certificate of deposit). Good debt has the potential to make money from the debt.

Bad debt is borrowing money to pay off other bad debts. There is no potential for other income to be made.

For simplicity's sake, by default, why are credit cards so important, particularly when we question our own ability to pay the monthly bill, and most of us have not yet learned to utilize those cards in a constructive manner? Credit cards, for most of us, are simply more bad debt.

But, credit cards do have some important fiscal factors attached to them that improve both their convenience and utility. For example, credit card statements can be used to serve as a tracking method of where and how your money is being spent, which in turn can help you see how to regain control of your spending.

One of the largest benefits of credit cards is their penetration into the economic market, which means their acceptance is almost universal. Therefore, we now have the ability to pay bills from home using a telephone and our credit cards; and, we can even make important purchases over the internet because of our credit cards.

In addition to the numerous rewards offered through credit cards, such as cash back, travel opportunities, special purchases and gifts, by being a part of a purchasing network, one of the biggest benefits of having a credit card, if used properly, is the ability to have an automatic emergency fund, if the need should arise.

Other card benefits include, card programs tailored specifically to the need of each consumer, the ability to make short purchases very quickly, such as a business owner needing to purchase inventory, and maybe the biggest benny of them all is the ability to shop around for better cards.

Referring back to the question posed at the beginning of the chapter, it is easy to see why it is so difficult to divest ourselves from credit cards because of the dominating role they play in our individual lives and in our overall economy.

An individual cannot even rent a car without a credit card, not a debit card with a Visa or MasterCard logo. So the absence of an actual credit card will prevent anyone from being able to rent a car. Unfortunately, that is financial power that cannot be denied.

While the most important of all reasons to own and not to own a credit card is their ability to extend one's income further than it might otherwise go until the time comes to pay the bill, there are some things you should clearly understand before this commitment.

Credit Cards 101

Debit card - Most of us have become familiar with this card by default, since their introduction in 1987. These cards allow customers to access the money in either their checking or savings account to make purchases electronically.

Credit card - These cards were first introduced in the 1920s and have steadily grown in popularity since. Credit cards have enjoyed widespread use because of their portability that allows consumers to make almost any type of purchase imaginable and pay for those items over time. Simultaneously, the cards have grown in popularity with card issuers because they have become cash cows for most financial institutions, bringing in several different types of streams of revenue for banks, just off of this one product. What has been forgotten by many consumers is that purchases made on a credit card are loans that must be repaid.

Charge card - Although there are very few true charge cards still in use today, a true charge card requires you to pay your balance in full when your statement arrives in the mail. The original charge card was issued by Diners Club in 1950 as a restaurant card. Diners could go to any restaurant that would take the card and eat without any cash as long as they paid their bill in full when it arrived – hence the name Diners Club. But the most popular of all charge cards is American Express that was first offered in 1958. Even American Express has succumbed to the pressure, and now offers credit cards in addition to their charge cards.

Maybe the old adage is true, if you cannot beat them, join them. Before anyone joins the ranks of credit card holders, they should understand the fine print associated with carrying those cards.

a. Every card carries an annual percentage rate (APR), which is the cost of your credit with a particular card carrier compounded over the course of one calendar year for that card, or the annual interest rate on your card loan. The lower the APR the better. However, there are some important factors to pay attention to.

b. The interest rate is the dollar amount you pay your lender for using their money expressed as a percentage. (Remember in 4th grade math when we thought percentages would not be important?)

c. Finance charge(s) are the all inclusive charges you pay the lender for using their card, from your fees to your interest charges.

1. Although many cards carry an introductory rate as a marketing tool to attract new customers, these are generally short-lived.

2. These introductory rates may apply separately or in totality against cash advances, purchases, and balance transfers.

3. Further, many card carriers have a variety of rates for the same card depending on the particular consumer that is the intended recipient of the card.

4. Many cards often come with an adjustable APR that can be changed at will, but generally kicks in if you are late

making payments, or even miss a payment. These kinds of APRs are considered penalty APRs that are almost impossible to lower once they start.

5. Then there is a delayed rate which does not have any interest attached anywhere from 6 months to 1 year. But the caveat is that the entire card balance has to be paid in full every month or within the 30-day billing cycle every month for the delayed period. Otherwise, the penalty APR will kick in.

d. A balance transfer is any balance due on one credit card transferred to another card, usually at the start of a new account with a new card carrier as a way to entice new customers.

e. Every transaction has a different grace period for each card carrier, which are all different for cash advances, purchases, and balance transfers. Also, each transaction type carries with it a different finance charge and calculation method, including a minimum finance charge.

f. Other important features include the ability to use any ATM to get an advance, limits on the amount, and the number of times during each billing cycle that you may access any ATM for your cash advance without triggering additional fees.

g. When it comes to repaying your card loans, it is important to know how your payments are applied. Are they applied to cash advances first and other purchases second or vice versa? This will make a tremendous difference in how quickly you repay your debt.

h. Also, are there any additional fees attached to your card, such as annual membership fees, return check fees, exceeding the credit limit fee, cash advance fees, late fees, and transfer balance fees; and, how are these fees triggered?

i. Finally, does your card(s) carry any other special features like frequent flyer miles, discounts, or rebates at special stores or for particular merchandise offers, to name a few? For others, some cards carry discounts on movie tickets so that is a big draw for them. If you have a special want or need, there is generally a card that can fit that want or need if you are willing to shop around.

When used wisely credit cards can reap you benefits just as previously mentioned, and maybe even a better credit score. But remember this, it is going to cost you something to be a member of this card-carrying club, so make sure: 1) what you get in the form of benefits is worth the costs, and 2) that you do not pay any more than your fair share of membership fees, if you will.

Club Leadership

Just as it is important to know the leadership of any organization that one may choose or not choose to join, it seems appropriate to spend a little time discussing the leadership of the card-issuing group.

Twice a year, sometimes more, newspapers in most major cities around the country publish a list of compensation packages of the largest public companies in their area. These lists are generally published in March and December, at least in my area.

Although it is a cliché, some clichés are both true and beneficial. We have all heard the saying, most people do not plan to fail, they just fail to plan.

If you are like me, you see the names of those corporations and their CEOs, and the only thing you can think about are their headline making mistakes that consume the news and influence our pocketbooks.

Let me refresh your memories with one of the most recent headliners

Monday, September 15, 2008, then Bank of America chief executive Ken Lewis was applauding his, "deal of a lifetime," referring to his then $50 billion purchase of Merrill Lynch.

Meanwhile, the rest of the stock market was not sliding, but rushing downward like a waterfall. Economic forecasters were predicting the worst financial crisis in history that had the potential to topple the entire U. S. economy. Jobs were being lost by the 100s of thousands and foreclosures were so prevalent that they were off the charts.

Then you find yourself wondering how do those CEOs make those glaring mistakes translate into huge salaries?

There is enough anger to go around. However, that is not my primary point here.

My point here is these CEOs have a plan. Despite what anyone thinks, no matter how their plan impacts individuals, other businesses, and even the country, these people have their plan, and they work their plan until what they want to happen is accomplished!

They have a plan for their lives and for their businesses. Sometimes, some of us find that their plan does not include us. That is when we our anger really sets in. But these CEOs do not care, at least as far as I can see.

Now, when these business plans do not go as planned, then these CEOs start re-working their plans – – delaying some projects, increasing revenue, and cutting costs. If you have ever listened to any number of CEOs, after a failed plan becomes public knowledge, they are not contrite, or sorry. Instead, they are resolute in what they are doing, and are already in the process of tweaking their plans, to compensate for obvious shortcomings; but, they are still forever forging forward to reach their goal, whatever that may be.

Of most concern to us, as employees, is that those cost cutting measures generally include pink slips that may impact our own financial plans.

Although these institutions can also get help from the Federal government, help that is not available to individual citizens, which gives them some extra leverage in maintaining their stability, do not count yourself out of the game just yet.

The first thing we all need to do, before things get tough, is to become resolute in what we are doing, and determine that we are going to complete our goal – in this case get out of debt and learn to invest our money in ways and activities that earn money, no matter what!

Despite this seeming disadvantage, there are things you, as an individual, can do to make sure that you can bank on a life that is free of stress and financial worries.

So while the U. S. economy gets back on track and banks retool their businesses and customer base to survive during economic tough times, along with some cash infusions, there are things you can do to bring in some much needed cash also.

If your garage and maybe even your entire household is overrun by "things,"

things that you do not need, use, or want any longer, let your old things help bring in a new you.

Although the traditional money outlets still exist with some planning – yard sales, consignment shops, and a source of last resort, pawnbrokers, do not overlook the internet.

There are even a few free courses or relatively inexpensive courses on how to sell on the internet. A little research goes a long way, including books that will teach you how to sell on the web. Ebay, for example, has its own training course for selling on their website.

Sometimes a combination of several selling techniques will help you reach your goals faster. So those items that you find hard to dispose of online can be sold at a yard sale and vice versa.

Listen carefully. I am not saying that you will not have to work because you will. However, you can go to work and not be concerned about your job, your bills, or the possibility of having to pay those same bills without a job by doing a little advance planning now. And the most important part of any plan is to put it on paper. (Habakkuk 2:2)

The Fine Print

Thus far, we have discussed the history and the basics of credit cards, debt management, and beyond, including what to do with our money when we no longer owe credit card debt, and how to take lessons from credit card issuers on how to become focused.

But, while you are working to get to those points above, we need to know the reality of what we are dealing with now.

When I last checked, the average outstanding balance for credit card debt in American households was $9,000 and rising. These payments are due by a specific time on a specific date. If you miss the deadline, the late fee is now $39 and climbing.

A few late payments and you will trigger that penalty interest rate increase previously mentioned, which may have a secondary effect of lowering your credit score. When your other card lenders see your lower score, then the interest rate can and probably will go up on your other credit cards also.

Recently, Federal bank regulators moved to reign in credit card companies.

On December 18, 2008, the Federal Reserve adopted some long-desired, sweeping regulations that will finally restrain some of the credit card industry's flagrant practices. These changes went into effect on July 1, 2010.

The new changes will:

- Impose a new rule whereby "0 interest" will really mean 0, which will end the deferred-interest practice.
- Prohibit card companies from raising interest rates on already borrowed money unless it was borrowed on a variable rate card.
- Prohibit card companies from raising interest rates on already borrowed money unless the minimum payment is made more than 30 days late.
- Prohibit credit card companies from charging a late fee if the cardholder's bill was mailed less than 21 days before the due date.
- Prohibit credit card companies from charging interest on amounts already repaid by using their two-cycle billing system.
- Prohibit interest rate hikes in the first year of an account. The only way these rates can go up in the first year is if the credit card company disclosed a future rate hike at the time the account was opened.
- Restrict financing fees on credit cards where the fees or deposits use up the majority of available credit on the account.
- Require payments be allocated fairly among their card balances with different interest rates. These payments must either be allocated to the highest interest balance or prorated.

Although the credit card industry has always touted itself as fair (for their self-preserving profitability interests), these new rules are supposed to establish new ground rules of fairness.

Meanwhile, while the credit card companies are working to find new ways to get around the new rules, to help yourself, if possible, you should limit the number of cards you have to two, high limit cards.

If you have four or more cards, you are in credit trouble, period, or fast approaching – maybe blindly.

Lots of card applications will hurt your credit score just as closing several credit cards at once will rapidly decrease your score.

But the solution is simple, 1) stop the applications, 2) pay your balances down to $0, 3) decide which two cards to keep, and 4) then close the other cards at the rate of one card per year, every 12 months.

Read. Read. Read. It truly is fundamental!

Read the fine print for all of your cards so that you can – 1) make the best choice of which two cards to keep, and 2) understand how your balances will be calculated as you execute your pay-down plan.

Therefore, know your interest rate, your grace period before interest kicks in, and, most of all, know your credit limit and your billing cycle. Billing cycle, typically, is the time between the purchase of an item and when the payment for that item is due.

Each company determines it own billing cycle. For example, a utility company I once worked for had a 25-day billing cycle, because a shorter billing cycle means more revenue, in shorter periods. So, credit card companies have various billing cycles from 21- to 30-days.

And whatever you do, make sure you know whether or not you have a universal clause in your contract. A universal clause means that your rate can be raised on your card if you are caught late paying any other bill.

Although, the new rules are designed to prevent universal clauses, do not be surprised if your credit card company sends you a newly worded universal clause that meets with the letter of the law, but not the spirit.

Translated, this means do not expect a dramatic change in your credit card fees for the foreseeable future, if ever.

Meanwhile, the time has now come for you to seriously improve your negotiation skills and to do it quickly.

Now if you are fortunate enough to have a 700+ credit score, you may have more leverage than you know because credit scores are very powerful predictors of future bill-paying performance, which may help any 700+-score consumer. By the way, these 700+ FICO scores, like all credit scores, are gathered from 22 separate pieces of data collected from the three major credit bureaus.

If in doubt, then do not exceed 30% of your credit limit on any card. Even if you pay your bill in full every month, you are driving your own credit score down if your utilization is more than 30%. Remember, credit bureaus are only interested in how much of your available credit you use – nothing more in this area matters much. What is good for them (the credit card issuers) is not good for you, so make sure you are a competitive comparison shopper.

One huge plus for all cards is that if you buy a defective item or protest changes, all card companies are obligated by law to investigate those claims and rectify the situation within a reasonable manner, at no additional cost to you.

On the other hand, if your carrier mails you some convenience checks, do not be fooled. Do not use these checks(!), unless you truly understand the details of their use.

These checks are very costly and generally carry additional fees of as much as 5% per check.

Also do not purchase the card protection that is so generously offered at a nominal payment to you. If you ever needed the plan, these plans are designed to pay the minimum monthly payment to the credit card company while you continue to build interest on your outstanding balance. What this means, is that you would be buying insurance that would dig a hole deeper and faster than you ever could, which no one in their right mind would ever pay someone to do.

The only way this insurance plan is good for anyone that becomes disabled or unemployed is if it: 1) stops all additional interest and fees on outstanding balances, and 2) requires the insurer to match your normal payment based on your highest three payments for the previous 12 months.

Now if you are an individual that likes special sales and private customer showings, then find yourself a local department store you like and stick to it. These stores generally only offer these kinds of deals to their cardholders.

Back in the Saddle

If you are using a credit card to re-establish credit, this may not necessarily come very cheaply.

If you are perceived as a credit risk, you may be allowed back into the credit game but with a very expensive card that carries with it excessive fees.

As clearly demonstrated, credit cards are your friends until you can no longer make those payments.

Now if you are a parent that has waited until your child is 18 years old or is already in college to have the money conversation, then it may be a little too late, but better late than never. The concern here is that one, well-intended, conversation may not be enough to undo 17, give or take a few years, of potentially bad spending habits.

On the other hand, it is completely possible to build credit without a credit card.

Whether this is for you or your child, you can start by opening a checking account or if your credit is that bad, you may have to start with a savings account and work your way up to a checking account.

Then add an ATM card to the checking account with limited withdrawal privileges to learn how to manage cash, and then change this over to an ATM/debit card, still with limited privileges, but more than previously allowed.

All of this will help to build a minimal credit profile.

If you already have some credit that is not very positive, and you are doing business with other creditors that do not report your history to the credit bureaus, then make sure that this information gets reported. This may be the break you have been looking for.

If not, you still have some options available to you.

Fair Isaac Corporation (FICO) has also taken some steps to make it easier for individuals to develop credit. According to the FICO Corporation website, approximately 25% of the U.S. population lacks enough credit to generate a traditional FICO score (Chapter 6).

Therefore, FICO has developed a new score – the Expansion score.

This Expansion score allows consumers to build credit using nontraditional information such as rent, utility bills, or similar recurring debts.

Payment Reporting Builds Credit (PRBC), as previously discussed, is another website dedicated to helping consumers build credit that is similar to the FICO Expansion score, which incidentally is probably part of the reason for the development of the Expansion score.

At the last check, PRBC does charge a verification fee but has some other features that may be worth researching for personal viability.

Finally, there is always the traditional method of establishing credit without a credit card, which is to apply for a secured card. Remember, a secured card is a credit card where the credit limit is determined proportionately by a customer's bank deposits.

Whether or not you are trying to get back in the saddle or have been riding in it for quite a while, all lenders use three things to determine if you qualify for credit – character, capacity, and other credit.

Your current or future credit decisions will be determined by your ability to maintain both stable employment and a reasonable household at a regular address (character); your ability to repay your debts, which is derived from your income and assets (capacity); and, your discipline to repay your bills on time without exceeding your credit limits (credit).

Regardless of whether you are new to credit or are more seasoned, as foolish as this may sound, the fact is that credit cards, like all monetary transactions, have an emotional attachment for most individuals. This is a particularly important point to remember when considering financial options, because many firms, including traditional financial houses, will prey upon individuals during their state of financial-emotional vulnerability.

Who Works for Who?

Banks have been in the news quite a bit lately, and it should have triggered all of us to consider or reconsider our reasons for using a particular bank.

Whether you have a bank, are searching for a bank, or are considering changing banks, here are a few things you should consider.

- Do you plan on getting a home mortgage or car loan in the future? Then you might want to consider opening your checking and savings accounts at that same bank. It will make your loan application process a little easier if you already have an established relationship.
- This kind of planning may earn you some extra benefits, such as free checking or an interest-bearing checking account and low-interest credit cards or platinum account holder credit cards.
- For example, when I was ready to get my first mortgage, instead of putting in blind applications, I did my research to find out who was the Vice-President of the mortgage department for my bank and paid him a visit. I had all my financial documents in order, and told him my entire situation. By doing so, I put myself in control of my own mortgage negotiation. We did the initial application in his office during that very first

meeting, and I was able to answer any questions he had. My first mortgage was done in less than 30 days! He is still the only person that I will sign a mortgage with today because of the way he treated me initially, no matter where he chooses to work.

- If you are currently one of those unfortunate individuals living paycheck to paycheck with no loan plans in your future, then choose a checking account with a no-minimum balance and no monthly service charge. This will help you save money as you start out on your new road to financial growth.

- Now, if you are currently racking up bounced check fees, then you need to add overdraft protection to this account. If you do not currently qualify for overdraft protection, talk to your banker to find out exactly what you must do to qualify for this protection, or ways the bank can help you stop inquiring overdraft fees.

- Make sure your bank has enough ATMs in the areas where you do the most business. If not, then find out where the nearest ATM is to your home and use it, but only when it is necessary – remember the more money you have in your hand, the more an individual tends to spend. As I previously stated, set a weekly limit and stick to it. When it is gone for that week, it is gone!

- If your bank offers online banking, make sure it is free, and then sign up! This will keep you from receiving paper statements that can be stolen (identity theft) and help you pay your bills on time, which saves you money and maybe your credit.

- Finally, it pays to be in-the-know, that is to know your bank's rules on everything from automatic deductions to stopping payment on a check, and everything in between because the penalty for breaking their rules may be a rude awakening.

Experience and history tells me that most individuals will get bored with their own financial planning and give up for no other reason than that they feel as if they are "living in a box."

The only thing that I have never known individuals not to grow tired of doing is eating, and one other.

So let me present you with the finest financial dining menu that is worth every penny of your money, one that will leave you fully satisfied, financially, for years to come.

The Life of Luxury Menu

The attitude of this menu is to live a life of no financial worries. To help you achieve this, we have developed this big, bold menu of financial options that when served will provide consistent, authentic moments of a life financially fulfilled.

Appetizer

Begin by taking 30% of your income. Set aside 10% for a savings that you cannot easily raid, 10% for investments that will earn money until you need it, and 10% for charity. This fresh mixture is just enough to whet your appetite.

Amuse-Bouche

Pair your appetizing savings by saving all of your sick time and vacation unless it is absolutely necessary. This fresh bite will save you money by saving you time, and satisfy that craving for that yearly family vacation you have been dreaming of. If you have any leftover, carry as much as allowed over into the next year so you will be ready when that rainy day comes.

Soup

A good hearty mix of insurance that protects your income and your family now, and well into the future, if you are not around. The good taste includes mortgage, auto, life, disability, health, and income-replacement insurance.

Salad

A fresh mix of greens and vegetables means you are paying attention to your long term physical prospects. A good lawyer, a living trust, a durable power of attorney, and a will is a good mix that will take care of your long term financial prospects.

Fish or Seafood

It should be seared into your mind that you should no longer be drowning in a sea of bad debt. If you are close to paying off any debt keep sinking those same payments into your savings and investment accounts.

Main Course

A lean cut of bright red, top round, trimmed of any visible fat. Your home mortgage should be equally lean, cost you less than 1/3 of your totally monthly gross income, and provide heart healthy benefits long into the future.

Dessert

This bittersweet symphony of tastes mixes common ingredients in an uncommon way, which brings the entire menu to a dramatic climax. Since you eat with your eyes, it is time to show off your job skills. Step up your performance at work. Make yourself that go to person, the person the company cannot afford to lose. Take every opportunity to learn a new skill, show off old skills, and increase your income while you are having fun.

Cheese, Fruit with Coffee, Brandy

Finally there is a platter full of fruitful and delicate choices available for you to pick and choose from to help you build your investment portfolio including real estate, gold, stocks, bonds, and other hard assets. Sit back sip and enjoy, you earned it!

The Money Trail

So now that you are indebted to your friend, and you better understand the inner-workings of this friendship, here is how the money works.

Each month when you make a payment, your payment applies first to interest, then finance charges, and then to reducing the debt, according to the card issuer's choice.

Therefore, of your payment very little if any money goes to actually reducing your debt while the credit card company gets rich off your efforts, because of your credit card friend.

It used to be that a typical card carried an 18% interest rate, and the minimum payment requirements were 3% of the entire balance due on the card. But that is no longer the case despite the fact that the Federal Reserve has cut interest rates to historic lows.

Despite the Fed cuts, interest rates on credit cards have dramatically increased as has the minimum monthly payment on all cards across the board without exception.

Now here's the good news; do not beat yourself up about the situation if this is you.

Estimates are that a minimum of 60% of all U. S. households are in the exact same boat. So that makes for a pretty big boat and lots of potential for lost income. This makes it a little easier to understand why credit collectors are so aggressive although it still may not feel very nice.

One way to take back control of this relationship is to start charging only items you can afford to pay off when the statement comes due in addition to the payment you are already committed to making.

For example, if you purchase a $200 interview suit on the 3rd of the month and your minimum monthly payment is $35, then at the end of the month, you owe the credit card company $235 plus interest charges.

Now if you really want to stay ahead of your scheduled payments, you should add an extra $25-$50 per month to your payment, which will dramatically decrease your overall balance even after interest and finance charges are added to the balance.

The general rule of thumb is:

- if you owe $10,000 or more in credit card debt, then you should pay an extra $200 per month to get out of debt in addition to your minimum monthly payment.
- if you owe $5,000 – $9,999, then you should pay an extra $150 per month in addition to your minimum monthly payment.
- if you owe less than $5,000, then you should pay an extra $100 per month in addition to your minimum monthly payment.
- Anything above these numbers is just icing on your cake!

By paying more each month, you reduce both the time and the amount of money required to pay off your debt. And by not using your credit cards for impulse purchases, you save even more money. For example, if you save one, $85 impulse purchase per month, you save $1,020 per year.

Now, if you are not yet in the position where you can afford to pay this much, then start paying as much as you can until you can reach an appropriate self-determined payment level that you can maintain, remembering that time truly is money.

And, most importantly, stop using your credit card! If you cannot afford to make the payment, then you certainly cannot afford to continue adding new debt to old debt.

Put the credit cards away in a safe place until you can use them responsibly!

Now start using your debit card instead. You cannot spend what you do not have, and your debit card will keep you from overspending and having unexpected bills.

Remember also, that in the overall scheme of financial payments, credit cards rank #7 on the pecking order of repayments behind: 1) family necessities (food) and medical expenses; 2) mortgage or rent (including taxes and insurance); 3) essential utilities (electric, gas, and water); 4) car loans (including taxes and insurance); 5) child support (if applicable); 6) income taxes (if applicable); and then 7) credit cards and unsecured loans.

Just because credit card companies lean the hardest does not necessarily make them the most important to get paid. Sometimes, just getting a clear understanding of your problem will help you see a solution, and stepping back to gain some perspective and get a plan can help you do both.

Before we close this chapter, we need to briefly mention student loans.

Because of Federal changes, necessary changes, in student loan programs, private lenders will be making numerous changes in non-federal loan programs over the next few years – from increasing interest rates to potentially requiring collateral for loans, such as liens on homes. If the current rate of non-federal lending continues, which was $11 billion in the 2008-09 academic year, the sometimes prohibitive cost of educating one's child or children is pushing the U. S. very close to a class society.

If you or someone you know has been paying for tuition on a credit card, and/or taking out additional loans on top of credit card debt, now may be the time to seriously reconsider your list of possible options.

There is surely more to come on this front, so buyers please beware!

To End This Relationship?

It is not uncommon for many people to consider canceling credit cards during a difficult time or financial strain. The reasoning is that closing credit cards will make one look more attractive on paper, i.e. credit report.

But according to FICO Corporation, once an individual acquires more than 7 revolving accounts, their FICO score starts to automatically decrease. The preferred number for debt is 30, as in 30%, not 30 accounts. This means the total debt on all lines of credit should be equal to or less than 30%.

Now if all you are looking at is your credit report, then let me give you some clear cut facts that are not listed on your report.

Lenders scrutinize the ratio between your total available credit and the balances on all revolving accounts. If you have, say 20 open accounts on your credit report, now is not the time to close those accounts. Any accounts you close will not be factored into your ratio. This means you have in fact caused yourself more damage because you have increased your debt ratio because the percentage of debt divided by available credit will increase.

For example: if you have 20 open accounts and your total debt load is $20,000, your total available credit is $50,000, an average of $2,500 available per account. Then you choose to close 10 of those accounts. Your credit score is going to go down because you have by your own uninformed choices done yourself harm.

20,000/50,000 = .40 or 40% debt load versus 20,000/25,000 = .80 or 80% debt load

You would also not benefit from the deletion of old closed accounts because these accounts do not have a negative impact on your credit report.

Actually old closed accounts that have a good history make you look better because you get the benefit of a long credit history and those accounts attest to that positive history.

Remember as stated in Chapter 7, 15% of your credit score is determined by the length of your recorded borrowing history.

On the other hand, if your lender does not share your point of view, then the lender may consider a penalty against you for having too much available credit. But the only way you are going to know this is to have a discussion with the lender either in person or in an email.

I do not recommend having this kind of conversation over the telephone because there is nothing to refer to should a dispute arise.

This penalty could be as simple as denying you any further credit, and, if so, then you may want to seriously consider putting some of your cards in the shredder. No one has to know this but you and your family.

Your shredder actions should result in you consolidating some accounts and/or simply closing those accounts as you pay them off.

But, and this is a big but, do not delete them from your credit report!

It is also easier to keep up with a few cards because then most individuals generally have a better idea of their debt load and do better at controlling their long-term debt.

One more important note to consider that consumers may or may not understand. MasterCard and Visa are associations not credit cards. Therefore, these associations do not directly issue credit cards or debit cards.

Instead each association collects membership fees from all their member banks, respectively, and it is those banks that are allowed the right to issue cards bearing either the Visa or MasterCard logo.

Discover, American Express, and Diners Club are individual companies and issue cards in their own name.

Transaction Maze

Credit card transactions are both simple and complex mazes.

When an individual decides to use their card either in person or otherwise, such as an online transaction, the process starts by the merchant contacting their transaction processor. They, in turn, contact the card issuer to confirm the validity of the transaction, that is to confirm if there is enough credit to cover the purchase. This entire process happens in a matter of seconds while you may already be eyeing your next purchase.

An authorization is created on your account when the card issuer approves the transaction.

Even though the money has not actually been paid to the store yet, your available credit has been reduced by the authorized amount awaiting payment, for example to your favorite shoe store. Basically, the credit has been set aside and cannot be spent somewhere else, which protects you and the merchant.

Generally speaking, this part of the transaction is completed between one and seven days but can take as long as ten days to complete and close.

The completion comes when the transaction slip that you signed is received and verified by your card issuer, and they then transfer funds to the merchant's bank account.

If the slip is not received within a certain number of days, then the authorization expires, and the "on-hold" amount again becomes available.

When you present your credit card as payment (either in person, over the internet, or by conventional mail), the merchant will typically contact their transaction processor, which will then contact the issuer of your card to confirm that there is sufficient available credit to cover the purchase of any kind.

A common confusion regarding authorizations occurs in situations where the total transaction amount is uncertain.

For example, a credit card is generally required for renting a car. But because of the unknown potential for extending the car rental period or driving over a certain number of miles, the rental agency will initially request the credit card authorization in an amount that they estimate will cover the expected total end bill.

Many hotels do this as well because guests often stay longer than planned, and having charged a card upfront actually encourages guests to stay longer than one night.

Most individuals believe that credit cards are required so that car rental agencies and hotels have a way to cover themselves for the cost of minor damages or, in the case of hotels, the theft of small items.

Often the customer may not be aware of the amount of an estimated authorization, and may be surprised to find the available credit on the card is lower than expected.

When the rental car is returned or the hotel guest checks out, the final bill will be calculated based on actual days and/or miles involved.

Upon checkout, the customer will be presented with a final transaction slip to sign for actual charges that will eventually arrive at the card issuer, which will pay the merchant and release any excess funds still on hold from the original authorization.

But since this can take days, the available credit on the card can remain on hold for the full amount of the original authorization even after the customer has signed the final authorization.

Any time you are about to initiate an unknown dollar value transaction when you present your card, be prepared for a large authorization, and ask the merchant to tell you the exact amount before you hand over your card.

If for some reason the transaction slip is not received within a specified number of days, the authorization will expire, and the funds that have been sitting in a hold status will become available for your use again.

Before you get too happy and think that a store is going to forget to turn in your signed slip and you get that new suit for free, stores are too sophisticated and in too much need for consumer spending to forget to send a slip to a card issuer.

Two quick notes about allowing authorized users on your card and co-signing. Do not do either!

Authorized users have the ability to charge your card to its limit, but are not contractually or legally responsible for any charges. Where is the logic of giving someone that kind of financial power?

Of Interest to the Wise

During a sluggish economy, the Federal Reserve may start dropping interest rates, but do not get excited about those interest rate cuts being passed on to you in the form of lower interest charges on your credit card.

Even if your bank does lower your interest rate on your credit cards, do not expect to see a huge change in your monthly bill.

If your card issuer does lower your rate, first it will take a few billing cycles for the change to actually show up on your statement. Second, card issuers all use different formulas to calculate their prevailing interest rates, so there may be no change at all to your monthly bill.

Experts advise that those with variable rates are most likely to see a reduction in the interest rate charged, and then only to the card issuer's best customers.

Just remember that most card issuers use the prime rate as of two business days prior to the closing date of your billing cycle. So if your cycle closes on June 25, and the Federal Reserve lowers the interest rate on the same day, then your card issuer would still charge you the prime interest rate as of June 23.

If you have a fixed rate card, then it does not hurt to shop around to make sure you are getting the best deal for your financial situation. But keep two things in mind as you shop for a new card.

Every application for a new card will be counted as an inquiry on your credit report, which could eventually lower your credit score. Secondly, if you do decide to change cards, remember to try and keep the card with the longest credit history open since credit history counts for 35% of your total credit score.

What Goes Up

If you are one of the very few who actually gets a reduction in their interest rate, count your blessings. Credit cards and bank fees are cash cows for these financial institutions since the Federal Government and State governments have lifted all ceilings on how much interest banks can charge their customers; and, you can best believe that these companies will not let the new credit card rules kill their cows.

According to a report released by the U. S. Government Accountability Office

(GAO) March 2008, ATM, overdraft, and stop-payment fees are all on the rise, to name a few. The report further states these same financial institutions are relying more often on these charges to make up income lost.

It is a fee line drawn in the sand between the government and the banks. The banks say these fees allow them to offer more services to their tiered customers' demands. The government suggests that banks are not forthcoming about their fees.

As of this publication, according to the GAO, the average stop payment was $19.41, the average overdraft fee was $23.13, average fee on returned deposited items was $12.31, and the average insufficient funds fee was $24.18.

Most individuals I know, if they are paying any fees, are paying fees far above the average.

In all fairness to the banks, most charge fees because a particular type of transaction costs them money or may require additional work behind the transaction to ensure the transaction is completed correctly and in a timely manner.

Most customers are angry because they see the fees as arbitrary ways the banks dig into their wallets to raise their profit margin.

However, there are some ways to avoid paying fees. Some of these options are more sophisticated than others, and others are more time consuming.

For example, in today's marketplace, you can get e-mail and mobile phone alerts to let you know when you are getting close to going over your balance or when your balance drops to a certain amount.

This gives you the opportunity to transfer money from one account to another before you incur fees. (But there may be a fee for the money transfer, albeit it is probably much cheaper than the overdraft charge.)

Here is a list of some other ways to avoid paying bank fees.

- Only use your bank's ATM to withdraw cash.
- If an ATM is not available, get cash back at the grocery store, etc., by using your debit card and choosing the cash back option.
- Stay on top of your account by immediately recording every transaction so that you always know what your actual account balance is.
- Sign up for overdraft protection either with an overdraft account

specifically attached to your checking account for this purpose or by attaching your savings account to your checking. (Be careful, this could lead to trouble if you do not have any self control.)

- Some banks have special accounts set up to target certain parts of the market, i.e., student accounts, senior citizens, and minimum balance accounts. Check into one of these and see if they are right for you. Remember, each comes with a certain number of restrictions which saves you fees and does not cost the bank any money.

So while the banks are paying you less money on your deposits because the Federal Reserve has lowered interest rates and the banks pay less to borrow other monies, do not expect your fees, which is non-interest bearing income of the banks, to go down anytime soon.

Even if you are a good paying customer, you still could see the interest rate increased on your card based on periodic reviews of your credit risk to the bank.

Again the banks are trying to work a delicate balancing act, just as you are.

They are attempting to squeeze each customer as hard as they can without breaking the customer, thus increasing their overall profits by keeping you in debt.

Unfortunately, as many individuals struggle to pay their bills on time, something may happen where they may be late once. It creates a revolving cycle.

The key is to call your creditors before your creditors call you. This will keep you from having to dodge phone calls later, as well as uncomfortable and potentially embarrassing situations.

In fact, if you were to pay late to another creditor, some banks would raise your rate on their card, although you have never been late on that particular card, because creditors are reviewing credit reports more often. If your score drops or a late payment shows up on your credit report, then your rate on their card goes up. This is the universal clause that was recently banned by the new credit card rules instated by the Federal government. However, in my professional opinion, this clause will be rewritten and reinstituted by credit card companies as quickly as they can to protect their profitability.

The lesson here is to be very careful who you bank with. If your bank happens to mess up in one area that costs them money, they may come back to you and charge you more money to make up for their losses.

Why?

Because bank contracts are written in such a way that allows them to change their rate at will anytime and anywhere.

If you feel you have a legitimate complaint, refer your complaint to the appropriate agency referenced in Chapter 3.

If you cannot find the agency you are looking for there, then contact your local better business bureau for additional assistance.

Instead of attempting to make an exhaustive list of all banks, credit cards, and their changes from different banks, please contact your bank to get the latest information on your credit cards, interest rates, and bank accounts. But do not be surprised about what you may find.

If you believe you have been wronged by your financial institution, take the initiative to call your lender and see if there is the possibility of coming to a mutual solution.

If it does not work the first time, persistence may be the key to your winning. Keep trying about once every 30 days until you get the answer you are looking for, or close to it.

Finally, if you get into the situation and you know you are not going to be able to pay, then call your lender immediately and put your cards on the table. Keep good notes of who you talked to, date, time, their location, what they said, and the final resolution, if any.

The Fine Print

For the past several years, arbitration has become a standard industry practice deeply hidden in the fine print of almost all credit card contracts, and the practice is growing in other contracts as well.

Arbitration by definition is the hearing and determining of a dispute or the settling of differences between parties by a person or persons chosen or agreed to by them or as provided by law.

The theory is that arbitration is supposed to be quicker in resolving disputes by using an impartial third party as opposed to lawsuits.

And credit card issuers are requiring mandatory binding arbitration. This means regardless of the decision, it is a final decision and there is no appeal process.

Realistically, arbitration only benefits the credit card companies, which is another way for those companies to keep you under their control.

And if you go to arbitration and you lose, you may also get stuck with the costs of that arbitration, including attorney's fees.

The process is supposed to be neutral, but arbitrators are hired by the credit card companies so there goes the neutrality.

And like most individuals, an arbitrator is most likely to decide a case in favor of the individual who can ensure they are paid. And since they get paid by the case, and, oh, they do get paid, it seems most reasonable to believe the arbitration is going to go in favor of the credit card company.

But the tide has been turned a little by the new Arbitration Fairness Act of 2007.

What this law does is allow the consumer to choose arbitration and it does not force the consumer into arbitration as the only option.

We will close this chapter just as we began this chapter by asking you what about your friends?

Before you answer, remember, since credit cards account for approximately one out of every four transactions today, these cards are here to stay. But you do have some choices, and the financial regulations making their way through Congress will help to stabilize and secure the financial system, which is critical to our economy, particularly when it starts growing again.

As I stated at the beginning of the chapter, everyone is watching the U. S. economy. Now it is time for you to start watching you economy more closely. And the answer to the riddle is – on your own terms!

Note: Most financial houses report updated credit information to the credit

bureaus at the end of each month. Even if you are making a late payment, always try to pay something on your accounts at least 10 working days before the end of every month so that positive information gets reported. And if you cannot pay the entire amount due, pay at least $20 or more so that the company cannot report that you skipped a payment.

Chapter Nine

A Place Called Home

When most of us think about home, we do not think about a mortgage, bills, or repairs. We think about having fun with our families, a place to rush to after a long day, or we think, "This is my castle where I am free to do as I please."

Truth is, owning a home is a dream that everyone holds. In my experience, the best way to achieve any dream is to write down your vision, dream, goal, or whatever you choose to call it.

Then you need to take small steps toward this dream every day no matter what.

And most of all, no matter how far away this dream may seem, make the decision to never, ever, ever give up. Go read Habakkuk 2:2.

Keeping this written vision in front of you will help you focus on the dream itself and not the obstacles that may lie in front of you.

One way to not focus on the obstacles to a dream is to be informed about the process required to achieve a specific dream.

When it comes to purchasing a home, in order to create a satisfied homebuyer, you must start with an informed homebuyer. If you do this, then you, as a prospective homebuyer are much more likely to end up in your dream home, if you understand the entire process from beginning to end.

Buy Why?

There are concrete, practical reasons why buying a home is often a better decision than renting. The primary reason for purchasing a home is that every time an individual makes a mortgage payment they receive an interest in ownership for their money. This is called building equity.

In simple terms, it means you inch a little closer to actually owning the home every time you make a payment.

Most people who are renters pay their landlords an amount that is comparable to a mortgage payment every month, but they do not have an ownership stake in that address.

So clearly, home owners receive much greater value for the money they spend on housing than do renters. Additionally, home owners get significant tax breaks for owning their home, including a home mortgage interest deduction on their income taxes for the interest paid on their home loan every year.

Therefore, with monthly payments that help build ownership equity in a property and interest payments that are counterbalanced by tax breaks, home ownership is one of the best financial decisions a person can make.

But we are still a little ahead of ourselves.

When an individual starts thinking about a home, one of the phrases most often heard is "my dream house."

But since dreams differ, it is up to each individual family to decide what that dream includes.

Not to discourage anyone, but, generally speaking, our dream homes are not necessarily equal to our initial home purchase.

However, after you have purchased your first home and built up some equity, then you may be able to purchase up. Repeat this a few times, and, before you know it, you may be in your actual dream home.

But, if you are not yet in that position, then let's continue this all important discussion.

First Things First

Before we get into the actual details and desires of your new home purchase, we need to start at the beginning, and have the most important, and most difficult conversation for many prospective homebuyers.

Here are the most common factors that derail home loans. I tell you this first so that you will be a better prepared shopper for the unexpected, which is the norm, when it comes to home buying.

1) Personal debt level. Although the mortgage industry is moving to more conservative levels of debt, i.e., how much debt is allowable to still be able to secure a home loan, before mortgage debt is added, the industry is not there yet. Therefore, you need to be responsible and make sure you have enough breathing room for other mortgage costs, such as maintaining the house, inside and outside, in addition to the mortgage, property taxes, and insurance. Total housing costs should not exceed 30% of your total budget. If your total housing costs, as explained above, are at 35% or more of your budget, you need to rethink this purchase, and cut your debt, because the total allowable

debt (housing debt + all other debt) cannot exceed 36%. If you have student loan debt, it may behoove you to see if you can qualify for a deferment, even if you do not need it, financially. A deferred debt for 12 months, on paper, will improve your debt ratio.

Caution: At the end of the deferment period, if you cannot afford to pay your home mortgage and student loan debt, then you need to work on: a) reducing your student loan debt first; b) securing a higher paying job; or c) finding a second job to supplement your primary income so that you can afford the home loan debt, with the understanding that this is going to be long-term employment.

2) If you do not know your credit score or have not checked your credit report recently, you need to check your credit score from all three major bureaus, a minimum of 30 days before you are ready to start looking. Since credit reports are considered report cards, let me show you how the grading system looks at your credit report card:

	Low Score	High Score
A	901	990
B	801	900
C	701	800
D	601	700
F	501	600

As for your credit score, in today's housing market, a credit score of 750+ is the standard for most home loan. Some lenders may have programs that will allow your score to be as low as 620 and still qualify you for a home loan. However, there are some special programs available for those with lower scores, so make sure you discuss these options with your lender.

3) Income. If you are self-employed or are paid on commission, you may either have to qualify on your spouse's income, be prepared to put down a larger down payment, and/or possibly delay your home buying plans long enough for you to discuss other, acceptable fiscal options with your banker. Make sure your income tax returns are in order. These returns may help save your loan, or they may raise more questions, depending on the numbers. (When calculating your total income make sure you include every verifiable source, i.e.,

alimony, inheritance, etc., so that your income will be as large as possible.)

4) Private mortgage insurance (PMI). Even if your home mortgage loan gets approved, your home purchase could still be derailed because you cannot secure private home mortgage insurance. PMI is extra insurance that lenders require from most homebuyers who put down less than a 20% down payment, unless you get a mortgage under some type of special authority, such as a Veterans Affairs (VA) or Federal Housing Administration (FHA) loan.

5) The property. If you are considering purchasing a condo, the homeowner fees may pose a problem, because these fees are additional debt that cannot be included in your home loan. Make sure you know how you are going to meet those monthly obligations and the annual increases. If you are already close to your debt ceiling, these fees may be a deal breaker, unless you can re-negotiate the fees, and/or delay the fees for a short period. If you are considering an older single family home, make sure the house does not require too much work, otherwise you may have to set aside a large amount of cash for repairs that the lender will require be placed into escrow before final loan approval; or, you may have to get a construction loan, in addition to the mortgage.

6) The appraisal. Banks have tightened their appraisal standards significantly, so your appraiser is going to scrutinize any property more closely than ever. Actually, this is to your benefit also because you cannot afford to pay more for a home than it is worth.

Having considered all of this information, one of the first decisions prospective homebuyers must decide is what type of home they are interested in purchasing.

Are you interested in an older home that was built when homes had much more structural character? What about a brand new home where you pick out everything from the appliances to the wall paint? Or how about something in between where it is old enough to have been completely decorated by the previous owners but new enough to not require any major repairs.

Knowing what you desire, what you need, and what you can actually afford is the entire home buying process in a nutshell. However, let me make one quick observation.

When you get to the point where you are actively looking for a home to purchase, do not let anyone talk you into "purchasing" a home.

What I mean is that when you are shopping for something as big as a home, if it does not feel right, does not meet your criteria list, and does not meet your sight appeal, then do not buy it – no matter how much someone tries to "sell it" to you!

If someone, anyone, has to talk you into buying a house or anything else for that matter, then it is not the house for you, because the house for you is one that you know is right for you without anyone saying one single word.

And this task becomes easier when you know your own affordable needs.

Without making any assumptions and regardless of where you live, if you have been paying any kind of rent and paying it comfortably, then you are likely to be in a better financial position if your mortgage is close to your present rent. Remember, the general rule of thumb is that most borrowers can afford a home loan that is about 2.5 – 3 times their annual salary. Following this rule of thumb, if your annual income is $40,000, then you should be able to afford a mortgage between $100,000 and $120,000.

At this level, you should have some breathing room to cover those occasional extra costs that come with home ownership.

So, the real question is, how does one get on the road that leads to a major part of the proverbial American Dream.

Follow the Yellow Brick Road

It sounds sort of corny, but it makes a major point.

When it comes to buying a home, an individual will be faced with numerous decisions. The first of which is whether or not you are actually ready to buy.

But finding the right home is not always as straightforward as it would seem, and this includes securing the right mortgage for you and your family.

There are some easy steps that will help you through this process, keep you organized, keep you informed, and maintain your sanity throughout this sometimes nerve-wracking process.

Step 1: Get Pre-Approved. This makes you a highly-valued cash buyer.

Pre-approved is completely different from pre-qualified, and far better.

Pre-qualified basically means that you have spent a few minutes on the telephone with a lender answering a few questions. Based on those answers, the lender pre-qualifies you and issues you a worthless letter that you can show to sellers.

These letters are worthless because none of the buyer's information has been verified. There are a whole hosts of problems that could arise that could prevent you from closing a deal. This is the great chasm between pre-approved and pre-qualified.

To be pre-approved means your lender has made a mortgage loan commitment to you before you ever find a home. The basis of this pre-approved loan offer was a review of your credit file and your financial situation (financial statements) that shows your information has been verified.

This pre-approval does three things. First, it shows sellers that you are a fully qualified buyer, and, second, it helps you establish a clear price range in which to work. Third, your documents tell your mortgage lender that there is a high likelihood that you will be able to keep your promise to repay their loan.

The credit pre-approval process is the same as a typical mortgage application with one exception. This loan application does not include information on the property you are looking to purchase. Therefore the only outstanding issue is the appraisal on the subject property.

However, your loan officer has already collected information on your credit, income, assets, and debts and sent this information through their mortgage loan department, just as he would if you were submitting a full loan application with the subject property listed.

This process of reviewing these documents is called underwriting, i.e., having the bank determine if they will "fund, endorse" or insure your loan against any potential defaults.

If the underwriting process determines that you qualify for a loan, you receive a loan commitment for up to a specific dollar amount, which is contingent on the property meeting certain criteria.

While there are some general guidelines that lenders are required to use when underwriting, there is some flexibility in those guidelines. Part of the strength of this process is that if you are weak in one area, but strong in another area the strong one may help balance out the weak area, and thus, get you approved through the underwriting process.

Now that you have made your way through the pre-approval process you will be in a much better position to purchase the best property you can buy and do so for the least amount of money possible.

This entire process, depending on your situation, can take anywhere from a few days to a few weeks.

But, the biggest benefit of being pre-approved is that it puts you in a stronger negotiating position when you find a home you like, because it is like having cash in your hand, which motivates buyers to lower prices and close deals more quickly, than not having a pre-approval.

Getting Your Docs in a Row

Providing these documents in advance will keep you on schedule and help keep your nerves settled. This list is for every borrower that will be listed on the loan documents.

1. A copy of your driver's license and your Social Security Card.

2. Complete copies of income taxes for last 2 years, including W-2s.

3. If self-employed, complete copies of last 2 years of business tax returns, a year-to-date profit and loss statement, and a balance sheet with all original signatures.

4. Copies of your pay stubs for the last 60 days.

5. Copies of the last 3 bank statements for all bank accounts, IRA, 401K, and stock accounts, including those held by your employer.

6. If you have made any unusually large deposits into any accounts within the last 3 months, or have opened a new bank account within the last 6 months, be prepared to provide proof where the money came from.

7. If any gift funds are involved, the giver will have to complete a gift letter affidavit, and you will have to provide a paper trail for the money, i.e., a copy of your bank deposit slip and a copy of the giver's bank statement, where the money was withdrawn.

8. A list of all your previous addresses for the last 7 years.

9. Copies of the last statements for all outstanding credit accounts currently held.

10. If you have any judgments, bankruptcies, divorce decrees, child support, and/or alimony orders, you must provide copies of all of these court docu-

ments and resolution documents.

11. If you are applying for this loan based on special programs, such as VA loans, make sure you provide proof of your qualifying information for such a loan. There is a whole new set of documents required for a VA loan, depending on your lender, so be prepared to provide these additional documents.

12. Copy of your executed sales contract, if one.

13. Copy of the canceled earnest money check, front and back.

14. Contact information for both your real estate agent and the seller's agent.

15. If purchasing a pre-existing home, a copy of an old survey or title policy when it becomes available.

16. If you are selling a current residence, a copy of the listing agreement or a copy of the sales contract.

17. Be prepared to explain how you will make a down payment, if required, and, how you will cover closing costs.

Again, depending on an individual's particular situation, there may be some additional documents required, and the mortgage lender should let you know.

Having gotten all your documents in order, there are many good reasons for getting a loan pre-approved before you begin shopping for your new home. Those benefits are summarized below.

- Preapproval makes your home search more efficient by allowing you to focus your time and energy only on homes you know you can afford. This allows the home buyer to quickly create an itinerary of homes to visit that are all within their price range, which saves time and makes the entire process easier and less stressful.
- Preapproval lets sellers know that you have a solid, verifiable offer, so there is no worry after the contract is signed.
- Preapproval addresses any problems early in the process so they can be fixed.
- Preapproval gets most of the mortgage process out of the way up front, so that you can complete the transaction quicker after you find a home.

In today's market, some builders and sellers might even require that you be pre-approved prior to reviewing an offer.

A Quick Word

Since we have already had an extensive discussion on credit, credit cards, and the totality of one's financial situation (Chapters 7 and 8), we just need to mention a few quick matters regarding credit.

Before you started this process you should have already pulled all your credit reports and scores so you know what is on your credit report before you go to the bank for that initial meeting.

If there are any problems or mistakes on that report, you also should have started working to correct those issues or at least be able to explain why those problems exist, and reassure your lender that they are all behind you.

If you discover that your credit report is accurate, but your credit score is extremely low, you may want to reconsider buying a home, get some financial counseling on how to improve your score, or seek out special assistance programs for individuals that need some extra help.

Most lenders will pull an average score of all three major credit bureau reports. Let me explain further. As we previously discussed, each major credit reporting agency has their own score, and some companies will only request a credit score from one of the three bureaus in particular, normally Equifax, located in the greater Atlanta metropolitan area. When it comes to certain large purchases, however, most lenders pull a combined average score to see how your credit is reviewed from a collective point of view.

If your score is extremely low, there are some benefits to waiting a few months or a year, because this time will give you the opportunity to improve your score by paying your bills on time and reducing your debt. During this time, you can also work on pulling together a very good down payment to help offset a low score.

Finally, waiting a few months for your score to increase can result in a better interest rate on your mortgage, which can save you a lot of money over the life of the loan.

If you do decide to go ahead with buying a home even if your credit is less than perfect, it is still important to work to rebuild your credit. Once your score improves, you can refinance your mortgage for a lower-interest loan, which could lower your monthly payments, and save you thousands of dollars over the life of the loan.

Other People's Money

The greatest mistake most individuals make when home buying is that they start shopping first and then try to force a loan situation to match their house after they have picked out a home...only to be disappointed by the outcome.

Since the vast majority of home buyers require a loan, securing the proper financing is usually the most important part of the purchase process, and as such, it should not be an afterthought or a second or third step in the process. It should be the first and primary consideration. As previously stated, the factors that determine how large a loan you need and can afford are your income, your credit history, your savings, and the value of the property you are seeking to purchase.

Because every loan involves some amount of risk, your mortgage lender, like all creditors, must determine the risk that you may not pay their money back.

Everything else being equal, someone who has consistently made payments on time is a lower credit risk than someone who has not. Because lenders offset risk with higher financing charges, having a better credit history generally means getting more favorable loan terms, i.e., lower finance charges. And because some loan options are riskier than others, good credit may even give you more flexibility in structuring your mortgage, again all else being equal.

Since credit is the use of other people's money, i.e., the bank, credit union, etc., the more you pay people their money back as agreed the more access to credit you will have in the future. This can be very valuable when you are buying a home.

Yet there are still those who believe you cannot purchase a home unless you have excellent credit. While good credit is always a plus, a flawless credit history is not a requirement for buying a home. In fact, the opposite might even be true in that homeownership can be a tool for getting past previous credit difficulties.

Buying a home gives you an opportunity to improve your financial situation by establishing a strong payment record. Paying your mortgage on time every month shows creditors you can manage good debt effectively and, it helps build wealth for your future. Each payment helps you build equity that can be used as leverage to reach other financial goals.

If you are building a home, custom or otherwise, you will have a two-part loan. This will come in the form of a construction-to-permanent loan. Again, this type of financing has two parts: a loan to cover the costs of construction and a mortgage on the finished (permanent) home.

Many individuals start their mortgage shopping with a mortgage broker. Brokers are supposed to be experts in mentoring individuals throughout the potentially complex lending process, and they should have extensive consumer choices and access to affordable home loans, all this while balancing their client's financial interests and goals.

However, since there is a fee for using their service, unless you are in a situation that demands you use a mortgage broker (i.e., someone who shops your documents/financial information listed above around to various lenders to see who can structure you the best deal), I recommend you continue working with your own personal banker. The one thing you do not need in the process is another fee that costs you money before you get into your new home.

Step 2: House Hunting. No more window shopping is required.

Now that you have had your credit pre-approved and you know how much you can afford, it is now time to go house-hunting.

You may look at one house or two dozen houses before you find the one that is right for your family. To help you focus on things that are really important, I have included a checklist in Appendix B to help you make sure you are getting the place you want.

The checklist in Appendix B is provided by www.hud.gov. Make several copies and use a different form each time you go out looking so you can compare notes when you are trying to making a decision.

Immediately after the checklist are a few other things to consider when looking to purchase your new home.

Since the neighborhood you choose will have a tremendous impact on your lifestyle, here are some additional tips to help you make a decision you can live with well into the future:

- Make a list of activities – dining out, recreation, House of Worship, etc. – that your family regularly engages in, and a list of stores that you visit frequently. See how far you would have to travel from each neighborhood you are considering to get to each of these activities. And you need to find out if you will have an easy commute back and forth to work, and if there is more than one way to get to all of these activities. Is there only one way in and out of the community?

- Check out the school district. The Department of Education and the local school district can provide information on test scores, class size, special programs, and the like. If you have school-age children, no amount of research can replace an impromptu visit to the schools they are likely to attend so you can see what the school is really like on a daily basis. In this case, seeing is believing!

- Visit the local police department for crime statistics on your new neighborhood, both for the overall frequency of crime and the specific types of crime that are most common. Overall trends of increasing or decreasing crime are important as well, as are the specific parts of the community where the most crime takes place.

- Is your neighborhood economically stable? Check with the city's Economic Development Office to see if income and property values in the area are stable or rising. Lots of apartment buildings in an area can mean a large transient population, while vacant businesses and homes that have been for sale for months might be warning signs of a struggling local economy.

- Is the community wise to invest in? Are price trends appreciating? Although past performance is no guarantee, it is a good indicator of home investments in the area.

- Go see for yourself. After you have narrowed your choices to two or three neighborhoods that best meet your criteria, go out for a family drive to visit them. Are the homes tidy and well-maintained? Are the streets fairly quiet? If possible, pick a warm day so you have an opportunity to chat with people while they are working or playing outside. Then make a second trip at night. The later at night the better. This way you can get a true feel of the neighborhood's goings on. Make two night visits, one on a weekday and one on the weekend.

House-hunters should keep in mind the familiar adage about the three most important features of a home: location, location, location. Finding the right home for you and your family has as much to do with the neighborhood as it does the house itself.

Factors like safety, school quality, and proximity to shopping and entertainment all contribute to both the demand and price for homes in a given neighborhood. Is your neighborhood located to more upscale neighborhoods or low-value areas?

Beyond price, what you look for in a neighborhood probably has a lot to do with your personal situation. How far are you willing to commute to work? How close do you want to be to family and friends? Do you have young children who would enjoy a neighborhood playground? If you can visualize seeing your family living day-to-day life in a certain neighborhood, then that neighborhood may be a keeper.

If you are single or a new couple, you may also want to look beyond the traditional detached single-family home. Condominiums, town houses, and duplexes can be more affordable options, especially if you are looking in a densely populated area.

These types of housing may not offer as much yard space or privacy as single-family homes, but these features may not be as important to you as the chance to own a home in the neighborhood of your choice.

If you have looked for your dream home without success, or you are just not happy with the market selections, consider building. This will give you the opportunity to customize the entire home's features and design, appliances, and building materials. And all of this comes with some warranties. This is especially a good option when you already own some land.

Most residential construction is done by builders who purchase large tracts of land and build a number of new homes to form developments. Others specialize in building custom homes for individual buyers, usually on land the buyer already owns.

Both options give you all the benefits of owning a newly built home, but there are important differences in the construction timeframe, level of customization, and the time and effort you need to commit.

If moving into your new home quickly is the priority, you will want to buy a home in a development already under construction. Each home usually takes less time to build since the floor plan is already prepared and the materials purchased. Depending on how long the development has been under construction, you may be able to choose from homes that are at different stages of construction. If you are on a tight schedule, then you may want to buy a home that is almost finished, or one that has already been completed.

If you choose to purchase a home in a development, you will have a few different floor plans to choose from, and each will come with standard amenities, its own preset options, and a list of other optional amenities that are available depending on the stage of construction and price. This, plus whatever upgrades the builder offers for materials and appliances, is basically the extent of your customization options.

Therefore, purchasing a new home in a development gives you the newness with some options and far less involvement.

A custom built home will probably take much longer — at least six to 12 months. With many more things to consider — designing the architecture, choosing the materials, and buying appliances, to name a few — you should be ready for an involved process, and for delays, which I can promise you, there will be some delays at some point.

But if you have the trifecta of imagination, luxury of time, and budget, then the appeal of a custom home is that it gives you an opportunity to live in a place that is built around you, instead of you and your family adapting to a pre-built house.

Since building a custom home is a much more complex and time consuming project, most individuals who build these types of homes tend to be those who plan to stay put for a very, very long time— which makes the time and money well spent.

Choosing the right builder is a big part of getting the home you want. Considerations like cost, location, and availability will all play a role in your selection process. But the three most important factors in choosing a builder are communication, experience, and reputation.

If you have decided to build a custom built home, then you undoubtedly have put considerable thought into the kind of home you want to live in — how much space you need, how you want to use each room, and what extra features will support your daily living patterns.

It is your builder's job to construct a home around your vision. And for this relationship to work, you have to be confident that your builder understands your needs and can deliver a finished product that meets or exceeds those needs.

The only limitations will be your budget and your schedule, especially if you are buying a home in a development rather than a custom home. So your builder must be able to set clear expectations and make sure you understand what your finished home will look like.

For obvious reasons, most people prefer to work with a builder who has a lot of construction experience. This does not mean you have to find a company that has been around for decades. It simply means you need someone who knows the process well enough to do an efficient and thorough job and will not be caught off-guard by any issues that are sure to arise.

If you are looking for a general contractor to help you build a custom home, you must also look at whether or not they have experience building houses like the one you want.

Perhaps the best indication of a builder's quality is their reputation among former customers. Other ways to verify this reputation is to check with the local builders' association and the Better Business Bureau to find out if there are any complaints. Also, ask each builder for verifiable references and make sure you follow up with each one about how satisfied they were with the construction process, their finished homes, and the builder himself.

Step 3: Make an Offer. Now you are truly committed.

Congratulations, you have found a house you want to buy. Now all you need to decide is how much you are willing to pay for it to make it a place you call home. In a normal market, it would not be uncommon for one property to have several offers, which means that your offer has to be very close to target for a buyer to accept it. However, in today's market, you most likely will have a lot of flexibility when it comes to making an offer.

In addition to sale prices for other homes, there are several ways you can determine the right price to offer:

- **The condition of the house.** Is the home in move-in condition, in need of paint and other cosmetic improvements, or a fixer-upper that needs some real work?
- **The market.** If you are in a buyer's market—where there are more homes for sale than there are people to buy them—prices are probably stable or falling. If you are in a seller's market—where there are more buyers looking for homes than there are homes for sale—prices are probably moving upward.
- ***Your threshold.*** Since you have already gotten a loan pre-approval, you know how much you can borrow for your home purchase. Although you may not be comfortable paying as much for the house as you have been approved for from your lender, you need to think carefully about your total financial situation before making an offer.

- **Area comps.** Before you ever get to the formal appraisal for any home, you should have some idea of what your potential home is worth. So, for a brief moment, you can do some of what your appraiser is going to do. If you use an online estimator such as Zillow.com or Zestimate.com, you can calculate the value of your home or a home you wish to buy, by putting in certain specific aspects of each house. Since some estimators over-estimate and others under-estimate, you will have to use two or three estimators to come up with a fairly reasonable offering or selling price. Here are a few critical elements that you will need to determine the value of your new home or the selling price of your current home:

    a) Location – similar houses in the neighborhood you are looking or a similar neighborhood somewhere else in town should be close in price to your potential new purchase

    b) Amenities – pool, mother-in-law suite over the garage, play house in the backyard, etc.

    c) Size – the number of rooms, size of the garage, and the total square footage will all make a difference in your offering price

    d) Age of the house – truly similar houses should have been built in the same general timeframe

    e) Special circumstances – marriages, divorces, death, major accidents (such as the BP oil spill), and natural disasters may all impact housing prices in a particular area

- So far, so good: You were pre-approved for a mortgage, hired a helpful real estate agent, found a beautiful home and submitted your offer. What comes next? Making an offer is exciting, but it's only the beginning of the home-buying process. Here are eight important steps that can guide you through to closing:

Wait with confidence. If you have done your homework this is not the time to worry. Once your agent submits your offer, the seller has three options: he or she can accept it, reject it, or respond with a counteroffer. If your offer is rejected it may be that your price was too low or that you included certain conditions that were unacceptable. Whatever, the reason you can submit a different offer or simply walk away from the deal. The ball is in your court. However, more often than not, sellers will send back a counteroffer, usually for a higher price. This could go on for quite some time depending on how skilled you or your agent are at negotiating. There are some limited circumstances under which you may cancel your offer without losing your earnest money deposit. Either way make sure cancellation terms are spelled out in your contract, and make sure you consult your attorney before you actually cancel, should the need arise.

Hire a closing attorney. Now that you have an agreed upon offer, it is time to begin the paperwork. The attorney will take care of the title search, obtain a property survey (if not already done by the lender), ensure that any prepaid taxes and utility charges are divided fairly, and handle any other unforeseen legal requirements of the sale. Your closing attorney can even handle the selling of your current home if you so choose. He/She may work with your lender to make sure you meet all your mortgage obligations and that all the funds are properly disbursed.

Insure your new home. Since you already have an insurance agent, getting coverage for your new home should not be an issue. The lender and your closing attorney can help fill in all the gaps that are needed to determine what kinds of insurance you need and how much. If you do not already have an agent, then get some recommendations from some people you trust and check prices before you make any commitments. Your lender may also be able to recommend insurance agencies to you. Remember some insurance companies now also check your credit report, so if you already have an insurance agent, do not switch unless you are unhappy with your current agent. A new home purchase is the perfect time to switch, if you must switch.

When you are making what is likely the largest investment of your life, you should know as much as possible about what you are buying. That's why it is a good idea to have a home inspection before you make your purchase. Most purchase contracts contain provisions for a home inspection to be performed within a certain timeframe, and sometimes they specify what action the buyer and seller may take if problems are uncovered.

One final word. A very wealthy man once told me if you are not embarrassed by your offer, then your offer is too high.

Step 4: Home Inspection. Time to find out exactly what you are offering to buy.

Now that you have made an offer on a new home, you need to make sure that offer is contingent upon the home passing an inspection. Even if you have an inspection, your lender may have the home inspected a second time, if it is an existing structure, before they order the appraisal.

It makes good financial sense to protect your money before you spend rather than trying to get protection after the fact. With that in mind, you need to hire a professional inspector who can identify trouble spots you would not otherwise be able to recognize. For an existing structure this inspection can and should include a termite inspection. The best part of the inspection is that a qualified individual is taking an in-depth, unbiased look at your potential new home, and, if the report is not truthful and accurate, they can be sued for damages. This assurance protects you and the inspector.

I cannot understand how anyone can spend hundreds of thousands of dollars on a new house but argue about spending $500 or so for a home inspection so that a specialized professional can warn them if they are throwing their money away. (Remember the movie *The Money Pit*?)

The home inspection gives you some contract remedies you might not otherwise have. This means if there are problems found with the house you have either the option of demanding that the seller correct these problems, or you can walk away from the contract and get your earnest money back (as long as you have made sure these stipulations have been written into your contract). If neither of these options suit you, you can always negotiate to have the seller reduce the price of the house by the dollar amount required to make the necessary repairs.

While most purchase contracts contain provisions for a home inspection to be performed within a certain timeframe, and may even specify what action the buyer and seller may take if problems are discovered, when it is a seller's market, it is not unusual for buyers to give up this option to increase their chance of having their offer accepted. This is purely a personal decision. However, from a pure business standpoint, I would never advise such an option.

Further, I just believe if a seller does not want you inspecting the home before you sign the final documents, there is something amiss about this kind of transaction.

Short of this, you should choose a qualified inspector who has plenty of experience with residential homes. Contact one of the national or state associations of home inspectors to find out about qualificications and if there are any members in your area. You may also pose this question to your real estate agent.

Here is where a membership on *Angie's List* may come in handy. *Angie's List* is a consumer-driven membership network organization that rates contractors and the work they do. So, instead of having to go it alone when needing some assistance, you have the benefit of documented satisfied customers.

Angie's List is also a great place to go when you need a contractor because the homework has already been done for you.

Since all of their contracting listings are based on referrals, they have already checked the contractor's credentials, visited job sites, documented insurance protections, looked at their sub-contractors, if necessary, and quoted some reasonable price ranges depending on the level of expertise.

The only thing you have left to do is to sign a contract and pay approximately ¼ of the cost upfront and the remainder when the work is completed, or some sort of payment schedule based on work completed.

Check out their website at www.angieslist.com. Angie's List is not in every area, but there may be a similar service available in your area.

However you choose to acquire an inspector, at a minimum, the inspector should examine the following components:

- Exterior structure, including the foundation, roof, siding, and chimney.
- Interior structure, including the basement or crawlspace, attic, flooring, and ceilings.
- Major systems, including heating, cooling, plumbing, and electrical, and estimate the remaining useful life of these systems.
- Identify any items that need to be replaced or repaired; and, identify any safety concerns associated with the structure.

Every buyer should make every effort to be present during their home inspection so that they will have an opportunity to ask questions and see first-hand what the inspector looks for. This is the time to receive first-hand information about the true condition of the property, i.e., how the house operates, where the main shut-off valves to the utilities are located, and much more. Remember you are paying for this inspection with the primary purpose being to find any and all defects and deficiencies in the house, so do not be surprised by the final list of recommendations.

All of the information uncovered during the inspection should be thoroughly explained to include possible causes and solutions. A few days after the inspection, the buyer(s) should receive a written inspection report with an overall description of the home, positive and negative aspects of the home, a detailed description of any problems and the way to correct those problems, and finally it should include photographs to support all findings.

I cannot stress enough the need to include a home inspection contingency in the contract for a property regardless of the market conditions, and this includes new construction homes. Although most home sellers have to provide either a disclosure or disclaimer statement regarding material knowledge of the property, there is the old adage "Buyer Beware." Whoever said it, did so for a reason.

While most sellers choose to disclaim, meaning they are selling the property with all its improvements "as is" with no representation or warranties as to the condition, this is one of those times when individual buyers need to be proactive and not fall victim to negligence or ignorance. Here is where an inspection can help you by gathering detailed information about the overall condition of the home prior to purchase.

Experience teaches that if you are building a new construction, then, you should have an inspector perform *a pre-drywall inspection* and a second, final inspection just prior to your taking possession. Most builders will try to discourage this as not necessary since their construction is subject to local building inspections and enforcement along the way. My experience teaches me that the local building inspector is not as concerned about the house the way you are.

A home inspection also has some clear benefits attached that include:

1. eliminating property condition surprises;
2. reducing the need for lengthy negotiations;
3. assuring fair market value and price;
4. providing valuable information regarding expenses one may incur after closing; and,
5. allowing you to budget for home improvement costs after ownership.

Here is a final list of reminders for your home inspection.

1. Focus on the big items, such as structural concerns, electrical issues, roof, and appliances.

2. Always ask for copies of receipts for work completed to correct the deficiencies.

3. The cost of the home inspection is usually based on various factors, such as square footage and sale price of the home.

4. A typical charge of $1 per $1,000 of the sales price is not uncommon. For example, a selling price of $500,000 should have a home inspection tag of $500 or more, depending on the particulars of the house.

5. If you have a particular desire about how some specific work needs to be accomplished, then ask for credit at closing so you can choose a contractor that suits your needs.

6. An inspector that can give you an onsite computer-generated report after the inspection, and one who is available for questions after the inspection are big pluses.

7. If your inspector suspects mold, then you will need to find a qualified professional to analyze the problem and provide remediation options.

8. For an existing home, a radon contingency should be a part of your sales contract; your home inspector will be able to refer you to a technician who can place and retrieve the testers that measure the radon levels. Make sure the testing firm is listed with either the National Radon Safety Board, or the National Environmental Health Association. The additional charge for the radon testing is about $100-$150, but this is money well spent.

No one would buy a car without first test driving it, and the same principal applies when purchasing a new home.

Although you have had the home inspected, it is not a bad idea to see if you can get some extra protection in the form of a home warranty either on the entire house and its contents or on specific items, such as the heating, ventilating, and air conditioning (HVAC) system.

Even a one year warranty on an existing home may be helpful because the first year is generally the time things do happen. But, if you cannot get a warranty on an existing home, only you can decide if the lack of a warranty is a deal breaker or not.

New homes should automatically come with both short-term and long-term warranties. Short-term for minor repairs and long-term for structural defects and other items like the roof. Just make sure these items are spelled out in your contract.

If you are purchasing your home from a builder let me give you a few tips that may help you get a deal that protects you.

- Never sign a contract the first time you see it. If you do sign that document just to get a particular house, insist that the following provision be added to the contract. "Subject to attorney approval without penalty." As soon as you leave the builder's office go straight to your attorney's office.

- While your attorney is reviewing your documents you should check with the Better Business Bureau in your area and the state attorney general's office to see if there have been any complaints against your builder and how those complaints were resolved. Second, you need to take a trip to the courthouse to see if your builder has had any lawsuits filed against them. Third, go visit some of your builder's other communities and talk with those buyers to see how satisfied they are.

- Do not agree to binding arbitration. If you must have binding arbitration, make sure it is structured where either the loser pays or the costs are equally split. If you can, talk with the arbitrator and do your homework on this individual as well.

- Do not sign any contracts that allow the builder to make modifications without your approval.

- Since you have been pre-approved, you have lots of power so use it to negotiate for things you want. Some of these things could be the builder pays all closing costs, appliance upgrades, and/or the builder pays all taxes in the first year.

- Make sure you get a drop-dead completion date that if the builder does not meet they have to pay some sort of penalty that increases the longer the project is delayed.

- Make sure you get a pre-drywall inspection and a final inspection written into the contract, by an inspector of your choosing.

Now that you have found your new home, agreed on a price, and had the home inspected, the time has now come to close the deal and take official ownership of the property.

STEP 5: Close the deal. Closing dates change sometimes for various reasons – the closing documents are not ready, your attorney finds a mistake that needs to be corrected, information has not been verified, or the final dollar amount needed at closing changes.

The closing date will also depend on when the seller is ready to move out and when you are ready to move in. Even if you are not yet quite ready to physically move, request a closing date near the end of the month in order to minimize the amount of interest you have to prepay on your mortgage.

Despite all of our technological advancements, the closing process is still paper-intensive. Try to set your closing for as early as possible in the day so that you will have time to do some moving or start on some touch-up projects in the new house in the afternoon. These projects could include such things as clearing away excess shrubbery, installing new locks, securing patio doors, installing outside security lights or motion lights, and installing an outside storage unit, to name a few.

Either way, clear your entire schedule for the day, wear some comfortable clothes, bring a snack and your driver's license, and be focused and prepared to sign a lot of documents – some of them in duplicate and triplicate. Most importantly, be prepared with your certified funds for your final closing amount (your attorney should have given you the final dollar amount for your certified funds a few days before the closing).

Although closing practices vary greatly, the attendees may include all or none of the following:

- the closing attorney
- both the buyer and the seller or their appointed representatives
- real estate agents for the buyer and seller
- lender's representative, however in most cases the attorney is acting as the lender's representative with the collection and disbursement of funds

Closing costs vary based on a variety of factors, but here are some of the items that will be included in that cost:

- Lender fees. Your mortgage company may charge for expenses related to making the loan, including the appraisal fee, a credit report fee, origination points, and discount points.
- Third party fees. These charges normally include title insurance,

settlement fees, and attorney's fees. These services are not provided by the lender.

- Prepaid items. The lender collects certain mortgage costs in advance. The most common of these are pre-paid interest, insurance, and deposits to set up an escrow account.

Please go to www.HUD.gov to familiarize yourself with the HUD Settlement statement that is a part of every home loan closing held in the U. S.

Step 6: Moving day. Although your moving day may be a few weeks away, make things easy on yourself and start boxing up items that are seldom used. Moving takes longer than you might think, and, if you are not organized it is going to cost you more money than you think.

Even if you are only going to use professional movers in a limited capacity, call around and get quotes from two or three companies.

If your moving budget is a little tight and you plan on doing it yourself, the more you can do in advance and have ready to pack (with boxes clearly labeled for which room), it will make your volunteer crew very happy, and you too.

Make sure you get plenty of moving supplies far enough in advance to do you some good, including strong boxes, padding, and other packing materials.

Make sure you have an inventory list of everything that is in each box so that if something is missing you know exactly what that something is (so if you are using professionals, it will be easier to make a claim).

Now is also time to do some spring cleaning so that anything you do not want or need you can either sell or donate to charity (for the tax deduction).

Pack a special box of items you will need as soon as you arrive at your new home, such as cleaning supplies, kitchen utensils, dinnerware, bath items, tools, and a telephone. If you have young children, have them do the same thing by packing some of their favorite items to keep them occupied while you get the remainder of the trucks unpacked.

While you are thinking about the kids, make sure you have all of their files from their old schools so that registration at the new school will be as easy as possible. Moving is generally not an easy adjustment for young children so they may need some special attention getting used to the idea of moving and settling into a new place, maybe even a new city.

Do not forget to go to the post office and have your family's permanent mailing address changed to your new address, including your newspaper and magazine subscriptions.

Do not forget to also notify both your old and new utility providers of your moving in and out dates as well as your financial institutions and anyone else who needs to know your new address.

Step 7: Out with the old.

The most profound decision a seller can make is whether or not to hire an agent to sell the home or be a do-it-yourselfer. While the FSBO (For Sale by Owner) route is attractive because you save the 6% real estate agent's commission, if you are either not prepared for some work or are not knowledgeable enough to sell your home, then 6% can be a bargain – – if you have a good agent.

Do not be misled. Most agents are not going to try and get you the highest price for your home. Instead they are going to get you the most reasonable offer they can get depending on market conditions. And the reason for this is because the sales commission has to be split four ways – between your sales agent and their firm, and between the buyer's agent and their firm.

How do you know if you have a good agent? A good agent will:

- first and foremost be a top-notch negotiator that knows how to offer creative options instead of letting a deal fall through.
- help you set the right price for your home based on recent comparable home sales in your area, and the overall local market. If the price is set too high, your product will immediately get passed over. And if it is set at a high price, buyer's may expect more than what you have to offer.
- do all the leg-work. This means they will create advertisements, screen prospective buyers, and show your home, all of which are very time-consuming and labor-intensive undertakings. One crucial piece of this puzzle is to make sure as much and as many pictures as possible are posted on the internet so that prospective buyers can get a good look and a good feel about your property. Words like beautiful, gorgeous, landscaping, and move-in condition will help your house move faster and increase the possibility of getting your asking price.
- make sure that the real-estate sales contract reflects your interests.
- know how to effectively and efficiently screen for the right group of

buyers who are most likely to want your house and be able to make a reasonable offer.

- make sure you have a way out of the contract if the relationship fails to yield positive results within a reasonable period, i.e., 6 months or less.

Although your home does not have to be a spectacular showcase in order to sell, you should do your homework so that you can maximize your home's benefits while minimizing its shortcomings at the best price possible. That means you should do the same thing prospective buyers are doing – check out your competition. By doing so you may give yourself an edge up. A good agent can help you collect information on comparables that have recently sold so you can drive by and get some ideas on how to enhance curb-appeal.

A dear friend, who happens to be a real estate agent, told me that one of the best ways to find out how well a home has been kept is to check the oven first. If the oven is not clean, then the house will not be clean either.

This means you should make all necessary repairs, that everything functions as it should, and everything is clean and presentable. While you are at it, go neutral and tone down those special colors that have limited appeal, clean up all the clutter in every room by making sure that the furniture in each room showcases the room's best features. This includes removing personal mementos and family pictures. Now might even be the time to have that yard sale you have been talking about for so long to get rid of those unwanted and unused items.

These relatively small and inexpensive improvements can make your home much more attractive to buyers — but do not overdo it. If you find yourself spending a great deal of money to remodel your home, you might as well stay in the house. And while a remodeled kitchen is sure to bring a higher sale price, a fresh coat of paint and a sparkling-clean kitchen can also make a valuable impression for less money. It also may be a good idea to hire a professional cleaner, depending on your time schedule and budget.

The easiest and best way to get buyers inside your home is to get them to notice the outside. A manicured lawn with the right flower patterns and color may be your best investment in this process. Make sure also that your siding is clean and the remainder of the exterior is neat and tidy.

If none of these work, see if you can get a free review by a professional house stager.

Another way to quicken the sale of your home is to hire an inspector before you put it on the market. By uncovering any potential problems ahead of time you will be able to set a more accurate price, make for a smoother process, and, most of all avoid any unforeseen surprises that might disrupt your plans. (Remember to keep receipts for everything you do because they may be tax deductible expenses when you are all done.)

Finally do not forget that there is a time and season for everything under the sun, including selling your house. In general, most home sales peak during April and May and main remain steady through July because that is when children are out of school and family vacation time can be built around the move. And, it is easier to move in the warm weather than in the cold.

Now if you do need to sell your home in the autumn or winter you might actually be able to get a better price because there are generally fewer homes on the market during this time of the year. Also, some buyers may be motivated by the calendar so that they can claim the year-end mortgage deduction on their taxes.

One final thought – – make arrangements to not be at home when your house is being shown. Nervous or over anxious sellers are not helpful additions to an already emotional and maybe difficult decision.

Worth Their Wait

While we have already discussed many ways to begin your new home search, we are going to singularly focus on real estate agents for a moment. A great source to learn more about real estate agents is the official web site of the National Association of Realtors (www.realtor.org).

However, I have found the two most popular ways of finding a real estate agent are either by word of mouth or by default. In truth, by default has been more successful for as many individuals as has word of mouth.

If this is true, then is there a better way to find a real estate agent that makes them worth waiting for while they sell your property?

Although there are times when a real estate agent is required, such as when purchasing a home from a builder, it is not always required that a real estate agent be used in this process.

The reason a real estate agent is required when purchasing from a builder is that most builders have already set aside real estate commissions for agents that cannot be used for anything else, and this money will either be used or the builder will take the money back.

So if an agent is required, then it is first necessary to understand who represents whom.

A buyer's agent is a real estate agent who exclusively represents you, the home buyer. Their counterparts, or traditional agents, also called listing agents (a property for sale is called a listing and the agent who is responsible for selling that property is the listing agent) or seller's agents, usually represents the builder or seller.

Whether you are buying or selling property, you want an agent who solely represents you throughout the entire real estate transaction. While there are some agents who represent both the buyer and the seller, I am not sure that agent can have an objective enough opinion to serve both clients equally.

So your agent, a good agent, will guide you through the entire buying/selling process from start to finish.

They will help you find homes that best meet your needs by narrowing down your choices in an organized manner. That individual will also be an expert at recognizing property problems that are not obvious to the untrained eye, negotiating prices on your behalf, arranging financing, and managing the closing.

In truth, the buyer is at a disadvantage in a typical real estate transaction because sellers both know the ins and outs of the property, and they have already had their team in place long enough to formulate a winning game plan.

Once you sign a contract and your agent is legally bound to represent you, make sure your representative represents you both in the spirit of the contract as well as the ink of the contract.

In order to get to a contract signing, you need to use all of your resources to gather a few good names of some potential agents to represent your interest. A good number is about five.

Then after some thought, you need to pick out two or three to interview. One way of determining who will work best with you is to give each of them a certain task to do, and, based on their response you can help narrow down your choices. Essentially, you are the employer, and are interviewing potential employees, real estate agents for the one position you have available.

Some other things any good real estate agent should do is:

- Click in personality with you so that this will be an enjoyable experience.
- Make sure they do not disclose your drop-dead price to purchase or sell a property.
- Take all of their directions from you or the criteria list you provide.
- Let you do some looking on your own, but if you are doing most of the work, that is not a good sign.
- Specialize in the home value range and neighborhoods that fit your needs.
- Provide full disclosure of all information concerning your home search, including true value, market/neighborhood conditions, obvious physical defects, and the owner's motivation for selling.
- Level the playing field for you with expert negotiation skills, for such things as requiring the seller to do a title search, and what beneficial contingencies should be added to your contract.
- Get you the lowest possible price with the best possible terms.
- Give you the straight facts so you can make informed decisions.
- Assist you with financing options.
- Present "what if" scenarios about the clauses in a contract and recommend possible contract contingencies to protect your interests.
- Give you the edge throughout the buying process, and know when to withdraw an offer even against their client's advice.
- Keep their eye on the potential resale value of your property.
- Have a comprehensive customer satisfaction plan in place that is followed by action, in addition to being able to preview previous customer rating reviews.
- Offer references from at least their last three clients. If they hesitate, then maybe they have said enough without saying a word.
- Be observant of your lifestyle and make recommendations based on your needs.
- Be confident and firm enough to tell you when you are making a mistake, for example a mistake of location.

- Help you prioritize your needs, followed by your primary wants, and then followed by your luxury list.
- Make sure your earnest money is protected.

Now that you have some idea of the qualities an effective agent should possess, it is up to you to determine which qualities, in addition to your own desires, best fit with you and your familial situation.

But also remember, no one is perfect so you should also decide which flaws you can live with, if they do not impede your ultimate goal – homeownership.

To Be or Not To Be Delayed

I started this chapter talking about the documents needed when you are ready to apply for a loan, but I have not spent much time discussing the details of the actual mortgage options in the market today.

I purposely delayed this discussion until now, because it is the actual mortgage underwriting process that will determine if your homeownership dreams are to be or are to be delayed.

The word mortgage gets it meaning from both the French word "mort," which means dead, and the Old English word "gage," which means pledge.

So in the 16th century when King James I reigned, if a debt went unpaid, the land pledged for that debt would be taken away from the mortgager and thus be dead to the mortgagee, as if they never owned it.

Every mortgage lender is going to require a loan application not much unlike most credit applications. However, it is imperative that every question on the mortgage application be addressed. It is so important that I again suggest a face to face meeting with your banker to start the application process.

In addition to collecting your application and financial documents, your banker will help you determine which loan program is best for you, the relationship between interest rates and points, the importance of locking in an interest rate, and other financial matters.

These matters are sometimes more complicated than a simple yes or no answer, which makes them better suited to be answered face to face so that you and your banker can talk through information to make sure that everything is presented in the best possible manner without bending the truth.

After the preliminary review of your financial documentation, your banker should be able to tell you if you will be able to get approved through underwriting, and, if so, at what interest rate.

So your first decision will be whether to lock in your interest rate or not. While keeping in mind that interest rates can change at any time and without notice, and that rates generally change a little bit each day or several times a day, the best rule of thumb to follow is quite simple.

Locking in your interest rate means the lender is guaranteeing your loan rate, even if market rates change once or more before closing.

The general rule is that you can chose to lock your rate for 30 to 60 days at no cost. However, if you need to lock your rate longer than 60 days, your lender will generally agree for an upfront fee.

If we are in a volatile interest market where interest rates are dropping dramatically, it may be prudent to wait a week or two before locking in your interest rate.

However, if we are in an equally volatile market where interest rates are moving up dramatically, I would lock in my interest rate immediately.

The exception to this would be if interest rates are dropping and suddenly start moving up, then I would lock in my rate as quickly as possible.

Most lenders have some general guidelines favoring the consumer that basically state if the interest rates fall beneath a certain point after a buyer has already locked in, they will give the buyer the lower rate. In the same respect, if the buyer does not lock in their rate and rates start to rise, the lender will generally give the buyer a median rate between the rate the day their application was submitted and the highest rate before they locked in their interest rate.

Lenders consider many factors when evaluating a loan application, but they usually focus on four areas:

- Income and debt. How much money does an individual make in conjunction with what other bills they have to pay, in addition to the new mortgage. This will help the lender determine if a mortgage is affordable for the homebuyer.
- Assets. The lender needs to make sure you have enough total assets, either in cash or hard assets that can be converted into cash, to cover the

costs of buying a home.

- Credit. Very simply the question is, does this individual pay their bills when due.
- Property. Is the subject property worth enough to act as the collateral for the mortgage.

A traditional mortgage is 80/20, where the lender puts up 80% of the money, and the buyer puts up a 20% down payment. While there is no minimum down payment required for buying a home, in general, most first-time buyers believe they must be able to put down as much as 20% of a home's purchase price in cash.

This is probably true for individuals with less than stellar credit and those with other issues. Although 20% may not be required in all situations, most home buyers should be putting in some sort of down payment because when an individual has something to lose, they tend to work harder to keep it than if they have nothing at stake.

Even so, there are many mortgage options available today that require little or no down payment. Some public and private lenders have programs available where as little as a 3% down payment is required. If you still have a need for additional cash, go back and look at some of the options for increasing your income (See Chapter 7).

One such program to help individuals gather down payment money is sponsored by the South Carolina State Housing Finance and Development Authority. The authority first helps individuals qualify for home ownership. There is a second program that can also help individuals with down payment assistance. See the Appendix at the end of the book, and then look to see if similar help is available in your area.

In those cases when a lender lends more than 80% of a home's value or, stated another way, the lender puts up more than 80% of the total mortgage, they generally require private mortgage insurance (PMI).

PMI is a way for the lender to recoup their investment if the borrower should default or is otherwise unable to repay their loan. PMI is usually required when the mortgage amount is higher than 80% of the home's value.

Probably the most common way of bypassing PMI – – that is without having to make a down payment – – is to use an 80/20 program, which combines a first mortgage with home equity financing.

In simple terms, equity is the amount of ownership value a homeowner has in any given property. It is computed by subtracting the total of the unpaid mortgage balance and any outstanding liens or other debts against the property, if any, from the property's fair market value. The ending dollar amount is the total equity in the property.

For example, if a homeowner had a first mortgage of $150,000, a second mortgage of $30,000, and a first lien of $22,000 against a house appraised at $325,000, then how much does the owner have in the property? The answer is $123,000.

This equity increases as the principal balance of the mortgage is paid down and/or as the property appreciates in value. When all the debts against the mortgage are all paid in full, the homeowner has 100 % equity in the property.

A home's equity exists in conjunction with the loan-to-value (LTV) ratio. The LTV ratio is a percentile used to express the value of your property compared to the amount of your loan. It is determined by dividing the loan amount of the property by the property's current value, selling price, or purchase price, whichever is lower.

For example, if a homeowner purchases a home for $300,000, makes a $60,000 down payment with their own money, and has a $240,000 mortgage, then the LTV is found by dividing $240,000 by $300,000. In this case, the LTV is 80%, the equity is 20% or the $60,000 down payment.

If the home is sold at a later date, the equity at the time of the sale will be determined based on the fair market value of the home, less any money still owed on the property.

Continuing on with the example above, if you own a home for five years after your purchase, and you made monthly mortgage payments that reduced the principal balance by $15,0000 ($240,000 – $15,000), and the value of the house increased so that it was sold for $345,000, then the equity would be $345,000 – $225,000, which is $120,000.

Your final profit would be the difference of the $120,000 less your costs, including any real estate commissions paid to agents for selling the property.

Conversely, equity can decrease in a real property, which was a huge part of the unusual recession from 2008 – 2010, and still continuing for some.

This means that an individual is "upside down" in their home because they owe more on the home than the home is worth.

Sometimes the equity of a property is increased or decreased by the type of mortgage attached to the property.

All mortgages have either a fixed interest rate or an adjustable interest rate.

While there are arguably a few cases when an adjustable-rate mortgage (ARM) makes financial sense, for most a fixed-rate mortgage is the better option.

A fixed rate mortgage has the same interest rate throughout the life of the loan, which better helps buyers regularly make their payments on time because of the stability of this type of loan.

That's okay, I know how you feel. I hated word problems in school too, but that doesn't mean they are going to go away.

Most ARM loans are written to the advantage of the lender because the interest rate moves upward at regular intervals, usually once every year, based on preset market indicators, until they hit a peak point.

In general, the ARM begins at a low rate for an initial period of one to five years, maybe longer in some cases, and then it begins moving up every year after that initial period until they reach a maximum rate. This was an abusive technique that agents and lenders used during the 2008 – 2010 recession to get people into homes that they could not qualify for otherwise. When these bad loans started to default (because most individuals could not qualify for refinancing for a fixed-rate loan), these defaults rocked the entire economy.

Basically, if you plan on staying in your home for a while, more than ten years, then a fixed rate is usually the best plan of action.

On the other hand, an ARM is good if you plan on moving during the initial period, are absolutely sure you can get refinanced before the end of the initial period, or you are having to buy at a time when rates are extraordinarily high.

Discount points are prepaid interest, which you can pay to your lender at closing in exchange for a lower interest rate on your mortgage.

Every 1 discount point is equal to 1% of the loan amount, and is known as "buying down" your rate. So if you take out a $100,000 loan, one point equals $1,000. The general rule is that for every point you pay for a 30-year loan, your interest rate is reduced by 1/8 or .125% of a point.

So, if you pay one discount point at closing on a $100,000 loan ($1,000), you could lower your interest rate from 6 1/2 % to 6 3/8 %. If you pay two discount points ($2,000 on a $100,000 loan), you could lower your interest rate from 6 1/2 % to 6 1/4 %.

Although not required, just remember the lower your interest rate the cheaper your loan, over the life of the loan; therefore, lower interest may potentially mean a quicker payoff.

The mortgage payment itself will include all of the following:

- Principal, the total outstanding balance of the loan
- Interest, the cost to you for owing the bank the principal balance on the loan
- Taxes, property taxes levied by the local government
- Insurance, which protects the owner and the lender from losses caused by fire or any other hazards

Total housing costs, which include your mortgage payments, property taxes, homeowner and mortgage insurance, and homeowner's fees, should total no more than 28% – 30% of your total monthly gross income from all sources.

Your Total Gross Monthly Income	$______
Multiply by 28 Percent	______x .28______
Maximum Allowable Monthly Housing Expense	______

To determine an individual's loan qualifications, one of the first things a mortgage lender does is to divide the monthly payment of the proposed loan by the gross monthly income.

This is the housing-to-income ratio or the amount of your monthly housings costs as a percentage of your gross income.

If this percentage falls within an acceptable limit, the next step is to divide the total monthly debt by gross monthly income.

This is the debt-to-income ratio, or the amount of monthly debt costs as a percentage of gross income.

Again, if this ratio falls within acceptable limits, the applicant will most likely qualify for the loan.

Normally, all mortgages require an escrow account for taxes and insurance. This is the easiest way for the lender to know their interest in the property is protected.

Because your mortgage includes an escrow account, your monthly mortgage payment will increase to include the necessary amounts to pay the taxes and insurance when they come due.

If your lender is one of those rare lenders who do not require you to establish an escrow account, you will be required to pay the taxes and insurance directly, and usually in a lump sum, when due. The lender will send you a formal letter each year requiring you to provide proof that you have paid both the home owner's insurance and property taxes on the property every year until the loan is paid in full.

If these items are not paid, then the lender will reserve the right to secure insurance for the property, and bill you for the premiums, plus interest, in addition to paying the taxes, and sending you a second bill for those also. If the lender has to resort to these kinds of transactions, you can rest assured that your loan will be adjusted to include these items in your future payments.

These expenses are necessary costs of homeownership, and you, as well as the lender, need to know that you can afford these associated costs.

If the lender has to purchase homeowner insurance for you, you can best believe that insurance will be much more expensive than any insurance you can obtain on your own.

An individual may have several choices when it comes to selecting a mortgage lender, from mortgage companies to banks to credit unions and others.

Each institution will vary in terms of the rules, rates and fees that each offers in relation to different types of loans, and the variations in which loans are structured and collected.

All these differences mean dollars in or out of your pocket.

When shopping for a mortgage there are several options that need to be discussed with your lender.

- Conventional financing
- Federal government programs
- Alternative financing

Here are some of the many different types of loans available in the market today.

The first group of eleven "conventional" mortgage loans are described as such because these loans are not insured or guaranteed by a federal agency, such as the Department of Housing and Urban Development.

1. **Fixed-rate:** This traditional mortgage is a loan with a constant interest rate and equal payments for most commonly 30 years. The biggest promotion point of fixed-rate loans is their regularity of payment amounts. These loans also are available in other terms, such as 15 years, 20 years or even 40 years. (See Amortization schedule in Appendices.)

2. **Adjustable-rate (ARM):** As the name implies, the interest rate changes throughout the term of the loan. These loans are generally popular when interest rates are relatively high and appear to be dropping. They are also popular when the difference between ARMs and the fixed-rates is greater than 2 to 3%. Each lending institution's ARM is based on an index, so make sure you know how the ARM is based and adjusted before signing up.

3. **Jumbo:** A jumbo mortgage is so named because this mortgage exceeds the maximum limit set by the Federal National Mortgage Association (FNMA, or "Fannie Mae") and the Federal Home Loan Mortgage Corp. (FHLMC, or "Freddie Mac"), the largest national investors in mortgages. Because of the greater risk exposure to the lender by the higher-than-average loan amount, some lenders charge slightly higher interest rates for jumbo loans.

4. **Balloon:** Balloon mortgages get their name from the large lump sum payments required at the end of the loan. Beyond that, these are fixed-rate loans with insufficient monthly payments that are not large enough to pay the loan in full, which forces the balloon payment at the end. As mortgages go, these

are short term loans, usually 5 to 7 years with the large balloon payment that must pay the loan in full at the end of the period. Many borrowers refinance their balloon loans at the time the balloon payment is due to avoid having to make such a large one-time payment. The advantage of the balloon payment loan is that their interest rates are normally below current market rates.

5. **Fixed/Adjustable:** This is a slightly different and the most popular of all ARMs because they begin with an initial period from 1 to as many as 10 years where the interest rate is both low and fixed. Then after that, the interest rate will go up every year until it reaches a maximum rate, and it may increase significantly. The problem is that most individuals who qualify for an ARM do not necessary qualify for refinancing because credit standards change or the value of the property goes down.

6. **Interest-only:** Interest-only loans are so named because the borrower is only required to pay accrued interest at the beginning of the loan up to a specified period of time, typically 10 years. At the end of the specified period, the borrower's monthly payments increase to include both principal and interest, which could be a considerable increase. (By the way, if this is an adjustable rate interest only loan, the payment may go up several times even before the required principal payments.) The benefit of this type of loan is that the interest payments are considerably less than a normal principal + interest payment. This type of loan is sometimes preferred over a fixed-rate loan because the payments are generally lower than that conventional loan also. However, it is imperative that the borrower try to make as many principal payments as possible to help lower both the principal and the new required principal + interest payment when it comes due.

Here are some other important reminders. (1) It is important to remember that interest-only payments do not reduce the amount owed on the principal during the interest only period, which is why it is necessary to pay separate additional payments on the principal. This may not be financially easy to do, and for that reason interest-only loans are riskier than other loans. (2) It is possible that an individual may end up owing more than their house is worth with this type of loan if the home's value declines. This would make it almost impossible to refinance the loan. And if the house were to be sold based on a lower value, the seller would have to pay the bank the difference between the sell price and loan balance in order for the house to have clear title. (3) These types of loans also have prepayment penalties because the interest rates are so low that if they are paid off early the lender loses money. These penalties are purposefully set high so that if the lender does choose to pay off the loan early, the penalty should cover most of the lender's potential losses.

7. **Graduated payment:** A graduated payment mortgage (GPM) starts out with low monthly payments, which gradually increase over time. The borrower starts off making the lowest monthly payment allowed by the lender's standard. After the initial period, typically 5 to 15 years, the monthly payments start to increase. These initial payments are less than the amount of interest, like in an interest-only mortgage. The unpaid "deferred" interest, called negative amortization, is added to the principal amount of the loan. This type of loan may be good for borrowers who know their future income is guaranteed to increase. However, this loan has no surprises in it because all the details of this type of loan (interest rate, payment amount, and time frames) are specifically scheduled and documented. The drawback to this type of loan is that over the life of the loan, borrowers end up paying more interest because the initial low monthly payments are not enough to pay the mortgage interest that accrues each month; and, since the amount of the monthly mortgage interest owed is determined by the principal amount, the interest and the principal grow at increasing rates. (Student loans are the best of the "worst" example of this type of loan.)

8. **Payment option adjustable-rate (POA):** A payment option ARM is a flexible adjustable rate loan that allows the borrower to make one of several different possible payments but only for a specified period of time loan. Generally, these loans are more expensive because of the flexibility built into the loans, and they also carry the combined risks of the other loans with the same name as the payment options. (1) During the first few years, the borrower may have several payment options. (2) Typically there are three payment options included in the loan: a principal + interest payment; an interest-only payment; and, a minimum payment.

9. **Growing equity:** This is a rapid repayment fixed-rate mortgage that rises yearly until the mortgage is paid in full. The good news is that each additional payment from the payment hikes are applied directly to the principal, so that a 30-year mortgage is paid off in less than 15 years. The bad news is that it may not be easy to keep up with those increasing payments.

10. **Temporary buy-down:** With a temporary buy-down, the monthly payment is reduced by a temporary interest rate deduction because the seller, which in

most cases is a builder, gives the buyer extra money that is used to reduce the interest rate for a short period of time. This extra money is generally an added incentive to purchase a home within a specific development.

11. **Bi-weekly:** This mortgage option is a good way to pay a 30-year mortgage down sooner with very little risk. Instead of making 12 payments a year, this mortgage is paid every 2 weeks which equals 26 payments a year or 27 in a leap year. The total interest paid is much lower, and home ownership happens in approximately 15 years instead of 30. However, not all lenders allow bi-weekly mortgage payments.

This next group of mortgage options is a good place to start for any borrower because these federal government, state-backed, or private programs can not only help individuals with problems, but they may also help save the users money even if they do not have any problems. Most of these problems may be limited to first-time homebuyers only, but it never hurts to ask.

1. **Federal Housing Administration (FHA) insured:** This federal government backed loan is offered by lenders primarily because if the borrower defaults, the lender will recover their funds from the federal government, so there is very little risk to the lender. While there are some specific qualification requirements, FHA mortgages can be used to purchase a new or existing single-family home with as little as a 3% down payment. Two such programs are listed below. (www.fha.gov and www.fhainfo.com)

   203(b): This program provides mortgage insurance that protects the lenders from borrower default. It may also be used to finance the purchase of new or existing one-to-four family housing unit. 203(b) is known for its low down payments, flexible qualifying guidelines, limited fees, and maximum loan amount limits.

   203(k) is another mortgage insurance program which enables homebuyers to finance both the purchase of a home and rehab cost, if any, via a single mortgage product.

2. **Veterans Administration (VA) guaranteed:** The VA guarantees lenders against loss if a property is foreclosed due to default. These loans are only available to veterans or their families, but be prepared for more paperwork. The benefit may be well worth the time. (www.va.gov)

3. **Farmers Home Administration (FmHA):** The FmHA is a department within the Department of Agriculture which makes these loans available to persons

of moderate to very low income in rural or non-metropolitan areas. But there are also other loans available under the USDA. (www.usda.gov)

4. **State/Local Government Programs:** Almost every state and most major cities have a housing administration department that administers some kind of state or local financing program to assist individuals in becoming homeowners. Make sure you contact both state and local governments for more information.

5. There are other mortgage programs that are offered by various organizations and the federal, state, and local governments that are geared to a particular need. Some of these are:

a. Down payment assistance programs: do not forget your 401 (k) retirement funds can be used for a down payment without a penalty (talk to your employer to find out which is more beneficial, the loan or a withdrawal)

b. 0 down payment 103% plans, which allow a borrower to finance up to 100% of a home's value + 3% more for closing costs

c. 0 down payment 80/20 where there is a first and second mortgage on the property

d. 203(b) Fixed Mortgage Rate Loan, the equivalent of the federal government's first time home buyer program

e. Other loans geared to law enforcement officials, teachers, the elderly, and helping out depressed neighborhoods, to name a few

f. There are even loans available to adapt an existing home for someone with special needs

g. Private programs such as Neighborhood Assistance Corporation of America [NACA] (www.naca.com)

h. Habitat for Humanity (www.habitat.org)

i. Grants from both private organizations, and federal, state, and local governments, primarily for first time homebuyers

j. Assistance with mortgage insurance

Finally, I will mention just a few of at least 50+ ways to do alternative financing.

1. **Lease/purchase agreements:** A lease purchase involves two documents – one contract is your lease to occupy the property, and the second is your contract option to purchase the property. So while you are occupying and renting the home, you are potentially, simultaneously, preparing to be the homeowner of this same property. The beauty of this option is that part of each rental payment is counted towards the purchase of the home as either a down payment and/or closings costs.

2. **Second mortgage:** A second mortgage is subordinate to the first mortgage lien, and may be used to take owner's equity out of the property or to provide additional funds for the purchase of the same or a different property. Sometimes these mortgages are used when a borrower assumes the first mortgage of a previous owner that has a lower interest rate and needs to make up the difference between the loan and the sale price.

3. **Bridge loan:** Bridge loans are also known as swing loans. It is a bridge because it is a short-term loan secured by the borrower's current home, which is up for sale, as a way to secure proceeds to be used for building or closing on a new house before the current home is sold. Thus it is a bridge from one home to another, or it allows the homeowner to swing from the old house to the new house.

4. **Not so empty nests:** Although this option may cramp your style for a while it is nonetheless a huge money saving option. Many young individuals and the not so young are moving back in with their parents while they save money for a deposit, cut their expenses, get their credit in order, or a combination of all of the above.

A few final reminders about mortgages. Make sure you ask your lender if there are any penalties for paying your loan off early. Second, be wary of low doc/no doc loans because you will pay a hefty price for the lender not verifying your income and other assets.

Since the size of your mortgage is important to both you and your lender, there are several website calculators you can check in advance of any meeting with your lender to determine how much you can afford. One such calculator can be found at www.bankrate.com.

Fannie Mae's website, www.fanniemae.com can also help you determine a loan that you can confidently pay comfortably and a proper level of housing debt, in addition to your other monthly expenses.

First, you should look at an income matrix that gives you an idea of how much of a loan you can qualify for based strictly on your income only.

Second, you should look at an interest rate matrix that helps you understand how much you can afford at a particular interest rate. This kind of matrix looks at principal and interest only.

However, the best mortgage loan qualifier I have seen on the market thus far is found at http://www.finansw.com/jesspeacock/calculators/calc3/MortgageQualifier.html.

This calculator combines all the previous information into one **printable** report that includes graphs and charts to help you get a visual idea of what the numbers actually mean.

Although you may qualify for a larger loan, you need to take into account not only your expenses but your disposable income. Whatever size loan you qualify for, you need to be prepared for more scrutiny than in years past, and you may need to provide more verification documents than before.

While a larger loan might interfere with your family's other interests, the most important factor to remember is that you, not the lender, will be making the payments each month. Although many individuals talk about stretching to afford a home that is beyond their comfort zone, it is important to consider the stress this puts on your finances and your family.

Even though there are a number of ways to reduce most monthly expenses with a few adjustments, a mortgage payment cannot easily be reduced, or delayed, and failure to make those payments can have very serious consequences.

Remember, a mortgage broker is completely independent from a mortgage banker or loan officer. The latter works directly for your lender and can only offer you products offered by your lender.

While you can get a mortgage from many different sources, like mortgage, commercial, and community banks, credit unions, and other financial institutions, mortgage brokers may be worth considering if you do not know where to start shopping.

A mortgage broker is an independent agent that may have access to several different lenders and many different loan programs.

These private professionals are compensated directly by you, in addition to any payments they may receive from lenders for promoting their products.

The broker is paid a yield spread premium (YSP) by the lender. The YSP is the cash rebate paid to a mortgage broker based on that broker selling an interest rate product above the wholesale par rate that the borrower qualifies for. Generally, the higher the interest rate on the loan, the higher the YSP.

Before seeking out a local mortgage broker make sure you understand the terms of the agreement including all fees. While this decision is left up to each buyer, my professional recommendation is to not use a mortgage broker unless you have been turned down by more than one other source.

Even though using a broker may entail more fees than getting a mortgage loan directly from a banker, these extra costs may be worthwhile if the broker can obtain a loan with an interest rate that is lower than a rate that you could obtain on your own by working directly with a lender.

Some questions that you should consider asking a potential lender include:

- Is there any benefit to having existing accounts here or to opening an account before I apply for a loan?
- Where should my credit score be to take advantage of your best mortgages?
- What fees can you waive?
- How quickly does it take to get a pre-approval letter?
- How much do you charge for an appraisal?
- If I set my mortgage up on automatic withdrawals, how much can I save in points or fees?
- How do you normally communicate, and what is the best way to reach you if I have questions, including weekends?

To Buy or To Buy Later

While I do not recall the original source of the following matrix, it does help make the point of displaying the advantages to buying a home instead of renting. In many cases, the amount of money a person spends on rent can be about the same as or more than the amount a homeowner spends on a mortgage. The tax benefits and savings help make homeownership a tremendous deal when compared to renting.

Some other factors that need to be taken in consideration when deciding to purchase or not to purchase a home are:

i.) What are the risks?

ii.) New monthly housing expenses may be more than old rental expenses. In addition to paying the mortgage, you will have to pay property taxes, insurance, and other expenses not associated with renting.

iii.) These extra costs include maintenance, repairs, supplemental insurance, lawn care, home improvements, and decorating. Also you may be looking at additional utility bills, (water, electricity, gas, garbage, cable and possibly neighborhood association fees) because these are costs that landlords pay, and you are now the landlord.

iv.) If you ever decide to move, you may have to sell your home in order to do so. This may mean the added expense of hiring a real estate agent to sell the property for you.

v.) Although property values do not normally decline, the possibility does exist that any property can decline depending on market forces. Also, if your property is not maintained as well as your neighbors' homes, this can cause your home to lose value.

vi.) You could get in danger of losing your home if you fall behind on your payments. If you need some assistance after trying to talk with your lender, contact a housing counseling agency through the local

	Buying	**Renting**
Pros	Property usually builds equity over time	Little or no responsibility for maintenance
	Sense of community, stability and security	Easier to move
	Free to change the decor and landscaping	No closing costs and other home buying fees
	Part of the mortgage interest and real estate taxes are tax-deductible	
Cons	Responsible for maintenance	Large non-refundable deposit
	Responsible for property taxes	No tax benefits
	Possibility of foreclosure and loss of equity	No equity builds up, no matter how long you stay
	Less mobility than renting	No control over rent increases
		Possibility of Eviction

office of the Department of Housing and Urban Development (HUD) or the housing authority in your state or county.

Note: As this book was in final preparations for publication, 40 states had launched investigations into the banks in their states and potential foreclosure fraud.

Annual Helpful Tips to Keep Your Home Beautiful

January

Make a list of projects you plan to complete during the year. Include small but important chores so you won't overlook them and big projects so you can budget ahead.

Check toilets for leaks. Add a drop or two of food coloring to water tanks at bedtime; if the water in the bowl is colored in the morning, replace the flapper ball.

Post important emergency info: Location of main gas valve, for instance, or contact numbers for heating and cooling service.

If you're planning a bath or kitchen remodeling project, visit the National Kitchen and Bath Association at www.nkba.org.

February

Organize garage or shed; clean, sharpen and lubricate yard tools.

Properly dispose of old paint. Add waste paint hardener, available at hardware stores and home centers, to partial cans of latex paint. Cat litter works, too. Information: www.wipeoutwaste.com.

Clean lint from dryer exhaust ducts and vents.

Early spring is a good time for interior painting. Visit www.glidden.com, www.benjaminmoore.com, or www.sherwinwilliams.com.

March

Repair window screens and check screening on porches before bug season arrives. Save old screening for future patches.

Build or repair fences and arbors, so they'll be ready for planting season.

Repair deck boards as needed; remove protruding nails and replace with coated or galvanized screws. Be sure to check and tighten bolts in deck supports.

Clean and seal wood deck as necessary. Deck stains with some pigment last longer than clear sealers; information: www.cabotstain.com, www.flood.com, www.olympic.com.

Check the operation of your garage door opener. Consult owner's manual.

Add a garage door keypad outside for convenience — but be sure to keep it out of reach of young children. Consider a surge protector for your electric garage door opener.

Move firewood at least 30 feet away from house; pull wood mulch away from foundation.

Check foundation for cracks caused by drought; if large cracks develop, call an engineer to check for settling.

April

Reverse ceiling fans — they should have been blowing upward during the winter — and clean tops of fan blades.

Check to be sure winter wind hasn't lifted vinyl and aluminum siding, and repair as needed.

Wash black streaks from roof. Use prepared cleaner (www.shingleshield.com), or mix your own: Combine one part chlorine bleach with three parts water and a handful of trisodium phosphate. Apply to small section of roof with garden sprayer, let soak 20 minutes, rinse with hose.

Wash siding and gutters with similar solution. You'll have fewer streaks if you start at the bottom. Always be careful with ladders around power lines!

Scrape and touch up exterior paint, paying special attention to window sills, gable vents, garage doors.

May

Complete larger exterior painting jobs. Follow the shade — don't paint in direct sun — and quit before dusk so the paint can dry before dew forms. Cheap paint isn't a bargain. For most exterior jobs, look for 100 % acrylic, and buy at least the "better" quality.

Clean gas grill and replace any rusted or damaged parts.

Check crawl space for moisture and remove debris. If you spot signs of termites, call a pro. For information on termites, visit www.agr.state.nc.us/str-pest.

Clean concrete drives, walkways and patios, and repair as needed. Information: www.bonsal.com or www.quikrete.com.

June

Prepare an emergency kit for hurricane and lightning storm season. Information: www.homesafetycouncil.org.

Vacuum coils behind refrigerators and freezers to ensure proper operation. (Don't forget appliances in basement or garage.)

Check supply hoses to washing machines. If hoses are soft or cracked, replace them. (They seem to break when you're away on vacation.)

Remove toe panel from front of dishwasher and check for leaks under the appliance.

Test GFCI circuit breakers, especially those that supply power to freezers in garages.

July

Be sure air conditioner condensation drip tubes are flowing freely. If they're clogged, clear with wet/dry vacuum. To prevent mold in pipes, add a little chlorine bleach.

Trim shrubs away from heat pump compressor, and trim those blocking crawl space ventilation.

Cut back tree limbs that are touching roof. Be careful around power lines!

Flush water heater as needed. Be sure to turn off power to water heater before draining, and refill before restoring power.

Open and close cutoff valves to sinks and toilets. You don't want to discover during a plumbing emergency that valves are stuck.

August

Call heating service to schedule fall heating system checkup; call propane company to fill tanks.

If you smell a musty odor during peak air conditioning season, check ducts for leaks. Repair leaks with mastic — not duct tape.

Add programmable thermostat if you don't have one. Information: www.energystar.gov.

Replace light bulbs with compact fluorescents. Information: www.gelighting.com, www.sylvania.com.

Check operation of door and window locks, and replace as needed before you go on vacation.

For vacation security, add motion sensor controls to exterior lighting.

September

Test smoke and carbon monoxide alarms, and replace batteries. Information: www.kidde.com and www.firstalert.com.

Caulk around windows and doors. If you're going to paint, choose a caulk that's paintable. Pay special attention to places where dissimilar materials such as brick and wood meet. Information: www.dap.com.

Be sure weep holes in storm windows are open to allow water to escape.

Add weather stripping around pull-down stairs and attic access holes; insulate backs of panels.

Vacuum gas logs, and be sure they're properly seated before operating.

October

Add new sweeps to the bottoms of exterior doors as needed to block cold air. Use a candle to determine whether drafts are getting through gaps around doors and windows.

Reverse those ceiling fans again. They should blow upward in winter, to push warm air across ceiling and down walls.

Clean gutters. Use hose to be sure downspouts are flowing freely; they can get clogged at bends.

Install gutter covers to cut work next year.

If your water heater is warm to touch, and in an unheated garage or utility room, wrap it with insulating blanket. Be sure wrap doesn't interfere with pressure relief valve.

Check depth of attic insulation, and make sure loose insulation isn't blocking soffit vents. For insulation guidelines, visit www.eere.energy.gov.

November

Check roof from ground with binoculars. Replace or repair any curled or missing shingles. (If you find some that match, buy a few extra for next time.) Information: www.certainteed.com, www.gaf.com, www.owenscorning.com.

Be sure well cover is tightly sealed to prevent pipes from freezing.

Drain and winterize irrigation system; the backflow preventer is most vulnerable.

Seal holes in foundation, especially spots around pipes and wires where rodents might enter.

If you're considering a home generator for emergency power, visit www.briggspowerproducts.com, www.kohlerpower.com or www.colemanpowermate.com.

December

Create a fire escape plan for family and practice it. Be sure fire extinguishers are properly filled. Information: www.usfa.fema.gov.

Get rid of old medicines, and make sure household chemicals are out of reach of children. Post poison hotline number near phone. The national hotline is 1-800-222-1222, which connects callers to local centers.

Make sure everyone knows location of main water shutoff and that you keep access clear. Show neighbor where to find shutoff too.

Clean grit and mineral buildup from shower heads and faucet aerators.

Check holiday drop cords for wear and tear, and replace as needed.

Where to go to find some help:

Hiring a contractor: www.nahb.org | www.RemodelToday.com

Whole-house surge protection: www.askthebuilder.com | www.thisoldhouse.com

Garage organizing: www.closetmaid.com | www.gladiatorgw.com | www.hyloft.com | www.rubbermaid.com

Chimney inspections: www.csia.org | www.ncsg.org

Granite and stone care: www.stonecare.com

GFCI (ground fault circuit interrupter):www.ul.com/consumers/groundfault.html

Power washers: www.briggsandstratton.com

How-to libraries: www.lowes.com | www.homedepot.com

Note: Annual Helpful Tips to Keep Your Home Beautiful provided by Real Estate Agent M. Newton, January 2008.

Chapter Ten

So You Wanna Ride?

Although most people do some homework before going shopping for a new car, something happens when they step onto the showroom floor. There is something about all those shiny new cars and that sales person whispering in your ear that makes most individuals throw all caution to the wind and renege on their own research.

Experience is the best teacher; and, I know those feelings firsthand. I have experienced those exact feelings a few times before, when I first got into the car buying market. And despite all of my knowledge (including my budget), when I saw all the cars that I could not afford as compared to those I could afford, I completely forgot about my research and focused on the shiny vehicles in the first group.

Like many of you, I sat there for several hours until their numbers matched my numbers (until the dealership found a bank that would take my bad credit, and I generally did not have a down payment), even when I knew the numbers would be bad for me in the end (very large monthly payments).

But at that moment, I did not care, I was glued to that seat, my mind telling me to leave, but my body refusing to go.

I was hooked!

Yet, when my feet finally did touch the ground, generally around the time the second or third payment came due, they landed with a thud of unmitigated disbelief!

Then the reality of the situation sank

How do you know if you are car-poor... quite simply, if you are cruising around town on a Friday night, trying to be seen, it is not because you are cool...it is because you do not have the money to do anything else except ride in your new car... Then you are car-poor!

in, and all of a sudden that shiny new vehicle had become an anvil tied around the ankles of a drowning man (me).

And that same joy that swept me off my feet hand long since faded.

So, the first thing I recommend for anyone that is remotely thinking about purchasing a new car is to visit several new car lots, and not just any new car lot but the high end car lots that you clearly know are your desire but not your budget.

When you go on these visits, it is very important that you do not carry any cash, credit cards, checks, or any of your preliminary new car research.

Instead, just go to the car lots and sit in as many new cars as you possibly can. And do this repeatedly until you have gotten beyond the shiny new car looks and smells.

There is only one caveat. Do not give anyone attached with the dealership your information, i.e., your driver's license or its number, permission to run a credit check, or sign any documents under any circumstances, period!

Your second task, and maybe your most important task while making these visits, is to be prepared against the subtleties of the sales people, and keep your guard up so that their seemingly small talk does not become your undoing.

If you are not prepared to push back against these persistent individuals, then do not go! A second option would be to take a budget conscience member of your inner circle with you, someone who does not mind embarrassing you, if need be, to make sure you do not get into any financial trouble with commitments you clearly cannot afford.

It is absolutely imperative that you keep your wits about you in these situations; otherwise, you are doomed to give into the new, shiny car smell and effect, and the gnat-like whispering in your ear.

Why is all this important?

These lessons will teach you three things: to know the value of your money; to be persistent in your negotiations; and, most importantly, they will help you build confidence in your ability to control your own financial destiny and your pocketbook.

Whether you have already taken my advice or not, if you are ready to purchase a new car then here are some easy steps to ensure you get the best deal for your money.

Step 1: Off to budget you go

The first and foremost thing you need to do is figure out if a new or a new, used car fits your budget.

While I do know a few individuals who can and have purchased a brand new car outright, and a few more who are so disciplined that they saved every single penny for a new car in less than four years, most people are not going to approach car buying like those individuals.

Therefore, it is off to budget work you must go.

At this point in the book, you should be fairly comfortable with a budget and paying your bills.

You can either refer back to Chapter 7 where we discussed budgeting in detail, or you can go online and find both a budget calculator and a car budget calculator.

The first two will help you tally up all of your obligations so that you will know if this new car fits into your budget.

The third one, the car budget calculator, is the one you should actually use first because it will help you tally up all the costs of owning a new car from gas and oil, to insurance and maintenance, to payments and repairs, to taxes, tags, and registration fees.

Once you have figured out the total cost of your new car by using the budget calculator, then you can see if the total costs of a new car fit into your overall household budget.

Many people fail the budgeting process because they only include the car payment in their new home budgets and have no way of making up the cash outlays required for all the other things that come with owning a new car.

So, after you have subtracted all of your current expenses from your income, the remainder is your disposable income.

Now subtract all of your new car expenses from your disposable income. If you have anything other than a positive number left over after subtracting all of your new car expenses, that is a positive number which is within your comfort level, then you cannot yet afford a new car.

There is one exception to the budget rule.

If you are currently making a car payment, and you can upgrade to a new car with the same or slightly higher payment (meaning ≤ $50 payment increase) and do so without being upside down in your old car, then you can afford a new car.

Being upside down means that you owe more money on your current car than the car is worth, which happens more often than it should because of those things discussed at the beginning of the chapter.

While you are adding up all the costs of your new car, make sure you know your true car or truck needs...Consider your primary use for your new vehicle, your job, and your recreation needs...Most of all make sure you do not purchase a vehicle only to find out later you are still not happy because, for example, your new car does not have towing capabilities or extra storage.

Finally, you must be able to do this without extending your new payments by more than 12 months and keeping your additional car expenses flat (at or beneath your current level of car expenses).

If you can do all the above, then you can afford a new car.

Here are a few quick ways to help estimate some of your new car expenses.

When estimating your mileage, estimate your monthly mileage, and estimate it on the high side. Then multiply that mileage by the price of gas in your area. This gives you your new gas cost per month.

Call your insurance carrier to get a quote for your new car, remembering that if you purchase a sports car, your insurance is going to skyrocket. And if you just happen to be young, it is going into outer space.

Now you need to get an estimate on yearly maintenance and repairs. Remember: if you buy expensive features like tires, tinted windows, sunroofs, and the like, they will cost even more when the time comes to replace them.

Although your first year of owning a new car should come with very few expenses, you should still continue to regularly put money aside for your expenses because they will eventually come.

Now if you are purchasing a used car, make sure the seller has service records to support the asking price, and to document the car's maintenance and upkeep. Having no maintenance records should translate into a lower selling price when it comes time to negotiate your price, because you will have no history on which to judge the car's performance; and, you may have to sink large sums of cash into the car unexpectedly.

Used car means just that – used! The question is how much use has the car had? If there are no records, then you would be better off to assume greatly used.

Whether new or used, once your warranty runs out on your new car, do not go back to the dealership for repairs. There are a number of reputable mechanics and non-dealership repair shops that can and will give you the same quality repair work on your car, including regular oil changes, at half the cost of any dealership.

This is not a hard and fast rule, there is certainly some wriggle room here, so call around and get some price quotes on repairs. Also, reputation and work guarantees may be reason enough to pay a slightly higher price for some repairs.

Try to find one trustworthy (relatively) mechanic or shop to do all of your repairs.

Finally, there are annual registration fees to consider so check with your state's department of motor vehicles.

Once you subtract all of these individual costs from your disposable income, you should have a clear idea whether or not you can afford a new car.

Step 2: To set a price

Now, the final calculation required of all your work is to translate your monthly car payment into a car price.

After completing your budget, and tallying up all the costs of owning your new car, now we are going to look at the car payment only.

If you determined that you could afford to pay $350 a month for a car payment, and maintain that same payment for 4 years, then you can afford $16,800 as the sticker price of your new car ($350 X 12 months X 4 years). Hold on, we are not finished yet. This amount does not include the interest – the cost of borrowing the bank's money to pay for your new car, taxes, and other fees associated with a new car purchase.

Since only you know your drop-dead price for a new car, when you go to the dealer you need to go prepared to negotiate downward from your drop-dead price. And remember to never give away your trump card, your drop-dead price, (this is called a poker face).

Any downward pressure you can put on your price is going to save you money in your financing, your monthly payment, and your total budget.

This is where a car calculator, found on the internet, can really help you, because it will help you to see what kind of car you can truly afford, at different interest rates, based on your predetermined monthly payment. Cars.com has one of the best calculators I have found.

For example: If you know you can afford a maximum of $350 for your monthly car payment, with no down payment, no trade-in, 8.5% taxes, and 6.26% interest rate for 36 months, then the calculator would show you that the maximum price of a new car based on these variables would be $10, 561. If you have a down payment and/or a trade-in, you may be able to afford a higher priced car without exceeding your $350 maximum monthly payment. The calculator will help you figure out which set of options work best for you.

While you are doing your research, before you physically walk into any dealership(s), it would be an even bigger victory if you could find out the actual dealer price of the vehicle of your interest, which is the best starting point for any and all negotiations.

You have a few options on how to get this number.

1) Competitors, same or different type care dealers, may be able to help you because they are all competing for your money.

2) Check the manufacturers' websites to check out their new and used car prices and the cost of available options for each type of car.

3) Find some local dealers and request quotes or request to see the Manufacturer's Suggested Retail Price (MSRP).

By the time you finish all of your research, you should be able to walk into any dealership, knowing the kind of car you want, the options you need (air conditioning, automatic windows, tinted windows, etc.), the price of the car, the price of any additional options, and various interest rate qualifications.

Although you are armed with a great deal of knowledge, your negotiations may be greatly enhanced by the time of day, time of the month, and the time of the year you go shopping for your new car.

Shopping for a new car on a rainy day can be a smart move but do not underestimate your counterpart, the sales person (team). They are probably thinking that if you are the only person shopping for a new car on a rainy day that you are pretty desperate, and therefore, they are going to get a high price.

However, since you are already prepared for that strategy, take your time and wait them out. You may learn to like rainy days.

If at first you do not succeed, try, try again, maybe with a different approach. But, remember you always have the option to walk away from any negotiations any time you like. And no dealer likes to see a paying customer walk away, so that might be all the motivation the dealership needs to negotiate with you.

If you are one of those last minute shoppers, you can try to pop into a dealership 15 minutes before closing, again be prepared to walk away if the negotiations are not going in your favor. Do not be backed into a corner by the staff shutting down operations for the night, locking doors, and putting up the closed sign, for example. They will be open again tomorrow, and may be more inclined to negotiate.

Car shopping on a Monday or Tuesday morning will catch the entire dealership off guard because the truth is most people car shop on the weekends, or close to it. However, if you go at the beginning of the week you may find a staff that is much more amenable because they have not had time to prepare a defensive plan against your offense, and if they give away "too much" they have the rest of the week or may be the rest of the month to make up the ground.

End of the month car shopping might be one of the best, well-known strategies for buying a new car yet. The dealers' needs are probably greater than your needs at this point, so they are already extremely motivated. If they are a few cars short on their quota, then they can make this up by discounting the car to you and make up the difference in their bonus – but they need to meet their quota, and that is the only thing that is of any concern to you.

Buying a new car during major holidays can be a plus and a minus. Dealers generally cut inventory during these periods, but a savvy buyer may still make a good deal. However, the last two weeks of December may give the buyer an added advantage.

There are a few other times that may be most advantageous to buy a car:

- End of January to lower inventory and not pay taxes
- End of model year when new cars arrive, June/July or August/September
- If still unsure, July through October is a good time to make a final decision and make a purchase
- End of a car's design cycle because the manufacturer is introducing a whole new design

So now that you know how much car you can truly afford and the best time to go shopping, there are only a few loose ends to tie up.

Step 3: Out with the old

Now, the time has come to decide if you want a new car or a used car, and there are benefits and drawbacks in either decision.

The biggest drawback for a new car is that the moment you drive it off the lot, it immediately depreciates.

If you decide to buy a used car, the biggest drawback is that you are going to be the one who has to find the truth about the car, i.e., leg work, because no one is either going to tell you the whole truth or the car's maintenance records will not be fully intact for you to know the truth.

If you are going to purchase a used car there are two things I would buy once you have a model in mind. I would buy one of the following guides:

- N.A.D.A. Official Used Car Guide
- Kelley Blue Book Used Car Guide: Consumer Edition
- Consumer Reports Used Car Buying Guide
- Edmunds.com Used Cars and Trucks Buyer's Guide

These guides may also be found in the reference collections of the larger libraries across the country, depending on where you live.

Remember the prices listed in these guides make some specific assumptions about the used cars in order to determine a price, such as:

- these cars have been driven an average of 12,000 miles per year, so they have very low mileage; and,
- these cars are considered to be in mint condition both inside, outside, and with a clean engine.

Now, if you have narrowed your used car purchase down to a specific vehicle, order a complete car history of that specific vehicle at www.carfax.com. You will need the car's VIN number to order this report, which is the equivalent of your Social Security Number.

This Carfax report will tell you some of the following, and quite possibly more:

- the number of previous owners.
- whether the car has been salvaged, stolen, or recalled.
- if the car was ever involved in an accident.
- if the car has had any previous mechanical problems.
- the maintenance history of the car.

The Carfax report will also help you determine if the mileage on the odometer is correct or if someone has made an attempt to roll back, change or falsify the car's true mileage and thus increase the car's value.

But one of the largest benefits of buying a used car is that you can often get a great deal; and, in some cases your used car may be relatively new, if you purchase from an individual owner.

Just remember, when you are buying a used car you need to know the seller as well as you know the car because most car buying horror stories come from used car buyers.

By now, we all know there are a tremendous number of resources available to help anyone find a new or used car. The internet, used car dealerships, and even new car dealerships may sell used cars.

Most important of all, regardless of your used car source, never sign an *"As Is"* contract, regardless of the hard sell that comes with the contract. Why not?

Once you take that car off the lot, any problems you find are yours and yours alone.

You should negotiate a minimum of 30 days to have the car checked by a qualified mechanic of your choice after you take possession to ensure the car has no major defects.

However, since car dealers have many ways of trying to cheat you out your money, make sure that an "As Is" contract has not been purposely mixed in with other documents for you to sign without your foreknowledge.

Step 4: Financing your wheels

Now that you have figured out all of the details about your new car purchase, and exactly how much you can afford, there is only one final thing you need to do before you go into that dealership.

You need to decide how you are going to make up the difference between your down payment and the balance.

When you go to sign a financing contract for the remainder of your car balance, remember your credit is going to be the first thing looked at by your lender (Chapter 7), and, depending on your credit report you may or may not need a down payment, or you may need a larger down payment than planned.

If there is any doubt in your mind about any of these important details, go look at Chapter 7 again.

Beyond your credit, your loan is going to be structured to include interest payments and maybe late payment fees.

If you are a first time car buyer, have excellent credit, or can get financing under another program (college loans for students with good grades), you may want to consider going through the dealership's finance department.

However, if you are going into any dealership based on commercials advertising those low Annual Percentage Rates (APR), remember those are teaser rates for the general public but in actuality are advertised by dealers and automakers for their best customers only.

Although this information is only in the fine print, you do not know those low APRs are simply enticements to get you in the door.

So, if you do decide to go into the finance office, consider these options while you are in there.

Financing is negotiable, so negotiate.

- Make sure you negotiate on the total car price, not your monthly payment (i.e., low monthly payments can turn into long contracts that cost you more money).
- Read, read, read the contract carefully. Make sure that you understand the conditions before signing. Do not let anyone rush you through any part of those contracts.

Finally, if you currently own a car that you have to dispose of, do not use it as a trade-in!

The dealer is going to give you next to nothing for any used car that is not good enough for their used-car lot. All other trade-ins are considered auctioneers, meaning they are going straight to the auction block for the highest bidder.

Even though you cherished this car probably more out of necessity than like, it is going to sell at an extremely cheap price at the auction where an even lower car dealer is going to snatch it up, then raise the price, and make a good profit that could have been yours if you had sold the car yourself.

Whether this is your first time or the tenth time buying a car, the sales person is going to try and sell you an extended warranty, and every other non-essential that will do little, if any, to add value to your vehicle.

These warranties are generally very expensive and not worth their cost in the long run, but if you think you need it, think about it carefully (i.e., make sure you understand every nuance of the contract and how it works for and against you, more so the latter than the former).

However, if you believe that you were sold a bad car or as commonly known, a "lemon," you do have some remedies under the law.

All 50 states have some sort of lemon law on the books that specifically pertain to new car purchases and in some cases used car purchases as well. In one way or another, these laws allow individuals to take action against any dealer for selling a lemon.

If you believe this applies to you, http://auto.howstuffworks.com, and then search for lemon law. You can also go to http://www.lemonlaw.bbb.org/ for additional resources. Finally, if all else fails, check with your state's Attorney

General's office.

True Alternative Financing

There is an alternative financing option that may be worth considering before you go into the finance manager's office.

As an alternative to traditional financing techniques, there are now peer-to-peer or person-to-person (P2P) lending options that is taking the bank out of the lending process, and it is all happening over the internet.

As banks continue to tighten lending standards, numerous consumers have been compelled to look for new lending sources.

As with any new program, P2P has its skeptics and critics, but none of those individuals matter if you can find a P2P lender that you can trust to meet your financial needs at a reasonable cost.

One such site is www.prosper.com, which is supposed to combine financial industry ambitions with the socialization of the internet to help achieve unrealized goals, and to do this on a more personalized individual basis.

Other such sites are us.zopa.com, www.loan-back.com, www.virginmoneyus.com, and www.fynanz.com.

These sites are designed to provide loans to good borrowers who have been purposefully hindered by traditional financial lending paths.

Again, the pioneer and dominate site is Prosper.com, which was launched in February 2006.

Prosper.com is a privately held company based in San Francisco and has roughly 50 employees.

Like other P2P lenders, Prosper.com makes its money by charging its borrowers closing fees on their loans and by charging its lenders annual servicing fees to continue lending through their website.

Here is how the loan process works.

Individual borrowers create a profile along with their photos, a detailed explanation of the purpose of their loan, and, most importantly, their financial information, income, and debt-to-income ratio.

What is truly unique about P2P lending compared to traditional lenders is that the borrower has the opportunity to tell the lender the interest rate they are willing to pay – instead of the other way around when the borrower has an interest rate dictated to them by the lender.

Based on all the application information, the P2P will assign the borrower a credit grade. At Prosper.com the credit grade is 1 of 7 grades that range from AA to HR (High Risk).

Once the application processing is complete, then lenders bid on the opportunity to fund a loan. For example, a $500 loan can have as many as 20 lenders putting up $25 each.

The maximum amount an individual can borrow from Prosper.com is $25,000. In most states, these loans can be used for business or consumer loans. However, business loans are unregulated and carry no interest rate cap.

Prosper.com requires all loans to be repaid within three years, and the monthly payments are automatically withdrawn from the borrower's bank account.

Now for those individuals that are not yet ready to step out of their traditional financial boxes, there is only one other decision you need to make about financing your vehicle.

To Lease an Alternative

If you are considering a new vehicle and you like driving a new vehicle every few years, especially if you drive a luxury vehicle, then leasing could be another option for you.

Leasing has some specific advantages, and the two biggest are a low monthly payment, and at the end of the lease, you turn the car in and get you a new car.

However, there are some other leasing considerations that need to be carefully considered.

Although leasing a vehicle means lower payments, which helps make driving expensive cars more affordable, there are some other charges you will have to pay during the term of the lease that cost more than one may anticipate.

During the lease period, you will also be paying for the vehicle's expected depreciation, plus interest, taxes, and other fees. If you terminate your lease early, you will also have to pay for any pay-off amounts, and you will pay for excess miles driven above the annual lease contract limit regardless of whether you terminate your lease early or at the normal lease end.

When leasing a vehicle, also consider:

- The agreed-upon value of the vehicle—a lower value can reduce your monthly payment;
- Any up-front payments (acquisition fees);
- The length of the lease;
- Any end-of-lease fees and charges (disposition fees);
- Interest rate and the capitalized cost (the price the financial institution pays the dealer for the leased vehicle);
- The cost of any excess mileage and excess wear and tear;
- The option to purchase either at lease end or earlier;
- Whether your lease includes "gap" protection, which protects you and the lessor if the vehicle is stolen or totaled in an accident; and,
- If your lease qualifies you to take advantage of any warranties, recalls, or other services that apply to the vehicle.

Again, it is important to remember that all aspects of a vehicle leasing contract are negotiable.

The Federal Consumer Leasing Act and some state laws may provide you with additional consumer rights that may not be covered in your lease agreement. For information on these laws, contact your state's consumer protection agency or Attorney General's office.

One of the best things you can do for yourself is learn as much about the dealership where you are thinking of purchasing your car as possible so you can deconstruct their scams before you walk through the door.

While I am not suggesting that all dealers are out to dupe you, better to be prepared than pay anymore than necessary for your new vehicle.

However, you should know that car dealers generally profit in a triangle from the bottom up. The further you go up the triangle, the more the dealership makes.

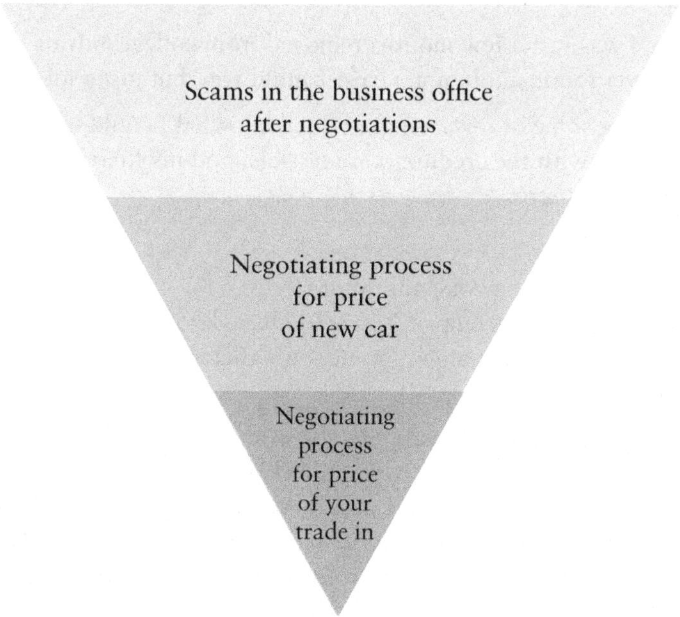

Step 5: Seal the deal

Car buying and car dealerships are in the business to make money, and of course they deserve to make a reasonable profit every time they sell a car.

However, your job, as the buyer, is to make sure you get the best product possible for your money, and you should because this one-time purchase is going to be a long-term investment.

Since an auto loan is the second largest consumer loan most Americans carry, doing your homework will help make this a sweet decision for years to come, or it could turn sour very quickly.

Unfortunately, too many individuals do not take car loans seriously. But today's lenders are savvy and swift to action when there is a problem with one of their loans.

So, let me emphatically state that if you have to struggle to make new car expenses fit into your budget, then you are not ready for that new car. And, if you go ahead and decide to make that purchase despite sound advice, then be prepared for the potential consequences.

The worst of these could be having your car repossessed, an experience I learned firsthand approximately 11 years ago.

At the time, I was just a few months removed from college (advanced degree), and had not yet found a job, not a career mind you, but just a job.

So, I was taking some of my savings and paying what I could here and there. My negotiations with the creditor were terrible, and my financial literacy at that time was near zero.

Then it happened!

One Sunday morning, I awoke and went to get in my car, and was stunned that my parking spot was empty. You could have knocked me over with a feather. It was the perfect comedy scene, only this was not a script. It was real life, my life!

By law, these individuals (the repo man or woman) may bypass or pick the car locks, or they may already have regular keys. While they are not allowed to break into a locked garage, they may come onto the car owner's property (driveway, carport, etc.), and can do so at any time, day or night. The only really restricted behavior by repossessors is that they may not "breach the peace."

So, the repossessor did not break the law in my case, but if had I been thinking and had more financial knowledge, my car would have been locked inside a garage, or I would have sold the car and paid off the creditor.

Worse, was the fact that I was in the process of helping a friend move, and half of all his personal effects (expensive clothing, shoes, and personal mementos) were in the trunk of my repossessed car.

I never did get the car back because the lender and I could never agree on the remaining loan balance for the car, and I also had to fight off a lawsuit for the deficiency balance, which is the difference between the amount of money the repossessed vehicle was sold for at auction and what is owed on the loan.

Now if you are currently under the threat of repossession here are some specific steps you need to take to move beyond the threat.

1. You need to find all of your original loan documents, payment receipts, and notices. This information will help you do several things. First, it will verify the exact amount of money that is owed on the vehicle. Second, it will tell you what your legal rights are. Third, it will tell you the steps the lender intends to take to recover either the car or the past due payments.

2. You also need to calculate how much money you are behind on the

loan. Sit down and figure out a reasonable way to catch the loan up within 30 days. One of the best ways is to do postdated checks over the phone with the lender.

3. You should call the lender and confirm your total loan value and the amount of money you are behind in your loan payments. Present your plan to bring the account current within 30 days.

4. If your plan is accepted, you have nothing left to do but make sure money is in the bank to pay the checks when they are presented to the bank for payment.

5. If your plan is rejected and if the lender is still giving you some time, call for an appointment with Consumer Credit Counseling to help see if they can get you through this situation.

6. Now, depending on how dire the situation is and your families' needs, you may also want to consider getting a hardship withdrawal from your 401K plan at your place of employment, if losing the vehicle is going to be a harder reality than the lost earnings on your 401K. But remember: this should only be used as a method of last resort! Make sure you understand the ramifications of this loan in a worst case scenario for tax purposes, like if you lose your job.

7. If you have access to a home equity line of credit, it may be a good idea to pay the entire loan balance off for the car, which may actually save you money if you have a low interest rate on your home equity line of credit.

8. Do not let anyone talk you into a voluntary repossession until you have consulted with a reputable non-profit credit-counselor or your legal representative.

As you are preparing to make your final choices, do not let the dealer increase your cost by charging you more money to get your car from another dealer or by charging you more to order your car from the factory.

Also make sure your dealer knows you are aware of his competitor's prices and are willing to go to his competitor if you cannot reach a reasonable deal. Pay attention to little details such as making sure your car has a pricing invoice sticker or a MSRP. It is illegal not to have one or the other on each car.

Most of all, do not give anyone your driver's license or SSN until you are ready to sign your purchase or loan documents.

Now, if all of this still makes you nervous, there is an easier way to purchase a new car. While you still have to do your homework to make sure you can afford a new car, there is a simpler way to get the best possible price.

Consumer Reports offers a new car price report that contains a detailed pricing list of all factory-installed options, equipment recommendations, unpublished dealer incentives, and much more.

For the low price of $14 per new car report and $12 for each report thereafter, you can find out what the dealer's invoice price (dealer's cost) was, and the true trade-in value of your actual trade-in.

Go to www.consumerreports.com or call 1-800-693-9582.

Bonus Material

While everyone needs an outside lending source at some point in their financial lives, most do not know that financial institutions maintain a complex and primarily secret scoring system that they use to raise their profits and limit their losses.

At this point, it has been beaten into all of our heads that our credit score is a vital number that is checked often by our creditors; truth be known credit scores are not the most used score among financial institutions.

Every time you make a financial transaction that transaction generates some kind of score. All consumers are judged by the types of transactions they make, how they pay their bills, and more.

So let me give you a rundown of 9 of the most popularly secretive scores kept by lenders:

1. **Credit-risk score.** This is the traditional FICO credit score that we have all become very knowledgeable about, remembering these scores are designed to predict the probability that an individual will miss a payment in the next two years.

2. **Behavior score.** This score provides a snapshot of how an individual consumer is managing their credit accounts. These scores are singularly-focused in that they are used by creditors to look at the account you hold with that particular creditor. From a broader point view, the lender looks at whether or not the user only pays the minimum amount due each month or carries a large balance each month; this information may be

used to decide if, for example, a past due payment is an anomaly or a sign of a deeper problem brewing. This is a score that is used to help collector's call customers in advance of customer payments becoming past due.

3. **Application score.** This score includes your current employer information, how long have you worked for that employer, how long have you lived at your current address, and your current income level, all data taken from your applications not included in your credit-risk score. This information helps a lender to decide whether or not to open a new account, the new credit limit, and the new credit rating.

4. **Response score.** This score is exactly as its name implies. It rates the likelihood that an individual will respond to a specific offer. This score is primarily used by credit card companies to decide whom to target and how to customize such offers as a balance transfer to appeal to a particular group of consumers.

5. **Bankruptcy score.** Again, this score is as its name implies. Equifax is the producer of the leading bankruptcy score, the Bankruptcy Navigator Index (BNI). This score predicts the probability that an individual will file for Chapter 13 repayment plan or a Chapter 7 liquidation in response to their total debt load. Equifax's BNI ranges from 1 to 300, and the higher the score, the lower the calculated risk.

6. **Revenue score.** This is the score each lender assigns to every account to determine how much profit each account is likely to generate; the lender does this to maximize their overall profitability.

7. **Attrition-risk score.** This score measures the possible risk a consumer will stop using a particular card. If your revenue score is low and your account is already not profitable, than the card issuer is probably not going to notice your usage stoppage. However, if your account is highly profitable, you may get a huge credit limit increase, a much better interest rate, and that may only be the beginning.

8. **Transaction score.** Every time you use your plastic, there is a score that is run to determine if that transaction should be approved. Mainly, the card issuers are looking to make sure the transaction is not fraudulent.

9. **Collection score.** If your credit card account has been unpaid for so long that it has been turned over to a collection agency, the collection agency will assess the probability of you repaying this debt by calculating

a collection score. These agencies use this score to maximize their minimal resources to collect on these debts by monitoring your credit report and other account data to see if your financial situation is improving.

Now you have a clear picture of how you look to various lenders and how your numbers impact their numbers. But if you improve your credit score, all the other numbers should automatically improve also.

Note: When it comes to automobile maintenance, whether new or old, www.motorwatch.com will give you an idea of what auto repairs should really cost. A yearly membership is about $12.95; however, a one-time membership should give you enough time to search the website and become knowledgeable enough to keep you from being ripped off by any mechanic shop for any future car repairs, which incidentally, will eventually come.

Chapter Eleven

And You Wanna Be Rich?

Circle of One

When I graduated from undergraduate school several years ago, I was heavily recruited by a major New York investment firm to join their broker's training program.

My problem was I could not see the forest for the trees.

You see, when you are fresh out of college, all you hear is that you should make lots of money. Therefore, any job offer that does not have big dollars attached to it normally gets turned down.

Needless to say, that training position came with a minimal salary and a bonus attached at the end of the training.

So I turned down one of the most lucrative opportunities in my life because of my own short-sightedness.

I gave up a lifetime of long-term earnings because the immediate earnings were $0, or so I thought.

Now I have come full circle. The same training I was offered for free 20 years ago, I am forced to teach myself with the same salary – – $0.

If that is not a lesson in investing, I do not know what is!

But, here's the kicker – – I have spent more than $150,000 in formalized education, only to realize the education I really needed would not come from a classroom but from the street (sounds a lot like sex to me, but that's a different book).

Despite the naivety of my early youth, I have never fallen into the mental trap of fear or belief in that classic cliché that opportunity only knocks once.

For me to accept those unwise self-imposed limitations, is to say that the creative abilities given to me by God are not working and cannot work in my life any longer.

That is a premise I absolutely will not accept.

As for me, as long as God has given us the changing seasons and the rising and setting of the sun, there will be opportunities in this world for me and whosoever will – and I am not just speaking of financial opportunities.

If you believe that opportunity only knocks once, then you will either allow fear to make you move when you should not, or the reverse. You will allow fear to scare you into staying when you should go.

One of the saddest examples of a life stolen by the kind of fear I have been describing is that of the reclusive billionaire Howard Hughes.

It is only when you let go of your fear that your opportunities begin to reveal themselves to you. One of my real estate instructors told me that fear and anxiety are debilitating emotions, and they are also interest paid in advance on a debt that one may never owe.

The greatest personal motivation I have ever known for not succumbing to fear has been having a plan, a purpose, a definitive goal to understand where I am going. The Bible calls this a vision.

Plain Vision

I have spent quite a bit of time with a number of different companies that are very good with helping individuals to catch "their" vision.

But a vision alone is not enough, and one of my repeated disappointments with those firms was that they are not nearly as good at helping bring those individual visions into reality as they are at inspiring the vision. So I ended up spending money to find out what I already knew.

There was a huge chasm between the vision and the reality or the fulfillment thereof.

After some years of service and further disappointments, I finally realized that the key to any vision is in its implementation!

Again, I have worked for countless public and private firms and government agencies that spend lots of money (i.e., millions of dollars) every single year to have their business analyzed and a new vision and strategic plan drafted.

It is no wonder that so many businesses fail, both large and small, because they have no true direction. And worse yet, that direction changes every year!

Most businesses are not structured to adapt to those kinds of changes so quickly. Therefore, they flounder about aimlessly until they fail.

One thing I have learned about investing, if you are considering investing in any firm, read their strategic plan, and research their history to see if it is the same strategic plan that they started out with as a new business.

Now, listen very carefully. If the strategic plan has changed, then the question becomes how often has it changed– every year, every two years...

My point is if the strategic plan has changed every year for a sustainable period, say five years, then that company is probably not stable.

My mother used to always tell me to stand for something or I would fall for anything, and I never quite understood what she meant until I was much older – like today.

What my mother was really trying to tell me is that you need to know what you believe in and why you believe it be true. And that truth is only truth if it stands the test of time.

The key to any strategic vision as an individual or as a company is whether or not that vision is easy to implement and whether or not implementation can lead you to your desired goal: in this case, can that vision help you gain wealth.

That said, most people stay away from the stock market because they fear it. And they fear it because they do not understand it.

However, anyone who desires to achieve wealth through understanding the stock market must first know what it is they want from the stock market.

It is not enough to just say I want to be rich.

You need to develop a strategic vision of what it is you want from the stock market or your investments.

For example, do you want to be able to afford to send your kids to any school of their choice? Do you want to start a business? Do you have long-

"...[2]Write the vision, and make it plain upon tables, that he may run that read it.
[3]For the vision is yet for an appointed time, but at the end it shall speak, and not lie: though it tarry, wait for it; because it will surely come, it will not tarry"
..Habakkuk 2:2-3

term health issues and want to make sure you can afford to stay in your home with 24-hour nursing care? Do you want to be able to take a vacation every year?

These are some ideas for creating a strategic vision that can be expanded as you reach your goals.

Now that you have a vision, how are you going to implement that vision, i.e., what steps do you need to take to bring that vision to reality?

The traditional method of implementing a plan involves three basic steps of integration:

1) Integrate plan into all aspects of operations

2) Training employees on new plan

3) Evaluating performance on regular basis

I propose a different way of implementing a plan across any business organization.

After the acceptance of the strategic vision and brainstorming the actual goals of the vision, then implementation becomes easier.

1) List all agreed upon goals

2) Quantify each goal

3) Determine timetable for achieving each goal

4) Use think bubbles to identify as many ways possible of how to achieve each independent goal

5) Periodic measurement of each goal against items 2) and 3)

Now when it comes to investment goals, you need to remember that your ultimate goal is to build long term wealth to achieve your strategic vision, and the best way to do this is to make sure that you have more than one source of income.

If you only have one source of income, be it a job or some other source, if you lose that one source you are in trouble.

Therefore, for long-term success of your financial stability, your goals should have multiple streams of income – several different sources (goals) to reach your strategic vision.

Although all of these steps can be overwhelming, they can be broken down into smaller steps. Each day, you should be doing something toward your goal(s) to move you closer to completion.

The most important point here is to continue doing those little things every day even when it looks like nothing is happening.

Example of One

The closest person I know had this long time dream that for an even longer time he would never tell anyone because...

The dream grew and grew inside of him, and everything he did just pushed him more toward his dream. But there was one problem.

He had no way of bringing this dream to pass.

But despite all the numerous obstacles in his path, he never stopped believing in his dream.

So every day, he would wake up and plug away at his dream a little more each day. And he never stopped talking about his dream or believing in his dream, despite all those around him who could not see his dream.

He kept knocking on doors seeking advice, and he knocked on some of the same doors over and over and over again.

Then one day, he was introduced to a gentleman, and, on his advice, the dream finally began to take shape.

Now if you really want to get rich, the first thing you need to understand is that you will not get there by working for someone else.

1. **Strategic Vision**
2. **Brainstorming**
3. **Goal Development**
4. **Break Each Goal Down into Small Daily Steps**
5. **Do Something Every Day Towards Your Goals**
6. **Enjoy your success**

In order to achieve this kind of wealth, there are some risks involved. No one, almost no one, just wakes up and decides they are going to be worth tens of millions of dollars, and then sets out to do just that.

To be rich, you have to be driven by pure desire. A desire that will definitely lead to sacrifice, and you just might be the one doing the most sacrificing. And it may lead to some heartaches. It will definitely stress some of your relationships.

Now many people have great ideas, but what they do not have is a plan of execution.

Many people say if I only had the money, I would do it. But experts say that is just an excuse to avoid failing.

But this close individual I am talking about did not do that.

Sometimes the shortest distance to a goal is not a straight shot. He began working on the most unlikely project, researching, writing, visiting people, reviewing thousands of documents, and rattling cages, but he won.

You see he had been wronged in the past, and he had the evidence to prove it. The decision was made in his favor and he had the seed money to start building his fortune.

But the important point here is that he was not sitting around waiting for someone to give him money or believe in his idea.

He believed in his own idea, and had the desire to succeed. And now he had the necessary tools to gain the much needed capital.

When he finally won, it was his tenth time presenting his evidence for a decision, but he never stopped believing that he would win!

And win he did, against the back drop of the laughter of his enemies.

So here are a few memorable steps – – taken from some very rich individuals – – to getting rich and staying rich after you build your company, (if that is your investment plan).

> **1) Do not trade shares of your company to anyone for capital. This is a decision that you will have to pay for over and over again. So find a way to maintain ownership. Read Tyler Perry's story.**
>
> **2) Ask friends, family, and maybe even some others you do business with to loan you some money, as long as you are up front with them**

that their investment in your company is a risk, which means they could lose all or some of their investment. You might be surprised how many people are willing to open their hand to you.

3) If you ever need to negotiate, make sure your negotiator is so ruthless that they are willing to walk away if the deal does not go their way. During serious negotiation, you do not want a compromiser. The person that is willing to walk away will always win.

4) Develop another passion other than money, one that can help you give all your money away before you die that will leave the world a better place than when you found it.

Think Like the Wealthy

I started *Funny Money Universe* by talking about the mind, changing your mindset, and thinking like the rich.

After reading, and rereading thousands of stories about the wealthy, it is abundantly clear that to become wealthy, you have to be able and willing to listen and learn before acting.

The wealthy are willing to learn and make themselves available to those who can help them learn how to grow their investments with little effort. And what most wealthy people have learned is that to be a great leader and investor, you have got to be a visionary.

You have got to learn how to get past the day to day activities and learn to see down the road.

So then, let's begin at the beginning. Investing is all about economics, primarily your personal economics and those of the firms you choose to invest in. But, I am getting ahead of myself.

Economics is the study of how the market forces of supply and demand allocate scarce resources. There are two smaller subgroups of economics – – microeconomics and macroeconomics.

Microeconomics studies the behavior of individuals, households, firms, and industries. These groups are considered a "small" part of a much larger, interconnected economy. So the prefix micro means "small" or "defined;" and, when we are talking about microeconomics, we are talking about taking a defined or specific look at a particular part(s) of the overall economy.

If you were sitting in my undergraduate microeconomics class, Dr. Belcher would have told you that we were going to study the theories of demand, of the firm, and of production (the demand for labor and other raw materials needed to produce a product).

In simplified terms, Dr. Belcher was teaching us to understand how prices and demand for a particular product are made in individual markets (such as women's shoes), and how these choices are coordinated across various markets (internet and/or different types of retail stores).

A market is defined as any place where buyers and sellers come together to exchange a product or some type of good. The consumer theory of the market is they are trying to maximize their options within the constraints of limited time and income. The producer theory of the market is they are working to maximize their profits with limited capital.

These decisions are based, in large part, on individual consumer choices, which are driven by economic factors of income, credit availability, and debt.

All of these factors combined comprise the study of microeconomics.

By comparison, macroeconomics is the study of an economy at the aggregate level (looking at the whole economy) instead of microeconomics that looks at individual pieces of an economy. For example, when you hear most newscasters talking about the "U. S. economy," they are really talking about macroeconomics because they are looking at the whole economy. Macroeconomics can also be used to describe an entire sector of an economy, such as the services sector or exports.

Macroeconomists are primarily interested in government policies and their impacts on such factors as unemployment, inflation, and productivity (industrial), in relation to the overall economy. This brings up one more important consideration about the study of economics – – economic analysis.

Believe it or not, economic analysis, is in part, what drives our division as a republic into Democrats and Republicans. Republicans tend to study economics from a positive analysis. This means they study the relationship of cause and effect. For example, why are African Americans willing to drive approximately three miles to the other side of town to buy a particular product when that same product is offered by a store within their own neighborhood or its perimeter?

Democrats study economics from a normative analysis meaning they like to look at things the way they ought to be, which imposes value judgments on economics (money matters).

The problem is despite either party's viewpoint, the end result is that both parties spend entirely too much money. Democrats tax and spend. Republicans borrow and spend.

Independents ask is there a reasonable medium between the two?

A second growth quality of the wealthy is that they have learned when to buy quality. If you have to keep replacing the same item, then you are not purchasing quality.

Thirdly, do not pay interest on anything that loses value.

There are a lot of millionaires that live on a budget. And these individuals do not pay interest on credit cards, car payments, or similar items.

They learned how to save for those items and pay for modest cars and others items in cash.

Then as their income rose, they gradually increased their purchases to higher priced items, like pricier cars, but this is not a requirement.

Also, there is a difference between being rich and being wealthy.

Wealthy individuals own repeating income-generating properties and ventures. Rich people have a lot of money that they can spend, but, when it is gone, they have no way to replace it; or, their money comes in from one source and, if that source is interrupted, they would have serious financial problems.

Most lottery winners are an example of rich people. The owners of football teams are examples of wealthy individuals. To take it one step further, most professional athletes are rich, but there are few former professional athletes that are wealthy, such as Michael Jordan.

Which brings me to my next point. Find new ways to make more money.

During my many travels, I have seen several households from various cultures do the same thing but with a unique twist.

Several families would move into the same household until they were sometimes busting at the seam. They would pool their resources and make major purchases like the biggest van they could find and maybe a couple of tattered but reliable cars.

Every morning, often before the crack of dawn, they would all leave for work and would still be at work hours after I had returned from work. But the coolest part was that as the house shrank, individual businesses grew.

What I slowly came to realize was these pooled resources would help each individual or group start a business, and then they would start the entire process all over again. When the house was almost empty, it would fill up again with a new group repeating the same process.

Although they did not have many resources, they learned to bundle those small pockets of money into larger resources to accomplish a specific goal, and they did this by working at whatever job they could find. Sometimes they all had more than one job.

But the most fascinating fact about these households was that many of them became financially stable through this frugality. They just were not caught up in lots of material possessions because those things were almost like a distraction.

It is not that they do not have nice things, they just do not need a whole lot of "things" to have a good life.

But these individuals are not frugal in their creativity, in the way they live, and in the way they make their finances grow.

For some of us, the desire to be financially stable has less to do with the distraction(s) of things and more about news headlines. Headlines like: wall street expecting to pay billions in bonuses and benefits; one large company is ready to buy another large company; and, companies pulling profits out of the market, all deter some of us from investing because we wrongly believe that by investing, we are giving those "big wigs" more money to steal or abuse.

But the truth is by not investing, you are only hurting yourself and your family because you may be, unintentionally, impeding your own potential for future financial security. Remember, "you cannot do what you have always done and expect to get a different outcome!"

Tap In

I believe every individual is born with the ability to be creative. But the difference is that some are in environments that encourage innovation, and others are in environments that stifle the same ability.

In order to achieve any kind of wealth, an individual has to be creative and look for multiple solutions to every single problem, and begin to practice creativity in everyday life.

Before you can reach your financial dreams, you have to identify those areas in your life that are negatively influencing your creativity. One of the biggest negative impacts on all creativity is society in general.

For example, we are taught to conform to rules, especially in the world of academia. And as children, we were posed with questions and problems that only had one right answer at the end, instead of being challenged by open-ended questions that had multiple solutions.

Other similar stifling influences include jobs, friends, and, maybe worst of all, our families.

Now while you may not be able to replace or completely remove those influences, there are some things you can start to do to help yourself:

- Shut the world out – stop telling your ideas to people who cannot grab hold of your vision.
- Let go of yesterday – you cannot change your past, accept it for what it was and move on.
- Learn to persevere – when you catch your dream, do not let anyone steal it from you. No matter how difficult it may seem, stand until that dream comes to pass!

Since creativity is really no more than finding new ways to solve old problems, an easy exercise to help foster individual creativity is to think of 10 different ways to solve every problem you face.

I learned this from an old Navy buddy who was killed in a car accident while we were stationed in Puerto Rico in the early 80's.

Now the first 2 or 3 solutions generally come very easily. The next 4 or 5 may take some real effort. By the time you get to the 9th or 10th solution, these may appear so outlandish that they make even you laugh.

However, if you really look closely at the last few solutions, you may actually find that you have a workable blueprint for a bona fide "creative" solution.

When it comes to investing and building wealth, some other creative ideas include pooling money together as an investment club.

If you are a novice who does not want to go it alone, then contact the National Association of Investors Corporation to find out how to start an investment club. The group, based in Michigan, also publishes a Better Investing magazine in addition to software for bookkeeping and stock analysis. All of this is designed specifically for clubs.

Their website is www.betterinvesting.org and the telephone number is 1-877-ASK-NAIC.

One of the most reasonable ways to start an investment club, particularly in the African-American community, is to use fraternities and sororities to build a club within a club. If this idea does not offend a club's bylaws, this is an excellent way to pool resources toward a common goal, something that fraternities and sororities are already very good at doing, in addition to knowing how to use creative ways to solve every day problems or challenges.

To push the envelope a little further, the fraternities and sororities can team up with each other to form some sort of unified investment club, whereby together they increase not only their investing power but their buying power as well – for such things as cars, mortgage loans, groceries, healthcare, mobile phone services, and anything else they desire. The sky is truly the limit!

One more idea is for fraternities and sororities to form group-buying sites. The idea would be that these sites would offer coupons to the finest restaurants in cities across the country, entertainment tickets, hotel discounts, and travel packages, to name a few options. Some examples of such sites are Groupon.com, LivingSocial.com, and dozens of others that are popping up as individuals try to stretch their limited resources. In fact, it is possible for groups to negotiate discounted investment advice for their site members.

Pooling buying power is a very creative way to access conventional services in a non-conventional manner, and to make money for the individual fraternities and sororities. Companies no longer hold all of the negotiating power in transactions.

Now if you have any doubt that creativity has anything to do with building wealth, then let us take a look at some of the investing philosophies of the famous Oracle of Omaha, Warren Buffett.

Admittedly, I have read quite a bit of what has been written about and by Mr. Buffet and his investing philosophy. The tenets I am passing on to you are some I have heard and read about over and over again in my research.

Mr. Buffett is a contrarian, or one that follows his own path. A prime example of this going against the crowd mentality is that when Mr. Buffet finds a company he likes, he invests in them heavily.

However, most money managers do just the opposite. They try to protect against risk by diversifying. And despite Mr. Buffet's unarguable success, I have heard him described as an average investor by a few money managers, who incidentally have not enjoyed half of Mr. Buffett's success.

However, to invest like Mr. Buffett does require a thick skin and a risk taking contrarian personality, despite the fact that Mr. Buffet would probably not characterize himself as a risk-taker.

A frugal investor has the luxury of patience and can think more clearly about when to buy and sell their investments. By comparison, individuals that live overly extravagant lives are rushed into making investments for the sake of trying to maintain their expensive habits. This is not true with a frugal investor.

Therefore, frugality gives the investor the ability to wait until good companies find their stocks trading very cheaply, and thus become a good buy.

In my experience and training, much like in real estate, investors make their money on the front end of most investment transactions. So learning when to buy a stock is key to your long-term success.

If you purchase a stock at a very high price, then it may be hard to sell it at an even higher price to make a profit. And if you purchase a stock at a high price and it goes down before you sell it, you will lose money before you ever have the opportunity to sell it. This means you will have to hold on to the stock for a very long time, or sell it sooner than you may have preferred in order to minimize your losses.

If you are a worrier, an individual that needs to have constant affirmations, or an individual that needs to see your money move up every day, then investing in the stock market is not for you, at least not yet.

This goes back to the beginning of the chapter when we addressed the idea that you must hone your creative abilities to grow your wealth, which will help you as you develop your own investment philosophy as a contrarian.

As I was saying, a frugal investor purchases a stock cheap, and the key is to find a way to determine when a stock is cheap enough to purchase.

Part of this means that you will have to become acquainted with large amounts of statistics and economic data. One of the best ways to accomplish this is to use *The National Data Book,* published by the U. S. Census Bureau. Although the book is published in retrospect, the most current is dated for 2007, it is still a good place to start your acquaintance with aggregate investment numbers. Section 25 is the banking, finance, and insurance section that you may want to study.

More recent economic data can be found online at the Bureau of Economic Analysis and/or the Federal Reserve's "beige book."

The beige book is a compilation of economic activity from the 12 Federal Reserve districts around the country that offers a portrait of the U. S. economy eight times a year. The beige book breaks down the macro – and micro – economics of each district into quantitative data that can be and is used to make short – and long – term investment decisions. The book can be found at www.federalreserve.gov.

You can be assured that any serious investor is well aware of the economic data produced by the Federal government, and how that data impacts the value of both individual stocks and the overall market.

Warren Buffet has spoken several times about the "intrinsic value" of a company. Once you understand the details behind this concept, it is quite easy to apply. However, in order to learn how to do this you should read *The Warren Buffett Way.*

In its simplest form, the intrinsic value of a company can be determined by what its competitors' stocks are selling for, or by calculating all of the cash a company may generate in the future in present day dollars. Not to mention that a stock's value is pressured from both internal and external forces.

For example, bank stocks are currently (October 2010) struggling because of several factors – 1) new government rules for credit cards have cut into their profit margins by cutting bank fees by some estimates as much as $5 billion; 2) the foreclosure fraud investigations by at least 45 states are forcing banks to reexamine their procedures, stop foreclosures, and may force banks to have to pay out huge cash settlements and/or give back some homes; and, 3) in my professional opinion, there are criminal proceedings forth coming for some banks and their employees for their actions leading up to the recession of 2009.

Although there are no short cuts in investment, meaning you must do your homework, you can be a copycat and do as Mr. Buffet does which is to ignore earnings per share and instead focus on return on equity (ROE).

By definition ROE is the amount of profit a company makes with the money invested by shareholders or expressed as a percentage and calculated as:

ROE = Net Income / Shareholder's Equity

So, if you are investing like Mr. Buffett, then you will look at about five primary factors.

1. ROE
2. The company should have solid operating margins.
3. The company should have no debt preferably, or a very reasonable amount of debt.
4. The company should make a lot of cash that is invested well.
5. The company should either pay shareholders good dividends or offer buybacks.

Since Mr. Buffett does not like startup companies, these five characteristics must be measured over a company's five-year history and by the company's performance in both up and down markets.

All these characteristics speak to a company's operating history, and probably the most clearly identifiable of these should be if a company has a sustainable competitive advantage.

A clear competitive advantage is one that keeps competitors from ever entering the market, such as a brand name, a distribution that cannot be easily replicated, high startup costs, or maybe a patent(s) on several high consumer-demand products.

Here are a few other quick McWarren's to consider when investing for the future.

1. Always reinvest your profits.
2. Make quick decisions (do your research beforehand).
3. Set your terms before the work ever starts because your leverage is greatest at the beginning if you have something others want.
4. Pay attention to the small things because small expenditures have a big

negative impact.

5. Probably the most important of all is to stay out of debt and borrow as little as possible.

6. Stay the course with diligence; that is, if you find an investment worth holding on to, be tenacious and do not let go.

7. Finally, imagine the best and the worst of a situation. Then decide if the risk is worth the worst. If not, quit and go in another direction.

Money is mentioned more than 140 times in the King James Version of the Bible, and, the word finances, is mentioned more than 600 times. Clearly, managing money and wealth were important to God from the beginning of time. Silver was first mentioned by Abram in Genesis 13:2.

Therefore, learning how to manage money and build wealth are important Biblical principles that encourage us to learn as much as we can about the subject. (Proverbs 13:22; Proverbs 21:20; Proverbs 22:7)

Two practical reasons for learning how to manage money revolve around statistics that show that more than 70% of U. S. households live paycheck to paycheck, and the average American family would have to find some sort of financial assistance to help pay for an unexpected expense of $1,000 or more.

Hopefully, the importance and benefits of budgeting and debt management is becoming increasingly clear. That budget needs to include 10%, weekly or bi-weekly (however often you get paid) payment to your own account for savings and investment purposes. No matter how tight your budget, you must find room to make this happen!

If you have a mental block against the word budget, then look at it as calculating your monthly cash flow. In other words, how much disposable cash do you have left over at the end of every month after you pay your bills, including savings and investing? Negative cash flow, no money left over at end of month – cut your expenses. Positive cash flow, money left over – continue cutting your expenses and increase your investing.

Put It Where?

In every country and every culture throughout history, the wealthy have owned real estate.

Although the current depression/recession makes this statement seem questionable, over the long-term real estate is a valuable commodity for one reason and one reason only – there is no more of it being made.

Now granted you must be smart about the details of any deal you make to own real estate, but the decision whether or not to own real estate should no longer be one for consideration.

One simplified plan to become wealthy is to buy five, six, seven properties or more. It is really quite simple to do. (Remember: I previously stated that good credit will help facilitate anyone's plan to build wealth, and, in some cases, it is an absolute must.)

Step 1. Define your area. It can be large, small, or a specific part of your city or another city.

Step 2. Do your research. Study the entire area's buying and selling for the past six months.

Step 3. Based on your knowledge, start knocking on doors and making offers. You will probably purchase most of your properties from as little as 10% below market value to as much as 45% below market value. Therefore, you will have already built up equity in your investments from the very outset. As I previously stated, you make your money on the front-end of investments, at purchase.

Step 4. No matter how many times the door slams in your face at your offer, keep going. If the door is not being slammed in your face, then you are offering way too much money.

Step 5. Make as few cosmetic changes as necessary and rent the property out and watch you money flow in.

Although you have the ending, the important part of any investment strategy is knowing how you got there. To this end, an investor needs to be like a really good scientist.

In other words, you need to keep some kind of diary about your investment thoughts, actions, ideas, and so on. This is not to be a cumbersome burden, but a tool to help you discover where you are going, and to learn from your own past mistakes. I knew this to some extent, but this lesson was recently reinforced by an older, African American real estate investor I met this past year.

Now if you are not a professional investor, in the beginning you probably only need to look at your investments once per month. Yet, you still may want to make notes on any trades you have made or thoughts you have about a particular trade for the future. Mainly these notes will help you gauge your own thought process.

As your investments grow, then you might also want to consider increasing the frequency of reviewing your investments.

When the time comes for you to measure your investments each month, make sure you review all your investments as a whole because a slow leak can sink the mightiest of ships.

Now, you have to determine what measure you are going to use to determine if your investment philosophy is working or not, which brings to mind another one of McWarren's rules of investment – do not lose money.

So, if you are not losing money, then that is good start, but not losing money alone is not enough to tell you how well you are or should be doing.

Therefore, you need to set some sort of goal, whether it be 4%, 5% per year, or some other sort of quantifiable measurement.

You need some pre-set objective standard by which to judge your own performance. And be brutally honest with yourself about what you have done wrong as well as what you have done correctly.

Finally, you need some sort of money management tool that will help you track your overall dollar performance. There are numerous options on the market so take your time to find the one that works for you. I will tell you that I have tried several of the most popular and most recommended money management tools over the course of several years, and I found all of those tools to be wholly inadequate. Unfortunately, I do not have a suitable recommendation.

The best way to know if what you are tracking is performing comparatively well is by reading. Each day, at the very minimum every investor should be reading something that gives them an overall idea of how the total market is performing, and, at the very least, each one should be reading the behind-the-scenes goings on of some of your investments for research sake.

Now while every investor would like to double their money in as short a period as possible, that is not as easy as it sounds, but, if that is your goal, then you might want to remember the Rule of 72.

For example if your money is earning 3.5% per year, then the rule of 72 is quite simple: 72 divided by 3.5 % is 20.57 years (72/3.5 = 20.57 years).

The Rule of 72 is straightforward math. Divide 72 by the interest rate your money is earning(whether it be 1.5, 2.0, 3.5, and so on), and the rule will give you the number of years it will take you to double your money at that rate of growth.

There are two caveats to the rule: 1) the rule is only applicable when interest and dividends are reinvested, and, 2) it does not take taxes into consideration.

The rule also works in reverse. For example if you know your money doubled in seven years, then divide 72 by 7 and you will see that you earned approximately 10.28% per year.

Also remember the rule does not work when using extreme numbers. If you were to divide 72 by itself that would give you one year, but that would actually take a 100% return and not 72%.

So when dealing with higher returns, use 76 instead of 72.

Now that you have learned a few basic investment conventions, principles, and practices, it is time that you began to learn how to apply this to your every-day real-life situation.

Before we move on, I want to point out one more critically important rule. Although we are quite sophisticated, as a nation, if you are thinking, "this information is not germane to me," because you believe that Social Security and other Federal programs will be around, you should reconsider that rule, immediately!

As sophisticated as we are, estimates are that 75% of the country cannot take care of themselves, they are not self-sufficient. And the government (Federal, State, Local) is taking care of 80% of those who are not self sufficient (80% X 75% or .80 X .75).

This means the government is taking care of 60% of its citizens!

This kind of financial assistance is not sustainable into the future without some major changes in our government (debt and deficit reduction, new revenue, restructured tax system, and a few others that are better suited for another book). Therefore, it is incumbent upon us all, individually and corporately, to learn how to take control of our own financial destinies.

Fill in the Blanks

Wherever you are today at whatever age you are, you need to start seriously thinking about the future.

If you are going to make any kind of money, the real reward is knowing what you are going to do with that money, unless you are like Warren Buffet who enjoys making money because it gives him the freedom and the luxury to do whatever he wants to do at any moment of any day, and to do it with individuals of his choosing.

Most individuals daydream about leaving their full-time job, and not ever having to work again. However, most of them have not thought about what they are going to do the next day, and the day after that and so forth.

Probably an equal number of individuals have dreamed about working from home, yet those same individuals lack the necessary discipline to work from home. Or they do not know what they would do if they ran into a problem they could not solve on their own, or worse, what they would do if they got bored!

If you have a desire to increase your wealth, then it is time you start to fill in some of those blanks.

One of the biggest blanks is that many individuals do not know their own needs or wants. I understand this perfectly because I too was so busy trying to make a living and stay ahead of the bill collectors that I did not have the luxury of time to think about who I was or what I wanted, or so I thought.

And like so many others, I did not think about these things until I was forced to think about them, for whatever reason. Let me tell you, it is hard to think about remaking yourself, financially, when you have lost your job, are faced with foreclosure, or you are sick and cannot work for a while, just to name a few.

So as you began to think about investing, you also need to think about who you are as a person, before a situation forces you to lament over why you did not do this when you had the chance, which is now!

There are a lot of personality tests that are available on the internet, through your employer, and maybe even through your church or house of worship that can help you achieve this goal of knowing thyself. One of the biggest parts of knowing thyself is knowing your core values versus your situational values.

Your core values are generally the values you learned as a child from your parents, teachers, the Bible, and so on. When it comes to investing, these values may be the same or different.

For example, one of your personal core values may be that you believe in giving back to your community. This may also be translated into an investing core value because you may only want to invest in companies that give back to the community in a very tangible way and are environmentally conscious.

These values should never change, except to grow stronger.

Situational values are values that are called upon or evoked based on a situation(s). These values are like "charm."

For example, some wealthy people are well-mannered, and genuinely likable no matter their surroundings. Others are well-mannered only when in the company of other wealthy people, normally their wealthy superiors (though most would never admit it). However, behind closed doors, they are vicious, nasty, and conniving people.

I hate to say this, but most politicians only have situational values. Literally, their values are dictated by the situation or whatever it takes to continue being re-elected (absolute power corrupts absolutely, I learned in the 6th grade).

In addition, look around your office, I am sure you will see or already know of individuals that only have situational values, and they make business decisions based on those values.

One of the best movies I have ever seen, quite by accident, that did a masterful job of displaying situational values is Ever After (1998) starring Drew Barrymore and Anjelica Huston.

Do not spend your time being upset about these kinds of individuals because according to the law of reciprocity, they will always get their comeuppance, though you may not be there to see it when it happens. And the reason why comeuppance is their just reward is because Romans 12:19 tells us, "Vengeance is mine; I will repay, saith the Lord."

While it is our duty to participate in our republic by voting against corrupt officials and policies, and, to assist those who are bound by law to adjudicate corruption, by no means am I suggesting that one has to be rich to be happy.

Happiness is the art of living well. Few people live well, and those that can afford to do it, are not happy because money, by itself, cannot make a person happy.

True happiness is learning to be content wherever you are while forever planning to move forward.

But, remember this. Happy or unhappy, content or not content, the wealthy make up 1% of this country, and they make their money from the other 99% of the country.

Regardless of how many years you have left at your job, here are some things you can start doing now to help you fill in the blanks when that day finally arrives.

1) Decide what it is you want now while there is no pressure and you have the freedom and the time to think clearly.

2) Make a detailed list of things you expect to do on a daily, weekly, and monthly basis, include any special items like trips, vacations, etc.

3) Decide what time frame you want to accomplish these things.

4) Now attach dollar values to all of your activities, including any special purchases you will need to make in order to fulfill your dreams.

5) Make a list of not just the bills you have right now, but add to that list those bills you will have to pay during retirement.

6) Make a list of those additional large purchases you plan on making during retirement, like a new beach front home.

7) Now you need to look at your income sources and list every single source and the dollar value; these include social security, and any pensions as well as your various retirement savings.

8) At this point you should have some idea of what kind of money you need to be saving to reach your goals.

9) You do have some options, like decreasing your current expenditures, maxing out your 401(k), adding some additional investments like a Roth IRA and Roth 401(k), and maybe even add a new job.

10) Now if you are working a minimum wage job or one not far from minimum wage, and do not have an asset base to build on, you still can start an investment program. You can get some help in achieving your goals by reading a couple of books, *Wealth on Minimal Wage* and *The Automatic Millionaire* with its accompanying workbook.

11) Whether you plan on staying in your current home or moving, now is the time to finalize those decisions and make all those major repairs and other upgrades to spread the cost out across your working years.

12) If you plan on working after retirement or plan on running some type of business, then now is also the time to shore up those plans as well, i.e., develop your business plan(s) or start your retraining program.

13) Finally, if you have not already done so, you need to make sure all of your final documents are in order.

As stated before, sometimes investing can seem overwhelming. We are all inundated by the financial information that is constantly streamed into our homes, with such acronyms as CD, ATM, BDD, and EFT, to name very few, being blasted at us from every media outlet possible.

But, do not let that idea scare you away from the huge earning potential that lies in front of you. Probably, the best way to overcome this fear is to keep it simple. The old adage, "if you can't beat 'em, join 'em," is truly appropriate in this situation.

There are two basic steps required for investing. First you have to identify any money that you do not need for the next five years. Second, you have to choose which investment best suits you – stocks, bonds, or real estate.

Here is a simplistic guideline to help you in your early decision-making.

If you are under age 50, stocks are the most attractive investment for long-term earnings. Although some years stocks lose money and other years they may have big gains, the longer your money is in the stock market, it will, historically, pay off to your benefit.

Since you are not a professional investor, the best way for most individuals to get into the market is by investing in a collection or grouping of stocks, which is called a mutual fund.

There are two basic types of mutual funds. There are index funds and active funds.

With index funds, the group of stocks changes very infrequently so the fund is more stable in this respect. Now, active funds are managed by a professional investor or money manager whose job is to pick the stocks that the fund will invest in. Therefore with active funds, there is a lot of volatility.

As a novice investor, probably the best basic place to start investing is in the S&P 500 index fund. This is a low cost fund, with little volatility, and is composed of 500 large American companies across different industries.

If you have limited resources now, mutual funds may be a place worth considering for your serious money, that is money you are going to need for your retirement. So while you are researching these funds (I listed a few financial websites that may be helpful later in this chapter), here are some factors to consider in that research.

Fund loads are the sales commissions that you must pay as part of your fund membership. In actuality, these are commissions paid to the professionals who actually buy or sell the fund. There are three types of loads.

The front load means you pay a fee when you buy shares in the fund. Deferred load means you pay a fee when you sell your shares in the fund. Then the third and best load is no load, where you do not pay any fees for buying or selling fund shares.

Morningstar.com, www.morningstar.com, is one of the best sites for tracking mutual fund returns, risk, valuation, and any other factors that may be of interest to you.

One more fund fact. Periodically, Consumer Reports Money Advisor will publish a model on how to build an all-index-fund portfolio. You may contact them through their website, www.consumerreports.org/money.

Finally, keep it simple. Try to limit your investments to 9 or 11 stocks and even fewer funds. Start slow and do not worry about momentum: that will come in time.

Let me be clear that investing is not like saving. There is a risk that you can lose some or all your money. However, the risk of investing is generally rewarded with a reasonable return on your investment.

Also let me remind you of a few prudent investing rules you should never forget.

If investing was easy, everyone would be wealthy. You should always focus on the long term, and invest in businesses or companies you understand best. For a number of individuals that is going to be your company's 401(k) plan. There is nothing wrong with starting where you are since you have to start somewhere.

Since your 401(k) may be the greatest benefit of working for your employer, behind your health insurance, and your salary being third, let us take a closer look at the 401(k).

I will not spend much time on how to get started investing in your company's plan because 99.5% of all firms will send you a rules handbook once you become eligible to invest in their company's plan. In fact, many companies will automatically enroll you once you begin, but you will not have access to the money until you become vested with the company, generally one to three years.

You already know why participation is important, but if you do not, then here is another reason to participate. The more money you put in your 401(k) plan, the lower your taxable income will be, the less tax you will pay in taxes, and the faster your investment may grow.

Some may ask, "how is this possible?"

Money invested in a 401(k) is pre-taxed income. This means that the 401(k) contribution is deducted from your salary before the income tax is calculated. Because it is a pre-tax deduction, you will be paying less taxes because the income tax is calculated on a smaller income.

Most employers have retirement calculators on their websites to help their employees see what would be the tax implications at different rates of investing. These tools are very useful, and I recommend everyone play around with these calculators to see what the possibilities may be.

In some ways, employers have made it easier for employees to invest by making some early decisions for the employees like the variety and type of investments that are available for their 401(k) plan. This is intended to make it easier for employees to join the plan by simplifying their choices, and, generally, it lowers the cost of the plan so that the employer may offer more investment choices to the employees.

Although most plans average a choice of investment options between 8 and 12, these options can include everything from mutual funds to stock funds to index funds to bond funds, and anything in between, or combination thereof.

While you may not have a voice in the choices that are available, you do have the choice of how to invest your money among the available options, including your employer's contributions.

Your investment options may change over time based on your age, risk tolerance, other retirement assets, and your tax bracket. We will demonstrate some of these options for you, graphically, later in this chapter.

The final three points I would like to make about 401(k)s is that they require some work. This means you will have to periodically check your investments, and rebalance your accounts as your needs change or if one of your choices starts to lose money.

If you leave your job, the law allows you to take your 401(k) with you to your new employer, if you so choose. The other options are:

1. You can leave your money in the old employer's 401(k) plan.
2. You can roll your money over into your new employer's plan.
3. You can put the money into a rollover IRA.
4. You can take a lump sum withdrawal.

All of these options are tax free options until you get to the withdrawal option. There are some heavy penalties for withdrawals unless the withdrawal is to purchase a new home, to pay for medical bills, and for some limited hardship withdrawals.

When stock prices are low, and companies are sitting on record profits and lots of cash (as many U. S. companies currently are), then it is possible to build a million dollar 401(k) plan. It will require some work, but since you have to manage your 401(k) anyway, manage it with the largest possible profit margin in mind, which will depend in large part on the quality of your research. This means you cannot be a passive investor, but instead, you are going to have to find an informational resource you trust. This may take a while, but it will be time well spent.

Now, if you are working for a company that you do not want to invest in, first of all you might want to reconsider your decision to work for that firm. That said, we have all found some product that caught our eye, that intrigued us, or we thought was really good. Here is your opportunity to do some research and find out if that product is worth investing some of your money.

One other option is to look at where you are spending your money. What are some of your favorite places to shop? These stores might be worthy of your investment since you trust them as a favorite retailer, and you might actually make some of your money back.

More people lose their money by acting on "tips" and trying to make a "fast buck." So do not start these bad habits and you will cut your problems in half. Do not forget the Parable of the Talents told by Jesus in Matthew 25:14-30 and repeated in Luke 19:12-28.

If you are still tempted to try and make a fast buck, then here is your opportunity to be a Buffett copycat. Mr. Buffet's favorite holding period is forever.

Just as it is important to know when to invest, it is equally important to recognize those times when you should not be investing in the stock market.

You should not be investing in stocks if:

- you need the money within the next two or three years
- you do not know the major product lines a company makes or know its competitors
- you think of investing like playing the lottery or gambling
- you are not good with handling change
- you think every stock you buy will go up
- you do not understand your own reasons for making a purchase or when it is time to sell

Finally, make sure stocks you purchase meet your preset investment standards, and if an investment interest does not fit, do not force it. Remember: just because someone else made money on a stock does not mean you will too, so do not go off following the crowd.

Most of all, do not invest with a stranger. Take time to develop a relationship and if you feel rushed, then that is not a person for your money. While you are at it, make sure to find out if the professional makes a commission off the products they sell to you. If they do, then you already know that your best interest is not their best interest!

I tell you all of this because every single one of us has to increase our financial intelligence in order to survive in today's financial environment, and into the future. If just having a job was the answer, then working families would not be living in borderline poverty, the middle class would not be losing their homes to foreclosures in record fashion, and families with healthcare coverage would not be struggling to pay medical bills because they exceeded their coverage and their savings.

Having two or three jobs is also not the answer.

There is no such animal called job security. You can be the best performer on any job, but if a company is sold or a new manager comes in and does not like you, without you even provoking that individual's anger, there goes your job security. Or, if profits start to suffer, there again, your job security may be on the chopping block.

In actuality, you do not have to do anything to be terminated from your job because most states are "at-will" states. The doctrine of employment at-will means that in the absence of an employment contract, employers generally may terminate any employee for reason or for no reason at all, as long as their reasoning does not violate any other statute.

Therefore, even if an individual was the subject of termination for an unfair reason, that does not automatically mean that one may have statutory recourse in the matter.

While I clearly understand the benefits of money and its importance to our daily lives, I absolutely believe in my heart that "the love of money is the root of all evil." (1 Timothy 6:10) Although some prominent financial writers have stated otherwise, I respectfully disagree. I believe the word of God that has already withstood the test of time is due providential reverence over a 21st century writer, no matter how popular the writer may be.

Money is a tool. It is a tool that can be used for good or bad, depending on one's education (or lack of) about that tool. However, if one becomes obsessed with any tool, that ill-placed love for that tool, in this case money, will drive men to do some unspeakable things to get that tool. This obsession was clearly and prominently displayed by some of the actions taken by the heads of a few major companies that lead up to, at least in part, the most recent global recession.

While it is my earnest desire to teach you as much as possible about money, the tool, I equally hope that you will learn to have a healthy enough respect to know that this tool can be a corrupting force, if one allows it to be.

So again, I return to the lessons discussed in Chapter 1. You have to change your mindset, and learn how to see things differently in order to increase your financial intelligence, and hopefully, your wealth.

Alexandre Dumas, the 19th century African-American French writer (grandfather married a slave from what is now known as Haiti), wrote *The Count of Monte Cristo,* and, the movie of the same name, in 2002, both vividly demonstrate the reality of I Timothy 6:10, and the evil of loving money.

The most important point of this entire book is not that assets can be bought and sold, but it is the information on how and when to purchase and/or sell these assets for the financial benefit of your family, that is the primary concept of this book.

Secondly, the recent global recession has forever changed the way our economy operates, and we all, individually and cooperatively, must change how we do business in this economy, if we are going to survive.

In my lifetime, this is the second time that our economy and the way of dealing with money has changed. The first time was when President Richard Nixon took the U. S. off the gold standard in 1971.

On August 15, 1971, President Nixon ended the stability of the U. S. dollar in one fatal swoop that ended the world's three hundred year history of stable money.

Under the gold standard, our government, like all world governments, were legally limited as to how much money they could print. For the U. S., this meant that the Federal Reserve could only print four times the value of our gold reserves.

The removal from the gold standard also guaranteed the U. S. would have inflation infinitum. Without getting into a discussion on U. S. monetary policy, inflation is when prices for goods and services rise, and purchasing power (the dollar) subsequently falls.

Simply put, it takes more currency to buy the same product than it may have cost in previous years.

Therefore, the U. S. dollar is no longer defined in financial circles as money, because money is backed by a specific value – for the U. S. that was gold, for

Britain that was sterling; currency, on the other hand, has a floating value which changes daily.

As I stated at the beginning of the book, currency has to forever move to be of value, which brings me full circle back to investing. Since the value of currency changes daily, it is important to invest because investing forces currency to move, and as such will make more currency that keeps moving. Perpetual motion creates wealth.

Now in truth, the stock market is not the only avenue for earning wealth in the world. If you have the entrepreneurial spirit burning deep within you, many a man and woman have gained enormous wealth by doing one simple thing – they all followed their passion.

Outside of our families and our religious beliefs, the only other thing that comes close to defining who we are is our job. So many times we are all in mixed company and people begin introductions with "she is an accountant" or "he works for XYZ Corp."

So clearly not only do we define ourselves by our job, but so do our peers and other outsiders.

Since this job determines how we spend most of our days and sometimes our nights and impacts everything from our anatomy to our zeal, then why are more of us not working in areas where our professional ambitions are aligned with our personal ones?

If you have an unfulfilled entrepreneurial desire, beyond having a good idea, here are a few other tips that may help you turn that one egg into a golden goose.

a. Become relentless in your pursuit, almost to the point of becoming fanatical

b. Make sure you do your homework – read everything you can about your dream and talk to every expert you can find

c. Learn every aspect of the market and learn how to exploit inefficiencies

d. Keep searching for new ways to improve

e. Learn how to sift through the extraneous fluff and get to the point

f. Learn to have fun with whatever you do

g. Become a little narcissistic, at least enough to find out what you truly want and be willing to put in the time and motivation to become great at whatever it is you desire

h. Learn to confidently accept the risk of your adventure – do not be a wimp or sheepishly back down under pressure

i. Phil Simms (NFL) says that you have to be mentally free enough to the point where your body is right on the edge of being out of control, but not quite, then your skill can come out

j. Learn to be prepared to walk through every open door before it closes by having your goals forever before you

k. Find a way to make sure your gift, your desire can also help hurting people somewhere else that may not otherwise have been reached if it were not for you

Pocket Change

While you are building your dream, if you want to grow wealthy and stay wealthy, you must learn when and when not to take on debt as you are working toward your true goals. As discussed in Chapter 7, debt can be a positive tool.

If used correctly this tool helps individuals purchase things they can afford but do not have the liquid (hard cash) assets to purchase outright.

When used incorrectly, this same tool can help people buy things they cannot afford. The latter is bad debt and the former is reasonable debt.

But remember this fact: whether rich or old, you are going to have money problems. Think of money as a mountain, if you are poor, you are struggling up the mountain; and, if you are rich, you are struggling to stay on top of the mountain – but either way everyone is on the same mountain.

Increasing your financial intelligence can help you if you going up the mountain, on top of the mountain, or sliding down the other side. So while your assets may change, your knowledge should continue to grow. The Wall Street Journal is another tool to help grow your financial intelligence.

I remember someone once saying that becoming a millionaire is easy. The first million is the hard part. This makes perfect sense because the mistakes are made in gaining that first million. But that is also the period where the most knowledge may be gained. After that, making the remaining millions is easy, by comparison.

So here is a simple exercise. Create a list of all of your problems. If you believe that money is going to solve those problems, create a second list detailing how money is going to solve that problem. Now, create a third list of ways to solve the problems without money. Finally, create a fourth list of ways you can make money from your ideas from list three. When you are all done, you will have solved your problem and found new ways to build your income.

When I was poor, I pined over my problems and drowned myself in my sorrows first in one thing and then another. When I moved to the middle class through education and securing a higher paying job, I dealt with my money problems by working 80 hours a week to stay one step in front of my creditors. Now that I am on the cusp of wealth, I still have money problems, of a different kind, and, I have learned to resolve those new money (currency) problems creatively.

A number of every day Americans who have earned their wealth are living a financially comfortable existence in part because of their frugal use of debt.

Money that is not required to repay old debt is money that is available for growing your wealth, and research has proven that second to your investment choices, the most important factor in wealth generation from investments is consistent, ever-increasing contributions. Lower debt helps you achieve this goal more quickly.

Wealthy individuals do use debt, but their borrowing is different from the average person's. A large majority of them do not carry credit card debt or other installment debt, which generally speaking is expensive debt.

The majority of all their debt is tied up in real estate holdings – primary home, and other investment properties. This kind of debt can help an individual make money and gain wealth.

Generally speaking your primary home will gain equity with each payment made, which is cheap money that can be used for other investments should the need arise (notwithstanding the recent global shift).

Investment properties have tenants that pay enough rent every month to cover the mortgage and all the expenses of the property with enough left over every month for the owner – profit.

One of my financial instructors taught me this same lesson in a very powerful way.

You have two sets of parents that are basically equal financially, but they have different mindsets. Both of them borrow money to send their child to school.

The second set puts the money in a low-interest bearing account to pay the education bills as they come in.

The first set takes the money and purchases an apartment building near the university, and puts it in the child's name. Now their child has free room and board for school, has a regular income coming in, and, most of all, has learned how to leverage debt to produce wealth.

The law of attraction teaches that you become what you think about. So if you think you are going to fail, then you will. And if you think you are going to succeed, you will do that also.

So that bill you are about to put in the mail or pay online, pocket change, can actually be used to produce some major results if you approach your decisions with a little creativity.

If you are ready to invest, but are not ready to be a landlord, then here are a few questions you should be able to answer before you buy any stock.

> ***Question1:*** What is the business of the company? This may be an obvious answer for certain companies but for others the answer may require some research. There are a number of websites that will help you discover this information such as www.msn.com, www.altavista.com, www.cnnfn.com, www.morningstar.com, www.bloomberg.com, www.bondsonline.com, www.marketwatch.com, www.investinginbonds.com, and www.hoovers.com, www.investors.com, and others to name a few.
>
> ***Question 2:*** How much product does this company sell every year?
>
> ***Question 3:*** How profitable is this company? Taking a note from the Oracle, ROE is the ratio to look at when measuring profitability, as long as the company does not have high debt or unreasonable debt.
>
> ***Question 4:*** How bad is the debt situation? How bad will the debt situation become if interest rates starts to rise? A common rule of

thumb to measure debt is the financial leverage ratio. No debt means a ratio of 1. If the ratio is above 5, then you should avoid that company. The financial leverage is computed by dividing total assets by shareholder's equity.

Question 5: Is there more money flowing into the company or is there more money flowing out of the company, which is related to questions 3 and 4 above? If cash is flowing out, is it an anomaly or a pattern of things to come?

On March 8, 2006, *Investor's Business Daily* published its own hit list for stock market investment success. According to the report, IBD built detailed models of all the most successful stocks from 1880 to 2005. The company analyzed those companies' characteristics and the factors that existed before these companies – -considered the best – – had huge advances, and how those factors changed when the stocks peaked.

Here is the website if you would like to review the entire list in detail: http://www.investors.com//editorial/editorialcontent.asp?secid=1000&view=1.

Here are a few more common measures of investment success:

(a) P/E, price/earnings ratio (discussed earlier)

(b) Growth in both sales and profits. If sales growth does not grow profits, look at the management group. If profits grow but sales lag, the profits will probably start to shrink also. Again look at the management.

(c) Yield is the price of a stock's dividend per share divided by the stock price per share. If the stock price is $30 per share and the dividend is $1.50 per share, then the yield is 5%.

(d) Volatility is a concern if a stock carries more activity by comparison to others in their grouping.

Stock	Price/ Earnings Ratio	Sales Growth (Current Year)	Profits Growth (Current Year)	Yield	Personal Knowledge of Compainy (1=no knowledge, 5= very knowledgeable) / Why
		%	%	%	
		%	%	%	
		%	%	%	
		%	%	%	
		%	%	%	
		%	%	%	
		%	%	%	
		%	%	%	
		%	%	%	
		%	%	%	
		%	%	%	
		%	%	%	
		%	%	%	
		%	%	%	
		%	%	%	
		%	%	%	
		%	%	%	
		%	%	%	
		%	%	%	
		%	%	%	
		%	%	%	
		%	%	%	
		%	%	%	
		%	%	%	
		%	%	%	

I have also prepared a 'Show Me Your Homework Sheet.' The purpose of this sheet is to make sure you are truly doing your homework and spending some quality time thinking about your money choices.

Taking Stock

I have always heard that if you want to know where you are going, you have to know where you came from. In the financial world that equates to computing your net worth by creating your own personal financial statement.

Later in this chapter you will see an example of a simplified financial statement taken from the Microsoft programs that I initially used to quantify my own numbers some years ago.

Even if you do not yet own any investments, you need to calculate your own net worth so that you can see your own potential for growth and start incorporating your lessons learned into your financial plan to help build up your net worth. The three-fold purpose of this exercise is to show you were your money needs protecting, areas where your budget needs to be tightened, and if you need to increase your income-earning potential. We all have to start somewhere.

This time, however, instead of giving you detailed instructions as I have in the past, I am going to leave it to you to figure out how to complete your financial statement. But know this; you already have access to all the information you need to complete the sheet.

Each of us has to start understanding our own numbers, because we all live in the world of money or currency, to be exact, and we have got to learn how to start using those numbers or we are going to get left behind.

There used to be an education policy called "social promotion," where teachers were forced to improperly promote kids to the next grade, even when it was known that those kids were not ready for the next level; and, today, many of those same kids are left behind in life.

There is no social promotion when it comes to finances and your financial intelligence. When you start to understand the financial world, by doing the necessary homework, it will show up in your increased finances; if not, then you will forever be at the mercy of the rich (Proverbs 22:7).

You should periodically do your financial statement, maybe every six months or once per year, depending on your individual situation. The reason for dating your financial statements is so that you can see your own progress, better be able to negotiate a loan, do a better job at managing your cash and paying down your debt, and, of course, know how much your investments are worth.

Again, there are money management programs that can be found on the internet that will do all the calculations for you. All you have to do is print the sheet out.

The statement can serve dual purposes by also helping to identify both where you derive your current income and potential new income sources.

Couple this income statement with your predetermined financial goals discussed earlier in the chapter, and you have a financial road map for your future.

You can start filling in that road map by setting short-range, medium-range, and long-range goals. Write all of these goals down somewhere so that each member of your family can see them often. Short-range goals are those things you want to accomplish within the next year, medium-range are the next three to five years, and long-range are the next 10 to 20 years. Remember that these time frames are all relative. For example, retirement is a long-range goal when you are 25, but it is an immediate goal when you are 60 years old.

While these goals have to be reviewed on a regular basis, these periodic reviews will help you identify the obstacles that must be overcome to achieve your financial goals, and/or, these reviews can help you identify what kinds of assets you might consider purchasing (what you can afford) to help you reach your goals.

Now you can start filling in all the details for each set of goals so that when you finish you should have a daily action plan whereby you can do at least one thing every day toward reaching your goals.

I am not trying to pretend that I have all the answers, because I do not. But, I do have enough knowledge (mistakes and my education) that I can pass on to others so that they can begin to educate themselves in the manner most conducive for them to learn this sometimes daunting material.

Look at it this way. If you were sick and you had to go to the doctor, or you find a new job and your boss has to train you for that new job, you would immediately begin to educate yourself about your illness or your new job. Well, if the financial world is new to you, *Funny Money Universe*, is a first-line tool and a continual reference to help you learn this all-important new body of knowledge.

Going back to your financial statement, somewhere on that list of things to do should be three very important things – increase your income, cut your expenses, and put all of your savings from lowered expenses into new investments. While we have already covered all of these items in detail in earlier chapters, some of that qualifies for repeating here.

We will take the easiest one first – increasing your income.

Now there are a few options to increasing your income. You can either get a raise, get a new job, or add one or more part-time jobs, and any number of other options that may available to help you reach your goals.

None of these should be that difficult since you know exactly what you are working towards and how important these goals are to you and your family. But – in truth, I have lied to you. None of these will increase your income, but they will increase your salary, temporarily or maybe longer.

To increase your income, you need to increase your assets on a yearly basis. This is how the rich get richer.

Working for a paycheck will not increase your income for several reasons. First, you will have to work more and more hours to get a single paycheck. Second, at some point employers are going to stop all the extra hours because those extra hours cost them more money. So any salary increase is temporary because employers are working to control their cost just as you are.

Adding assets means adding income, passive income, without having to work harder. By now, it should be clear how all of the information from the preceding chapters is necessary to accomplish your financial goals – – such as your credit score and resolving debt issues.

The other side of the equation, cutting your expenses may not be quite as easy because each family member has something at stake that they do not want to give up. A modified list was presented in prior chapters.

Six major ways of cutting your expenses are, first, to use a shopping list every time you go shopping and do not defer from the list under any circumstances. Businesses do this all the time. There are regular budget meetings to decide which projects need to be funded, machinery purchased, etc., and once the decision is made that becomes their shopping list.

The second way is to have a cooling off period for every major purchase over $50. If this is an impulse purchase, wait 48 hours before discussing it again. But if it is a predetermined family purchase, then wait 24 hours before discussing the purchase. If no compromise can be reached, the leader of the family, just as in business, has to make the decision for the entire family.

The third way is to give everyone in the family a weekly or bi-weekly allowance, and once that allowance is gone, it is gone until the next allowance is issued. There is one caveat. Family members can borrow from future allowances, but make sure they are held to the terms. But remember, it is not a good idea to borrow from future allowances, just as it is not a good idea to borrow from future paychecks in the form of payday loans. Incidentally, these kind of lending offices are only located in either African-American, Hispanic, or any other neighborhood other than the suburbs.

Do not purchase a daily newspaper in your area but get a used one every day, and start searching for consignment shops, top notch thrift stores, garage sales, and estates sales.

These passed over groups, oftentimes have hidden gems in the rough. Who knows, you may actually find a new job or an alternate source of income (when coupled with online selling skills or reselling to consignment shops). At the very least, you have a new shopping hobby at less than 75% of the cost for new items.

If you or your family member cannot shake the urge to shop in the malls, then make sure you shop for sale items only. And if you do make a purchase, make sure you pay for those items in cash, which brings us to number six.

Cost cutting item number six is to cut your credit card bill purchases, or stop using the cards altogether.

Personal Financial Statement

Name: **Date:**

Assets	Amount in Dollars
Cash - Checking Accounts	
Cash - Savings Accounts	
Certificates of Deposit	
Securities - Stocks/Bonds/Mutual Funds	
Notes & Contracts Receivable	
Life Insurance (Cash Surrender Value)	
Personal Property (Autos, Jewelry, etc.)	
Retirement Funds (IRAs, 401k)	
Real Estate (Market Value)	
Other Assets (specify)	
Other Assets (specify)	
Total Assets	

Liabilities	Amount in Dollars
Current Debt	
Notes Payable	
Taxes Payable	
Real Estate Mortgages (Describe)	
Other Liabilities (specify)	
Other Liabilities (specify)	
Total Liabilities	

Net Worth	

Landscape Design

There is no better time to get your feet wet like the present, and since the stock market is not going to wait for you to learn how it operates, you might as well learn how to move at a fast pace now. Find the nearest public library on your regular route traveled and start using its resources you pay for with your tax dollars.

While there are a number of different ways to measure a stock's performance, my primary goal is to give you a broad overview of some of the most widely used investment terms and philosophies as a building base for your future financial growth.

Bulls and bears! These are terms you will constantly hear in discussions about the stock market.

Bull markets are markets when stock prices are moving increasingly higher. Bear markets are markets when stock prices are declining sharply and at a rapid pace.

So if you are a bull you are optimistic, and if you are a bear you are a pessimist.

Now let's take at look at some of the primary investments and strategies that are used to identify bargains in the marketplace.

1) Income stocks – these are the stocks of the giants in their respective industries. These are financially stable companies that are also profitable, and pay a reasonable share of those profits as dividends to their investors.

2) Growth stocks – these are fast-moving stocks that show good strong growth in most years. These companies consume a lot of income and pour that income back into the business for future growth. Therefore, they rarely pay any dividends, but are attractive because of the hope that their growth will generate hefty capital gains.

3) Large cap (capitalization) – capitalization is defined as the market value of a stock ([the number of outstanding shares] X [the price per share]). For example if XYZ has 150 million shares outstanding at $75 per share, then the capitalization is $11,250,000,000. That makes XYZ a large cap. As of March 4, 2009, the most familiar of the largest cap stocks is McDonald's.

4) Small cap – ABC Corporation has only 30 million shares trading at $20 per share. Their capitalization is $60,000,000. One of the most well known small cap stocks is Netflix.

5) Growth vs. value – the main difference between these stocks is how they are perceived in the marketplace. Growth stocks are considered high-quality stocks which have a high P/E (price-to-earnings) ratio and whose earnings are expected to grow at an above-average rate. Value stocks generally have low P/E, but are purchased because investors hope that these stocks are bargains that have not yet reached their full potential. Both stocks tend to run in cycles, but there may be room for both types in a portfolio.

6) U.S. vs. Foreign – the stock market is not limited to the United States, and, in fact, some of our most famous brand names are foreign owned.

7) Bond philosophy – it its simplest form, a bond is an IOU, whereby the issuer promises to pay you for the use of your money for a specific period of time, which is your interest rate, and to also return your money to you when the period of time has come to an end, i.e., when the bond has matured.

8) Bond market – there are basically three groups of bonds. (a) Treasury securities issued by the federal government; (b) Municipal bonds issued by local governments and other similar entities, where both are exempt from federal income taxes; and (c) Corporate bonds issued by corporations which tend to pay a higher rate of interest than Treasury or municipal bonds.

9) Treasury securities – there are three groups of these securities. (a) Treasury bills mature within one year. (b) Treasury notes mature between one and 10 years. (c) Treasury bonds mature in 30 years. One of the attractive features of Treasury securities is that all interest is exempt from state and local taxes, and you can purchase these directly from the U. S. government.

10) Stock options – options allow you to bet on the stock market without buying or selling any stock. With an option, you are buying the right to buy or sell a particular stock at a set price at some point in the future, if you so choose.

11) Two options – there are two types of options – call option and put

option, both with a lifespan of 9-months. Options are not only for stocks but can be used on virtually all securities and commodities.

12) Call option – this contract affords you the opportunity to buy 100 shares of a particular option at an agreed upon price within a 9-month period. The owner of the contract pays a premium for the option, and does not have to buy the stocks. However, if the owner decides to purchase the stocks, the seller is obligated to sell those 100 shares as long as the option is still valid. The reason for an option is to lock in the price of a stock that you think is going to go up in the future so that you can buy it at a lower price. If the stock goes down, then all you have lost is the premium.

13) Put option – this option contract gives the holder (owner) the right to sell a specific quantity of stocks to the option writer (buyer) at a specific price for the life of the contract. The owner does not have to sell, but if the owner decides to sell, the buyer is obligated to buy. For example, if an individual is concerned that a specific stock is going to drop, then they write a contract to sell their stock at a specific price so that if the stock does go down, they are guaranteeing that they will only lose a certain amount of money. Now, if the stock does not go down, then the owner does not have to sell their stock but does have to pay the premium fee for the option contract.

14) Leverage – this is when a little money controls a lot of money, like when buying a piece of real estate. But for now just know that options give a professional investor a lot of leverage.

15) Futures – are forward contracts because they represent an agreement to execute a specific transaction at a future date. Unlike options, futures contracts are obligations to buy that last for 18 months. The buyer (the person on the "long" side) and the seller (the individual on the "short" side) are both at equal risk. So if one wins the other loses the equal amount. In a futures contract, what you are betting on is that the price of the commodity rises or falls enough to make it profitable to either (a) execute the futures contract or (b) sell the contract rights to another buyer and take your profit immediately. Futures are sophisticated leverage documents for skilled investors. However, you should at a minimum be aware of their existence so you have some understanding when you hear the name.

16) DRIP – this is a Dividend Reinvestment Plan offered by some corporations that allows shareholders to purchase additional shares without using a broker or paying a commission. Here is how the plan works. The first share purchased must be purchased through a brokerage firm. After that the company allows additional optional cash purchases at any time, and the company will automatically reinvest cash dividends and capital gains distributions. So instead of receiving dividend checks in the mail, those will be reinvested to purchase more company shares. The only downside is that the investor has no control over their dividend money as long as they are part of the DRIP program.

17) Dollar-cost averaging – although this sounds complicated it is one of the easiest ways to continue to ensure your investments grow. The concept is quite simple. Automatically investing a fixed dollar amount each week, bi-weekly, or monthly into the purchase of additional securities is dollar-cost averaging. In other words, build your investing into your budget or have the money automatically deducted from your paycheck each pay period.

The fact is that your money will never grow unless you take some risks. When it comes to investments, there are all kinds of risks that are both known and unknown. But instead of concentrating on risks, we want to focus on acting intelligently and ways to minimize those risks.

Also, by not taking a risk, you are actually taking a risk -- you are risking that your financial situation will not change for the worse. This is a bigger risk than investing, because when a person invests, they at least have the possibility of gaining something in return for their risk. By standing still and doing nothing, there is no potential for a gain.

For most individuals this boils down to two strategies – diversification and asset allocation.

Diversification mixes a wide variety of investments within a portfolio and within asset classes to minimize risk exposure. This means you can choose different types of investments or you can choose different securities within the same investment classification.

You can choose different assets such as stocks and bonds, or you can choose different types of stocks, for example, across different types of businesses.

For example, let's assume that there are only two retail stores in a town, one is a man's suit store and the other a woman's dress shop. You have the option of investing in one or the other, but diversification means that you would invest some money in both firms.

The second strategy for risk aversion is asset allocation – – not putting all your eggs in one basket. Asset allocation means you spread your investments across different classes of assets – stocks, bonds, cash, commodities, real estate, and so on.

As an investor you can chose a mutual fund that makes all of these decisions for you or you can develop your own mix that would most likely include some growth and income stocks; small-cap and large-cap stocks; U. S. and foreign stocks; and other investments to start.

Since investing is not like a one-size fit-all robe, every investor also has to remember that different investments do better at different economic times and asset allocation will help weather those periods of economic turmoil.

But remember this: bonds tend to perform well when stocks are not performing, and stocks tend to perform well when bonds are not performing.

Here are four different investment mixes that will give you some examples of what diversification and asset allocation may look like. Every individual needs to take into consideration their risk tolerance and their goals, as well as making sure the various assets are spread across different types of businesses within each asset grouping.

Conservative Mix

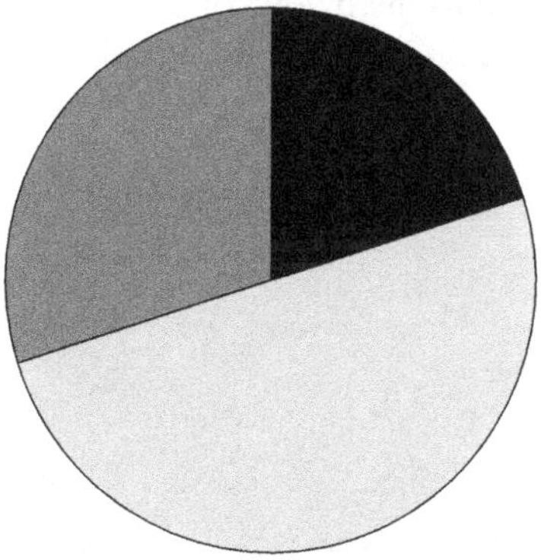

- 20% Domestic Stock
- 50 % Bonds
- 30% Short-term Investments

Balanced Mix

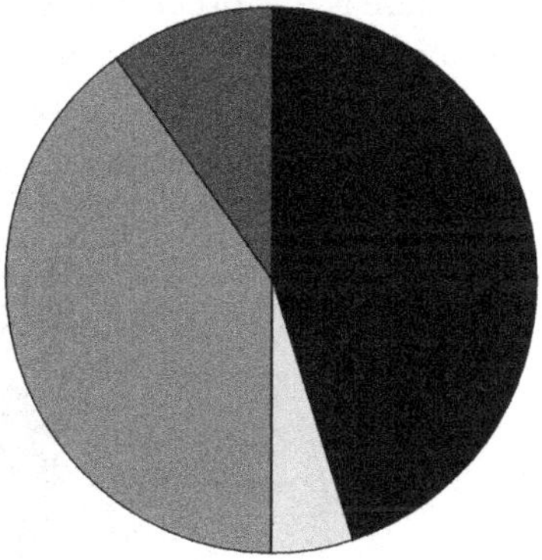

- 45% Domestic Stocks
- 5% Foreign Stocks
- 40% Bonds
- 10 % Short-Term Investments

Growth Mix

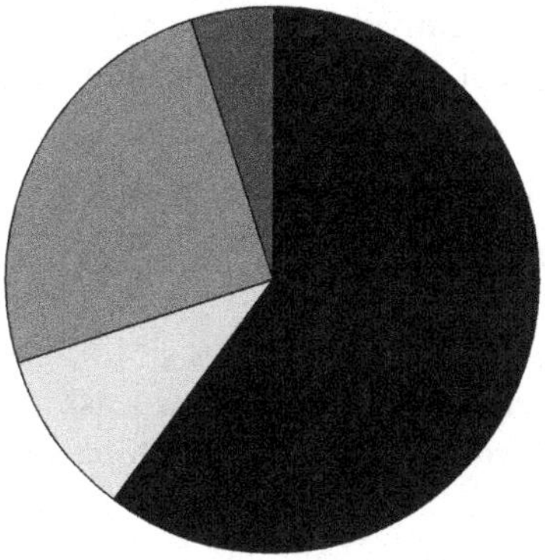

- 60% Domestic Stocks
- 10% Foreign Stocks
- 25% Bonds
- 5% Short-Term Investments

Aggressive Mix

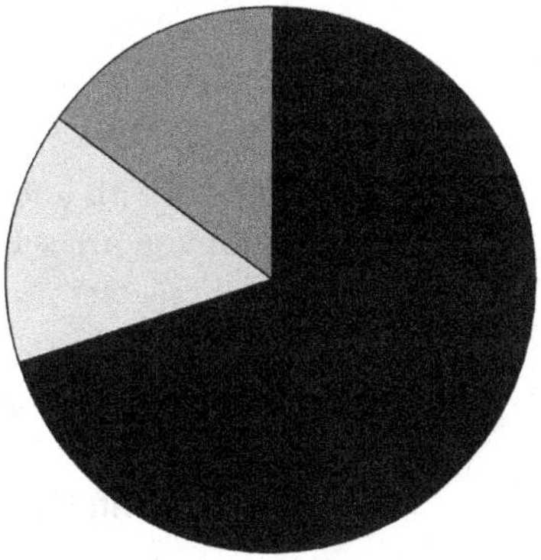

- 70% Domestic Stock
- 15 % Bonds
- 15% Short-term Investments

Definition: Short-term investments may include cash, U. S. Treasury notes, and other debt that by definition should mature within 1 to 10 year

Here is one other portfolio mix that was presented to me by one of my financial instructors. This mix is different because it requires a little more work to fill in the various selections for the different asset classes. This graphical mix just provides a broad diversification strategy.

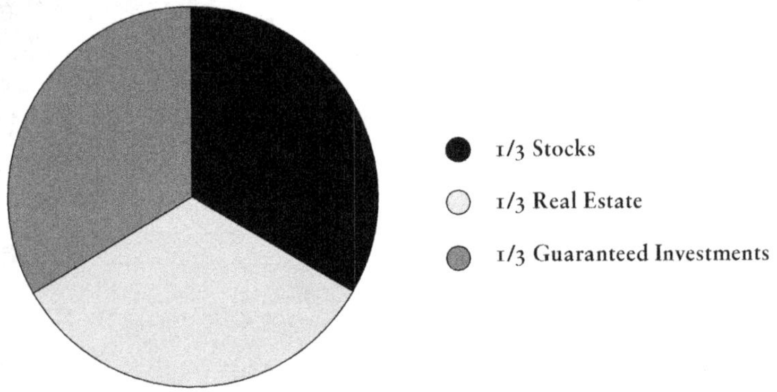

As important as it is to get into a market, it is equally important to have an exit strategy. When you get to a point where you are ready to sell a stock, here are a couple of pointers to consider when making that decision.

- Have some kind of preset target. This target may be when the stock reaches a specific price, or when the stock has gained 30, 40, or 50%. It could also be when the stock has lost 15, 25, or 35% of its value. This target may also be a time target associated with a specific goal.
- These are all good reasons for selling. But more importantly make sure that you are selling for your reasons and not someone else's pre-imposed reasons.
- Side note, if there is a market panic, it is hard to sometimes sit by and do nothing. So one idea is to sell off between 5 and 10% of your least favorite assets. This will make you feel like you have done something to help your mental and financial state.
- If something dramatic that has happened in the marketplace that directly impacts your stocks value, like a foreign government has made overtones about taking over a specific company.
- Finally, when considering selling any investment do not forget about the tax consequences of such actions.

One of the most important considerations that can reduce a portfolio's overall performance is the capital gains tax that must be paid when assets are sold. While long-term investing will help you avoid unnecessary taxes, whenever an asset is sold at a higher price than was paid at purchase – a capital gains tax must be paid on the profit.

Research shows that frequent traders are less successful with their portfolios than long-term investors primarily because of the tax consequences involved.

Because the tax code changes so often, be sure to consult your tax accountant about your individual situations.

While these are some overly simplified reasons for selling some of your investments the point is to make sure you have a well defined exit strategy, should it become necessary to execute that strategy.

So now that you are a disciplined investor with your own investing style, it is time to start investing. As an investor, you will be inundated with weekly economic reports released by the Federal government, businesses, and numerous other sources. Although these reports have been regularly released for decades, they were not important until now because you were not paying attention to them. They will now have your undivided attention.

Probably, the four most important market indicators, the factors that contribute to the market moving up or down, are: employment, inflation, consumerism, and investor confidence in the market.

The primary key of the four indicators is employment. The U. S. Bureau of Labor and Statistics releases its monthly unemployment report on the first Friday of every month. This report is so important because the level of employment is the clearest indicator of the health of the U. S. economy.

The unemployment report is so vital to the U. S. economy that both the bond and stock markets sometimes have the largest one-day gains or losses based on this single report. The report publicly announces how many jobs the U. S. economy gained or lost in the previous month.

This report has tremendous influence on the other indicators primarily because the U. S. economy is 70% consumer driven. Unemployed consumers do not make purchases, thus lowering company profits, which triggers more layoffs, and increases unemployment. Additionally, if employees are in fear of losing their jobs, they withhold their spending which in turn impacts consumer confidence and investor activity.

Consumerism (the study of what people buy and where they buy it) has a direct impact on both corporate profits and stock prices. Although there are several ways to measure consumer spending habits, the most used method is to measure consumer confidence.

This confidence quotient is important because it is a forward looking index, which complements stocks because the stock market is a forward looking market. The other two separate indices that are looked at to give an overall snapshot of consumer confidence are retail sales (historic buying patterns), and, new housing starts and new home sales (future confidence).

The third most important market indicator may be investor activity. This includes foreign investors who purchase U. S. Treasuries. When foreign investors purchase Treasuries, this drives interest rates lower and stock prices tend to move higher. The reverse is also generally true – – higher interest rates generally means lower stock prices (which as a buyer is a good time to purchase stocks).

Contrary to popular belief, during a bull market, when everyone is rushing to purchase stocks, may not be the best time to purchase new stocks because the bull market is driving prices higher. I believe, one of the best times to purchase stocks is in a bearish market (lower prices), when everyone is reluctant to make stock purchases.

The fourth major market indicator is the Consumer Price Index which measures inflation by looking at how expensive items have become for the average consumer. The second index to help measure inflation is the Producer Price Index which measures the cost of raw materials for makers of products.

These two indices, less the volatility of food and energy, help to formulate the inflation percentage. However, everyone watches the price of oil because it impacts the price of all products, globally.

Historically, inflation has averaged about 3% per year. This means your investments will have to earn a little extra to reach your goals because inflation is going to cause prices to rise (it will take more dollars to pay for things like college).

Now that you are aware of these indicators and their importance in the marketplace, the real trick is to learn how to read these indicators, and more importantly, what does the market expect of the indicators. Once you can do this, then you are ready to make sophisticated investment decisions that could pay huge financial dividends for you and yours.

If you only have $20 to start and can commit to $20 per month, considering looking into DRIPs, discussed earlier in the chapter.

Over time you will have graduated to $100 or have a couple of hundred to invest. Go research some index funds for a low-cost way to establish your presence. Two excellent resources in this price category are www.ishares.com and www.sharebuilder.com.

Do not be put off by the acronym ETF, because basically these are exchange-traded mutual funds that trade like stocks. While there are fees charged for each investment, regular investments will make for a good way to see your starting money grow.

Now, if you have $500 in seed money, consider opening a brokerage account. There are a lot available and their fees may be reasonable. The key here is to keep your costs down to 2% or less for all transactions.

If you have $1,000 available for starters, considering setting up a ROTH IRA. With regular yearly or monthly contributions, you can build up a considerable nest egg for your retirement. You can also go to Google and look for ROTH IRA calculators to get an idea of how your money will grow, or talk to your banker. One resource that I have found to be very helpful is www.mint.com. Once you log onto the website, go to "Find Savings," at the top of the page, and then look for IRA, Roth IRA, and IRA Rollover.

One of the best resources I have ever read about small investors getting into the marketplace was *How To Invest $50 – $5,000* by Nancy Dunnan. The author provides a systematic way to gradually invest your money as it grows across a variety of low-cost investment options or good places for starter funds at various investment levels.

The best interactive tool that I have used to help find stocks and funds that meet my investing objectives is the MSN Money Investment Toolbox. This toolbox can be downloaded from www.msn.com.

This tool will help you regardless of whether you are trying to invest a $1,000 in mutual funds or $10,000 in stocks. Another tool that is designed specifically to educate online investors can be found at www.investingonline.org.

Regardless of where you invest, everyone has to learn how to manage risk. But do not let this idea scare you because this is something we all do every day.

For example, when you get up to go to work every morning, you manage risk by paying attention to the road, driving defensively, controlling your speed, obeying traffic violations, and so on.

Managing investment risk is just like driving. You have to first learn the rules of the road (driver's education), then you have to practice driving until you build your parent's trust to let you drive alone, knowing you are going to make some mistakes, hopefully not too serious or expensive (learner's permit), before long you are a seasoned pro (driver's license). But for those of you that want a more formal way of learning how to manage risk, there is a college course called "Applied Quantitative Analysis: Decision Making Under Uncertainty" that can help your investment risk skills.

Now that you have all of this information, it is time that you learn how to read a stock chart. Instead of recreating the wheel, there are two very good sources to help you learn how to read the charts. The first one is found at www.swing-trade-stocks.com/support-files/howtoreadcharts.pdf. The second one is a video that can be found at www.youtube.com, search for "How To Read Stock Tables For Dummies."

While there are a number of different ways to measure an investment's performance – yield (measures the income paid by an investment during a specific period, generally a year, divided by the investment's price), return (the money you make or lose on an investment), capital gains and losses, or other benchmarks such as the Dow Jones Industrial Average, S&P 500 Index, Lipper Fund Indexes, and so on, there are two other options also available.

There is a course or group of courses called "Evaluating Financial Performance," that is taught at colleges and universities all over the country, including some community colleges, that can teach students in detail the various methods of evaluating the performance of an investment, and the reasons why one method may be better than others, depending on the type of investment involved.

The other option is to order free prospectuses from www.orderannualreports.com/kiplingers to learn how to read and evaluate an investment's performance firsthand. Practically speaking, a combination of all the above-mentioned methods is probably the most reasonable approach.

Some individuals are turning to day trading classes to learn how to invest better or better understand the changing marketplace landscape because they have heard about someone who made a whole lot of money day trading. If you choose to go this route, make sure you are studying under a reputable instructor and know exactly what you are getting for your money. Check out any day trading firm with your state securities regulator or at www.nasaa.org/QuickLinks/ContactYourRegulator.cfm.

Day traders are so defined because they buy and sell stock on the same day. Admittedly, there are those who have made or do make money day trading, but for the vast majority of individuals, day trading is like gambling because day traders purposely do not hold stocks for more than a few minutes or a few hours during the 8-hour trading day that the market is open.

There is another huge, but seldom mentioned, hurdle to jump for those who would consider becoming day traders. The minimum account balance for a patterned day trader, one who is recognized as a day trader by profession and according to their transaction activity, is $25,000. And anytime the account falls below $25,000, then no trading is allowed. There are a number of other financial requirements for day traders that you should read up on, if you are contemplating day trading.

If you enjoy a high stress job where you will spend the entire day sitting in front a computer looking for stocks moving up or down, a job that requires you to spend lots of money before you make any, and, one that you will generally lose lots of money before you make any, without ever getting a vacation, than day trading may be for you.

But, if you have that kind of money to lose, why is it not invested in a less risky investment that at least has the opportunity to make a reasonable return?

Just as there are things you should do to learn how to invest, there are things you should not do as well. Here is a brief, but important list of things not to do.

1. Do not destroy any documents received regarding your investments.

2. Do not ignore fees or transactions you do not understand.

3. Do not be pressured into anything based on a sales pitch by a broker, even your own, like, "you are going to miss out on an impor-

tant opportunity."

4. Do not ever send a broker money without thoroughly checking them out.

5. Do not rush to invest in "penny stocks." These stocks are inherently risky!

To Broker a Deal

Although you may not yet be ready to hire on a broker, it is, nonetheless, prudent to plan for the service before you need it. And since I did train, in part, to be a broker, I do understand what a good broker looks like, and you should too. Here are a few questions you should ask any potential broker.

1. What are your business credentials? Your education?
2. Which licensing exams have you passed? Did you pass each exam the first time? Since most exams require re-certification every few years, when was the last time you were tested?
3. Have you ever been reprimanded by the Securities and Exchange Commission or any other regulatory board?
4. Have you ever been employed by any financial institution that was bailed out by the taxpayers?
5. What is your investment strategy?
6. Do you have any references?
7. How are you paid?
8. What is the minimum account size you work with?
9. Do you work primarily with individuals or institutions?

As you grow in your investing savvy, you will surely develop other questions that you will want to add to your list of potential questions. In the meantime, as you start out investing, you will start out working with a discount broker, someone who gives you zero advice, executes your orders, and nothing more. However, I would recommend you having at least one meeting with a full-service broker so that you can get a better idea of how to match your wants and needs to various investments.

Later, you may want to change to a full-service broker – someone who gives you personalized advice, places your orders, and more.

In the end, the decision to use a broker, full-service or not, is completely your decision. Just make sure that whatever you decide works for you. If you are unsure, continue shopping until you find the right shoes for you.

What You Don't Know

There are a few empirical rules of investing that I accidentally stumbled upon in college, which means I learned them while I was in college, but they were not a part of the formal curriculum. In truth, I learned them from an acquaintance who had extremely wealthy parents.

I have already told you about the **Rule of 72** earlier in the chapter. Let's look at the **Rule of 120**.

The **Rule of 120** states that if you take 120 and subtract your age, that is the percentage of your investments that should be in stocks (120 – (48 years old) = 72).

Very similar to the **Rule of 72** are the **Rules of 70** and **69**. **Rule** 70 is another rule to calculate how long it takes one's money to double. The formula is 70/X, with X being the percentage rate a particular investment is earning (70/4.5% = 15.5 years or 70/.045 = 15.5 years).

Rule 69 is a third doubling rule to help guide investing growth, but with a slightly different formula. The formula is 69/X with X being the percentage rate a particular investment is earning + .35 (69/4.5% +.35 = 15.7 years).

Most individuals are aware of these rules, even if they have not been exposed to them in great detail. However, I was particular shocked when I learned of the next three rules.

Rule 114 is an estimate of how long it would take to triple one's money. The formula is to take 114 divided by the interest rate of one's expected rate of return, then you will have an estimate of how long it takes to triple your money (114/8% = 14.25 years or 114/.08 = 14.25 years).

Rule 144 is an estimate of how long it would take to quadruple one's money. The rule works the same way that **Rule 114** works. (144/8% = 18 years or 144/.08 = 18 years).

Rule 78 does not directly apply to investing, but it is a practice that may still be utilized by some lenders. The rule or the practice is that lenders front-load the interest on loans to guarantee their profit margin is maintained in case a borrower decides to pay the loan off sooner than is contractually required.

Legally, any loan that is calculated under **Rule** 78 cannot exceed 61 months. Some states have actually outlawed this lending practice. The rule is so named because the sum of 12 payments in a one-year loan is equal to 78 (1+2+3+4+5+6+7+8+9+10+11+12 = 78). Therefore, one would pay most of the interest on the loan before any substantial repayment of the principal was made.

Bedrock Gold

While it pains me to say this, but when it comes to business, one man's loss is another man's gain, which is proving to be true in the mortgage crisis sweeping across the U. S.

If you are looking for investment options other than the stock market, commodities, or bonds, something that is more tangible, then you may want to consider foreclosure properties.

Here is a simplified layout of how the process works. If you are looking to purchase a property not in foreclosure, the traditional way or after the foreclosure process has run its course, you can refer back to my detailed housing instructions in Chapter 9.

Although the foreclosure process varies in each state, basically, once a homeowner misses three or more payments, the lender sends a letter to the homeowner and a copy to the county where the property is situated. This letter is actually a default notice.

Some states require a judicial foreclosure and others follow a non-judicial foreclosure process. Judicial requires the lender to sue the homeowner to take back the property, non-judicial does not have this requirement.

Either way, the default notice alerts seekers that the property is now available for possible purchase. Since this is the easiest and quickest way to acquire a foreclosed property, a serious shopper may want to get a subscription service to www.Foreclosures.com and/or www.RealtyTrac.com.

Both of these and other services may offer short trial periods for newcomers to browse around and try these services before actually committing any funds. Before you sign up for these or any other services over the internet (or elsewhere), make sure you understand exactly what it is you are committing to; and, make sure you know exactly what you expect to get out of these services.

If you are an old fashioned individual, you can simply visit your local recorder's office (court records) to search through the notices by hand (time consuming).

Once you find a prospective property now comes the delicate task of convincing the owner that the best action is to sell their home to you. While a lot of individuals do this in the form of a letter, I do not recommend sending an unsolicited letter to an already skeptical homeowner.

Instead, I recommend making a face-to-face house call to sit down and explain the benefits of you purchasing their home, which the primary reason may be that they get from underneath the debt with their credit still intact. Some investors may also buy the house and then lease it back to the owners so that they continue to live in their home without the future threat of ever having to leave it again.

But before you start making any offers you want to make sure there are no other unpaid debts on the property including any kind of liens, tax or otherwise.

At the same time, you want to move quickly to beat any competitors, and before the disgruntled homeowner trashes the property.

But do not start celebrating just yet because even if you get the property before the bank steps in, you will still have to get that lender's approval.

A short sale, which is a sale short of the bank's investment in a property, may take a while for approval even with the threat of foreclosure because banks are simply reluctant to lose money.

The owner of the property normally negotiates an agreement with the lender to sell the home for less than their loan's value, but even if a new buyer is found, the sale is still subject to final bank approval.

But if a property goes through the entire foreclosure process, then it will end at the steps of the courthouse. If a property reaches this point, there will be public notices of an auction to be held whereby the proceeds will go to repaying the lender, after fees are deducted.

The bank sets a specified time period in which the sale must occur, otherwise the property will go into foreclosure. The bank will way the short sale losses against the foreclosure costs, which can still be a considerable amount of time. And for the seller, there may be some tax consequences because this sale may constitute forgiven debt.

However, if the property goes through the complete foreclosure process, for the buyer, they must show up at the courthouse prepared to pay their bid price in full that very day, and they are going to be purchasing this property sight unseen. If you are the winner, you may also have to pay off other debts, so your hope is to find a home that is worth both the mortgage and any other outstanding debts on the property.

The buyer may incur other costs such as eviction services and repair costs as well. Therefore, if you plan on attending an auction, make sure you have done your homework and have some price limits in mind based on comparable homes in your area.

If the auction does not produce any buyers, do not despair. An interested buyer can go straight to the bank at this point and negotiate directly with the bank for a post-foreclosure property that has been cleaned up legally, financially, and physically.

In the event that a bank still has not been able to get rid of a foreclosed property, some banks hire auctioneers to sell the house directly. This gives you a chance to see the property before it is sold, but it will also probably add a 5% fee to any price you pay.

The big question is how does one decide what to offer for a piece of property?

The typical formula is as follows:

> ((After Repair Value) X (.68%) – (Total Repairs Cost) – (Anticipated Profit)) = Maximum Allowable Offer (MAO)

The MAO is the highest price a buyer can afford to pay for a property and still make a profit. So when making a bid, do not start with the MAO, start lower and work up to the MAO if necessary. The ARV is the future property value after all repairs are completed.

This offer is most likely based upon a conventional appraisal. However, since the real estate market has changed, a buyer should consider other factors when determining a property's value that includes the local supply and demand, interest rates, and other localized market data that can help you purchase a property at what most closely resembles a true market price.

The old adage is true, you make your money on real estate at the beginning of the deal. This means buy low and sell high.

If you are the one facing foreclosure, be aware of wolves in sheep clothing, but if you cannot tell by their clothing, you sure can tell by their actions.

If you are facing foreclosure, DO NOT:

- sign your deed over to anyone under any circumstances.
- make your mortgage payments to anyone but your lender. Make sure you communicate with your lender during this period.
- be pressured into making a decision in a hurry.
- give anyone any cash for any reason.
- be talked into paying for any services before they are rendered.
- hesitate to call the police if you have any questions or doubts.

Meanwhile, while your property is in the pre-foreclosure stage, here are some other options to consider.

- Do not ignore any written correspondence from your lender. Answer every single letter and be prepared to provide financial documentation.
- Do not leave your home under any circumstances. If you leave you may hurt your chances for any assistance.
- Contact the U. S. Department of Housing and Urban Development (HUD) for their assistance and to find a HUD-approved counselor in your area.
- You might qualify for a special forbearance, mortgage modification, or a partial claim which may be a one-time payment from the FHA-Insurance fund under certain circumstances.
- Do not sign any documents, discuss your situation with strangers you do not absolutely trust based on the above criteria, and make sure you do not give anyone your personal information.

Research shows that most foreclosures sell for approximately 5% below market value. But there may be some additional incentives offered by the lien holder such as waiving some closing costs, offering a better interest rate, and some flexibility on the down payment.

But what really determines if this property is worth investing your money is location, location, location.

If the house has been trashed or neglected, as most foreclosures have been, but it is in the right location, do your homework to determine a reasonable offer. Remember, if you are not embarrassed by your offer, then your offer is too high!

Depending on how motivated the lender is to move the property, you have more bargaining power in the negotiations. But do not blow a good deal by asking for too many little things that will not improve the property's value or your loan terms.

Also do not forget about those hidden foreclosures that are on the books. These are new homes built by builders that the bank has taken control of because the builder did not have a buyer at the end of the loan so the bank took the home based on the construction loan that was given to the builder. But no one associated with the property is ever going to call it a foreclosure because it sends the message that the property needs to move, and do so quickly.

While I have served as a property manager for the Federal government, and have taken some classes in furtherance of that job, most of this in-depth information came from sitting up late nights looking at infomercials, over and over again.

Between my formal training, my professional experience, and my insomnia, I have developed a list of things to do when considering real estate as an investment.

1. Take time to learn the real estate market in your area. Two ways to do this is to, one, drive around town and see where the construction is happening. The second, more sophisticated way, is to visit the public planning board, which maintains the public plans for growth. These details will help you know where you should be looking to invest your money, before prices skyrocket in any one particular area.

2. Make sure you put together a reliable team that includes an attorney, an agent, an appraiser, and a handy man.

3. There are a number of available options to acquire property, including lease options, rent to own, and contract assignments, to name a few.

4. Learn how to negotiate with confidence.

5. Learn how to evaluate properties and make an offer.

6. Learn the basic must have clauses for buying, selling, leasing, and rent to own contracts.

7. Learn how to creatively purchase property with little or no money down.

8. Spend some time volunteering and shadowing property managers so that you can gain experience and ask questions.

9. Learn how to read bankruptcy filings, these will help you get an idea of properties that may be coming on the market, and their early potential value.

10. Homes can be broken down just like cars and sold off in pieces, sometimes the sum of the pieces is greater than the whole.

11. Do not purchase more real estate than you can afford to pay for should you lose a tenant for a long period or just a few months. These "assets" are not yours until they are paid in full!

12. Use your skills to solve problems for other people. People pay a great deal of money to others who can solve problems for them. Learning how to save someone's home from foreclosure can make you a very wealthy person.

13. Local governments may have a surplus of distressed properties and may be open to creative ways to dispose of these properties, including land leases for agricultural purposes.

14. Real estate is a viable alternative for creating wealth when compared to stocks for those who do not like investing in paper assets. With some skills on how to improve a property, learning how to control costs, and knowing how to leverage one's money, real estate can be another way to build a highly profitable portfolio.

15. A good real estate investor controls the value of their property by the improvements made to the property, and other variables that can be controlled with a little attention to details. (The U. S. Navy taught me it is the little details that end up causing us the most problems.)

For me, I made the best of being poor by using it to motivate me to learn, by any means necessary, the crucial skills to be better able to control my own financial destiny, and to be more appreciative of even the smallest financial gains. Life was hard because I had to make some very difficult choices, which oftentimes required me to acquire new skills, not always an easy task. But the dedication and hard work paid off. Once you learn how to put together your own strands of financial gains, you too will appreciate the hard work that you put into building your own impressive portfolio.

There have been hundreds of books written, each dedicated to the above points in great detail. While I am not going to tell you what to read (this time), I think it is a good idea to read a lot of books written from different points of view, even opposing viewpoints. This knowledge will help you get a more well-rounded understanding by teaching you how to create a solution list like the one I proposed earlier in this chapter. Reading will also help you to see that there is no right way or wrong way to solve a problem; but, there is a way that works best for you.

Most of these resources are available at your local public library, online, and maybe at your local community college. If you happen to be near a college or university, that is an even better access to people, resources, and knowledge.

I have worked hard digging ditches, loading and unloading trucks, and a few other back breaking jobs that took a lot of labor with poor returns, comparatively speaking. But for me, it was either use my back or my brain. I chose to save my back.

As you grow in your investor savvy, you may learn to find homes before they go into foreclosure. Homes in default may be a rewarding challenge with a little homework.

One final fact is worth noting here. Some states have what is known as a "Redemption" law whereby the owner can, under certain circumstances, get their property back. So before you spend any money or write a contract, make sure you know the laws in your state.

If you are interested in purchasing a piece of real estate for investment purposes, you still have to do your due diligence and:

- use all available sources to find foreclosed properties, including HUD's website, www.hmbireo.com.
- research the property and the neighborhood before bidding.

- talk to a lender before making a bid to ensure that getting a loan on a foreclosed property is not going to be an issue.
- hire a lawyer to do a title search.
- hire a home inspector, if you have access to the house prior to the sale.

There are basically three options to purchasing a pre-foreclosure property.

1. Purchase the property from the seller at a discount, and if there is much equity in the property, this may open up some other options for the sellers like possibly getting cash back at the end of the deal.

2. Take over the loan and make up any back payments. The advantage is that this stops the foreclosure process, and the new owner will make the payments while the original owners get to still live in the property. The only drawback for the seller is that the loan will remain in their name until some future date. Purchasing property this way is a "subject to" purchase. Title transfers, but the occupants do not. Although most banks have a due on sale clause in all of their contracts, as long as the payments are being made on time, most banks will not enforce that clause until and unless a problem arises. This is a powerful leveraging tool for any buyer because it avoids all sorts of fees, requires little out of pocket cash, and their credit is not impacted or at risk.

3. Negotiate with the lender to purchase the property at a discount, commonly known as a short sale, accepting less than what is owed on the property. The challenge for the buyer is to figure out what is a reasonable discount. Most lenders are motivated to sell property because they do not want to be property owners and as long as they hold the property they are responsible for taxes, insurance, fees, closing costs, and realtor costs, among others. The biggest motivator for most banks, especially in today's market, is that cash now is better than cash later.

If you are taking over a loan there are some very important documents that need to be prepared in order to make sure the deal is legally secure. Although you may not yet be ready to enter into this sophisticated transaction, I am providing you with a potential document list so you will be ready when that time comes.

1) **Standard Purchase and Sales Contract** that sets the terms of the sale.

2) **Authorization to Release Information** allows the buyer to contact the bank, discuss the property and loan details, and negotiate payment arrangements.

3) **Letter of Intent** states that you, the buyer, will make every effort to stop the foreclosure, but are not making any guarantees to the seller.

4) **Warranty Deed** conveys ownership of the property to a trustee and must be signed in front of a notary (preferably the lien holder's notary).

5) **Declaration of Trust** creates a land trust and keeps your personal name off of public records.

6) **Trustee Letter** identifies the trustee and indicates that individual will be responsible for all future payments, including trustee financial information. The letter also indicates that the trustee is taking ownership of the property "subject to."

7) **Escrow Letter** requests the lender to apply all escrow funds to the loan balance when the loan is paid in full.

8) **Power of Attorney** that applies only to the property in question, signed before a notary, and gives the trustee authority to handle all situations arising regarding the specific property.

9) **Residential Real Estate Disclosure Form** discloses any property defects in compliance with all federal and state laws.

10) **Hardship Letter** gives the seller the opportunity to explain in detail to the lender why they are unable to make payments and thus require the assistance of a third party.

11) **Financial Statement** of the seller will be reviewed by the bank to make sure that the seller does not have the ability to repay the loan now or in the future.

The same logic holds true for a short sale, so here is a list of documents that should be included in a short sale package to the bank.

1) **Cover Letter** requesting a short sale and why your offer is the

right offer for the lender and the property.

2) **Authorization To Release Information**

3) **Standard Real Estate Purchase and Sale Contract**

4) **Borrower's Hardship Letter** including evidence of attempt to sell.

5) **Borrower's Financial Information** (Tax Returns, Bank Statements, Financial Statement)

6) **HUD Statement** that shows the money disbursements as proposed to the seller.

7) **Value Opinion** shows the property value based on comparables, using the lowest valued comparables available.

8) **Repair Estimate** that proves why the property should be discounted.

9) **Trustee Sale Notice** shows the lender that you are aware of the foreclosure process, and includes a copy of the foreclosure notice as a reminder.

10) **Color Photos** that highlight the problems on the property.

During my research of real estate investors, I discovered several traits that were repeated over and over again in their investment strategies.

1) They know their real estate market better than most professionals. They have a tendency to compare property values and rents against the sale price of comparables.

2) They understand tax implications of an investment, and work the right property at the right financing to lessen tax consequences. They have a good tax accountant on their advisory team.

3) These individuals focus on what they know – commercial properties, apartment buildings, condos, fixer-uppers, foreclosures, and so on.

4) They know the cost of every project going in – all of the financial statements, vacancy costs if any, loan payments, operating expenses, cash flow, insurance costs, utility costs, etc.

5) They know their tenants – whether they are short-term or long-term, and their financial patterns.

6) They have their own property inspector on their team.

7) They have learned to use technology to their advantage. BB&T has some of the best investment calculators I have tried on the internet, and you do not have to be a current customer to use them. (www.bbt.com/bbt/Financial-Education/calculators/investment.html)

8)They are avid readers.

Although there are some similar traits that are maintained by all investors, there are as many varied ways to purchase properties with no money down. But as a way to help get the creative juices flowing, Robert G. Allen lists 50 different no money down techniques on his website, http://www.multiplestreamsofincome.com.

Once you get to the website, click on "keyword search," and then look for "nothing down." This same list can also be printed from the website.

Another hot real estate topic is flipping houses made popular by the television show of the same name. For those who are interested in flipping houses, you can go to the internet and research some of the most popular tips recommended by the experts to save you both time and money, and some may even help you locate properties and financing.

While we are discussing the potential for profits in real estate, let us not forget the benefits of investing in raw land.

Now the difference in investing in raw land and speculating in raw land is that the latter involves purchasing land in an undeveloped area with hopes of development in the future.

Investing in raw land is buying tracts of land in developed areas and waiting for the development to reach your parcels.

But in a way, both purchases are investing and speculating, simultaneously. Neither purchase guarantees to generate a profit and both are hoping that development eventually reaches their parcel, barring any unforeseen circumstances.

However, with a little preliminary research both of these purchases can be turned into profitable ventures, given a little time.

Conventional wisdom shows there are four primary factors used to evaluate the investment potential of raw land purchases. Those factors are zoning, utilities, the number of acres, and whether or not the land lies in a flood plain.

One of the first things that any investor of raw land needs to find out, before making this type of purchase, is whether or not the land lies in a flood plain. Any land that lies in the flood plain is obviously unusable, and, therefore, must be subtracted from the available land for development purposes, and also subtracted from any profit.

This problem resolved, the second major issue is zoning. While zoning can be changed through a sometimes difficult process, the current zoning will tell the buyer what restrictions come with the land, and how the land may be subdivided.

The zoning office will also tell you whether or not there is a building moratorium on the land, the reason(s) why the moratorium may exist, and how to get that moratorium removed.

Utilities are the next major hurdle because if they already exist on the property this could be a tremendous savings; but, if they have to be extended to the property across already subdivided lots, this could be a tremendous but worthwhile cost, depending on the merits of each property.

Now, as the owner of the property you have two choices. You can either prepare, subdivide the land, and then sell it to builders all at your own cost. The second option is to hold the raw land and sell it to a developer and let them incur all the costs of development.

The latter is called wholesaling and presents a whole different option for making money by simply buying and reselling land.

Either way, all of these factors are necessary to determine the MAO for an undeveloped piece of land. To more precisely calculate the MAO, a buyer must first determine the exact number of buildable acres. Then, according to zoning regulations, the buyer must determine how many separate lots will be allowed per acre (if a housing development for example). But the process is the same for a shopping center or any other development.

Of the available land, approximately 20% of this land will be required for utilities, retention ponds, roads, sidewalks, and maybe some common land such as parks and recreational space. So, if an individual owned 100 acres of land that were all suitable for development, then 20 acres are not going to be available for individual lots (100 x .20 = 20 acres; 100 – 20 = 80 acres available for development).

Now using 80% of the land's total acreage, this will give you the total number of buildable acreage. Multiply the buildable acreage by the potential number of lots per acre. Then multiply that number by the asking price per lot.

In the example above, there are 80 buildable acres, which is equal to 43,560 square feet, which is equal to the size of a football field. If the zoning is medium density this could mean anywhere from three to seven homes per acre. In this example, this would mean 5 houses X 80 acres = 400 houses total.

Assuming a price of $30,000 per lot with a 400 house total would be a price of $12,000,000.

But do not forget to add in your other 20 acres that will be used inside the housing development. Divide $12,000,000 by 80 acres and you will get a price of $150,000 per acre. Then multiply $150,000 by 20 acres and you will get an additional $3,000,000.

Thus your total asking price would be $15,000,000 for 100 acres.

Then the buyer needs to estimate the developer's total costs by figuring out those costs on a per lot basis. Assuming really cheap costs for a developer of $5,000 per lot for a total of 400 lots, means a total cost of $2,000,000.

Finally, subtract the developer's total cost from the total dollar asking price for lots, and this should give you a MAO.

After subtracting the developer's total cost from the asking price, this leaves a $13,000,000 price tag.

It is important to remember that most builders will only pay a developer 20% of the total price of the house he expects to build on a property. So if the builder is going to build $300,000+ valued homes on the lot, then he will expect to pay about $60,000 per lot, for a total builder price tag of $24,000,000.

At a $300,000+ price tag for 400 homes, the builder would expect to make $120,000,000.

So it is easy to see how raw land pays off every step of the way, all the way through to the end.

Now if you require the services of a real estate agent at any time during a real property purchase, here are a few primary questions you need to have answered correctly to ensure a profitable working relationship.

1. Is this individual a novice or do they have some true experience in the business? By definition a novice in this case means less than 5 years experience.

2. Is the agent an investor, trader, or a salesperson? Investors are owners of real estate and understand the challenges. Traders buy and sell property for quick profits. A salesperson, in this case, is much like a stockbroker, when the deal is done they move on to the next customer.

3. Do they have any particular expertise, i.e., foreclosures, raw land, fixer-uppers, particular neighborhoods, particular price ranges?

4. What is their normal commission? Remember everything is negotiable depending on the level of service provided.

5. What kinds of marketing and advertising plans do they provide for their clients?

6. How many deals do they close on average and how quickly do they close?

7. Are they good at negotiating sticking points?

8. Do they work on weekends, and what is the best way to contact them?

9. Are there any potential conflicts that the client should be aware of such as family or other interests?

10. Do you have an assistant, and if so who is going to be handling the details of my purchase?

11. Do you already have an established relationship with a title company and escrow company?

If you are considering using a real estate agent for any reason, you should interview three different agents. Once you make your final choice, make sure you have an exit strategy in case the relationship changes.

Back to the Beginning

But with or without an agent, a successful investor in real estate or otherwise, must learn to ask questions rather than draw conclusions, despite what may seem obvious.

For example if you are presented with a choice of paying 10% for a loan versus 12%, do not assume the lower number is better. You need to ask questions.

It may be that the 10% comes with a 90-day repayment period and a huge penalty if not repaid. But the 12% may come with a 2-year repayment period, no penalty for early repayment, and the possibility of additional funds without raising the interest rate.

But you would not have known this if you had jumped to a conclusion without asking additional questions.

By asking questions you release your mind to think creatively as opposed to shutting down the creative process before it even begins.

Let me give you a few examples of creative thinking that will hopefully help you learn how to both ask questions and improve your creative thinking process.

Some years ago, this gentleman I knew purchased a 40-acre mobile home park with seller financing. He had no money and bad credit, so it was a challenge to come up with the $40,000 down payment.

He called a few lumber companies and made them some offers, and finally one company accepted what he was offering. He sold the company the right to cut down what turned out to be some very valuable lumber at one end of the property, and take it away once he took ownership of the property.

In exchange for this privilege, the lumber company paid him $40,000 which he used to make his down payment on the mobile-home park.

Quite some time ago, while living in Washington, DC, I had a friend who lived in a co-op building where everyone collectively owned the building and were responsible for all of the maintenance, like roofing, etc.

Then there was an outsider who wanted to purchase the building and turn the co-op units into condominiums. By a majority vote, those who did not want to sell would be forced to purchase a condominium in the new building and make the necessary repairs to bring their units up to the new standard, all of which they could not afford.

A group of them got together and offered to buy out those who wanted a quick sale (condominiums), but only if they would sell their units at a discounted price. In exchange for the sale, the sellers would get all cash at the completion of the sale.

Then the entire group went to the bank and borrowed against the building, and paid those who wanted their asking price but only if they collectively agreed to subordinate their mortgage to the new bank loan.

Once everyone that wanted to sell was out of the building, the remaining owners turned the several small units into a couple of huge units and sold the individual units and made a huge profit, and the buyers also keep their homes and improved the entire building's exterior as well.

Now that you have established yourself financially, you need to make sure you and your family are protected now and in the future. Seek out a reputable estate-planning attorney and look into establishing a trust to help you achieve your goals, without losing the shirt off your back, including making sure your taxes are paid in full.

Contact the College of Trust and Estate Counsel or National Academy of Elder Law Attorneys for referrals, (www.actec.org, and www.naela.org, respectively).

If you already have a will make sure you name a guardian for your minor children and an alternate; make sure all property is specifically named with a beneficiary; settle any family feuds that could become court issues; and, finally name an able-minded executor and an alternate, in addition to the guidelines

To Look Within	
Truthfully look at yourself	Assess who you are and where you are today. Now dig deep and find out who you are supposed to be and find out what gives your life purpose
Small Beginnings	Make yourself a promise and keep it. Get up early. Study your bible. Exercise. Eat Better. You become the controller of the environment instead of a puppet.
Homework	You skipped in high school, do not skip it now. With enough research you can get any job you want, build any dream you want. Start by studying what is already in front of you - the industry, individual company failures and successes, their needs, suppliers, customers, employees, and most of all their financial backers.
Write your own mission statement	This is not what you are doing now, this is what you want to do, and this is what you ought to be doing. Writing bridges the conscious and subconscious mind so that when you put something on paper the words become a creative force in your life because they are your words.
Over the Top	Stop accepting mediocrity in your life, your job and your family. "Just Okay" is not okay. When you decide to grow, the world will grow with you. Look at Moses, David and Joshua, to name a few who had to grow into their calling.
Concentrate	Sometimes concentration in your life and your finances will require big risk and yield bigger rewards!

they must follow along with a possible overseer.

If you do not have a will, get one! (www.nolo.com or www.legalzoom.com)

Finally, let me give you a few thoughts to help you find work you enjoy, a life that is financially secure, and a more hormonal existence with your environment. These rules are structured from various incidents from my past, and my own introspective research using some of Stephen Covey's work that was required by a previous employer of all their managers.

To Heir

The harder you work at building your portfolio the more important it becomes to protect those assets, even when they no longer belong to you. Although you pay taxes on your investments every step of the way, when it comes to passing assets to your heirs, it is critical that you understand the federal, state, and local tax impacts upon any gift, large or small.

I have endured the double heartache of losing a loved one and having to fight for their estate in probate court, and I did it all by myself. That entire terrible situation consumed my every waking moment for almost two years. I had to learn the process myself by spending hours doing legal research, and interviewing officers of the court so that I filed all the necessary papers correctly (this was all the easy part of what I was enduring at the time). I also realized that I should have gone on to law school. I am equally convinced that I would have been a judge today had I pursued that career path.

I also had to learn this process because I could not afford to pay for attorney services, and I could not get access to the estate to pay for those much needed legal services. So, I did what I had to do! If there is something you can do to avoid that heartache for your heirs, I recommend you do it for them, not you.

While numerous estate loopholes exist, it is important that you consult with an estate attorney. Although there are a number of options available for anyone to gain the proper legal advice -- membership legal networks, attorney services offered by your employer may be a little known benefit, the internet, church, and reduced consultation fees offered by the state bar association in your area -- I will tell you that one way the wealthy have avoided passing huge tax bills on to their heirs has been to create life insurance trusts.

A life insurance trust is a legally created entity (created by the owner of the assets) that owns the policy so that the value is kept out of the estate, unless and maybe until the law is changed. Then the individual names their designated beneficiaries as the trustees and makes annual gifts to the beneficiaries that they (the beneficiaries) use to pay the insurance premiums. These gifts are tax deductible up to a specific dollar amount.

The other gift you can give your heirs is the ability for them to take care of themselves whether they have $100, $100,000, or more. While I do believe I learned as much from my financial mistakes as I did my formal education, my formal education opened doors in some places that I may not have gotten open otherwise. I also believe that a college education can help one's future, when properly utilized.

However, let me make it absolutely clear that college is not for everyone, but it most cases, some college is better than none. That said, there is no reason why your family has to go broke trying to help prepare your children for a brighter future.

When it comes to a college education, there are a number of options, including community college for a few years, Peace Corps, community service, internships, apprenticeships, trade schools, military reserves, and, many employers will reimburse employees for college courses under certain conditions.

Therefore, if saving for college or pulling out your checkbook are not immediately available options, then you may want to research one of the options listed above in more detail.

But if you are looking for ways to invest and fund college education, then start by looking at financial aid. This process can help guide your investments and outlays.

First of all, it is important to note that under current rules, any money collected outside of tax-sheltered retirement accounts is going to decrease your availability for Federal and state financial aid because those accounts will be counted as assets against you for financial aid purposes.

So, the first thing you must do is to accumulate all college savings in protected accounts. This includes not putting any money into custodial accounts in your child name, except under limited circumstances. This is all necessary because many middle class and some modestly affluent individuals also qualify for financial aid, even if they do not demonstrate a financial need.

But before you rush off to sign up for this aid, remember grants do not have to be repaid, loans do; and, the financial aid formula does not favor students with assets, but it does favor their parents.

When it comes to tax-sheltered plans for college education, there are education savings accounts and 529 plans. These plans come in a lot of different shapes and sizes, so it might be worth it to shop around, particularly if your child has their eye on a specific school.

These are two of the most liquid options that are both tax free contributions and are still interest-earning accounts.

The only drawback, that I am aware of, regarding both plans are that the money in either account may be counted as an asset by a college, if it is held in your child's name (custodial account) and not in your name.

As for the 529-plan, if we are talking early teenage years, 12-15 years of age, then still look into putting your money into a 529 within your state, if your state offers tax deductions for these contributions.

Continue putting money into the 529 the entire time your child is in school, if your state's plan allows continual contributions. This will help lessen the financial impact on your child, and it will help decrease your need for outside financing that will have to be paid back after college (loans).

And when the time comes to start paying those university bills, pay them from the 529 account. This could be a tremendous savings on your end-of-the-year tax bill.

Now, if your kids have not yet reached those teenage years, here is a different approach to consider. You may want to look at investing in target-date 529s, which automatically adjust as your children get older.

The beauty of target-date funds is that they self-guide your investments between stocks and bonds as the college years get closer.

Finally, if your children are six years old or less, then start with whatever amount you can, and then make regular monthly investments into the 529 over the next 12+ years. The recommended investment plan mix for this age group is roughly 25% bonds and 75% stocks.

Also remember that you can sign up for any 529 plan in any state without being a resident of that particular state. However, if your state offers a 529 plan, then you will most likely not get a tax deduction for an out of state plan. So you can live in Florida, invest in a 529 plan in California, and your child can go to school in Iowa.

If you choose a broker-directed fund, which means you have to use broker services, you will obviously pay commissions. So stay away from those types of funds whenever possible, and use what are called direct funds – those that do not require a broker's services.

Here are two of the best websites I have found to help make college investment decisions – http://www.collegesavings.org/index.aspx, http://www.savingforcollege.com; and, here is one that has the possibility of some education grants, http://www.kn.pacbell.com/products/grants/locate.html.

Check with your state to find out what is the limit allowed for each of these accounts for yearly contributions and the maximum total contributions. You should also go to the U. S. Department of Education's website, www.ed.gov , to read up on the new rules regarding student loans.

Now that you have taken care of your children's education, it is time to turn your attention to your own future stability.

According to the Melbourne Mercer Global Pension Index, the U. S. ranked last on its pension-plan stability compared to 14 of our peer nations. The 2010 rankings were as follows:

1. Australia
2. Brazil
3. Canada
4. Chile
5. China
6. France
7. Germany
8. Japan
9. Netherlands
10. Singapore
11. Sweden
12. Switzerland
13. United Kingdom
14. United States

To read the report in its entirety, you may go to www.mercer.com and draw your own conclusion about the adequacy, sustainability, and integrity of our retirement system.

While you are at it, there are a few other things you may be able to do to help boost your retirement income, including delaying your Social Security withdrawals, if you can financially afford to (if the system is still intact by then), because the longer one waits to make their withdrawals, the more money will they collect.

Another option is to focus on no more than 6 mutual funds because by doing so you will have a far-reaching, diversified portfolio. And try to focus mostly on dividend-paying stocks because these will add more money to the bottom line of your portfolio, as long as you continue to reinvest those dividends.

There are also some new financial products that are available only to those individuals 55 and over that guarantee a specific income stream annually. However, these investments are not FDIC insured (investment that can be lost based on market conditions), so you have to do your due diligence and investigate these products carefully.

One of the best resources I have come across for those budget-conscious, thrifty shoppers is Consumer Reports: Money Adviser. Check out their website at www.consumerreports.org for subscription and back ordering costs.

Finally, when it comes to making sure that your retirement income is well-supported, you need to look very closely at your current healthcare costs and future needs. A couple of ways to help you understand the potential impacts are to: a) contact your current healthcare provider to see how you can get a copy of the new healthcare law and read it for yourself; b) consider purchasing some term life insurance and additional healthcare insurance while you are healthy; c) begin taking better care of yourself today – making better decisions about food and lifestyle choices.

One company that can help you with your lifestyle choices is Back-To-Eden, LLC, founded by Ed Brogdon. Ed can be reached at EdBrogdon@gmail.com.

Here are a few additional websites that may help those seeking medical attention or other assistance during tough times.

- www.helpingpatients.org
- www.aoa.org
- www.adea.org
- www.neweyesfortheneedy.org

Although you may have retired, I know retired individuals that work harder and smarter than younger individuals, not because they have to, but, because they want to. These individuals have found work they enjoy, believe in, and are committed to doing every day. How did they do this? They took their interests, experience, knowledge, and maybe some money and put all of these resources into defining a new career – – a career, for most seniors, that has made them the most profitable group during 2009, and continuing recession.

Everyone has dreams, regardless of whether or not they have money. If you do not believe me, go read wealthy Michael Jordan's journey to majority ownership of the Charlotte Bobcats. Although currency can solve a lot of problems, it does not solve all problems. So, I think it would be good for you to read his story to see his drive and determination in action, and to see how those intangible traits can bring in some very tangible results. Even with all his money, he still needed to do quite a bit of additional work before his dream came true.

For those of you who are still doubting your dreams and your wallets, I would like to close this chapter with three short stories about dreams and to demonstrate how a little adds up to a lot.

A few years ago, I closed a particular investment account with a major firm. Several months after I closed that account, I received a final check for $.26. That's right 26 cents!

I put the check in a drawer, not with my regular financial information that I reviewed daily, and forgot about it. One day, I stumbled across that check, sat down and calculated how much money that company made on the millions of others who did the exact same thing.

If only 1 million people did exactly what I did, the company made $260,000 for doing nothing! (1,000,000 X .26 = $260,000) If you were to add in interests and reinvestments, the company made more than several million dollars on our 26 cents!

A little goes go a long way.

I cannot recall who told me this story, but as it was told to me, there was this female bank teller who was well-liked and had been with the bank for quite some time. Every day for several years, this teller would take $.01 from every account she touched every single day. She would then funnel that $.01 into her own account.

Again, I cannot recall how her deeds were uncovered, but someone stumbled upon her account only to find out that she had more than $1 million stashed away. After the investigation, needless to say she does not work for the bank any more.

The love of money is the root of all evil!

One day, I had taken a relative to a drug store to pick up their prescription. My relative's change was one penny. But, instead of giving my relative her penny, the cashier just closed the drawer.

I went over to the cashier and asked her where was our change? She did not apologize, but in fact, she gave me a nasty stare, opened the drawer, gave me the penny, closed the drawer, and said, "It's only a penny!"

I was fine with everything until she made her comment. After her comment, I was livid because her objectives were abundantly clear.

I immediately went and got the manager. After I finished explaining the entire situation, the manager assured me he would discharge the matter.

A couple of weeks later I went back to the same store, alone this time, to pick up another prescription. That pharmacy technician was no longer employed with the company.

The company and the manager knew, just as I knew, that there was no way to calculate exactly how much money this young lady had taken from her customers and/or directly from the company's register (not a very sophisticated accounting system).

You cannot have a dollar without having a penny.

My point is that dreams are very powerful motivators. You can let them motivate you for good, bad, or nothing at all. But in the end, they are still your dreams!

All I wanted to do in this chapter was give you enough information so that you could see that your dreams do have some options.

Chapter Twelve

To Thine Ownself

I have heard a number of people jokingly state their credit was so bad they wished someone would steal their identity. Although misguided, I understand the sentiment behind the statement. However, the reality is that if a thief can get their hands on your vital information, they will find a way to exploit that information for their gain. Maybe the old adage is true, "one man's trash is another man's treasure."

I personally know several individuals, with "seemingly" bad credit, who had their identity stolen and were later arrested for traffic violations and other serious charges. Some of those individuals are still fighting to recover from those problems more than ten years after the fact.

Although most of us understand that identity theft (ID theft) occurs when someone uses your personally identifying information to commit fraud against you and quite possibly others, it is hard to grasp the idea that we are sometimes unwitting accomplices to these same crimes that are perpetuated against us, in part, because many of us have not been taught how to protect that which is truly important.

I recently read somewhere that the net gain to thieves for these kinds of intrusions on our privacy was approximately $13,500.

For example, if you are one of those individuals with "supposedly" bad credit, then, someone else has figured out a way to make roughly $13,500 off of that same bad credit. That is astonishing!

To put this in a proper perspective, this means that a thief can steal your personally identifying information, which includes, your name, Social Security number, credit card numbers, and any other financial information, and earn more money than a hard working individual who is considered poor by the Federal poverty standard (somewhere between $9,000 – $11,000).

Another reason ID theft is so prevalent is that our identities may be the hottest products for sale in this "new" global economy because every identity is a one-of-a-kind product. These kind of unique products demand high prices, so thieves will do whatever is necessary to meet (supply) that demand (remember the economics lesson from Chapter 11).

The Federal Trade Commission (FTC) estimates approximately 9 million Americans have their identities stolen each year. According to my math, ID theft is worth $121.5 billion (9 million X $13,500), at a minimum.

If my geography is correct, there are currently 195 countries in the world.

ID theft is large enough to be the 53rd largest economy in the world. Simultaneously, ID theft operates as a sub-economy in the overall U. S. economy because that $121.5 billion is productive money that is pulled out of the U. S. economy.

The most likely primary source for identity thieves is the internet where online data brokers collect and sell everything from utility records to current and former addresses. In fact, armed with only an address, a thief can search your homeownership information, tax payments, home value, and other vital data simply by logging into your county's tax information through the internet.

These data brokers gather all of this information from any variety of available sources and compile it all into one file on you or whomever. Then, they sell their compiled dossier to information seekers, without care or regard to whether or not they (buyers) have a legitimate purpose, notwithstanding the fact that the brokers may not have a legitimate purpose in gathering the information. They then resell it again and again, as many times as buyers will purchase it.

The worst part of all is that a great many of these information files are found to contain multiple, egregious errors that can be further exploited against the identifying individual, a true two-edged sword.

If you think that ID theft or other similar crimes are not serious, let me give you a true story, worse-case scenario, from a newspaper story I read a couple of years ago. At least one major news network, CBS News, also reported on this story.

In July, 1999, the then 21-year-old Liam Youens contacted Docusearch, an online-broker still doing business today, to retrieve the work address of one of his former high school classmates.

According to court records, Docusearch hired a private investigator to illegally acquire the work address for Amy Boyer through a practice known as "pretexting."

The court defined pretexting as the practice of collecting information about an individual using false pretenses. In Amy Boyer's case, the Docusearch private investigator pretended to be Boyer's insurance company, called Boyer's workplace, obtained the address – all over the telephone.

Youens waited until Amy left work, at the dentist office, then drove up beside her car, called her name, and shot her dead. All with information provided by the online data broker.

While this is the most tragic case that I am personally aware of, it is obviously clear that identity theft can take many criminal forms. Regardless of whether the thief has obtained a credit card, or rented a private home, most individuals do not find out about the crime immediately, unless you have a specific service such as *Lifelock*.

However, while an ID theft protection service may be helpful, to protect yourself from this kind of theft does not specifically require the purchase of an ID theft protector service.

But for most individuals, the crime goes unnoticed unless a bill does not arrive when normally expected, or when unexpected statements start coming to their address. Yet, the crime may still not be noticed at this point if you are one of those individuals who does not open their mail until it is time for you to pay the bills.

When unknown creditors start calling your home, unexpectedly, then most individuals start to take notice and panic. Unfortunately, by then, the damage is generally done and repair may not be as simple as one may think.

While some victims end up resolving their problems quicker than others, many spend hundreds of dollars making those repairs but still may end up with some significant financial losses for an unknown number of years. I have a personal friend who spent an entire weekend behind bars because of an ID theft situation that is still not completely resolved after four years of litigation.

Despite my sometimes violent recommendations that every home should have a diamond cutter paper shredder for all of those preapproved mail-in offers and other personal information that needs to be destroyed, those times where my cries have gone unheeded have resulted in years of financial torment. Let the chips fall where they may.

Probably, the second most prevalent way for information to be stolen is through dumpster cruising. But instead of cruising the main drag or the boulevard at night, these thieves primarily do their cruising during the day. Although some of them have given a new meaning to 8-to-5 job, there are those who still cruise at night, generally on the nights that the trash is put out for the morning pick up.

Whether it be day or night time cruising, the plan is the same. Drive through the targeted neighborhood, scout the better looking houses in the neighborhood, rummage through the trash for documents, score their find and leave. It really is that simple.

Most cruiser thieves know certain neighborhoods better than most of its residents know their own neighbor's comings and goings. They also know such menial details as the trash schedule and those who put their trash out at night versus those who put it out the morning of.

Once the thief has made their first score with your documents recovered from your trash, they increase their leverage over your financial life by changing your address so they can get credit card statements and bank statements sent (to you) at their address. All they need is one statement to increase their illicit financial empire and destroy your good name.

This is known as account takeover ID theft because it occurs when a thief acquires existing credit account information to garner the necessary means to purchase legal and illegal goods and services by simply redirecting critical correspondence.

Critical correspondence may not only contain names and account numbers, but they may also contain something even more important -- your email address. Your email address is important because it gives individuals and companies direct access to you!

From here, they generally begin to phish your email because they have new weapons of information about you and your financial situation. Then, they brazenly contact you via email, armed with your stolen information, and eventually dupe some individuals into releasing the critically important missing piece of data -- your password(s). Thus, their financial control over you and your money becomes complete.

Most of these thieves are relentless until they succeed. It is this same relentlessness (in the form of emails) that should be a sign that something is amiss.

Some thieves are not willing to rummage through trash, day or night, so they do what is known as skimming. A skimmer is a device that can be purchased over the internet by anyone with no questions asked.

There are several different types of skimmers. Some are free-standing devices, and others are attachments that can be slipped over the card slot of an ATM or credit card machine, which then reads the magnetic strip of any card once it is in place.

Skimming is hard to detect until the card is actually used by someone other than the owner. Anyone's credit card can be skimmed or compromised any time the card is out of the owner's sight (restaurants).

Even worse is that the skimming may only be the tip of the iceberg. Skimming could be a small part of a larger more intricate web of crimes that can go as far as terrorism. And skimming is usually an inside job, or at least has an accomplice on the inside.

So identity thieves are not your every day run of the mill thieves. Many of these individuals are smart, sophisticated, smooth-talking salespeople who know their way around banks, the internet, and know how to manipulate people into doing exactly what they want them to do. However, some are also old fashioned thieves who know how to steal, pick pockets, and break into establishments.

Ill-Gotten Gain

Why is your personal information such a sought after commodity? Once thieves have your personal information, here is a brief list of some of the things your information does to help these strangers.

- They may open new credit card accounts in your name or get duplicate cards on existing accounts.
- They may use your name and credit to get all of their utilities connected, including mobile phone service.
- They may open a new bank account in your name or write bad checks on your existing account with counterfeit checks they made; or, they may clone your ATM or debit card and in a matter of days and drain your account(s).
- They may use your name and Social Security number to get welfare benefits or other similar government benefits.
- They can give your personal information to police during an arrest. And since you do not know about the arrest, you are obviously not going to show up for court, which is going to cause an arrest warrant to be issued for you.

This kind of ID theft is known as application fraud, which is also called "true name fraud" by most experts because the thief actually uses the victim's personal information to open new accounts in the victim's name.

Again, unless an individual check's their information on a regular basis, most victims are not likely to learn of any fraudulent applications for at least 30 to 60 days or longer because the imposter has had the monthly account statements mailed to an address other than the victim's true address.

So in the end, your personal information is proven to be quite valuable, or maybe more valuable to others then it is to you.

The best way to avoid or at least short-circuit ID theft attempts on your personal information is to:

- monitor your bank accounts regularly – daily.
- check your credit reports regularly (Chapter 7).
- have a fraud alert placed on your credit report that requires the credit reporting agency to contact your personally before any new credit is granted.
- shred any and all sensitive information before discarding it, even if it means you have to tear every document by hand (go to the nearest office supply store and purchase a home-office shredder, under $50.00).
- do not leave receipts of any kind laying on a counter or inside an ATM machine or gas pump.
- never give out personal information over the phone, even to a known creditor. If they do not already have it, either end that conversation or ask to speak to a manager.
- do not carry your Social Security card with you or any documents that have the number listed on it. If you do need it, take it with you to your business and then take it right back home.
- never click on any links in an unsolicited email of any kind!
- immediately notify your bank, credit card company, or any other financial institution when a bill does not arrive as it should. Better yet, set up all of your accounts for paperless billing.

Even though most ID thefts are found out after the fact, there are still some prudent steps that can be taken to begin righting this wrong.

First, if you have any verifiable details about the stolen information, even if those details seem insignificant to you, file a police report. But you must file another, even more important, report beforehand.

This detailed report is known as an Identity Theft Report (ITR), which entitles you to certain legal rights once the ITR is provided to the three major credit reporting agencies.

This ITR can be used to permanently block fraudulent information from appearing on your credit report(s) that is/are a direct result of the identity theft, and, it will help you ensure those debts, if any, do not reappear on your credit report in the future. One way this is accomplished is by allowing for an extended fraud alert to be placed on your credit report.

But the biggest benefit of all is that the ITR prevents companies from making any attempts, whatsoever, to collect on any debt that came about as a result of the ID theft. This means that the victim will also not be receiving any telephone calls from any collection agencies based on those debts.

The initial fraud alert placed on your credit report generally last for approximately 90 days. This is the one that is placed on your report when you first suspect your identity has been stolen, such as if your wallet is missing.

To place this alert, you only need to call one of the three major credit reporting agencies listed below. That agency is obligated to notify the other two. However, if you do not get a confirmation within 30 days, then you should contact the remaining two agencies directly. Or better yet, call all three agencies on the same day and ask for confirmations over the telephone.

Make sure you keep excellent notes throughout this entire process – the date and time of every telephone conversation made or received, names, titles, telephone extensions, and specific statements made by any and all parties, in case further legal action is required. If you must send any correspondence, send it certified return receipt so that you have evidentiary support that you mailed the letter.

- Equifax: 1-800-525-6285
- Experian: 1-888-EXPERIAN (397-3742)
- TransUnion: 1-800-680-7289

Once you have placed your fraud alert with each of the three agencies, then you are entitled to one free credit report per company. If you have to order a report, make sure you request that only the last four digits of your social security number appear on that report, in case your mail is being targeted.

With an ITR in hand, an extended fraud alert may be placed on all three credit reports for seven years. You can also go to the Federal Trade Commission's website, www.ftc.gov and file an ID Theft Complaint.

Once you have filed your complaint with the FTC through their website, you need to take that report down to your local police station and file a police report to ensure you are entitled to all the legal rights mentioned above, if you have not already filed a police report. In this case, one report supports the other and vice versa.

If you have already filed a police report, it does not hurt to take a copy of your FTC ID Theft Complaint to the police. You can never have too much evidence.

By completing the FTC's ID Theft Form, you are further justifying the need for an extended fraud alert, and you may also be helping law enforcement officials across the country in similar investigations.

The major benefit of the police report is that it allows you to track any dealings the actual thief has with any creditors and law enforcement officials. If you choose to make this request in writing, you may get a copy of a sample letter from the FTC's website.

Additionally, by placing an extended alert on your credit report, you are entitled to two free credit reports from each of the three credit reporting agencies for twelve months. Your name is also supposed to be removed from all pre-screened marketing offers for up to five years, unless you make a written request directing otherwise within that period.

However, as always, if you should start to receive pre-screened offers before the five years is up, you need to contact each credit reporting agency again to make sure that your fraud alerts are in place as they should be.

Just as with the initial 90 day alert, the extended alert carries the same requirement that requires potential creditors to make personal contact with you anytime an application for credit is submitted or before any credit can be extended.

Even if you are able to work out any ID theft charges with a specific company, you still need to file an ITR to protect your future financial interests and take advantage of the protections afforded you by law.

The number one reason why it is necessary to take all of these steps after your identity has been stolen is because it is virtually impossible to predict how long the effects of identity theft may impact one's life. There are so many unknown variables that determine ID theft's lingering effects that it makes good money sense to monitor financial records for several years after the crime is discovered.

As for your credit reports, they should be monitored once every three months after the first year; thereafter, the reports should be set on a staggered schedule of monitoring, since everyone is now entitled to one free report per credit reporting agency per year (Chapter 4).

Even after the victim has filed all of the necessary reports, they must make sure that they follow up on every single request to correct any and all records, and shut down any fraudulent accounts.

Beat 'Em at Their Own Game

The best weapon against ID theft is awareness. Monitoring your accounts and credit reports on a regular basis, knowing your neighborhood mail carrier's schedule, and other similar activities can save you money and heartache.

If you are the victim of ID theft involving credit card fraud, generally, you would not be liable for more than the first $50 of the loss because of federal protection in the Truth in Lending Act, and Fair Credit Billing Act, 15 USC sec. 1601. In most cases, the victim will not be required to pay any part of any loss.

However, debit card users do not have the same kind of protection against fraud. Depending on how quickly the theft is found out and subsequently reported to the financial institution, an individuals' checking account could be completely wiped out, and in some cases could be liable for the total amount of the loss.

Even if an ID theft victim is not forced to pay a thief's bills, they still may find themselves fighting bad credit for years, while simultaneously struggling to get deserving credit and possible even get hired. Keep all evidence nearby because you may have to refer to it on more than one occasion.

More times than not, ID victims may find it difficult, if not impossible, to receive any assistance from law enforcement officials. So much of the work to repair the damage must be done alone, by the victim. This is why it is so important to keep excellent notes of even the most trivial events throughout this entire process.

While no one can guarantee that you or your family will never become victims of ID theft, here are few rules that will help you stay as secure as possible.

1. Reduce the overall number of cards you carry on your person. Avoid debit card usage as much as possible because of the potential exposure they present. Try to limit the number cards you carry to one card, two cards at the most. Report any fraud or suspected fraud to your financial institution on the spot!

2. Go to the website of every single card carrier, register your accounts online, and make sure you read the fraud liability coverage for each in its entirety. If you do not understand something, make sure you ask questions in writing, email or handwritten letters, so that you can have a written response from the company as your evidence.

3. Whenever you give your card to someone to swipe for a purchase, keep your eye on your card at all times.

4. Use credit cards when shopping online, not debit cards, because credit cards offer you more protection in case of fraud.

5. Keep a photocopy list of all your credit cards, debit cards, bank accounts, and investments — the account numbers, expiration dates, and telephone numbers of the customer service and fraud departments — in a secure place, like a safe deposit box or another secure location.

6. Never allow your credit card number to be written on your checks when writing a check to any business. It is against the law in several states. If you are not sure, ask the clerk or ask to speak to the manager.

7. Watch the mail when you expect a new or reissued credit card to arrive, or negotiate a delivery date beforehand. For more security, you may also request that the card be delivered to a local branch office, or if delivered to your home, request a signature confirmation so that it cannot be left on your front porch. Contact the card issuer immediately if the card does not arrive as planned.

8. Some financial institutions have certain branches across the country where they can print new cards on the spot. Check to see if this option is available where you live.

9. In seven states residents can obtain free annual credit reports under both state and federal law. These states are: Colorado, Maine, Mas-

sachusetts, Maryland, New Jersey, Vermont, and Georgia (two free reports per year in Georgia). If you reside in one of these listed states, take advantage of this extra protection afforded you for more extensive monitoring of your credit reports.

10. As of November 2007, the entire nation is able to "freeze" their credit reports with one or all three credit reporting agencies, which means that credit issuers cannot access your credit files except by your specific permission. There is no fee for ID victims, but there may be a small fee for others. Please check with each agency before making any decisions.

11. There are many ID theft insurance products available on the market and many carry with them credit monitoring services. While I do not personally recommend any particular service, there are some that are better than others and, of course, carry a higher cost. If you have been a victim of ID theft, have reason to be concerned about potential ID theft, or simply cannot make the time to check your accounts regularly, then the fee may be worth the service to you. Just make sure you know what you are agreeing to if you do sign up for such a service.

12. Do not use your mother's maiden name, your Social Security number, or any other easily found or obvious personal information when creating passwords and/or PINs (personal identification numbers). The best passwords use a combination of letters, numbers, and maybe one special character (@, #, $, %, ^, &, *, <). Another possibility is to take a line from a poem, movie, or song, and then use the first, last, or combination of letters from each word as your password, similar to a pneumonic device or limerick. The longer the password, the harder it is to crack. You can also ask your financial institutions to allow you to add an additional code or password to access your accounts.

13. Commit all of these passwords to memory, but, if you have to write them down, hide them in an inconspicuous location. Make sure when you have to use your PIN or password in public, that you use your other hand to shield your entries. You can either feel bad for protecting yourself now, or feel worse for not having protected yourself later.

14. If you have to use your password in public, enter the number as quick as possible, so as not to give anyone time to recognize the numeric sounds. If you have not noticed, each number on most key pads makes a different distinctive sound; and, if you take too long in between entries, some individuals are keen enough to know which sound corresponds to which number, and they can remember your code just that quickly. After that, you will become a target so they can get your card.

15. Although you already know not to carry your Social Security card in your wallet, you should also ask any business that requires your SSN if there is any other way to transact this business using another identifier. If you must use your SSN, make sure it is never said out loud or written on any public documents, including your checks. If you have to give it to someone, write it down and retrieve the paper when complete. Double check to make sure your driver's license number is not also your SSN.

16. As for your home computer, make sure you have a firewall installed and updated virus protection software to prevent access to your files by hackers, especially if you connect to the Internet by DSL or cable modem. Password protect as many files as possible, and encrypt those whenever possible, so if there is a breach you can limit its impact.

17. Make sure you know your online shopping partners, and make sure they have some sort of acceptably recognized protection logo prominently displayed on their website. If the website is a secure website, you will generally see a small yellow lock in the lower right-hand corner of the web page, a yellow lock in the address line of the page, or you will see https://www.anywebsite.com. If you have to dispose of your computer, purchase a wipe clean utility program before getting rid of it or set it back to the factory settings before disposal.

18. Scan your computer often for file-sharing and file-swapping programs that expose your computer to illegitimate access by hackers and fraudsters.

19. Other prudent moves would be to have your name removed from the marketing lists of the three major credit reporting bureaus — Equifax, Experian, and TransUnion. Call 1-888-5OPTOUT or go

online to www.optoutprescreen.com.

20. Sign up for the Federal Trade Commission's National *Do Not Call Registry.* Your name is added to name deletion lists used by nationwide marketers. You may also need to register for your state's "do not call" list, if it has one.

- National Do Not Call Registry, www.donotcall.gov, (888) 382-1222

21. Sign up for the Direct Marketing Association's Mail Preference Service to have your name added to name deletion lists used by nationwide marketers.

- Mail Preference Service, PO Box 282, Carmel, NY 10512 (Include $1 money order only, no checks.)
- Opt-out online ($1 fee, pay by credit card only not a debit card, not even if it has the Visa or MasterCard logo), www.dmaconsumers.org/cgi/offmailinglist

22. Considering speaking to your local telephone company about the options of having your name and address removed from the phone book and reverse directories, using only initials, or other available options to shield your identity.

23. When given an opportunity to have your information shared with other firms, always decline the requests.

24. Consider installing a locked mailbox at your residence, purchasing a post office box, employing a commercial mailbox service, or installing a mailbox on your front door. Remember, whenever you are away from home for any extended time, have your mail held at the Post Office until you return.

25. When it comes time to order new checks, pick them up at the bank. If you still pay bills the old-fashioned-way, do not leave your payments, or any other financial or personal mail at your mailbox for the postal carrier to pick up, or in open boxes at public desks in a workplace. If you do so, you are one of those willing participants in ID theft I addressed previously.

26. Experts suggest check writers use a gel pen (found at any office supply store or drug store) for writing checks because gel ink contains tiny particles of color that are trapped in the paper, making check

washing more difficult .

For More Information

Federal Trade Commission Identity Theft Clearinghouse

- Phone: (877) IDTHEFT (877-438-4338)
- Web: www.consumer.gov/idtheft
- FTC's free identity theft guide "Take Charge," www.consumer.gov/idtheft

While the goal of *Funny Money Universe* is to inform and enlighten its readers, I have merely scratched the surface on this all important conversation. ID theft happens in a number of different ways, and each case may present its own set of unique problems. Therefore, if you need further assistance, contact your state's attorney general's office through their website for additional guidance, such as sample letters and other guiding principles because there may be some other protections and actions required depending on whether the theft is from an investment account, brokerage firm, or involves a passport or other similar types of transactions.

One final thought.

Every account is not governed by the same rules of ID theft. Some accounts may be replaced in whole, some in part, and some not at all, so make sure you speak with your financial representatives very carefully about these matters and have a clear understanding of how your money and your good name are protected should you become a victim of ID theft.

The old sports adage makes good sense here – sometimes the best defense is a good offense.

Chapter Thirteen

Working for the Man

Several years ago, when I was very unhappy with my employment at a particular firm in North Carolina, a very dear lady friend who I greatly respect sent me the most inspiring email, without us ever discussing my disappointment. Although I am going to share this email with you in a few moments, I wanted to first tell you why the email was so important.

That email did three things for me. It reminded me of how talented and skilled I was despite the appearance of my current situation. Secondly, it told me to stand up and get over the pity party! Third, it showed me that I always have choices in my life, and if I did not like the available options then I could always create new ones.

That email was the beginning of the end of me working for someone else, and the final push I needed to start me working for me!

Among other things, here is what her email said, "Everything I need to know about life, I learned from Noah's Ark. One: Don't miss the boat. Two: Remember that we are all in the same boat. Three: Plan ahead. It wasn't raining when Noah built the ark. Four: Stay fit when you're 600 years old, someone may ask you to do something really big. Five: Don't listen to critics; just get on with the job that needs to be done. Six: Build your future on high ground. Seven: For safety's sake, travel in pairs. Eight: Speed isn't always an advantage. The snails were on board with the cheetahs. Nine: When you're stressed, float a while. Ten: Remember, the Ark was built by amateurs; the Titanic by professionals. Eleven: No matter the storm, when you are with those you love, there's always a rainbow waiting."

From that day forward, I started taking on small projects, outside of my normal job, so that I could enhance the skills that were already a part of my work life, although they were not being utilized by my current employer.

To that end, one of the first projects I took on was helping a friend resolve his car loan that had several months of payments in arrears. After spending several weeks talking to the local branch officer, with false promises and no success, I decided to make direct contact with their headquarters in Mullins, SC.

This telephone call was necessary because my friend gave me his working file on the account that had a great many unanswered accounting questions about payments already made. So I called the bank, unexpectedly got the loan officer's voice mail, and left her a list of questions that needed to be answered, all with my friend's written approval.

Now, I do not know about you, but if someone leaves me a detailed voice message or sends me a detailed email addressing specific concerns, I think it only makes good business sense to be prepared with those answers before I reply. It is also a huge timesaver in today's rat race.

Nonetheless, she calls me back completely unprepared for our discussion.

Now, what Ms. Incompetent could have done was say Mr. Bolden, I do not know the answers to your questions, but if you will give me some time I will find out those answers and call you back in a day or two. But that is not what she did.

Instead, Ms. Incompetent wanted to have the conversation, so I began asking the exact same questions I had previously left on her voicemail, based on the records given to me by my friend. She was clearly flabbergasted, and so was I, to tell you the truth!

She could not answer one single question about the loan, their policy about certain transactions, or questions about how their bank's accounting system tracked loans.

Now the true insult was that Ms. Incompetent had written a note at the bottom of a piece of correspondence she mailed to my friend that said, "please call me so that I may help you with this loan."

When Ms. Incompetent realized that she could neither type fast enough to find the answers, nor did she possess the necessary skills to find the answers, and that I was not going to be deterred by anything less than the full truth, she blurted out, "let me get you a manager."

After an untenably long wait, I suddenly hear a gentleman screaming in the phone like a 12-year-old kid having a temper tantrum.

Clearly, I was shocked to realize that Mr. Tantrum was the "managerial assistance" she went to get to help me with this loan. At this point, needless to say, I was very concerned about anyone who did business with this financial institution – a loan officer who does not know her own bank's loan tracking system and a bank manager who screams and yells at his customers?

In the midst of Mr. Tantrum screaming at me and continuing to refuse to answer any of my questions, I politely tried to interrupt him several times so that we could have a civil conversation. My attempts were futile. But I could not help but laugh at the behavior of this bank manager.

If we were standing face to face, I am sure that I would have needed a handkerchief to dry my face after being showered with such affection.

It was like a cartoon of Dagwood Bumstead's boss yelling at him with all the bleeps above his head, except this manager was no cartoon. There was no doubt in my mind that this man was screaming pure hatred at me!

Although I have my beliefs as to why, I will leave you to draw your own conclusions. But I will say that the friend I was helping is Caucasian.

But for the sake of my friend's automobile (job and family), I could not let these screaming, tantrum-throwing individuals keep me from my appointed task. My friend had legitimate questions that deserved to be answered regarding his money. And I had to prove to myself that I had the ability to navigate tough negotiations if I was going to be successful as an entrepreneur.

When Mr. Tantrum was finally too winded to scream anymore, he stopped long enough for me to interject. Nonetheless, he still continued to follow the lead of Ms. Incompetent and would not take ownership of the problem that was documented in their correspondence mailed to my friend at his home address. Before the conversation ended, I heard, "it's not my fault," and "I don't know," several more times during that call.

Now, if you see yourself in either Ms. Incompetent or Mr. Tantrum, then you only have a job, and clearly it is a job you either hate, or do not have the necessary skill set to perform optimally, or a little of both.

While I have taken into account that everyone has a bad day or an off day, I have been a manager long enough and in customer service even longer to know how to recognize a disgruntled employee and/or an individual who hates their job.

It does not matter whether you are an atomic engineer or a zoologist, if you do not enjoy what you are doing it is eventually going to come out in your performance and in your interactions with your customers.

We continuously hear about companies reinventing themselves, redesigning their products, and developing new marketing campaigns to capture or recapture market share, but none of these repackaged ideas ever reach low enough to be of any really help to those that need it the most -- like the bank manager or their staff.

However, most employees can no longer sit idly by and hope their employer will help them become more relevant in today's marketplace. Individuals must do their own reinventing!

Once upon a time this meant finding a mentor to help one navigate the corporate world, but today, most mentors are too busy -- protecting their own jobs from those who would desire to be mentored; and, therefore, those who need a mentor most are the least likely to have one.

In my more than 20 years in the corporate world, in a variety of positions, I observed every tactic imaginable from individuals, like myself, struggling to get ahead. During those very difficult times, I discovered 12 basic requirements that are critical skills for anyone who wants to succeed in the corporate world. These same 12-steps, if you will, appeared to be the qualities most sought after by senior management.

But before you take on this list, let me give you one piece of critical advice. My mother used to always tell me, "Don't start something you are not willing to finish."

I. Become results oriented.
   A. Learn how to set clear job objectives.
   B. Learn to prioritize work goals.
   C. Learn how to complete tasks and meet deadlines.
   D. Learn how to overcome obstacles.
   E. Develop some sort of verifiable evaluation system to monitor your progress.
   F. Keep a list of every assigned and completed task along with pertinent details.

II. Excellence must become your mantra.
   A. Learn how to plan your work and anticipate potential problems.
   B. Follow through on every single task. Do not leave any task undone, no matter how small.
   C. Push yourself to strive and excel above others.
   D. Yield yourself to a higher standard. You are not in high school any more so do not allow yourself to be bullied by peer pressure.

III. Prove you are a team player.
   A. Learn how to assist other team members without stepping on their toes.
   B. Learn how to build a network of support.
   C. Learn how to work out conflicts directly.
   D. Volunteer to work late or come in early.
   E. Learn to be genuine.

IV. Become the top notch professional.
   A. Confidentiality is of utmost importance here.
   B. Do not conduct personal business on company time.
   C. Always speak the truth; and stay away from gossip.
   D. Become known as a problem-solver, not a complainer.
   E. Join the professional network so that your name can be raised to those in positions of influence.

V. Develop a customer focus.
   A. Volunteer to handle difficult customer situations.
   B. Learn the art of active listening.
   C. Learn how to respond to customers in a timely manner.
   D. Learn how to meet the customer's requests without costing the company money.

VI. Prove diversity works without becoming divisive.
   A. Make it your business to learn the culture of all the countries where you firm does business, and find new ways your firm can become relevant in those societies.
   B. Learn how to state your views in an honest and open manner without appearing aggressive.
   C. Learn how to respond in a non-defensive manner when others disagree with you, even when they attack you personally (and they will).

VII. Demonstrate efficiency.
   A. Learn how to delegate tasks.
   B. Learn how to get others to become better users of their time, to your advantage.
   C. Find areas of duplication and eliminate as many as possible, in addition to taking the initiative to resolve recurring problems.

VIII. Become more flexible.

A. Look for ways you can become more amenable to office change.

B. Demonstrate you are a competent follower and leader as the situation requires.

C. Get in the office early. Go to bed an hour or two earlier than usual so that you can get up 30 minutes to one hour earlier and be in the office 30 minutes to an hour before your start time. Once you arrive in the office, go to work immediately, this will surely pay off in time. But the best reason to get to work early is because most managers are more accessible before the work day begins, and this may be the time to fish some of your ideas and thoughts, but be discrete and do not step on any toes. If you do get this privilege, keep your discussions to yourself, even if you are challenged by other employees.

IX. Be a fun co-worker without being a clown.

A. Demonstrate that you know how to laugh (including laughing at your own mistakes).

B. Enthusiasm for the future. Finally, your presence should lift up your co-workers, which, hopefully, will help steer the company and you into future endeavors because you are spending your time learning how to make both more viable in any market or trend. The more you help one, the more you help the other, and both bottom lines.

X. Become an expert in continuous improvement.

A. Learn how to question policies without appearing insubordinate.

B. Review previously completed projects for continuous improvement ideas.

C. Seek out constructive criticism from peers and others. Inside of every criticism is something good.

D. Listen to everyone's grips and begin to think of ways to resolve those grips and improve the company's bottom line performance. Make sure you document and keep notes so that when your changes are implemented you will get the credit you deserve.

XI. Become an innovator.

A. Learn how to spark creativity in everyone you meet.

B. Develop new ideas and approaches to problems. Keep a log of all of your suggestions.

C. Learn to do a risk analysis for as many company processes as possible to prove you are ingrained in the company's culture.

D. Volunteer for new technology projects and pilots. Be the first to vol unteer for new and difficult projects, as long as you understand the requirements up front. Being organized can help in this manner so that you can do more without becoming overworked or stressed out.

XII. Step up your personal learning.

A. Ask for feedback, whenever possible, written is even better. Do not wait until it is time for the annual performance appraisal to be blind sided by something that happened at the beginning of the year. By the time your annual performance appraisal comes up, you should be more than prepared with highlights, your own areas of improvement, and a justifiable raise/bonus proposal.

B. Learn to use every assignment as a growth opportunity, and a new resume skill.

C. Learn how to become a decisive decision-maker based on solid reasoning.

D. Constantly re-evaluate yourself.

E. Video Gaming. Learn to use new technology and cutting edge ideas before they are introduced into the company. Video games help im prove eye-hand coordination, timing, and help players to think fast on their feet, to see around corners, and other valuable workplace skills.

If you pull all of this information together, you will have an impressive portfolio to show off when the time comes. When opportunity knocks you have to be prepared to answer by doing your homework in advance.

Everyone wants a chance to succeed, but how many put in the necessary hours to prepare themselves? (Read Joseph's story – Genesis 37 – 50)

Before I learned the 12-steps listed above, I sought the help of a professional headhunter.

At the initial meeting, I was told that the agency would videotape all of our meetings, and that I would have to review those videos, as homework, to identify my strengths and weaknesses so that I could learn from my own mistakes.

The company would also teach me how to interview better, also videotaped in full interview attire. They would also redo my resume and create me a professional portfolio, which I did not own at the time.

All of these services would be provided over the course of 12 weekly sessions at the small fee of $6,000 up front, with no guarantees.

I thought the firm had an excellent plan, so I went home and re-created their plan for myself for less than $100. I went from a customer service telephone operator to a customer service manager in less than one year.

If you were anything like me, you did not go into the workforce prepared with a career choice in mind. My problem was that I had a lot of different interests and a lot of different skills. But I did not have anyone who took an active interest in coaching me onto the right career path.

So, I made up a resume, went on a few interviews, and took the job offer that paid the most money with daytime hours.

This was after I had gone to college for four years.

It was still almost ten years later before the dream or idea of who I was and what I wanted out of my life's work began to take shape.

Whether you are a new entrant into the workplace or have been in it for a while, it does not hurt to do a career test periodically. One good website for such a test is http://www.futureproofyourcareer.com/.

Despite getting my first job when I was 17-years-old, going to several excellent institutions of higher learning, and being in the military, I did not come into my own until I had been in the rat race for more than 20 years.

Let me make a few things clear.

Even though I was intelligent and a A- student, I had no direction and no sense of what I wanted to do, so I just worked.

I do not now nor did I then blame anyone for my choices or my experiences. In fact, when I was working for the man (in several jobs I hated), I had to find ways to encourage myself to keep seeking higher ground, better experiences, and, of course, a better paying job. So I began to take stock of who I was, what I had to offer, and what I wanted my future to look like more and more.

I now know that if I could have done anything else other than what I am doing today, I would have become an attorney.

So if you are working in a job that you hate, or your skill set is lacking for a new job, then the first thing you need to do is be honest with yourself and determine your strengths and weaknesses.

First, you need to take a piece of paper and make two columns.

The first column is going to be a list of all things you hate about your current job situation and why. Be specific and give vivid details.

For example, if you hate your pay, then why specifically do you hate it. Saying you are not paid enough is not a reason why (we will address this later in this section). A reason to hate your pay is because you have been in the same department for more than five years and are the lowest paid staff member.

The second column is going to be all the things you do like about your job situation. For example, you like the flexible hours because they give you more time to spend with your family.

Now on another sheet of paper you are going to make two more columns.

The first column is going to list of all the things you can do, I mean everything whether it be tasks you do in your job, at home, at church, a volunteer position, or just for fun. This really is a list of your skill sets, and again you need to be brutally honest and creative.

The second column is going to list all the things you cannot do. Again be brutally honest.

You may be surprised to learn that all things you hate about your job is connected to all of the things you cannot do. Additionally, you probably now know that all the things you do like about your job are all the things you can do.

Now, the third thing you need to do is design your perfect job or name a specific job that you would like to have either within your current company or in a different one.

See if you can find a job description about this perfect job. You can start by searching the Occupational Outlook Handbook, which is produced annually by the U. S. Department of Labor.

Some other options are to check your employer's organization chart, your employer's current list of open positions, and look at other companies who do what you are interested in doing. See if you can set up a few information interviews with one or more of these other employers to get more data about your dream job and how to move into that specific area of interest.

As a last resort you may ask someone in human resources, but be mindful of your asking. You do not want to alert anyone to your actions prematurely because you do not want them to have the opportunity to label your efforts negatively to those of influence, nor do you want to jump the gun on your efforts.

What you have done for yourself is to create both an individual self assessment and managerial feedback gap analysis. You may find copies of each on the internet or online at your company's internal document repository.

This self assessment and managerial feedback gap analysis are both documents that employers and hiring managers use to determine where an employee or applicant's skills rate in comparison to their peers.

So by completing these documents, you have already begun your assent to a new and better position because you have identified what kind of job you would be best at (your dream job), you have inventoried your current skills, and you have listed your areas of weaknesses that you are going to start working on. Better to find this information out now then when you are sitting in an interview.

Now as you go to this job you hate every day, you have more of a purpose or direction, and you are not only giving, but you are getting in return.

As for those skills that you are lacking, you now need to focus on how you can obtain those skills in the least amount of time.

Here are a few options to help you obtain those skills.

See if these skills can be gained through company training, outside training paid for by the company, on-the-job training assignments, temporary job assignments, volunteer assignments, or some combination of all of the above.

Once you have started on this road to gaining your new skills and you have been steadily improving for four to six months you may consider asking for an information interview with that particular individual or someone who knows that individual's job requirements (with your current employer), and/or asking if you can shadow that individual for a specified period of time.

This will accomplish two things. First, it will make sure you are on the right path and that your efforts are not being wasted. Secondly, these efforts will demonstrate to senior level officials that your change is real and deserves to be considered.

The fact that you are even remotely interested in growing your career is going to increase your stock in the company. However, there is one caution, make sure you understand exactly what you are agreeing to before you take on any new task, because the unspoken is oftentimes more important than the spoken.

Do not be discouraged if you do not get an immediate response to your request or your requests receive a cold welcome when first mentioned. It may take some time for others to warm up to your change of heart, if you do not have a good reputation within the firm, for whatever reason.

Remember the old adage, "actions speak louder than words." From this point forward, let your actions be the right actions even when you are in challenging situations. Do not take things personally (even when they are purposefully intended to be so), business is business, and until you own the business, it is not personal, no matter how personal others try to make it.

The Bucket List

After 20+ years in the workforce, I have had numerous opportunities to pick up a few bad habits that potentially could have derailed my career had I not had enough sense to recognize the potential damage before any real damage was done.

If you are looking for a job or are already employed, here is my list of pitfalls to avoid in order to have a much more financially rewarding career.

1. **Stay away from the (scuttlebutt) water cooler.** Do not join any cliques regardless of their reason for existence. These groups never have anything good to add to your career or to say about any changes happening within the workplace. Their negativity will eventually become your negativity, and then you will look up and find yourself stuck in a rut. Be as nice as possible, but decline any offers to join any groups. I have seen people fired while standing at the water cooler.

2. **Frequent travelers** are quick to recognize they cannot change the culture of a foreign location. They simply accept it for what it is. If they like it, they can participate, if they do not, then they travel to a different locale. This is the attitude most need to have at work. One cannot change the culture or the people, you can only change yourself. So take all of that good advice and keep your mouth closed!

3. **See no evil. Hear no evil. Speak no evil.** Be observant enough to see what needs to be done, and what is not getting done. If you listen quietly and long enough your co-workers will eventually tell you everything that

is going on in the office, and why they are where they are. People love to talk and tell. All of these skills can help you tremendously as long as you keep your mouth closed!

4. **Money, Money, Money, Money.** When the O'Jays sang For The Love of Money back in the 70's, they completely laid out all the motives for and against money. Not much has changed in 30 years. Do not think you are going to get a pay raise or a promotion just for doing your job. Further, that is not the money you should be concerned about in today's environment. Getting a salary is easy (although it may not be the salary you want). Retirement dollars are the ones you should be concerned about because: 1) even if you have a retirement plan, does your employer have the ability to back-door bankrupt the plan; 2) do you know if you are even going to get the opportunity to retire? This is the parachute that you really want to know what is its color?

5. **Who's the boss?** No matter how many "friends" you have at work, friends come a dime a dozen, and most of them, when squeezed, will hang you out to dry. If you are working for the man, then you need to decide if you are going to make money or friends. Your only loyalty is to provide for your family.

6. **What's truly important.** Above all else do not lose your integrity. If you ever compromise your integrity you will never be respected throughout the company again. So let your skills speak for themselves and no more.

Is Pink Your Color?

Research shows that job loss is the 5th greatest stress individuals face during their lifetime, and because job loss is so stressful, individuals may actually suffer the four emotional stages of loss – shock, anger, grief, and acceptance.

While I must confess that I do not know where the strain of working and simultaneously having to file for bankruptcy falls on the stress meter, I can tell you, without a shadow of doubt, that I endured the same emotional stages of loss as I was fighting for my financial life in court and also fighting to hide this fact from my employer (and the derailment of my career).

During the initial stage of shock, I found myself wondering why this was happening to me. I felt abandoned even though I was the one who chose not to discuss these details with anyone. And just like those who lose their jobs, I felt my personal importance, safety, and security were forever gone when I had to file those papers.

Although these feelings are all normal reactions to an unfortunate part of the business cycle that happens during both good and bad economic climates (job loss), there is no getting used to filing for bankruptcy. While I clearly understood that the bankruptcy would stay on my credit report for ten years, I did not know that it would take me ten years to get over it emotionally.

It is natural for individuals to go through a brief period of blaming themselves as they get closer to the end of stage I, shock. It makes perfect sense that anyone would try to desperately figure out what they did wrong so they can fix it and save their job.

For me, my blame was natural and probably well deserved. I tried everything possible, and I do mean everything, to fix my financial problems before I filed for bankruptcy. But I failed miserably! All of this added to my feelings of embarrassment and depression.

Stage two is the anger phase. It is natural to be angry when one believes that they have been betrayed by someone they trusted implicitly. But one may also be angry with oneself for allowing themselves to trust so completely in a job or their boss. A worse type of anger is the self directed anger that they did not do a better job in preparing for such a possibility.

This anger may show up in everything they do after the loss, unless it is taken under control and taken fairly quickly. Although I had not lost my job, I was so angry with myself that I sat in a dark apartment every day after work for almost 12 months. It was all I could do to get through the work day.

I have heard that many experts, if you will, suggest that individuals get into some kind of exercise program that forces them to work hard and hopefully release their frustration. I do not know if this is true or not, but I can tell you that I believe everyone is going to react differently. And each person's response is going to be decided, in part, by whether or not they have had the support of a confidant. (I am reminded of an episode from *All In The Family* when Archie Bunker lost his job and his wife Edith picked up the broken pieces of his manhood, no easy job if you know Archie.)

But before an individual can get to the calm, rational talking, they may still have more grieving to do. And because grief, stage three, comes out in so many different ways or may not come out at all, this could be a particularly difficult period for the individual and everyone in their immediate circle.

One way to help get through this period is to call a local or national grief hotline where your identity is anonymous, and the individual is free to talk about their grief in detail. Getting past the grief of a job loss or bankruptcy is critical to securing new employment. If this grief is not dealt with decisively, it will have a negative impact on your next job interview.

While there is no exact timeline of how long it will take to overcome this loss, depending upon individual resilience, it can be anywhere from a few days to a few months. But the sooner they can get to the final stage the better.

I have seen numerous people get fired and I have also had the unfortunate managerial responsibility of firing several individuals, and no matter how many times you do it, it never gets easy. Although I strove for the most positive experience as possible, grief is an inherent part of the firing process.

The final stage of acceptance is the recognition that life did not end here and that one has to find a way to move forward. This is where the individual can begin to do the truly important work, such as reworking the family finances based on unemployment benefits and maybe a separation package.

I have been unemployed four times in my life. Fortunately, for me all four times were of my own volition.

But in all four situations, before I left the company, I took the necessary time to evaluate all of my options, pay down my debt, ensure my reserves were sufficient enough to sustain a reasonable period of no employment (two years was the longest period), and I worked every day I was unemployed. That is to say, I got up every single day and worked on my plan just as if I was going to work for the man. In fact, I worked harder because I had more at stake.

But I also recognized that acceptance meant I had to make some lifestyle changes and cost cutting measures; yet, I came out on the other side stronger and smarter.

The loss of one's job is a valid crisis so do not hesitate to call your creditors (all of them) immediately to see what programs they have available to help you until you can return to work.

Also, remember that there are a number of nonprofit agencies available to help with cash management and debt repayment programs during this period.

In addition, one may consider new ways to raise cash, like sell your skills (i.e., preparing income taxes, construction skills, lawn and gardening), selling some valuables, selling some luxury items, and having a garage sale.

It is important to note that if you are unemployed you are also entitled to a free credit report from each of the three major credit reporting agencies, which may be more helpful then is immediately seen. Check out the individual websites of the big three for further details.

Before we leave this section, I want everyone to know that I clearly understand how devastating a job loss is, of any kind, in terms of one's self esteem and the ability to take care of one's family. But I recently heard a sermon by Joel Osteen that I thought would help so many hurting people today and in the future.

In this sermon, Joel stated that he had recently heard of a medical survey where a team of doctors looked at the value of every single body part of the human system -- the blood, the cells, the molecular structure, I mean every aspect of the body was included. The doctor's determined that the value of every human system is $6 million. (Truly we are fearfully and wonderfully made. Psalm 139:14)

So, while many of us determine our value by the jobs we have or do not have, your true value is so much higher. No matter your job title, hopefully this will help you to hold your head higher and walk with more pride in who you are as a person!

Now that you have started to map out your family's survival plan, it is time to turn your eyes toward reentering the workforce once again, if that is your desire.

The first thing I am going to do is give you a few unscripted pointers to consider in your new job search.

> I. Do not limit the amount of time you spend looking for a new job. This project is as important as any assigned by your boss, and this one also has a deadline – the date your current financial reserves will expire.
>
> II. Since you do have some time, use that time wisely to make sure you are a good fit for any potential new employer. Try not to repeat the mistakes that caused you problems with your previous employer or those things that may have gotten you fired.

III. Do not leave a single stone unturned. Most people look in the same place over and over again for a new job. But there are more than 40,000 different job boards on the internet. These are the kinds of stones that need to be turned over in anyone's job search. Additionally, do not become a hermit and hide behind your computer. Get dressed up and make an impromptu visit to some offices with your resume in hand. Get involved in some of the professional networks in your city. If you belong to a fraternity or sorority, utilize those networks also.

IV. You know people that work at all kinds of places, recruit them to anonymously start spreading your resume around. But, if you must submit an application on line, make sure you have bold statements that make you a stand out. For example, the question may be to list your qualifications for this job. Take the job announcement and number your qualifications based on those needs listed in the announcement, then give one sentence on how you meet every single qualification. Such as, "I coach a little league team and manage 30 parents every Tuesday and Thursday afternoon."

V. All email should be considered professional correspondence. You may also want to disable all of your social networking sites until you procure new employment. Depending on how high in an organization you are looking, you may want to have your spouse and children do the same thing. Sometimes, an organization does not just hire you, but they hire your entire family's image.

VI. If you live in an area that has absolutely no job growth, you certainly need to consider relocating your family, or leaving your family put and you move to find a new job. These are unusual times, which may require unconventional solutions to problems.

VII. You should get a copy of basic interview questions and practice them every day so that you are not surprised by any question, and so that your answers will come across as a natural part of you. (Lawyers do this all the time to prep their witnesses.)

Whether or not you have been a part of any marketing campaign, the important thing about selling oneself to any employer is not to sell your skills, but to sell the sizzle.

Have you ever been to any restaurant and was either undecided about what you wanted or maybe you had already made up your mind about what you wanted to eat, until something happened.

A member of the staff walks in your area, and not even close enough by you for you to see what is on their serving tray. All you hear is this overwhelming sizzling.

Immediately, you order the exact same thing, sight unseen.

You were sold on the sizzle!

If you still have any doubt about the sale of the sizzle, let me give you one more, even more powerful sizzle selling example.

While we all have different opinions about too much skin in advertising, the fact still remains that sex sells, and it sells in a huge way.

One of the best originals of selling the sizzle that I can remember is Calvin Klein.

If you have any doubts go back and look at any of Calvin's advertisements on the internet, you will be instantly attracted to the advertisement without first knowing what product he is selling.

According to my research, Calvin Klein's sales were a whopping $52.2 million per year as of January 2007. And if you still are not sure about the sizzle, remember this – Calvin Klein makes more money lending his name to other products than he does creating new products himself. Now if that is not selling the sizzle then I do not know what is.

The same principles apply when you are selling yourself to a new employer, you must sell the sizzle of your product, which is you.

Since your resume is going to be the first part of your sizzle, you want to give the potential employer just enough information to be interested, but not enough information to make a decision without calling you in for an interview. This is a fine line to walk, but one that can be done.

The fact is that you only have about four to five seconds to catch an employer's eye with your resume, so the top 1/4 of your resume must hit the spot, just like a fine meal, but with less time to savor the flavor.

Be different, be unique. For example, instead of starting out listing all of the things you have accomplished and all of your skills, start out talking about the brand and how the position you are applying for will directly improve that brand.

To do this, take a page out of the television advertising handbook and use the philosophical techniques they use to sell their brands to you, the consumer, to sell your brand to a new employer.

For example, if you are applying for a senior customer service position, instead of listing the standard objective at the top of your resume, try this approach – ***"are you searching for an average performer or an individual that is in the top 1% of all product sales for three years running?"***

You now have the hiring manager's attention, make sure you KEEP IT!

How?

Remember your words paint a picture for a not-so-blank canvas, i.e., an individual whose job it is to find a reason to discard your resume. Most human resource managers have already made up their mind about who they want before they advertise for a job. Make sure that every word (every artist's brush stroke) counts.

If you are applying for a management position, then here is an idea – ***"is the hiring manager more comfortable with someone who is good at being micro-managed, someone who gives regular updates by email, or someone who is only seen when summoned by the hiring manager?"***

This shows flexibility without having to say the word and a willingness to be governed by the hiring manager's preference instead of some pre-set preference of your own.

Finally, one more example.

If the position is at the executive level, here is another possibility – ***"understand the company's current financial position, therefore, am willing to negotiate a minimal salary with bonus options tied to previously agreed upon contract objectives."***

This tells any employer, you know what you are doing, and that they can take a chance on you without it costing them any money.

That is how you sell the sizzle!

The remainder of the resume will be one page and no more than one page, with only one method of contact listed.

Do not give your home address, home telephone number, mobile number, and work number. That is too much information for a human resources manager to absorb, even if they are interested in you as a potential new employee. This will also keep you from driving yourself crazy by checking every contact device several times a day.

Then only include two brief statements on the rest of the page, and include no more than two sentences per section. These two sections will support your objective statements (examples) listed above with some detailed information.

The first statement should focus on the essential aspects of the position. Again you should only have two supporting statements to drive your understanding of what are the essential aspects of this job. All of this information comes from your research about the company, the brand, and the current situation. This makes your resume relevant with the current corporate climate.

The second statement focuses on the benefits of hiring you over all the other candidates. What particular value are you bringing to the company to meet their need? In this situation, the potential employer, for now, is your customer. Again, the same rules apply as they did for the first statement.

Close your one page resume with a statement like, ***"career portfolio of accomplishments will be made available for review at personal meeting."*** Here you are making it clear that you expect an interview, and that the interview will not be a waste of time on either party's part. See the sample resume on the next page.

James E. Bolden

Street Address City, State, Zip Code

List only your primary telephone number Your email address

Pioneer – history of working and succeeding in unknown territory

Regional Management (2 years)

- Overall managerial responsibility for two largest geographic offices in region
- Provided technical and administrative guidance to local office managers
- Assisted local office managers in understanding, determining, and implementing necessary recruiting targets to meet staffing goals, included pre-employment testing
- Monitored turnover and staff replacements to ensure minimal disruption to operations
- Direct observation of field operators
- Weekly detailed ops reports that included resolution of field discrepancies
- Prepared managers and subordinates for regular audits

Program Administration (12 years)

- Built several programs from ground up where program previously did not exist
- Took over several problem programs and revamped into successful programs
- Created a programmatic infrastructure for microenterprise small business development program
- Provided technical and financial assistance to private, public, and non-profit partners to maximize the efforts of each organization within at large community
- Negotiated critical compromises
- Responsible for safety of field personnel

Fiscal Operations and Real Property Management (8 years)

- Managed $20 million+ real estate portfolio and personal property portfolio
- Developed and administered $2 million annual budget for 150 incarcerated members of Navy brig
- Helped secure $20 million in Congressional appropriations for street and neighborhood improvements for the Long Beach, CA strategic base reuse plan
- Navy property leasing administrator, regularly reviewed contract proposals and bids for development of outlaying properties at Naval installations
- Helped acquire capital infusions for existing businesses

Human Resources Administration (2 years)

- Responsible for payroll management and all personnel transactions for more than 2,600 employees on a daily basis
- Analyzed demographic characteristics and information to determine potential recruitment sources
- Supervised 3-shifts
- Charged with 6% increase in productivity, achieved 8%

Employee Supervision (10 years)

- Trained, supervised, and built operational talent in groups of employees from 5 to 100
- Responsible for every aspect of relationships from hiring, performance review, and removal from service
- Motivated and inspired teams to high performance and responsive service
- Wrote individual improvement plans for employee advancement opportunities

Microenterprise Small Business Development (6 years)

- Spearheaded community redevelopment efforts within communities negatively impacted by Navy installation closings

- Taught independent, competing community groups how to collaborate and build economically viable, comprehensive community reuse plans for base closure facilities in California, Hawaii, and Guam
- Improved business climate for minorities desiring to start a business or acquire capital for expansion projects
- Helped develop new business openings
- Trained and counseled potential business owners on how to write business plans; and how to establish, build, and maintain new and existing businesses
- Designed and implemented a variety of economic development and revitalization strategies for communities impacted by military base closure
- Jobs Creation – Expanded strategies and solutions to combat high unemployment, low income-earning levels, and severe long-term economic distress for underserved and under resourced groups

Education (15 years)

- Classroom Instructor/Corporate Trainer for OJT that included software instruction, operational instruction, situational (specific issues) instruction, and new employee in-processing; taught 6 such classes for the U. S. Census Bureau
- Graduate Teaching Assistant for 100+ graduate and undergraduate students
- Developed course syllabi and overall course structure where none previously existed
- Prepared lesson plans, and graded all written work; proctored and graded exams; calculated final grades; provided classroom instruction
- Taught microenterprise classes to novices and potential business owners
- Taught customer service skills and classes to new contract employees in Charlotte, Atlanta, and Montgomery, AL

Customer Service Manager (15 years)

- Customer service provided in collaboration, consultation, and partnership with customers, agencies, and stakeholders
- Customer needs identified, and issues are clarified in communications with the customer
- Customer expectations managed to ensure that customers understand the type and level of service available and expected time frame for inquiry resolution
- Work product reflected thorough research and consideration of customer issues and concerns
- Managed inbound call team; email and fax requests team; and, escalated call team
- Responsible for service level, employee work assignments, time management, and scheduling issues in support of smooth daily team operations
- Managed competing demands between internal and external customers
- Monitored employee availability (amount of time signed into telephone and compliance with scheduled hours)
- Monitored employee AHT (Talk time + wrap time + work time)

Public Relations (10 years)

- Knowledge of principles of public relations and outreach in order to establish and maintain good relationships and strong partnerships
- Built and developed community-wide relationships (including faith-based organizations, media outlets, businesses, and other grassroots groups)
- Established collaborative relationships with state and local governments, regional planning authorities, public and private nonprofit organizations, and higher education
- Conducted workshops and seminars; made presentations; and, worked at exhibit booths

- Promoted programs and benefits to a skeptical and sometimes reluctant general public, including microenterprise programs
- Supervised public relations staff across 46 counties
- Consulted with business community to identify needs, recommended marketing/growth strategies, and facilitated acquisition and transfer of resources
- Print media – accustomed to giving interviews to print media
- Radio – Community talk show
- Public presentations to military commanders and staff members, state officers, elected officials, and community organizers
- Negotiated with reluctant partners

Business Administration and Retail Store Operations (15 years)

- Primary decision maker responsible for independently carrying out all the duties, programmatic and administrative, for assigned team
- Coordinated, managed, and worked with staff members; interpreted policy in terms of established goals and objectives, as well as methods and techniques to be employed
- Developed overall project objectives that were concise and accurate with the highest level of technical clarity
- Managed interdepartmental relationships, commitments, and collaborative efforts
- Member of strategic planning team
- Analyzed and resolved unexpected data or inconsistent findings
- Obtained resources (materials, time, and space) to support organizational projects

Education

Master of Theology – A.B.D.
Oral Roberts University, Tulsa, OK

Master of Public Administration
The George Washington University, Washington, DC 1995

Bachelor of Science in Business Administration, Finance
The University of North Carolina at Charlotte, Charlotte, NC 1989

Military

U. S. Navy

Author

Funny Money Universe, 2011

Volunteer Operations

Lead and directed 40-member volunteer committee for command EEO activities for two years
Sat on human resource selection criteria committee

Industry Served

Federal Government • City/County Government • Nonprofit • Utility • Mobile Telephone Service • TV Entertainment • Restaurant • University • Primary Education • Military • Fast Food • Retail Credit • Civic

This is only a sample resume to demonstrate how an individual may highlight his/her individual skills so that their resume showcases their talent in the best light in order for them to get an interview, and land the job of their dreams. My resume is longer because I have been employed in a wide variety of capacities.

Now here is where you go in for the final push for the sale.

Your portfolio should be organized as follows.

Part 1: Centered on the page should be all of your personal information: name, home address, email address, home telephone number, mobile number, and work number, if a direct line to you (do not give any potential new employer permission to contact your current or former employer until you both have reached a tentative agreement).

Part 2: Starting with your formal education, list your highest degree first, and then go down the list (ex., Masters, B.S., Associates, etc.). Then list every formal training class you have ever taken outside of your degrees, then the informal classes, then any other training you have done on your own. Make sure under each entry you list two things -- 1) the main focus/purpose of the course, and 2) your main accomplishment from having taken the class, i.e., how have you used what you learned to further your career.

Part 3: List all of the positions you have held, how you expanded the role – meaning how you went above and beyond every single day, and your major accomplishments while in the position regardless of whether those accomplishments were personal or professional. For example, if you completed your undergraduate degree while working full time, you want to list that so that the employer sees you not only have drive but you have outside interests that relate directly to your career. Did you have the opportunity to train other individuals, and if so how you did that, and how successful are they as company employees today? However, do not list any employers in this section. Now if you have any emails, letters of accomplishments, awards, and any other documents that would verify your accomplishments include those in this section. Awards, special bonuses, or anything that shows you are a stand-out employee is to be included here. Also include dates under each position.

Part 4: List all of the employers you have ever worked for and the time frame. Make sure you include the address where you worked, the person you worked for and their direct telephone number, and list the human resource officer's contact information. As an added bonus, include a copy of your last performance appraisal from each of the employers or something as close to a performance appraisal as possible, like a competency assessment of your skills.

Part 5: This section should show off any other accomplishments you have achieved like professional association memberships, newspaper articles, certifications, or anything else that shows you have or are being recognized.

Part 6: This is your salary history listed chronologically starting with current salary and working backwards. Your salary is the total amount of money you made that year, and then the pay rate. Under each salary include your benefit packages, your normal work schedule, i.e., 40 hours or 30 hours, etc. Then if you worked overtime include how many hours averaged per week, and especially do not forget to list any bonuses received.

Part 7: Be creative and write three different letters of reference, and ask individuals (not your previous supervisors) within any of your previous companies to sign those letters. Most times in the past when I needed a letter of recommendation, I was told to write it and they would sign it. So I am passing that same direction on to you.

Part 8: This is a copy of your own individual development plan. A plan that lays out where you are, where you want to go, and how you plan on getting there. Be specific, give good details and timeframes for reaching each step.

Now if you can think of anything else that needs to be included in your portfolio, make sure to add materials that highlight your skills and improves your negotiating value.

Showtime

Okay, you have all of your documents ready for your interview, now is the time to prepare you for the interview. This means everything from your appearance to your mental preparation.

The day before the interview make sure you have chosen appropriate attire for the position you are interviewing for. If you are interviewing for any kind of management position, you need to have on a business suit, whether you are a male or a female.

For men, this means a gray, medium-colored brown, or blue suit. Stay away from black for an interview. For women, gray, blue, or something along these lines should work in a nice business suit that has a medium length skirt and is not tight-fitting.

Do not wear any perfume or cologne and minimal jewelry, not even a watch, but maybe a wedding band. You do not want anything to distract the interviewer from your face or your answers. You also do not want to be distracted by anything.

Make sure you get a good night's rest the night before because you need to be focused on the interviewer and the questions asked. You also need to be able to think on your feet without looking like you are struggling for an answer.

Most of all, you do not want to have to ask your interviewer to repeat themselves. Your listening skills are being interviewed more than anything else. These skills will help an interviewer make that much needed connection that is necessary for you to get a job offer.

Arrive at least 30 minutes early for your interview so that you can see at least one or two people exiting from the interview and get a feel for how things are going. This should also give you some time to relax and become familiar with your surroundings.

Be nice to everyone you meet, you never know what their role may be in your future. This means that you should turn off your cell phone until you are safely back home where you can have detailed conversations about your experience. If there is an emergency going on in your family, tell your interviewer up front so that they will understand, if the mobile phone should ring, or, if possible, try to reschedule the interview.

If your interview is short, generally speaking, you will not get the job because the interviewer did not make the necessary connection to continue wanting to talk. If the interview is longer, you have a better chance of making a lasting impression. That is why practice makes you a better candidate because you will be a better prepared. A longer interview gives you the opportunity to display your confidence by answering more complex questions.

Regular practice of the most frequently asked interview questions is the only way to portray the kind of confidence I am speaking of, and this practice will make sure you are prepared to answer any questions about your portfolio that may arise. Meanwhile, you need to have some questions prepared to ask so that when your turn comes to make your inquiries you can do so competently. Remember you too are interviewing the company.

Here are a few pertinent questions you should consider for your list.

1. How well do you know your department's employees? How many are college graduates? (The purpose here is to find out how you will be treated if you decide to take the position.)

2. Ask the interviewer how did they get into the position they have?

3. How does senior management view this department?

4. If you were told this department was going to be cut, how would you help your employees deal with and move beyond this kind of news?

5. **Do not ask any questions related to money – salary, retirement, or other benefits. There will be time enough to discuss those details if and when you are offered a position!**

You want to ask questions that show you have thought critically about this position and your future with this organization.

Below are some of the most basic interview questions that will be asked of you, depending on the length of the interview. You may need to be prepared for a group or panel interview where you are interviewed by anywhere from one to three individuals.

I once was interviewed by a board of 15 individuals, and they were shocked that by the end of the interview it was clear that I was interviewing them better than they were interviewing me. By the way, I did get the job.

Do not be taken aback by the notes being written before, during, and after you answer a question. Answer every question forcefully and honestly, as if you own the question and its answer. In truth you do own them both, at least for that moment. Make sure you look the interviewer directly in the eye every time you answer a question. This demonstrates that you stand behind your words.

Potential interview questions may include:

1. Tell us about your educational background – the subjects you enjoyed most and ones you enjoyed least. **Refer the interviewer back to your portfolio that may include a copy of your college course work and your grades. If you made a bad grade in a particular course, use that course to show how something you did not like has turned out to be very useful as an adult. Then use one of your elective courses to show how you can build your personal interests into your career goals.**

2. The same thing applies to your work experience.

3. Do you have any experience dealing with irate/unhappy customers? How did you handle it? **Write this answer down and rehearse it several times before you go into the interview. They are looking for you to stumble upon an answer, your preparation, and how fast you think on your feet.**

4. What are you looking for in a job? **Open-ended challenges, growth potential, and opportunities to be a part of a team while still being rated as an individual.**

5. What are your short term and long term goals? **The purpose here is to see if you are forward thinking, looking into the future to see if your are organized and driven. Give two short term and long term goals, and two examples of each that you completed in the past, and how you completed them.**

6. Type of supervision you like or dislike. **Everyone dislikes a certain type of supervision, but here show that you know how to give and take under any direction. For example, if you have someone who wants to stand over you and micromanage everything you do, then show your fun side and state that you perform well with or without pressure, that your skills are adaptable, and the more outside variables that are added to a situation the more your skills shine.**

7. What areas or what personal qualities need improvement for you to be fully effective in your job? **I believe in perfection and as a result I am my worst critic. Or if the job is a lower-level position that requires typing for example, say that you need to improve your typing skills, right now I only type about 75 words per minute.**

8. Was your previous position a good fit for your interests, skills, and qualifications? **If yes, give some details if not explain how you compensated and turned a negative into a positive.**

9. What were/are your major responsibilities? How well do you deal with changes in responsibilities? **What do you do to help you manage those changes? Again, write these answers down, here is an opportunity to shine and show off a whole variety of skills, so make sure you spend some time on this one.**

10. Why did you leave or are planning to leave? **Growth under the existing structure is limited or non-existent. Do not make this per-**

sonal and start talking about all the things that are wrong. Instead be professional and talk about moving forward. Find out your interviewer's interest by looking around the office for clues, then try to relate your answer to that interest – football, soccer, family, business, etc. The interviewer is really looking to see if you are a negative individual that is going to disrupt their environment. If there was any hostility, that should have all been handled during the four stages of grief as previously discussed. If not, maybe you are not ready to work again, just yet.

11. Finally, you may have some pointed group questions that focus on such things as customer service, integrity, practical learning, teamwork, and job motivation. **Make sure you can speak intelligently on any subject presented to you. If you get stumped on any question either ask for more clarification, such as: "I am not sure I understand your question," or "Please tell me exactly what it is you are looking for?" If neither of those are appropriate, then when all else fails, simply tell the truth. "I do not know the answer that you are looking for. I apologize."**

12. What kind of salary are you expecting? **Your answer will show off your negotiating skills. Just because an employer opened the door does not mean you have to walk through it. While I would expect everyone would do some research to find out what is the going salary for a particular position in their area and then add in a reasonable one to two percent premium, I still would not give the interviewer a number. I would state, "my primary focus is to find a job that is interesting and challenging, and offers me an opportunity to grow and learn. Even if a starting salary does not quite meet my desire, I am sure that I can grow into a responsibly larger salary in a reasonable amount of time."**

As a way of practicing, here are 25 of the most pressing interview questions that may ever be faced by any interviewee, http://www.datsi.fi.upm.es/~frosal/docs/25mdq.html.

Sometimes the seemingly obvious questions are the most difficult ones to answer. Make sure these questions do not become your undoing at the interview.

1. Why are you here?

2. What is your greatest achievement to date?
3. What unique skill(s) can you bring to the firm?
4. Tell me what you know about our company.
5. Why should I hire you over any other candidate?

The same attention to detail applies to a telephone interview as it does for a face-to-face meeting. The only differences are that you should try to use a landline for obvious reasons, and, find a quiet place with no distractions or interruptions. Beyond that, you already know how to sell yourself.

Finally, one more thing. If you were fired from your previous employer, now is the time to own up to what you did, even if it was not all your fault. Take a brutally honest and objective look at your actions without becoming defensive and without rambling on and on. Practice your answer until you have a short, but truthful answer that focuses on what you have learned and how you are a better person from that experience.

Above all, do not lie!

It is easy to spot a liar. Most liars will not look you in the eyes when they are talking (the eyes are the windows to our soul, Mathew 6:22-23), and they will become defensive to protect themselves by folding their arms tightly or by some other nervous body gesture. Repeating the question several times, long hesitations, inconsistent stories, and over the top answers are also indicators that an individual is lying. Just don't do it!

Great job!

You have presented your package well and as best you can.

Enjoy your new position. But, if you did not get the job, send an email to the interviewer to find out where you may be weak, in their eyes, so you can work on those things for your next interview. This shows great strength of character, even if you do not get a response. Just do not ever give up on you, no matter what anyone says!

But

If you are not interested in working for the man again, or at least right now, there are some other options.

Within every loss there is an opportunity, if one is willing to search for it. As

Lebron James once said, "you have to be willing to fail in order to succeed."

So during this period of restructuring after a job loss, once the issues of finances has been answered, at least temporarily, now is the time to decide if:

- a new occupation is worth seeking by seeing if those same skills can be used in another career field. Here is that opportunity to make your wish list. See if you can get a free career test from your unemployment agency, previous employer, or a nearby college or university.
- looking at the same job from a different perspective can be helpful. For example, if customer service is your forte how about becoming an instructor at your local community college or elsewhere.
- you can divide up all your work skills and specialize in an area, and turn that into your new job.
- now is the time to start that business you have always dreamed about (Chapter 14).

If any of these thoughts have crossed your mind, then here is what you do with whatever options excites you most.

- First, start out with your greatest fear, write it down and make it plain.
- Second, decide what is the worst thing that could possibly happen if your greatest fear came true.
- Third, think of the greatest opportunity that could happen if you were to succeed.
- Fourth, decide how you can put that opportunity into motion with a step by step plan.
- Fifth, is to work your plan, and find a job that meets most of your financial requirements but with less demands on your time so that you can work your plan.

But if you are still not yet ready to step outside of your box, then here is another sample resume builder you can use until you decide that you no longer want to work for the man, or, no longer need someone else to validate your skills and you, as an individual.

HEADER

(Name, complete address, telephone number, email address)

OBJECTIVE

One single sentence explaining what type of job you are looking for and why. This is hard, so you must give it some serious thought. You may have to write this one sentence 50+ times.

ACCOMPLISHMENTS

Show how your past positions have prepared you for the job you are currently seeking. List four of five standout accomplishments,

WORK EXPERIENCE

Give the employer's name, job position, number of years in position, city, and state location. Be brief, focus on the important details of what you accomplished in each job. Do not rewrite your old job description or tell all the things you used to do. This is a new you!

EDUCATION

Give year degree completed, type of degree awarded, school's name, city, and state

SKILLS & ABILITIES

Every job has at least three skill sets attached to it, list the highest level skill sets that you have mastered that can be easily transferred to this new position.

Personally, I do not subscribe to the cover letter approach, except under limited circumstances such as executive applications, or when a cover letter is adding some truly unique information not perfectly suited for or already mentioned in the resume.

However, if you believe a cover letter is in order and you are using an updated version of Microsoft Word, then you may go online and retrieve a pre-designed cover letter from several cover letter sample templates from Microsoft

Office Online templates. You can even mix and match several templates to make one that is truly your own.

But, if you do not have the exact experience that is called for in a job announcement, then you might want to use a cover letter to identify those skills you do have and the unique way you attained those skills. To do this, you need to think outside the box, but be very specific.

For example, you may work well under pressure, a skill you gained as a volunteer firefighter. You may be an excellent negotiator from being a volunteer parent at your child's school; or, you may be an excellent organizer because of your children's active school and extracurricular schedules. Finally, you may be a strict disciplinarian because your father or mother was in the military. If you think strategically, you should be able to come up with at least ten different skills that you have gained just by doing what you do every single day.

If there is no new information to add or you cannot find a way to substitute the cover letter for the resume, then the cover letter is not for you because the human resources clerk is only going to read one or the other.

Now that you have prepared these all important documents, there may be a few more matters of consideration before you take that final plunge into leaving your current job or seeking a new one, and particularly for those unemployed individuals.

Just as with anything else, you should have an exit strategy. When it comes to job hunting, an exit strategy is similar to an interview or resume follow-up. Regardless of whether you were invited for an interview or not, you should send a thank you email, or thank you card (if your job search budget allows for the costs) approximately 15 days after your resume was forwarded to the human resources office or 1 day after your interview.

Try to come up with a generic card that only requires you to change the company's name or its representative, and the other statements, minimally. Thank the individual for the interview or for looking at your resume. Please, make sure you spell the interviewer's name correctly! "Thank you for the opportunity to discuss your company's plans for expansion with me on September 25, 2010." **"Thank you for reviewing the resume I forwarded to your office on May 29, 2010."** These statements could possibly prompt the manager to take a second look at you, if they have not yet made a hiring decision.

If you had an interview, try to remember some obscure detail about the hiring manager that you can make reference to, as long as it relates to the job or your positive personality, and then tastefully close the note. If you are only at the resume stage, the same thoughtfulness applies in your thank your letter, without the personal reference of course, and then move on. **"I enjoyed chatting with you about your love of fly fishing and how it relaxes you. I have been reading up on fly fishing and may one day have the opportunity to try this relaxation technique."**

All of these efforts show a well-mannered, respectable individual whether you win or lose. Follow-up is so important in today's marketplace because it is these kinds of niceties that create positive memories for new relationships. It is true that sometimes it is not what you know, but who you know. Your one act of generosity may be all it takes to get that new job.

If you are like most individuals with reasonable expectations, the good news is that if you are working for the man, you are earning a regular salary and benefits, even if they are not to your liking, and you should also have the ability to earn even more money over time, if you choose to stay with your current employer.

But, if you are at that point where you would consider making a leap, just remember that some of our greatest gifts are not displayed until a crisis demands their appearance (David, Moses, Samson, Joseph, to name a few).

Yet, while many would strive for something greater, there will forever be those naysayers who would hold one back wherever possible.

For example, I used to have a friend who worked at a popular fast food restaurant for several years. But, many of our mutual friends ridiculed him every day, despite the fact that he always had a job when others were unemployed, and he would feed most of them when they were in between jobs.

Little did the naysayers know that an employee had to work at this corporation several years before they could own their own restaurant.

But those who wanted to ridicule my friend did not care. So much so that they even refused to work for him when all other job offers were non-existent.

There is no shame in taking a lower paying position in order to take care of one's family. I have known several individuals who lost their job for a variety of reasons, and they took much lower paying positions for the sake of their family. Several of them performed their jobs with such pride and attention to detail that they ended up doubling their salary, from the one they lost, in less than two years time.

As this chapter draws to a close, I am reminded of an article published in *Parade Magazine*, September 14, 2008. Doris Kearns Goodwin, a historian and author, listed ten qualities a good leader possesses, and she used Presidents Abraham Lincoln and Franklin Roosevelt as guides. Here is the gist of what she said.

Presidents have the courage to stay strong and withstand adversity while motivating themselves in the face of enormous frustration. President Lincoln did not use his poverty as an excuse, nor did he let it keep him from achieving his desired goals, despite his repeated failures. President Roosevelt, on the other hand, grew up with great wealth. His test came when he was stricken with polio at age 39. Although it crippled his body, it did not cripple his spirit or resolve.

Good leaders know how to surround themselves with smart but diverse people without being intimidated and without threat of retaliation when they disagree with them. Lincoln hired three of his chief Republican rivals for crucial cabinet positions and filled the remaining positions with former Democrats. FDR also created his cabinet by appointing competing critics of the New Deal into key positions. Then, and he reached over 34 names to appoint George Marshall chief of staff because the straight-talking general once disagreed with him in a meeting. Of course, we all know the story of the "Marshall Plan," from 10th grade history.

For those of you who cannot quite remember, many European cities were demolished and their economies were devastated at the end of World War II (1945). Working to prevent a repeat of the world economy, 1929 depression, the U. S. implemented the Economic Cooperation Act of 1948, which later became known as the Marshall Plan.

This plan not only saved the European economies, but it also laid the foundation for the North Atlantic Treaty Organization (NATO) and the ultimate unification of of the European countries to form the European Economic Union.

Successful leaders have the ability to acknowledge and learn from their mistakes without losing their perspective. Lincoln and FDR both had the opportunity to revamp their strategies after defeats, Lincoln at Bull Run and FDR after his first New Deal failed.

Leaders also know when they need to change. FDR, when faced with war, made peace with the industrialists he had alienated with the New Deal. He relaxed anti-trust regulations, and brought in business executives to run the war effort to build the necessary assets to win – – planes, tanks, and ships.

Presidents and good leaders encourage their closest advisers to be loyal and give their best by sharing their successes and shouldering part of the blame for failures. This makes people want to do a better job.

Presidents Lincoln and Roosevelt had more than enough opportunities to let their emotions run wild. But both knew how to keep calm when facing dire circumstances, Lincoln during his battle to hold the union together, and FDR when the Japanese attacked Pearl Harbor, HI.

Both presidents were keenly aware of public sentiment. Lincoln knew just when the time was right to deliver the Emancipation Proclamation, and FDR knew when the nation needed a fireside chat.

Strong leaders have the courage and integrity to follow their convictions, even at the risk of losing great support. Senior Republicans tried to force Lincoln to renounce emancipation as a condition for peace talks, but the President refused. FDR sent weapons to England to battle Hitler despite tremendous opposition within his party.

FDR and Lincoln each had their own way of relaxing, and these rules were never ignored by them or others.

Finally, good leaders, like good presidents know how to inspire people. That means shaping public opinion behind their goals. Go read Lincoln's second inaugural speech when the North was about to win the war against the South, and FDR's first inaugural address given at the height of the Depression to see graciousness under pressure.

One more thing, that friend's car that I was working to save, the one I discussed at the beginning of the chapter, it was saved along with lots of his money.

Chapter Fourteen

God Bless the Child

Owning your own business or being an entrepreneur is a dream many individuals have or have had, but few are able to bring their dream into fruition. Statistics indicate that less than 20% of the U. S. workforce is made up of self-employed individuals. However, this same 20% makes up more than 75% of all millionaires in the country.

According to the Small Business Administration (SBA), small businesses, those that have less than 500 employees, represent 99.7% of all employer firms in the U. S., and employ half of all private sector employees.

It is reasonable to extrapolate from this data that every small business in the U. S. began as some sort of entrepreneurial enterprise. For that matter, I would go as far to state that every large corporation began as an entrepreneurial endeavor (Sam Walton, Ray Kroc, Charles Schawb, to name a few).

These numbers also help us to understand why the 2008 – 2010 recession was and still is so devastating for entrepreneurs and employees already in the market, and those wishing to enter or re-enter the market. But, no amount of explaining is going to change those lives ravaged by the recession. Notwithstanding the collective pain of those hurt by the recession, entrepreneurship is more than just numbers.

Entrepreneurship is one example of the embodiment of a definitive goal that an individual has a burning desire to achieve. Once determined, opportunities for personal initiative are then easy to find. This idea of personal initiative was also espoused, in part, by Napoleon Hill.

A very close friend of mine, who happens to be a high school teacher, once told me a story that, I believe, exemplifies this essence of entrepreneurship.

One of her former students, a varsity football star, chose not to play football his senior year, and she wanted to understand why. As I understood the story, this 18-year old young man had three priorities: his father, football, and school.

His father had painstakingly taught himself how to restore vintage cars; and, whenever he was working on a car, he had his three sons there with him so that they too could learn some skills.

So, her pupil, who was a better than average student, had paid so much attention to his father's work that his father was able to use him as a subcontractor. This ongoing business had proven to be very profitable for everyone involved.

The last time I checked, the son was still his father's only subcontractor for any restoration contracts $30,000 or less. Her student, in turn, hires his two brothers, at a premium rate, to do the work while he oversees all of the details as the general subcontractor. That is keeping it in the family through entrepreneurship!

By the way, the father has sold more than two dozen cars at a going rate of more than $167,000 per car, not including those cars the son has sold as his father's subcontractor. And, the business is still growing.

From an entrepreneurial viewpoint, her student made a decision of passion, because he chose the priority that he cared about most. I agree with Martha Stewart that when an individual is so passionate about their work it is no longer work, but an enjoyment. And, besides, he already had ownership in a thriving business enterprise that catered to a high-end clientele, all before he even graduated high school.

He decided that in the long-run he could make more money and save his body (potential dangers of football), along with numerous other benefits, by staying in the family business. A decision he and his family are clearly enjoying.

Although the entrepreneurial landscape of the U. S. is the best in the world, still, the transition is not necessarily an easy one to make, primarily, because most individuals do not know where or how to start the process to entrepreneurship. And contrary to popular opinion, I believe that a recession may be a better time than any to start a new enterprise.

There are several practical reasons why I believe that a recession may be a good time to start a new business, if one is prepared. First, I believe that start up costs may be lower during a recession, because most businesses are reducing prices on everything to entice customers to make some kind of purchase. Bargain buying may yield such things as office/warehouse space, slightly used office equipment, and contracts with partners that one may never had access to if it were not for a recession, just to name a few.

Second, large companies do less marketing in a recession. This means that there may be an opportunity for a new, cutting-edge company to impact market share, to reach a particular segment of the market with less opposition. Sometimes, this may be easier in a down market, because customers are less loyal when prices are an option and when fewer marketing dollars are competing to influence customer purchases.

Finally, a larger employee pool can help new employers secure top-notch labor at much lower, initial costs. Unfortunately, skilled labor is plentiful in a recession. These are a few, but, important reasons why beginning an entrepreneurship in a recession is an idea worth considering, all things being equal.

Most of us have heard the term, "necessity is the mother of all inventions." This may be the best reason of all to start a new enterprise during a recession. UPS began in 1907 and FedEx began in 1971.

Let's examine an enterprise a little closer to home.

I started working on this current work more than ten years ago. It had little organization and no name. I was simply committing my experiences to paper. The more I worked on it, the more I realized that it was not enough to just recount my own stories. I needed to find a way to help all of those individuals who shared my same experiences and were also without help.

The more I worked on the project, the more my responsibilities grew at work. There were several times during this ten year period that I did not work on this project for more than two years at a time. The competition between my work and the project forced the project to take a backseat to my family's survival.

I then willingly transferred to a job with far less responsibilities, and from there, on to a temporary position, which finally lead to a period of unemployment, knowingly. Although I was already on a debt elimination plan, as I got closer to the end of each job, I increased my debt reduction payments to pay off as much debt as I possibly could. I also set aside money for my monthly expenses during my expected period (s) of unemployment.

I worked lots of extra hours, and took on several additional duties to increase my weekly earnings. This way, I paid for individual aspects of the project as they were completed, or set money aside to pay for future aspects of the project. This was critically important to me, because I did not want to take on any debt to produce this project.

Finally, when I had enough of the project completed, I presented it to several major publishers, but they could not see the appeal and impact of this kind of project. However, I had so much faith in God, the project, and my overall plan that I took all of my own money and self-published the book you are now reading.

President Theodore Roosevelt also gave me hope, even before I was born, in a speech he gave at The Sorbonne, Paris, France on April 23, 1910. The title of the speech was, "The Man In The Arena."

Here is an excerpt of that speech that has encouraged me for a number of years.

"The credit belongs to the man who is actually in the arena, who strives valiantly;...who knows the great enthusiasms, the great devotions,...and spends himself in a worthy ... cause, who at the best, knows the triumph of high achievement; and who, at the worst, if he fails, ... at least fails while daring greatly, so that his place shall never be with those cold and timid souls...who know neither victory nor defeat."

The necessity, for me, during the aftermath of this most recent recession, has been that so many people are still hurting, and have not been able to find practical answers to their collective financial pain. I also hope that this book helps to prevent similar pain in future years to come.

Additionally, I have had enough adversity in my lifetime that I have learned that everyone gets knocked down. But it is not being down in the mud that counts. It is what you do when you get out of the mud that really matters. Napoleon Hill said it this way, "No one has failed until he accepts the defeats as failure."

Many individuals are tired of the same old message -- go to school, get a good education, find a good job, have a family, work hard, and then retire. There has to be more to a working adult's life than the rote existence described above. And, there are too many barriers to that stated plan in this new economy we now live in.

But, the idea of going it alone, or at least, the idea of leaving corporate America appears to be the continuation of a trend that began in the 1980s. A trend that started, in part, because of the two recessions in the early '80s -- 1980, and, 1981 through 1982, and all the other economic bumps or hurdles (depending on your market and job positioning) over the past 30 years.

Which tells me, that other individuals have already recognized those barriers – job loss, financial instability, inability to increase income while working in a traditional job, income that lags behind costs of living, archaic rules that stifle creativity, uninformed supervisors, and so on. So, while the economy has changed, the rules for surviving in the economy have not changed, which is the reason why so many individuals are coming up with their own financial survival plans, i.e., owning their own.

Having served as a microenterprise-small-business-development-manager, I have seen, firsthand, and, participated in the decision-making process of those contemplating a business venture and those trying to grow a micro-enterprise. I have also sat in my office and heard the detailed reasons why owning their own business was so important. Their reasons mirrored those already listed.

Despite what others may say, those who were most successful, in this transition to private enterprise, did so because they were beyond being angry about the impact factors listed above. They decided they were going to be successful before they put the first word on paper. In their minds, they did not have a choice. Failure was not an option!

Regardless of when one decides to pursue their entrepreneurial dream or why, a business plan is going to be a critical part of that decision, before and after.

Accordingly, I have organized this chapter in the same systematic way that I counseled each of my former clients. It is designed to help anyone analytically transfer their ideas from the creative (mental) phase to paper.

A step-by-step format that presents a logical, well thought out, documented plan in a clear and convincing manner is similar to a decision matrix, except that a decision matrix is a table of qualitative or quantitative values. A business plan uses both qualitative and quantitative analysis to systematically identify, analyze, and rate the strength of relationships, based on some predefined, business criteria.

In the end, this document, whatever form is used, should give any reader a clear understanding of the decision criteria and the available options used to formulate this plan, even when one has to create the options before they are yet available. Further, based on those details, the plan should explain why the specific course of action presented in the plan is the best choice for the business at hand. However, the plan does not just stop there. It should also detail the interconnectivity of those options, i.e., how different combinations of options change the expected outcome.

All of this is no easy task when one considers all the work of writing and re-writing the business plan, and all the hours of behind the scenes work that goes into that entire process. Therefore, as much of this work as possible should be accomplished while one is still employed -- in a semi-relaxed environment. This way a potential entrepreneur can create an authenticate plan to present to their family, their financiers, and potential partners, without feeling pressured, and without feeling that they have lost anything, i.e., quitting one's job prematurely.

Some individuals start this process very early in life, others start in the middle of their lives, and still some start at the end of a long career. There is no one path that works best for everyone. However, there are some basics that can help anyone regardless of when they start their journey.

According to the SBA, entrepreneurship may be considered the true engine of the U. S. economy, because these enterprises provide approximately 75 % of all new jobs added to the economy. Together, these enterprises employ more than half of the entire country's workforce, and are more than 25 million businesses strong.

Before I continue this discussion on entrepreneurship, I would like to focus on the entrepreneur, the individual, for a moment.

Napoleon Hill, in his great work, *Think and Grow Rich,* listed twelve great riches of life that I believe are embedded, in one way or another, in the moral fiber of every individual that would aspire to be an entrepreneur. Those twelve riches are:

1) Positive mental attitude.
2) Sound physical help.
3) Harmony in Human Relationships.
4) Freedom from fear.
5) The hope of achievement.
6) The capacity for faith.
7) A willingness to share one's blessings.
8) A labor love.
9) An open mind on all subjects.
10) Self-discipline.
11) The capacity to understand people.
12) Financial security.

The reason I paused to look at the individuals behind these businesses is, generally speaking, that the individuals get lost in the micro-enterprise, whatever it may be. Contrary to the advice of "experts" who say that the entrepreneur needs to have a life separate from their business, every successful entrepreneur will tell you that there is no such thing as a "personal life" when starting a new enterprise, and possibly several years after.

I can also emphatically state that during all my years as a contract manager and a small-business manager, I found out there are a lot of experts, but few entrepreneurs; and, most of those experts have never owned their own business.

Everyone that I have spoken to, without exception, said that their business was their life. And, they had to work twice as hard to build a successful business in the beginning, no matter how long it took. This is necessary because the owner has to do everything, or almost everything, themselves, in the beginning, to save money and build clientele. It is not uncommon to hear of normal work weeks being 80+ hours a week or more, whether at the office or at home.

Therefore, it is critical that this individual knows who he or she is, where they want to go, and what actions are required for them to achieve their goals, and all this before they start. Because, once they have begun or when that final decision is made, there will be no time for introspection or turning back. Besides, you do not need to be second-guessing yourself or your business, because there will be enough people doing all of that for you.

Napoleon Hill stated this same fact in his 1928 work, *The Law of Success In Sixteen Lessons*. Hill stated that once an individual has attentively defined his personal goals, he can then focus on achieving those goals. This prevents wasted energy, because having defined his goals, he can now create the environment and circumstances necessary to achieve those goals, instead of letting life "happen" to him.

But, regardless of whether you stumbled into success or planned your way into it, it still has to be managed to be sustainable.

Many individuals, throughout history, have had tremendous business ideas. But, in the end someone else came along and actually became the owner of an idea that was another individual's dream child. Why? Because they either did not know how to market their idea or manage the process of owning their idea before they tried to sell it in the public domain.

If you doubt this is true, there is a current popular movie that speaks to this very subject. You decide. But remember this, inside of every rumor there is some truth.

Whether you have found your business idea or are still searching, statistics show that most entrepreneurial ventures are outgrowths of individual past experiences, i.e., work, personal, or otherwise – – and maybe from more negative experiences than positive. So then, the question becomes how does one discover a hole, a vacuum, or an unmet need in the marketplace and then fulfill that need with a superior product or idea?

Since most individuals, that consider starting a new business, start right where they are, here a few pivotal questions to pose to yourself to help flush out your business ideas? Start carrying a writing pad everywhere you go so that you can write down your findings whenever and wherever they occur.

- Can I do my current job (industrial psychologist, for example) as an independent contractor for several companies?
- The maker of this product has ignored several details of a specific product, the market, and/or their service. Can I correct these errors and make a profitable business?
- Who is/would be my competition? What can I learn from the competition?
- Most new inventions are derived from products already in existence, for example, from customers who regularly use a product. Is there such a product in your life? (The Italian inventor Gugliegmo Marconi improved several patents belonging to Nikola Tesla's for the radio.)

Since you are still in the idea mode here are a few other places to look for business opportunities.

- Become a copycat – do what someone else is already doing but do it better. (Sandra Lee and Semi-Homemade Cooking)
- Look around the country and see what others are doing. Can you bring a new type of service into your area? (Angie'sList.com)
- Purchase a franchise. (Popular for veterans)
- What about purchasing a business you already frequent or one that is doing exceptionally well in your area? (Where I live, that would be an Italian restaurant named Stefano's.)

And above all else, do not forget that the Federal government is the largest purchaser of goods and services. Therefore, you may want to consider becoming a supplier of the Federal government. There are three ways to find out more information about the Federal government.

1) Directly through an agency's purchase officer, such as DoD, or HUD.

2) Through the General Services Administration purchase program.

3) As a Federal contractor, www.ccr.gov, or use the clearinghouse of information at http://www.usa.gov.

Regardless of where your brainstorming takes you, there are a few characteristics that are common amongst almost all entrepreneurs. However, this is not an exhaustive list. I have listed a few of the primary characteristics that I believe are of primal importance to entrepreneurial success.

- Driven for financial success – because this time you are going to have to prove that you are worth what you are asking for.
- People person – because you are going to have to know how to manage your people, your customers, your suppliers, and everyone in between.
- Manage the intangibles – some other very important factors to consider may include your overall personal health, perseverance, creativity, and the ability to take calculated risks, to name a few.

The SBA also has an excellent online course with print material that will help you in developing your small business, and some important considerations about the type of business (i.e., partnership, corporation, or sole ownership) structure that is better suited for your idea, initially. Just go to the SBA's website. www.sba.gov, and the first tab is *Starting & Managing a Business.*

How to Say Goodbye

If you are currently employed and are trying to find a way to leave your current employer, here are a few thoughts that might help you break out of that rat race.

Your work experience with your current employer, although underpaid, may turn out to be one of your biggest assets as an entrepreneur, because this experience gives you credibility.

Many new businesses have a problem gaining clients, because their clients are not sure that these new owners know how to handle their business. Your credibility may serve a dual purpose at a critical stage in your career. Not only may it serve as your departure ticket, but it may simultaneously be the key ingredient to your new success, if you know how to package and market this information.

So, think of your job as on-the-job-training for your next career move. Make it your job to learn everything you possibly can about being in business, especially the financial side — because in the end, this will be your true lifeline.

If you have never done so, despite our conversation earlier in this chapter, now may be the right time to take an entrepreneurial self-assessment to determine if you are emotionally, physically, and fully committed to the idea of being your own boss, and how this is going to impact your familial unit.

You can find several different types of these self-assessments on line simply by searching for "entrepreneurial self-assessment." All of these assessments are pretty much the same, except that each may be intended to measure a different aspect of entrepreneurship. Therefore, it would not hurt to take stock in yourself, by taking a few of these assessments, to help you decided whether or not to press forward or not. And, if you are going to pursue this, be brutally honest with yourself!

But remember this, no individual or an assessment can tell you if you are ready to own a business. Only you can do that!

There are similar self-assessments for skills also. However, if you already know that you are going to be needing some specific skills, that you have not yet attained, here are three ideas for attaining that all-important help.

First, you might want to consider partnering with one, two, or three or more individuals to help strengthen your new team. Second, you may include the expense of acquiring this skill as an employee cost in your business plan. Third, you might want to consider contracting with an individual or firm to provide this skill as a service to your firm.

However, if you are lacking in both skills and experience, for example, legal matters, then it might behoove you to partner with an attorney that can help you with both your direct business needs and other inexperienced legal issues that may arise.

Finally, if you have an impenetrable business plan, know how to raise capital, and have a ready cash reserve to live off of for six months to a year, then the last thing to do is say your goodbyes.

Let's review your checklist items thus far. You should have some business education or are getting some either on the job or in a classroom. You should have picked a partner or two who can give you advice, complement your strengths, and shore up your weaknesses. You should have already met all the criteria listed in the previous paragraph. If you have accomplished all of these tasks, then you have succeeded in completing a very impressive pre-business checklist.

However, if you have not been as successful in completing your checklist as you would like, then here is a website that may help you do just that — http://archive.sba.gov/teens.

This website was specifically chosen to encourage everyone to open their minds to all the possibilities; and, the best way I know how to do that is to encourage everyone to think like a child.

A second checklist that may prove helpful is http://www.score.org/business_toolbox.html, which is the website for SCORE. SCORE is the acronym for the Service Corps Of Retired Executives, who serve as small business counselors to the SBA. This group offers free advice to individuals in the areas of finance, human resources, legal, product development, and many other areas, to help individuals develop the best small businesses possible.

Even if you have not completed a pre-business checklist, the matrix below, taken directly from the SBA's website, may help guide you in your strategic development. This matrix is found under the Small Business Planner on the website. It may also help you think more critically and strategically as you are writing your business plan.

Plan Your Business	Start Your Business	Manage Your Business	Getting Out
Get Ready	Find a Mentor	Lead	Plan Your Exit
Write a Business Plan	Finance Start-Up	Make Decisions	Sell Your Business
	Buy a Business	Manage Employees	Transfer Ownership
	Buy a Franchise	Market and Price	Liquidate Assets
	Name Your Business	Market and Sell	File Bankruptcy
	Choose a Structure	Understand Fair Practice	Close Officially
	Protect Your Ideas	Pay	
	Get Licenses and Permits	Get Insurance	
	Pick a Location	Handle Legal Concerns	
	Lease Equipment	Forecast	
		Advocate and Stay Informed	
		Use Technology	
		Finance Growth	

These matrices, also taken from the previously designed SBA website, under the Services tab, may help you in your business development and later on as your business grows.

Financial Assistance	Contract Opportunties	Disaster Assistance	Online Training
Note on Grants	For Small Business Owners	Basics	Free Online Courses
Intro to SBA Finance	For Government/ Contracting Officials	For Businesses of All Sizes	New Courses
Basics		Military Reservists Loans	Most Popular Courses
Loan Application		For Homeowners & Renters	About SBTN
SBA Loans		Office Locations	Online Universites & Colleges
Surety Bonds		Disaster Preparedness	
Equity Capital		For Media	
SBA Partner Topcs		2005 Gulf Coast Hurricanes	Compliance
7(a) Lender Programs			
Counseling & Assistance	Special Audiences	Laws/Regulations	Compliance
SCORE	Women	Small Business Advocacy	
Small Business Development	Veterans	National Ombudsman	
Women's Business Centers	Native Americans	Law Library	
National Training Events	Opportunity Gaps	Hearings & Appeals	
	Young Entrepreneurs		
	International Trade		
	En Español		
	50+ Entrepreneurs		

The SBA also produces an annual magazine entitled, Your Small Business Resource Guide, which is chocked full of information for start-ups and existing business owners. Check with your local SBA office for a copy in your area.

In addition to the SBA, check with your state's department of Commerce and see if they produce an annual Small Business and Entrepreneurship Resource Guide, which offers some additional resources beyond the SBA guide listed above.

Now, if you are interested in starting a business, but not ready to leave your comfort zone, then try researching a small home-based business that does not need much start up cash, such as a medical transcriber, to name just one example. Here is a website that may help you do just that – http://www.business.com/directory/small_business/getting_started/.

Remember this, some of the most lucrative businesses today had their start as a home-based business (Martha Stewart).

First Things First

Now that all of the preliminaries have been addressed, it is time to look at the business road map, game plan, plan of action, or whatever name you choose to call it.

This business plan gives everyone who reads it insight into your thought process and your business' innermost workings. It also helps potential investors or business partners evaluate the feasibility of your business idea in an objective unemotional way.

In addition to serving as your baseline marketing, management, and operational plan, it may also serve as your strategic plan, which will help you identify both opportunities and avoidable mistakes.

While I am going to give you a few thoughts on some matters that need to be highlighted in your plan, the best business plan workbook I have ever seen was given to me some years ago at a SBA small business course. At the time I was given this booklet, I was researching a new business venture, and had no idea that this book would include this subject matter.

The 35-page booklet can now be found at www.mastercard.com/ca/wce/PDF/bro_develop_business_plan.pdf. (A quick web note: the spaces in the website tag above should actually be underscores, and look like this in your browser, www....bro_develop_business_plan...). The booklet can be printed for free from this website.

Here is the basic business plan outline that I used to help my former clients began the transfer process from their head to paper. Every item on this outline may or may not be required for your business plan. So do not feel pressured to include a particular item. For that matter, if there is a need to include an item that is not listed below, then, by all means, make sure that information is included.

I. Executive Summary
   A. Vision Statement
   B. Mission Statement
   C. Credentials
II. The Business
   A. The Industry
      i. Competition
   B. Your Company
      i. Competitive Edge
   C. Your Product or Service
III. Market Research and Analysis
   A. Customers
      i. Objectives
      ii. Target Audience
   B. Market Size and Trends
   C. Competition
   D. Market Share and Sales
IV. Marketing Plan (www.knowthis.com)
   A. Overall Market Strategy
   B. Pricing
   C. Sales Strategies
      i. Outlets
      ii. Distribution
   D. Advertising and Promotion
V. Operating Plan
   A. Location
   B. Facilities and Improvements
   C. Strategy and Plans

D. Labor Force

VI. Management Team

A. Organization

B. Key Personnel

C. Management Compensation and Ownership

D. Board of Directors (if required)

VII. The Financial Plan

A. Business Budget

i. Overhead Costs

ii. Employee Costs

a. Labor Force

iii. Marketing Costs

iv. Material Costs

v. Insurance Costs

vi. Taxes

vii. Capital Equipment Costs

viii. Technological Costs

ix. Other Costs

B. Sources and Users of Funds

C. Pro Forma Cash Flow Analysis

D. Profit and Loss Forecasts (Income Statements)

E. Pro Forma Balance Sheets

F. Breakeven Analysis

VIII. Appendix

A. Loan Application(s)

Footnote regarding the financial statements. All of the financial documents listed above have free templates that can be found in any number of programs, on any number of sites on the web, and/or at Microsoft online templates. Each of those documents should be prepared in three different forms, unless otherwise instructed by someone, such as your accountant. They should each be prepared in monthly detailed reports for the first year (12 monthly reports for each document). Secondly, they should each be prepared in quarterly details for the second and third years (4 quarters X 2 years = 8 quarterly reports for each document listed above). Finally, each financial document should have a three-year summary.

Here is a list of some other documents that may become necessary as you continue through this process. Make sure these documents are in order, if the need should arise.

I. Most recent three years of tax returns for all principals
II. Three years personal financial statements for all principals, on bank letterhead
III. If a franchise, copy of franchise contract
   a. Copy of all additional documents required by franchisor
IV. Copy of proposed building lease or purchase agreement
V. Copy of licenses and other pertinent legal documents
VI. Copy of resumes for all principals
VII. Copies of letters of intent from all suppliers
VIII. Operational flow charts to show exactly how the business will work on a daily business.

Of course every business plan has to have an introduction which also has three sections. The introduction comes before the executive summary listed in the above outline.

I. The Cover Sheet
II. Statement of Purpose
III. Table of Contents

Although your business plan is developed for limited eyes only, the primary group that you want to see your plan is your financial supporters, because your plan will show your budget projections, balance sheets, and, most importantly, your breakeven analysis, and income projections.

One of the primary purposes of the financial section is to help you raise cash from private and public investors. And the most important part of any plan, for investors, is how soon will they realize the return on their investment? In addition to showing your liquidity, the financial section demonstrates your ability to both repay your debt and keep your overall debt within a reasonable limit.

Therefore, writing your business plan is not a task to be taken lightly, because its consequences are clearly far reaching, as you are already well aware. Plan to spend upwards of 300 hours or more (roughly 7.5 weeks in total, but if you are working, then these 7.5 weeks may not be consecutive) researching, writing, and rewriting this plan, because every detail must be perfect. Make every single word count!

If your business plan is a complex one, for example, like a childcare education facility, production and distribution of a particular type of food product, or a non-profit organization, then you may want to add an executive summary at the beginning.

The recommendation, in this case, would be to remove the statement of purpose and insert the executive summary just after the table of contents. This summary should be short and concise, about 3-5 pages, and, give a broad overview of the details contained within the business plan.

Your outline should also serve as your section headings for your readers and to help you stay on subject. Once you have done your research and are ready to start writing your plan, your initial draft should contain as much detail as possible. Do not leave anything out of this initial draft. It may take you several different writing sessions before you have a complete business plan.

Once you have a completed plan, put it away for a day or two, but not more than a week. After this much needed rest period, go back and pick up your plan. This time, however, you are going to start cutting as much as you possibly can. But, you must make sure you maintain clarity and uniformity in your presentation.

The goal here is to cut as much extraneous material as possible. By this, I mean, you want short declarative sentences that are exact and to the point. Use as little flowery language, or as few adjectives and adverbs as possible.

For example, instead of saying, "The beautiful red boat will be stored in a dark abandoned warehouse." State it this way, "The boat is stored in a warehouse."

Regardless of the color of the boat or its beauty, it has to be stored somewhere. The same goes for the warehouse. This way, using declarative sentences, each sentence has only one focus, one main point!

Business plan writing is very difficult for many individuals, because it is a different type of writing. For those who can succeed, there is the potential for a very lucrative, independent career. For those who simply want to get their own plan completed, it is a doable, but formidable task.

I know this to be so, because one of my former clients walked into my office one Monday afternoon, and presented me a top-notch business plan that she had written completely on her own, over the course of several months. This lady was a volunteer, a teacher for deaf children by day, a mother, wife, and childcare giver by night, and a student on the weekends; and, when everyone had gone to bed at night, she would stay up a few hours each night working on her plan. It was abundantly clear that she had mastered her subject matter, and that she knew how to turn her skills into a profitable business enterprise. Her plan was flawless!

In some ways, business plan writing it is very similar to writing a legal brief – – it should contain only facts and be concise, to the point. I remember reading a comment that Justice Antonin Scalia once made, that basically said, legal briefs brought before the Supreme Court were too verbose. Think of your plan in this same respect. It is going to be judged by several people, so the shorter and more to the point it is, the more of it will actually get read.

Sometimes a picture may do for your plan what words cannot, so do not ignore the practicality of using pictures and/or graphs whenever possible. That old saying does have validity, "a picture is worth a thousand words."

If you have any doubt about your presentation at this point, there is what is commonly known as the elevator test that you can use to judge the clarity of your argument.

If you can fill in the blanks for the six statements below by the time your elevator goes from the first floor to the sixth floor, then your presentation has met the standards of simplicity and clarity. If not, well then you have a little more work to do. Sometimes it may help to write the first part of the plan last, because then you have a full picture of what you are envisioning, which may make it easier to see the beginning after you finish the ending.

1. For [statement of need or opportunity]
2. Who [target customer]
3. The [product name or product category]
4. That [key benefit, compelling reason to purchase]
5. Dissimilar [primary competitive edge over alternatives]
6. Product [what differentiates product from others in market]

Here are three websites that may offer you some additional help. Always remember to check out these and all other recommendations for yourself before making any decisions, regardless of the source of the information. The first website offers some sample views of different types of business plans, and some other options for purchase, if you so decide, http://www.bplans.com/sample_business_plans.cfm. If you want to order some additional business planning assistance, you may consider, http://www.newgroundpublications.com/index.html. If you need some business finance assistance, here is a website that was referred to me by another colleague, www.businessfinance.com.

Oscar Wilde once said, "Experience is the name everyone gives to their mistakes." So if you make a mistake in your business, you will be in the experience of good company. Here are seven of the biggest business "experiences," thus far.

In 1858, Edwin Drake developed the oil drill. Investors, oil companies, and even foreign governments have made trillions off the invention Drake failed to patent.

In 1962, Decca Studios rejected signing The Beatles, and stated, [they have] "no future in show business."

In 1979, Ross Perot had the opportunity to purchase Microsoft from Bill Gates. However, the negotiations broke down and no deal ensued.

In 1983, Apple co-founder, Steve Jobs, was forced out for two years or more. The company was not profitable again until Jobs returned several years later, to which we have to thank, at least in part, for the iPhone, iPod, iTunes, and the iPad, thus far.

In 1984, ABC network turned down "The Cosby Show." NBC picked up the show for little or nothing, and the show stayed in the No. 1 spot in the Nielsen ratings for five straight seasons.

In 1999, Google founders, Larry Page and Sergey Brin offered to sell the business to Excite for $1 million. But, Excite's CEO George Bell refused the offer as too high.

In 2000, Time Warner merged with AOL for a colossal $350 million blunder. All of the major players came to their senses in 2010 and agreed to separate the companies.

These business decisions had some obvious gaps, that proved to be their downfall. To help you find and fill in the gaps of your business plan, SCORE has some excellent templates to get you on your way at their website, along with pertinent questions to help you derive at the necessary answers to fill in those gaps, http://www.score.org/template_gallery.html.

In addition to those websites listed above, you may also check with the local Small Business Development Center in your area to see if they have any additional free tools to assist you with your individual plans.

One such center that has an excellent outline for the business plan is located at Georgia State University, http://www2.gsu.edu/~wwwsbp/Busplan_Outline.pdf. The university's website is www.gsu.edu/sbdc.

Make sure you do not undermine your own credibility and hard work with a few senseless mistakes or simple carelessness such as:

- attempting to paint too rosey a picture without due consideration to potential downturns in market forces.
- using outdated financial information or impractical assessments.
- showing a clear lack of comprehension of financial documentation and information.
- a lack of specifics and unsupported assumptions.
- a financial section that shows the owner not only has nothing at stake in the business, but, is also unwilling to personally guarantee any possible loans should the loans default.

These are but a few mistakes that could doom your business before it ever gets off the ground.

Although every question in a business template will not apply to every business plan, the basic idea is to convey the belief to all your readers that you have given considerable thought to every single aspect of your business and that nothing has been overlooked.

Some of the best business planning assistance, in this manner, I have personally ever received was from the SCORE chapter located in Charlotte, NC. To give you some idea of the vastness of the information covered in those meetings, here are a few subjects that were covered, according to my historical notes.

The training covered the 12 crucial questions of marketing.

1. What are you selling (from a customer's perspective)?
2. Who would want it?
3. Why (Where/what is value)?
4. How many of these people are there (potential customers)?
5. How much money do they spend?

6. Who/What is the competition (find their weakness and make that my competitive advantage)?

7. What are their strengths?

8. What is your advantage over the competition (in the customer's mind)?

9. How will you make sure the market knows you exist (shotgun or rifle approach; the 2nd is more direct, but need a hook – reason for customers to come in)?

10. What share of the market can you expect to get?

11. How much sales revenue can you forecast (timeframe to reach goal; if demand goes up, how will survive; how will competitors react)?

12. It costs less to retain a customer than to acquire a new one. How to retain disgruntled customers?

Here are a few quick low-cost ideas on how to market your business.

- Develop a relationship with local media through news worthy stories, not advertising. Look into services of a publicist.
- Get involved in the online community. There are chat groups, bulletin boards, blogs, email discussion list, and more on a variety of topics. Find those that connect to your business and get in on the conversation.
- Use your business to sponsor a major cause you care about, or a major cause within the community (youth events, senior citizens).
- Get involved with trade shows and conferences.
- From the very beginning develop a electronic customer list to stay in contact with you customers, without harassing them.
- Make sure your name stays in your customer's homes with magnets, bracelets, etc.
- Create ways to connect to the children, this will keep parents attached to your business.
- Learn how to make customers feel special.

I used to have a chiropractor who employed several of these strategies, and he had the most successful practice in the city for more than 40 years. No other practice came close to the level of business that he did.

In addition to marketing, we discussed how to identify costs (initial and ongoing), payroll, taxes, utilities, professional services, and insurance, to name a few. Additionally, we discussed ways to save money from delaying expenditures, purchasing used equipment, 2nd hand furniture, and planning for growth instead of spending for it.

To help offset some costs, for example, if you have to build or purchase a facility to house your operations, considering checking with both your state and local economic development offices. Both governing bodies employ business site selection specialists that can help you identify the best place to locate your business and at no cost. Cities and states are both interested in growing their business community and tax base.

I also learned an important lesson about cash flow that I had never recognized before. Loans only shift cash situations to get to profitability, in the short term.

Although I intuitively knew that loans have to be repaid, I had not considered the fact that a loan only looks good on the books until the money is completely expended. Generally, this is a very short period. Businesses and individuals only apply for loans to pay debts that are due immediately or past due, and cannot be paid without an immediate cash infusion.

While the loan is used to pay bills and keep the business going, the real fact is that the loan and its interest payments are debt that has to be managed, along with the business' pre-existing debt, or that portion of any remaining debt that was not paid off with the loan.

Therefore, throughout this entire process, the business looks profitable because of the loan. But, this may only be *Funny Money*, because the loan is a long-term liability (payments will extend more than one year), and the cash money (loan) is a temporary asset.

The profitability of a company has to be measured over time. The real determinants of profitability are going to be if the loan can be repaid as required and if the company continues to grow. If neither one of these factors is true, then the loan was *Funny Money*, although the loan was probably sought with good intentions.

Again, while I knew this, I had not really thought as clearly about it until that training class. That is when I began to really see that loans only shift debt from one obligation to another. So on paper, a business may look profitable, but what is behind the numbers?

And, if a business owner takes out a loan to get through a rough period, and the business continues to taper off, that is when we began to see business closings as we saw in the most recent global recession. Loans cannot be part of a long-term business solution; and, a loan cannot help a bad business idea.

Beyond loans, we discussed sources of money (raising capital), and other financial considerations that business owners should at least be aware of, including maintaining a primary and secondary debt repayment source, controlling proprietary information listed in outside contracts, and having an exit plan.

As for an exit plan, this does not necessarily mean a business failure, but it can mean turning the business over to your children or grandchildren, and how the business will survive if the owner dies.

By the time the training was complete, it was quite clear to me that continuous planning is an essential key to the health of any business, new or otherwise. Any business owner should always be able to answer the Big IF(s) that will arise. For example, how will changing government regulations impact your business?

Lastly, if you plan on using your business plan to help acquire financing, here are the general requirements for most financial institutions, before they will even look at your business plan. And, here are some ideas for creating this kind of financial liquidity— retirement plans, and some other short– and long-term investment options.

- In the midst of these considerations, the 10,5,3 rule may provide some guidance. Remember, this is the rule of expectancy that basically states that one can expect a supposed return of 10% from equities, 5% return on bonds, and 3% on highly liquid cash or cash-equivalent accounts.
- 20% equity by owner
- Most banks will require 120% collateral
- Credit score 640-650+ (larger loans = larger credit score)
- Personal Financial Statement (separate from business plan)
- 3+ years tax returns (contained in business plan)

While writing your business plan may be some of the toughest work you may ever do, it may also be some of your most rewarding work. It should be unique and draw individuals into your idea with ease, including your financial calculations. If done properly, it will showcase you, your products, and your services. So make sure it does that in the very best way possible. By addressing the risks and creating some reasonable forecasts, you are addressing some of the most fundamental problem-solving challenges facing all businesses today.

Whether you have or have not had the opportunity to build a long credit history, this plan can help demonstrate to others that you are financially dependable. By creating a document that shows sound financial judgment, you can kill two birds with one stone – – fill in any credibility gaps and sell the business to potential financiers.

To this end, your plan should overestimate the amount of money you will need in the beginning, within reasonable limits of course. It is always easier to raise money before you need it than to have to come back and get more money, after you have failed to properly project what was actually needed.

Finally, if you are completely uncomfortable with the idea of writing your business plan from scratch, there are a number of business plans software on the market. Many of these program will walk you through the entire process, including cash-flow projections and other useful financial tools. Also, check to see if your state has a small business advocate who may be able to assist you in this and other business formation matters.

The best business plans, I have found, can be purchased for just under $200 at http://www.goodtogobizplans.com.

Once all of this work is complete, if you discover that your business is either not as sensible or as profitable as you once thought it to be, then the plan achieved its goal, and did what is was supposed to do. It revealed the vulnerabilities of your business idea, and its flaws without costing you much money. It also has sparred you even more huge losses on the other side.

Show Me the Money

The first lesson in small business money management is that everything in this business, from the first paper clip to the last piece of paper is going to come out of your pocket. As such, the true success of a new or existing small business primarily depends on one thing – your creditworthiness as the owner.

So, when you are putting together your financial data, you must consider such obscure facts as employee training, office equipment, 401k plans, insurance plans for the business and individuals, office supplies, and so on. And, the reason you need to consider all of these expenses is because you are the one who has to pay all of those bills.

Now, when it comes to financing all of these business needs, there are a multitude of ways to achieve positive end results. Some turn to private investors, and others to family, friends, or business networks for the capital. And, still there are others who use their own personal credit cards to fund their businesses or some sort of combination of all the above.

The main point here is that whichever financial road you decide to take, it should be well thought out, you should have the ability to repay the debt within a reasonable period, and above all, you need to be comfortable with this debt in the worst of situations.

If you are considering any type of financing that involves outside sources, the SBA can help you prepare these documents. Of course, these loans will have to be secured by the business assets. You will also need to calculate the actual cost of the loan (intangibles). By this, I mean, if you are taking your profits and repaying debt, then you are having to forgo other things, such as, a possible expansion, enhanced technology, or an assistant that keeps you on schedule.

But, do not be discouraged if your loan package is not well received by any bank. Almost 79% of all new businesses collapse within the first three years of opening their doors. This statistical fact obviously makes any banker skittish about taking on a new business loan, and, in particular, a loan for a startup company.

An alternative to conventional financing is the SBA, if you can withstand the Federal paperwork attached to any loan. Appendix C is a quick reference matrix for the entire SBA loan program.

If you decide that an SBA loan is right for your business, here are six things you need to know about getting this loan.

1) This loan is going to take some time and some paperwork. Getting the Federal government in your finances is certainly going to take more time than a non-government loan, which will make for a longer loan process overall.

2) You may not get all of the money required at one time. Although you have been approved for the loan, the lender may require documentation to prove that the disbursement of funds is both necessary, and is going to

pay bills acquired by and for the business. The lender may even require to see canceled checks to be sure that funds previously disbursed have been utilized before issuing any additional funds.

3) If you are married, your spouse may also be required to sign the loan documents as a personal guarantee before the funds are released. Generally, anyone having more than a 20% interest in a business will be required to sign loan documents. If your business assets are not enough, the SBA may also look to your personal assets for security.

4) An SBA-guaranteed loan may carry a higher interest rate than conventional loans. Although there are some cases where SBA-backed loans have lower carrying costs. What the SBA-guarantee does provide is the incentive for banks to loan, since these loans are not counted against the bank's reserves, and it allows the bank to extend a loan beyond their normal limits.

5) Getting an SBA-backed loan is going to come with some fees. The SBA normally charges lenders a guaranty fee of anywhere from 1% to 3.5% of its guaranteed amount, and an annual servicing fee of .25% of the outstanding balance. The SBA does allow these fees to be passed on to the borrower by the lender. However, the SBA prohibits lenders from charging application, processing, origination, and brokerage fees.

6) Minority-owned enterprises do not receive any special treatment when applying for an SBA-backed loan. Although the SBA does work to make sure that minority-, women-, and veteran-owned businesses are aware of SBA programs, there is no special treatment when it comes to their loan programs.

In addition, it may not hurt to review previous chapters where we discussed peer lending (P2P) options as a way to finance your new business.

To help you manage the risk of being a small business owner, the SBA has a Small Business Risk Management Guide that breaks down the risk factors associated with various small business decisions, for both the novice and the seasoned business owner.

Now, if anyone is considering other options for financing their business beyond the SBA, here are a few poplar credit cards that may be worth considering. This list is not to be construed as a recommendation of any one product over the other.

- Discover, Citibank, Chase Business Cards

- American Express
- Advanta (www.advanta.com)
- Ace-Net (www.ace-net.org) – Fee service where small businesses can put their plans and funding requirements on a network for investors to review
- SBICs – Small Business Investment Corporations, check with SBA on funding guidelines

Besides the SBA, there are some states that offer microloan (small business loans) programs – – Iowa, Maine, New York, North Dakota, Ohio, South Carolina, and Texas, to name a few.

If you are not sure your state offers any such assistance, contact your state's Office of Economic Development.

There is one more unique funding program that must be addressed because of the financial possibilities attached to it. The U. S. Department of Housing and Urban Development (HUD) is the controller of the Community Development Block Grants for the Federal Government (www.hud.gov).

Basically, under this program, HUD gives annual grants to cities and counties. Under the right circumstances, this money can be used to establish credit, issue direct loans and loan guarantees, create revolving loan funds, expand microenterprise programs, and more, as a way to improve communities, revitalize neighborhoods, and spur economic development.

Here is a list of some of the types of funding programs that may be available at the state or Federal level, above and beyond conventional low interest rates loans.

- Loan guarantees at the state level are co-signed by the state government.
- Interest rate subsidies where the state subsidizes some percentage amount of the interest on a loan.
- Industrial Revenue Bonds or General Obligation Bonds can be issued by a state to finance fixed assets like equipment or real property assets.
- Agricultural loans/Farm loans (www.fsa.usda.gov).
- Loans to exporters.
- Energy conservation loans.

- Regional loans for underdeveloped or economically depressed areas.
- High tech loans.
- Expansion loans.
- Loans set aside specifically for women, minorities, and other designated groups or help to get Federal contracts (http://osdbuweb.dot.gov).
- Sell products to the Department of Defense (www.dla.mil/db).
- Start a business in a small town (www.rurdev.usda.gov).
- Women only (http://www.womensbusinessgrants.com/how.shtml).
- Venture Capital Networks.
- Various Inventor Associations.
- Annual Governors' Conferences (opportunity for small business owners/associations to state concerns to captive audience).

Final Review

Let's do a quick review checklist for a new business, to make sure we have not left out any pertinent details, again taken from SCORE training notes.

- Can you describe your business idea in 50 words or less?
- Have you established the market for your product/service, identified your potential customers, and decided how best to advertise and promote your product?
- Have you determined the total dollar amount you will need to cover your personal and business expenses for the first 18 months?
- Will you require office, retail, or production space? If so are you familiar with zoning requirements?
- How many employees will you have? Are labor market conditions favorable for your enterprise? Are your familiar with the human resources requirements and other legal requirements for having employees?
- Will you carry any inventory, and if so, have you identified your suppliers?
- If you have equipment needs, have you investigated their costs?
- Will your require permits and/or licenses? (check to see if your state or local government has a one-stop-shop that helps with licensing, regulations, and permits)

- Do you need research and development assistance? (If considering a high technology-related business, this may be a free service offered by state or local government as well as procurement programs to help sell to other governmental entities and technology assistance centers.)

As part of this final review there is quite a bit of legal ground that needs to be covered depending on your state of residence. But, regardless of where you live, here is a brief list of some of the legal considerations or agencies that can have an impact on your business.

- Zoning and Sign Permits
- Fire Prevention Inspection
- Health Department Inspection
- Assumed Name Acts (business name not already taken)
- Tax Administrator (Local)
- Unemployment Insurance Tax
- Workmen's Compensation Insurance
- Sales and Use Tax
- Privilege License (check with your state's department of commerce)
- Employer Account Number (Federal and State)
- Federal Income Tax
- State Income Tax
- U. S. Department of Labor
- State Department of Labor (wherever you reside)

As you are considering the legal structure of your firm, Appendix D, a matrix taken from the former SBA website, will help you see some important considerations of each structure that any business owner needs to be familiar with.

Chapter Fifteen

Taken for Granted

When most individuals think about grant money, they immediately think non-profit organizations, and maybe rightfully so, because most grant money goes to those types of organizations, second only to federal grants given to the individual states. Since most grant monies go to non-profits it only makes sense to address non-profits before addressing grants. Notwithstanding all of this, there are a few grants that are given directly to individuals.

Starting a non-profit organization is much like starting a small business venture. One has to decide what is the mission, the purpose of the non-profit, and the problem the non-profit is going to address. Although this may sound daunting, it might be easier than you think, and it may only cost a few hundred dollars.

To start a non-profit may begin with something as simple as a meeting with a few close friends or advisors to talk about a simple plan, or it may just be you sitting down at your desk and making all the plans, alone.

This kind of serious soul searching will keep you from having to beg people for money by answering such questions like, "What are you really going to be offering? What targeted group or community are you going to serve? Is there anyone that can do this better than your organization? Can you just team up with someone else to do this service under their direction?"

Most reputable, non-profit organizations are incorporated entities. That is to say, these organizations, if properly run and managed, can exist long after the original starters have died or are no longer officially affiliated with the non-profit. But there are also a lot of very important financial considerations for becoming incorporated, such as owning property and maintaining bank accounts, to name a few.

Normally, when anyone thinks of a non-profit organization they think of a church or some other sort of religious organization. However, there are a number of other organizations that also hold the IRS 501(c)(3) status as a charitable, non-profit organization, which is exempt from federal and maybe other taxes.

This status has huge financial implications for both the non-profit and its donors. By having a tax exempt status, any donations given are also tax deductible for the giver. This makes it easier for the non-profit to collect the necessary funds to remain viable.

If anyone has any interest in forming a non-profit, there are ten basic categories of groups recognized by the IRS. They are:

1. Charitable organizations
2. Social Welfare organizations
3. Fraternal societies
4. Business leagues
5. Veteran's organizations
6. Employee's associations
7. Political organizations
8. Social clubs
9. Labor and Agricultural organizations
10. Others (catchall designations)

Here is a website that will help you get started in your planning, http://www.managementhelp.org/strt_org/strt_np/strt_np.htm.

An additional website that may lend you some assistance is http://www.managementhelp.org.

One other note may be important here before we move forward. An upstart non-profit can operate under the auspices of an already formed non-profit, as a subsidiary until their 501 papers are approved. But be careful, because this relationship can have huge implications for both non-profits.

Although this legal loophole exist, if at all possible, it may be better to wait for the approval on one's own 501 papers than to pursue your mission under someone else's management. There may be financial, managerial, structural, and community perception concerns to consider so be careful of any partnerships.

Where's the Money?

The five largest sources of grants are the federal government, foundations, other non-profit organizations, corporations (sponsorships), and individuals, in that order. There are literally hundreds of thousands of websites that may or may not help you write a grant to get some of that money.

In the meantime, here is a list of the largest Federal government grant programs.

The Catalog of Federal Domestic Assistance – a searchable compendium of all grants and public assistance programs currently funded by the U.S. government. Eligible groups, application processes, and contact information is listed for each program.

- The Federal Commons – "An Internet grants management portal serving the grantee organization community."
- Inter-Agency Electronic Grants Committee
- Department of Commerce's Federal Grants Page
- e-GRANTS, The Department of Education's (ED) portal site for electronic grants
- Department of Education's – CFO Grants and Contracts Information
- Department of Education's "School-to-Work" Grants Resources
- Department of Health Resources and Services Administration (HRSA) – Grants and Contracts
- Department of Justice – Ten Grants
- Department of Labor (DOL) – Employment and Training Administration
- Department of Transportation – Federal Highway Administration
- HRSA – Office of Rural Health Policy – Grants
- Department of Labor – Grant and Contract Information
- Department of Transportation (DOT) – Hazardous Materials Emergency Preparedness grant program
- DOT's State Highway Program Grants
- EPA's Grants Information Overview
- EPA's Environmental Research Grants
- EPA's Region IV Grants and Financial Assistance
- Housing and Urban Development (HUD) – Grants
- HUD – Community Development Block Grants – CDBG is the largest single federal grant program.
- National Cancer Institute – Research Projects Grants

- National Endowment for the Humanities – Grants and Applications
- GrantsNet – U.S. Department of Health and Human Services
- National Institutes of Health – Grants and Funding Opportunities
- Native American Programs – Grant Programs
- National Oceanic and Atmospheric Administration (NOAA)
- NOAA Sponsored – National Sea Grant
- NOAA's National Marine Fisheries Service Grants Information
- National Park Service (NPS) – Grants and Tax Credits
- National Science Foundation (NSF) – Overview of Grants and Awards
- Office of Electronic Commerce – Grants
- Office of Naval Research – Grants, Contracts and Acquisition
- OSHA's Susan Harwood Training Grants Program
- Social Security Administration – Office of Acquisitions and Grants
- U.S. Geological Survey's (USGS) Grants and Contracts Resources
- USGS Contracts and Grants Information
- U.S. State and Local – Housing: Competitive Grants

For a free list of the largest foundations in America, I suggest you visit your local library. Most libraries keep an informational copy of the largest grant directories in their reference section, along with directories of the largest non-profits, corporations, and possibly individual donors for in-house use by their patrons.

No matter the reason for the existence of your non-profit, there are five basic goals that need to be achieved on an annual basis in order to maintain financial survival.

1. Serve the targeted population
2. Keep the organization vibrant – visible, relevant, and attractive
3. Keep the finances healthy
4. Keep the organization in front of the community
5. Grow donor population

And, in order to achieve each of these goals, there must be an annual action plan that helps to prioritize the issues, assess their impacts on the goals, define the resources needed to successfully implement the action plan, and clearly identify the results achieved, based on resources allocated and predetermined goals.

These are all factors that must be dealt with in the beginning, because many of these same issues will have to be addressed in any funding applications for future grants.

Now if you are an individual seeking a grant, do not believe for one second you have been left out of the equation. Here is just one website that is designed to focus on you, the individual grant seeker, http://foundationcenter.org/getstarted/individuals.

The Proposal

Although grant sources are different, every grant proposal has five to seven basic elements, or sections, in each application. They are:

1. Executive Summary (may or may not be included)
2. The Mission Statement, Statement of Need, or Problem Statement
3. The Justification
4. The Procedures
5. The Evaluation
6. The Budget
7. Conclusion (only place where emotional summation is allowed, but do not over dramatize)

Before anyone attempts to start writing a funding proposal, I would recommend that you jot down a few notes under each area to get an understanding of what will be required in each section. Keep this pad handy throughout this entire process.

Now, starting with the mission statement -- it needs to cover goals, objectives, and a brief overview. Included in this section should be some organizational information. A few paragraphs of your organization's history and how structured, the population served and how needs are met, a descriptive list of programs offered, and how all of this meets the organization's mission statement. The mission statement along with the expertise of key staffers gives your proposal immediate credibility.

Adding one or two brief paragraphs about how the grantor's financial support will help you continue to meet the stated needs and fulfill the foundation's position of interest should close the mission statement section. Do not be cavalier (arrogant or careless) in this section. Even if your organization has received grants from this grantor before, fully describe how both sets of priorities will be met, just as if it was your first application.

The justification section needs to focus on the reasons why this proposal should be funded, the benefits to be received, and the expertise involved to accomplish all of this.

This portion could be seen as the main course of the proposal, because this is where you convince the grantor that your organization is the right one to fulfill their goals. Further, the manner in which you organization proposes to do this is the best and most cost-effective way to accomplish the desired outcomes!

Whether or not your organization already has an existing relationship with the grantor, take the time to explain why this is an important issue that needs to be addressed. Demonstrate your research in this area, some possible solutions, and why your organization's proposal is the solution of choice.

In the justification section, you have the opportunity and the obligation to explain how your organization came to recognize that this problem existed, the exact nature and extent of the problem, and the problematic impacts.

This means your proposal must have as much historical hard evidence as can possibly be gathered from local and state offices, any regional authorities, and studies completed by local colleges and universities. This kind of evidence should not only be geographical but quantitative and statistical.

The procedural section focuses on who will administer various portions of the proposal, how will this be done, and a timeline of events.

More specifically, the procedural section offers up details of your plan discussed in the justification section. You will spend approximately two to three paragraphs on the targeted audience and the specific activities that will be undertaken.

Included in this section should be a brief discussion on the planning that has already taken place so that the grantor knows your organization is well-prepared, in addition to letting them know who will do the work and how well qualified they are.

A further, more detailed discussion of the actual project is also appropriate here. This is the opportunity to explain the project in detail like where will it take place, and the start and ending dates.

A flow chart may be helpful in this area because it shows inputs, how the various parts of the project are interconnected, personnel functions, support services and facilities, and of course outputs (outcomes).

The evaluation section will describe how the agency's results will be evaluated based on the funding received. Will this be in house or outside firms, or both, and how often? Although I do not recall very much of my operations management class from my undergraduate days, I do recall PERT charts being touted as one of the most viable ways to measure any operation's success.

While I remember this class to be one of my more challenging courses, the Program Evaluation and Review Technique, while difficult for me personally, may prove very beneficial to some because of three important aspects of a PERT chart.

Those three aspects are the ability to chart specific sequential activities with milestones, the ability to construct an integrated network timeline, and the ability to chart critical paths. Then, one overall table to chart the project as it progresses. Another possible benefit of the PERT chart may be that it can be used to help justify your application's budget, at least in part.

One more point of consideration about the evaluation section is that there should be at least two parts to any evaluation. Not only should the project outcomes be evaluated and to what extent, but the process itself (the how to) must be judged and to what extent the process helped bring about the outcomes.

One of the best hidden benefits of any evaluation is that if it (the evaluation) has to be redesigned, it is cheaper to modify it if it has a good project design.

Because grantors want to know how well their dollars are spent, and that those dollars spent actually did some good, it is going to be necessary to decide how to assess the impact of your project early in the design phase. This includes data collected, records kept, and how both independently prove your outcomes. This kind of hard data will also help you in your future grant applications.

The last section, the budget, tells everyone how much is needed and what will this money be used for. So as they taught me in basic training, pay attention to the details!

The budget should not only include the cost of the project, down to the very last penny, but it should also contain data collection costs and recordkeeping costs.

Any good budget shows expected expenses and income, and breaks down the expenses into personal expenses, direct project expenses, and administrative and other overhead expenses.

It should also address whether or not other funds have been committed by additional sources, including in-kind contributions, such as free office space and technological donations.

The final portion of the budget section will address future funding needs and financial sustainability. While one should ask for more money than is needed, if your organization is fairly new without a long or no track record, be prepared to address this both in the budget and in the organizational description.

Grantors need to know that you will be around for the long haul, and one way to do this is to serve a need that no one else is interested in, or that no other grantor wants to fund. Both of these requirements can be partially fulfilled by making sure your organization has low facility and overhead costs.

The last section to be written should be the executive summary. This should be so compelling that it invites the reviewer to read further because it poses an indubitable recognition of a particular issue, contributing factors that may also be addressed, and the overspill effects of not addressing this issue, and/or the reverse.

This summary should be no more than two paragraphs, three at the very most. It should be the keystone of your entire proposal. This one-page document could be the critical decision factor in your project's acceptance.

As you are writing, do not forget your 7th-grade advanced English grammar lessons to always start each paragraph with the most important information first, and then use the remainder of that paragraph and the subsequent ones to strengthen your premise. After that, the only thing left to do is to proofread your work one, two, or maybe even three different times before the final submission, just like in 7th grade English class.

As one considers the possibility of a grant submission here are a few questions that should forever be in the forefront of the writer's mind.

- Is this a truly competitive grant?
- How qualified is your organization for this specific grant?
- Can your organization meet all the requirements?

Since grant reader's only have a limited amount of time to read numerous submissions, to help improve the overall readability of any grant proposal, it is a good idea to consider adding a short one-to-two sentence synopsis to give the grantor a quick peek at what your organization is proposing. Because this synopsis is so important, make sure this is the absolute last thing that is written, after the entire application has been completed, to both drive home your point and wrap everything up.

The synopsis should be placed just after the cover page and before the table of contents. This way the reviewer has a clear idea of what they are about to read and why. Also, since this is the first thing that is going to be read, remember the rule about first impressions!

While not everyone is up to the challenge of putting together a grant proposal or financing request, there are some impressive tools available to help individuals learn how to write a proposal and so much more.

However, one of the easiest ways to put together a grant proposal is to go directly to the source. Using the Freedom of Information Act Request, anyone may go to any Federal agency and request original copies of previously submitted successful business plans that were used to obtain grants, loans, and venture capital, as long as the requesting individual has a legitimate and verifiable need.

But, if one chooses to go it alone or as part of a group, remember, do not rush to give one's personal viewpoint. Instead, tell the story from the grantor's perspective as a way to demonstrate your understanding of the grantor's interests and not your organization's needs. All the while, you or your writer needs to remember that no matter how beautiful the prose, words cannot conceal a weak proposal.

An expert reader can tell from your proposal how much time actually went into planning and researching your project, so as they say in the neighborhood where I grew up, "come correct or do not come at all."

How To Propose

If you want to do more than lead your own non-profit, like be an impact grant writer, not unlike any other career, you need to be an informed individual of the goings on in the grant writing community.

To accomplish this means one must regularly network with other successful writers by joining professional associations, and spend a great deal of time in the library reading the latest periodicals and other pertinent literature.

People have a tendency to do business with individuals they know on a personal basis. Therefore, it would behoove any aspiring grant writer to try to maintain a travel budget. This way they can regularly meet with decision-makers at the Federal, state, and local levels, in addition to meeting with foundation board and staff members.

Attending optional grant writing workshops (meaning at your own expense), and other similar meetings can be very insightful and chocked full of helpful hints. So, if you do go, be prepared to take thorough notes to rely upon after the meeting. An added benefit may be that most, if not all of these expenses may be tax deductible.

If you are going to write a grant for yourself or someone else, you must do your research about the foundation or government agency. Not only do you need to be well-versed in their application guidelines, but you should also read their annual reports, and previously approved applications, if possible. Some groups will allow you to review previous applications while in their presence, because many do not allow photocopying of prior year submissions.

Talk to some previous award recipients to get their take on the grantor, and see if you can get a copy of the scoring sheet that is going to be used for the current award. If not, then see if a previous version is available for your review.

Two of the largest sources of grant information on the internet are found at www.grants.gov for Federal grants primarily (this site combines most of the Federal offerings listed at the beginning of the chapter), and www.fdncenter.org for private foundation grants. One may also want to search for state directories of grants such as http://www.foundations.org, which services the

Northern California Community Foundation, Inc.

Most foundations, like government agencies, have either a grant program officer or several key staff members who are key players inside the organization and in the grant decision making matrix. Do not be afraid to approach this individual or staff members with questions or to clarify details, because the more precise the proposal the better.

If you can get a meeting with a program officer or their staff, remember to again ask if you may review or copy as many previously approved applications as possible to help improve your own chances of receiving an award.

Whether or not a grant writer is a veteran, the U. S. Department of Labor publishes a 155-page guide that may help anyone develop a grant proposal for public or private funds, http://www.dol.gov/vets/grants/Final_VETS_Guide-linked.pdf. The Federal government also provides a user guides for anyone interested in Federal grants at http://www.grants.gov/assets/GDG_AppUser-Guide_0207.pdf.

For all practical purposes, most grants are a one-shot, no-second-chance deals, which means, an effective grant writer is not going to leave any detail unchecked. The exigency of the situation and the highly competitiveness of grant funding demands a no-excuses, no-mistakes tolerated attitude.

Writers will read and re-read every RFP (requests for proposals) and their subsequent application over and over again to make sure their submission has meet every requirement, and has done so at the highest levels of attainment. Grantors want to choose the application that has the best chance of long-term sustainability.

Remember, the grantor has already identified a specific gap that needs to be filled, and they do not want to see applications that duplicate others' work. Therefore, it is imperative that your organization is aware of what other non-profits are doing, in addition to initiatives being headed up by elected officials and other citizen groups that may duplicate or overlap on your proposed project.

The skilled writer knows how to build a team of primary stakeholders to do the same thing before, during, and after the application is completed, and all of this before the application is submitted. Together, all parties will highlight areas of concern, make notes, and ensure format and transmittal requirements all meet the grantor's stated guidelines of the RFP.

When all is said and done, there may be more than three or more separate individual reviews of the total package happening simultaneously. Have an expert read for content substance, a second one read for grammar and style, and a third read for guideline and criteria compliance.

Other important review considerations should be to make sure that the use of jargon is minimized, that core goals are continually emphasized, and resources are clearly identified. But the most important task of all is to ensure that all the major areas of the RFP are thoroughly addressed, and, in particular, any area that is scored in the application process is meticulously detailed.

One way to make sure these kinds of issues are addressed is to ask questions on any instructions that are unclear or ambiguous. One may even ask for an informal review by the grantor before final submission. The grantor's staff has the ability to address any potential shortcomings before anyone else is forced to point out the same, in a formal written assessment, which would mean that you did not get the grant.

In the end, the grant writer should be crafting a vision that clearly details who the organization is, where their strengths lie, why their goals are in tandem with the grantor, and how they expect to meet all the requirements and when. All of this has to be accomplished while following explicit details, even if the same question is asked repeatedly throughout the application, but in different ways.

To do this, an impact grant writer is a beautiful wordsmith that uses strong and colorful words to paint a vivid picture that motivates others into positive actions. To help drive home poignant points, I would recommend the use of pictures, because that old adage is true, a picture is worth a thousand words.

Photographs drive home emotional points, put a face on your project goals, and help promote your organizational direction in a way that even the best words cannot do, because photographs speak to both the hearts and minds. So make sure you use photographs whenever appropriate with a hard driving caption or maybe a powerful quote from an infamous moment in history, that are both substantiated by verifiable facts.

In the same way, a variety of graphs and tables should be used in place of narratives whenever possible. Not only do they fulfill the old photograph adage, but they also conserve space, same time for the reviewer, and may be used to convey complex data, economic or otherwise, that have significant impact trends.

If it is a short application, graphs, tables, and photographs will definitely conserve vital space.

Remember, the grant writer is telling a story, albeit in a little unconventional manner, and, as such, every piece of the story (the numbers, pictures, and words) must be unequivocally convincing.

Therefore, the organization's vision, mission, and leadership must be tied to outcomes, and their inputs; and, other activities must have a direct impact. Basically, this means including a logic model within your proposal.

By simple definition, a logic model is a diagram which simply describes the process of your program, and shows the links mentioned above with expected program outcomes; and, it details how those outcomes will be evaluated.

For more information or templates on logic models simply search for 'logic model' in Google, Bing, or the search engine of your choice, or checkout a few templates from the University of Wisconsin, http://www.uwex.edu/ces/pdande/evaluation/evallogicmodelworksheets.html.

When designing a logic model and thinking about outcomes, make sure that these outcomes are first tied to specific activities; second, outcomes must not only be measureable, but are also verifiable; and, third, identify as many measurable outcomes as possible. This will carry a great deal of weight with the application committee, because they can see how exactly how their money is going to impact the particular problem you have defined in your application.

To improve their credibility, a good grant proposal may include IRS tax exempt status letters, any strong letters of support, and a list of board members, including their relevant background histories, and their affiliations.

Although not required, a precise table of contents would help your readers navigate the proposal more quickly, and, a copy of last year's financial statement could provide that final piece of credibility.

All of this is to make the reviewer's job easy to read and score, and to help multiple decision-makers to focus on each criteria without distractions, to see the interconnectivity of the entire proposal.

Finally, a bound presentation signed in blue ink seems to make a very favorable impression; and, if you have an accountant, it would not be an unreasonable idea for that professional to review the document as well, if they are experienced. If not, see if they can recommend one that is experienced in this area.

Make sure your final product is delivered with a succinct cover letter before the due date and in time enough to reach the actual decision-maker's desk.

Now, if one is applying for a Federal grant, it may be worth careful consideration to explore the possibility of taking on a partner. A faith-based organization would be a good place to start because many already have some type of relationship with the Federal government, and, the government is always looking to increase these community organizers to help resolve and impact some social issues. Plus, it looks good to know that there is community collaboration or support for your application.

But, remember, they are not the only partners available. Do not forget there are citizen groups, individual players within a community, corporate sponsors, and maybe even a different type of organization than the one you represent, but, together, you two can collaborate on this one project.

In the end, a grant is a calculated risk that a grantor is taking based on the story of one's proposal, so make sure that your plan is credible and represents the best risk for the decision-makers.

To prove this to the decision-maker, there should be an action plan included that has clear benchmarks, a reasonable time schedule, and clear lines of accountability. Of utmost importance is that both the evaluation and managerial oversight plans must show true accountability, again to let the reviewer know that their risk is well-founded.

In the end, the grant, and the subsequent proposal are quid pro quo transactions in that both parties expect to get something of value for an exchange of some sort of interests. Even after the proposal is accepted (if it is accepted) there is no guarantee of equity in the end. This is one reason why grant writing is a true art form because the writer has to help the reader see what is not obvious.

The Art of Letterwriting

But before anyone rushes off to write a proposal, there are some private foundations that require grant-seekers to write a letter of inquiry (LOI) before submitting a complete proposal.

What the LOI does is to allow the foundation to quickly scan potential funding applicants to make sure their ideas are an ideal fit with the mission of the foundation. If there is a fit based on the LOI, the foundation may actually extend an invitation to the nonprofit to submit a full proposal.

So what is in this LOI?

Notwithstanding any guidelines published by the foundation, here are the basic requirements for any LOI, which is typically about three pages long and includes a budget.

1) At the top of the letter in the center of the page type, "Letter of Inquiry." [Part I]

2) Then you should have an unforgettable title that grabs the reader's attention. [Part II]

3) Next should be a one-, not more than two-sentence synopsis that is clear and compelling. [Part III]

4) These few sentences should tell the reader exactly who you are and what you do. Brainstorming will serve you well here.

5) Now comes the summation. Give the first sentence of this summary your greatest attention. It should be rewritten several times, because you need to strike an immediate tone of balanced selling that shows you know how to partner with the foundation to address a particular need. [Part IV]

6) Make sure to not know use any flowery language or vague ambiguities that sound good but do not add any true value.

7) Instead, give your reader concrete facts and use action verbs. Write in the active voice and not in the passive (7th-grade English). Make sure to give some specific details about how the project will operate.

8) Finally, this summary should definitively explain the issue at hand, and, more importantly, how will your organization address it, with the foundation's support of course.

9) Now comes a brief description of your organization that gives a full account of the management, the history, successes, and other relevant and pertinent facts. [Part V]

10) The final piece of this two – to three-page LOI should be an organizational budget, although it may not be required. This shows a commit-

ment of openness and gives the foundation an early look at how well your organization manages money. [Part VI]

11) Now make sure that you do not simply cut and paste from your proposal to your LOI. Your LOI should be fresh and inviting, because, remember, the goal is to get an invitation for a proposal from the foundation. Make every word count!

12) Think of your LOI as your resume. It is only a tool to get you an interview.

Money in the Bank

Although foundations do give away millions of dollars each year, getting that money is not necessarily a guarantee, even for the best of proposals.

So, before any organization starts putting together a proposal, they need to do their research. Since most foundations publish their philanthropic interests, one might check into purchasing a foundation subscription or check with your local library, because most major libraries have a subscription purchased for public use.

However, there is one other free option that is available for fundraising seekers, http://www.fundsnetservices.com/.

Most foundations are formed because their founders want to make sure things they care about continue getting attention long after they have passed away. There are almost approximately 100,000 foundations operating in the U. S., building relationships locally, across specific states, and across the nation.

So, when it comes to submitting a proposal to one of these foundations, you need to make sure that your proposal lines up with their published interests and shows your organization's history of success. Finally, your proposal needs to demonstrate strong reporting that will honestly measure your outcomes, even if those outcomes are not what was predicted or expected.

Finally, remember that most foundations receive exponentially more applications than those that are funded, so an organization may have to submit several applications to the same foundation before they are ever funded. Therefore, there are two characteristics a grant writer and a non-profit should have – persistence and a thick skin.

While foundations are a major source of funding for non-profits, do not forget that there are some matching grants available at the state level that may be used to abet both Federal and private grants.

The Council on Foundations, www.cof.org, while not directly supporting grant seekers, is still an excellent informational and networking resource

So when it gets right down to asking for money, here are a few strategic guidelines that need to be maintained.

- Do not ask for such a low estimate that it is unrealistic. This shows a lack of planning and research.
- Do not artificially inflate your estimates, because this too will be received as an ill-conceived project.
- Do not ask a grantor for an unreasonably high amount of money when their history shows that they only give modest amounts of money. This fact should be uncovered in your research. For example, if the grantor has a normal range of $10,000, then do not submit an application for $20,000 or more. But, maybe $12,000 – $13,000 might be a reasonable application request.
- Be prepared to address the possibility of receiving the funding in increments, quarterly or otherwise.
- Be prepared to issue milestone reports or have clear milestones identified that justify future funding allocations.
- Do not forget to address the question of is there going to be a need for additional funds from other sources?
- Will your organization be able to stand alone financially in the future?
- Are there going to be regular/annual fundraising campaigns for the future? If so, how? And how often?

When all is said and done do not forget your manners. If your application is approved and funding is granted, make sure to write a thank you note. If your application is denied, call and politely ask why was it rejected. If this does not work to your satisfaction, follow up with a written letter to ask for some specific guidance or pointers for future applications.

The Last Word

Everyone has money challenges. And the truth is that these challenges are all the same for the rich and poor alike – too much money and/or not enough money. I know some of you are saying to yourself, "Yea right. If you are rich, how can one have too much money or not enough money?"

But consider this. If you are rich, you are forever asking yourself if those around you are there for you or because of your money. Money also gives people individual and immediate notoriety, which makes the owner of the money an instant target. Thus, one may have too much money. So then, one begins to serve the money, by spending so much time trying to protect the money, instead of the money serving the owner. Money (mammon) becomes the master.

Further, if you are wealthy, you still do not have enough money. Again, consider these facts. If a wealthy person used only their money to maintain their lavish lifestyles that money would slowly dwindle away to nothing.

As much as I love Michael Jackson's talent and music, as an outsider looking in, Michael appears to have been a victim of his own success. Tragically, it now appears that Michael is worth more dead than alive. Cars, servants, airplanes, property, professional advisers, and so on all cost money; and, therefore are expenditures or bills to be paid at some point in the future. Thus, one may not have enough money. Again, mammon becomes the master because one has to work harder to make more money to spend more money. And yet again, the Bible proves itself true (Matthew 6:24).

But remember this. Money is neither good nor bad, it's just is. It is what one does with the money that is either good or bad.

So the wealthy learn how to use other people's money, at a much reduced rate (interest rate), to finance every aspect of their lifestyle.

At the beginning of the book, I spend some time teaching that money is forever on the move. It moves when people borrow money, lend money, and spend money. By borrowing at a lower cost and lending at a higher cost, income increases, as a general rule, as money is shifted around the world for any and all sorts of reasons. In a simplified manner, spending money increases one income while simultaneously decreasing another's income.

All of this money movement is *Funny Money.*

When I first pitched the idea of *Funny Money*, most people laughed me right out of their office. I was told my idea was too – *something*. It was too *black*. It was too *ghetto*. It was too *street*. It was too *unconventional*. It was too *narrow*. It was too *broad*. It was too *womanly*. It was too *corny*. It was too *poor*. It was too *simple*. Finally, I was told it was just a losing idea because there have been too many books written about the subject already and from well-known authors.

Although I clearly felt otherwise about my idea, the next several days were difficult for me. While none of the words were directed at me personally (or maybe they were and I was just too naïve to know any better), I did not feel very good about myself. Despite those words, they did not change the fact that I knew that *Funny Money* was also too real and so present, and it knew no color or gender boundaries. In sense, *Funny Money* had moved from the street to the boardroom.

After taking some time off to gather myself, I prepared to return to a job I hated, which was no different from the same plan I had if the comments had been positive. I am sure it was a mutual feeling shared by my employer because I was an outspoken employee who was not accustomed to being a "yes man." But I was tired of being thankful for scraps. Little did I know my journey was just beginning.

It wasn't long after those meetings that I found myself standing in line at the unemployment office. Then the feeling was real. I felt like a loser.

Most people do not that I am a very shy introverted person. So this unemployment experience was very intimidating for me. It was like my personal feelings or failings were being put on public display for some unknown reason.

As I sat down and waited for my name to be yelled out across open space filled with strange faces, I decided that I could not go through with it. Even then, I had to muster up the courage to stand up and leave. But when I finally did make that decision, I immediately made a beeline for the door!

Just as my hand reached for the rail, I heard my whole name being yelled out across the expanse of space and strangers. I stood there motionless for a moment. I slowly turned around and found everyone in the room staring at me. I had only felt this kind of shame once before. But this time, I had no reason to be ashamed. I had done nothing wrong. But that did not help me shake off those feelings. As I turned to walk toward the little woman with the big voice, I stumbled.

What else could happen? In retrospect, I have to admit it was funny, if it was someone else. But it wasn't anyone else, it was me.

I fell right there! All of my papers flew out of my hand and my face was full of dirty carpet. Everyone burst into unanimous laughter.

The remainder of that meeting was a complete blur. Afterwards, I was numb the entire ride home.

When I finally realized the totality of everything that had happened, there was only one emotion remaining – rejection. Rejected was the only feeling left for me to feel. It was the most liberating feeling in the world!

Although no one had said these words to me directly, they might as well have called me a loser. Then I remembered the most important and most overlooked fact of all. God only used losers to change the world, or so it seems.

Adam lost the garden. Cain murdered his brother. Noah was a nobody. Moses was a throw away who was convicted of identity theft. Then he became a slave, a murderer, a runaway, and a highly criticized leader. Rehab was a strumpet.

David was the apple of God's eye, and he was an adulterer and a murderer. Solomon had the wisdom of God and he had several wives who worshipped pagan gods. Job was considered a friend of God's, but he did not know how to pick his own friends. Jonah was food for Moby Dick and God's emissary. Paul wrote half of the *New Testament,* after he had persecuted the disciples of Jesus. And all of Jesus' disciples, the true Apostles, were the original rejects.

Everyone that God used had a flaw, a very human flaw, in their personality somewhere, and maybe some pride. But, they also had a heart, a yearning, to do the right thing even when it was the most unpopular thing. And, they were all considered losers by the world's standard in one way or another.

And consider this, Noah, the amateur, built the ark that was beat down with wind and rain for 40 days and 40 nights. And, he ended up on a mountain top saving lives. The Titanic was built by professionals. It ended up at the bottom of sea taking lives on its maiden voyage.

But here is the liberating part.

When people already expect you to fail, it frees you up to live. And once you believe or know something to be true, no manner of words can stop you!

This is a lesson most people do not learn until something tragic happens. There are three very good movies that make this point so well, although each movie does it from a different viewpoint.

In the *Last Holiday,* Queen Latifah was in love with LL Cool J, but she was too shy to tell him so. Actually she was too shy to do anything until she hit her head and received a diagnosis of death. She makes a dramatic statement about walking around with your head down all one's life, waiting for something big to happen. But, it wasn't until she hit her head that she could lift up her head to see, suddenly, the beauty of the world opened up to her in an amazing and brand new way. And the entire time all of this was happening she had only one confidante – God.

Jim Carey and his wife had everything, the perfect life, if you will. But they were dead inside. But when they lost everything, they started living life in a whole new way. Then they realized that helping themselves was not enough. That is when the *Fun with Dick and Jane* really began. The impossible became the only possibility.

Morgan Freeman had the right idea about living, but no money because he always did the responsible thing by his family. Jack Nicolson had the money but no life. It was only when death brought the two together did they change the worlds around them, and themselves. Their *Bucket List* was actually a prescription of what a life fulfilled looks like. I think it was a *Bucket List* because they were trying to squeeze a lifetime into a few months. So when they each died, all they carried with them was what they could fit into their buckets of memories – happy memories of a life fulfilled with no regrets.

My point is only when we have nothing to lose do we start living. That is why my initial rejection was so liberating. I was finally free, but freedom comes at a cost. I had a choice. I could go home and sulk about my circumstances or I could play the hand I had been dealt and use it to my advantage. I chose option number two. In truth, all things lined up as if the choice was already made for me.

So, I became the poster child for *Funny Money.* Using the same teachings I explained in this book, I went home and did two things. I rearranged my debts based on my new wages, and I intensified my efforts in finishing *Funny Money.*

Knowing that everything is negotiable, I renegotiated a temporary reduction in my monthly mortgage payment, I reduced all of my living expenses, and I even managed to regularly help my best friend, all while drawing unemployment. Mind you, prior to all of this, I had paid my debt down to as little as possible; and, I had managed to secure a monthly recurring income from a prior investment. I also called all of my creditors and explained my circumstances before they ever had to call me.

I am not saying it was easy, because it truth it was very hard. But, I had to put all the shame out of my mind and determine to succeed. I learned how to make better financial decisions on less than a shoestring budget; and, I learned how to mix and match decisions and programs to fit my needs for the moment, much like we all do with clothing.

Then, I got up every single day just as if I was going to work, in whatever attire suited my mood. I diligently worked on finding a new job, as required by the unemployment laws of my state; and, I worked doubly hard on getting every detail of *Funny Money* correct and complete.

Even though I could have given up on *Funny Money* and my dream, it would not have been authentic because I would have been giving up based on the words of others, and not by my own choice. That would have left me with all kinds of doubts and questions for the remainder of my life. That was a risk not worth taking. So I diligently applied myself in every way possible to all the tasks at hand. I have never been challenged more in my life thus far. And I have never been happier. I learned how to use laughter instead of tears, and I learned how to encourage myself instead of seeking the approval of others.

All of this leads me to the point of the power of words – whether they are words you speak to yourself or words that others speak into your life. Words are important. They can build you up or tear you down.

If they were not so important, why do you have to sign so many documents at closing for the purchase of a home or a car? If words are not important, why is there a legal disclosure sent with every credit card offer in the mail? If words are not important, why does the stock market move on the words of a few select individuals (when compared to the masses of people)? Why do gas prices move higher on pure speculation – words? Why is Congress full of lawyers? And why does every law have a loophole in it? Behind all of these words are, you guessed it, *Funny Money!*

If I had let the words of others take root in my spirit over my own words, I would have failed without ever starting. Although my words did not appeal to some, for whatever reason, my words clearly define the situation for some 42 million individuals.

According to the U. S. Census Bureau, in 2009, there were 42.9 million people living in poverty. That was 14.3 percent of the U. S. population. But, I believe a great deal more Americans would consider themselves to be poor today with 8.8 percent unemployment, a trillion dollar housing problem, and pocket books that are completely subject to the whim of gas prices.

These individuals know the power of my words!

Consider this, Wall Street made millions putting people into homes they knew they could not afford through adjustable rate mortgages. That's *Funny Money.* And Wall Street stands to make millions more by foreclosing on those same homes, sometimes with fraudulent documents. That's *Funny Money.* The federal government having to come to the rescue of Wall Street, big businesses, insurance companies, and automakers, all at taxpayer's (your) expense. That's *Funny Money.*

But here is what's not so funny – a single mother goes to work every day and struggles to take care of her children on nearly minimum wage salary; and, they live paycheck to paycheck. That's *Funny Money.* A father works more than two jobs to provide for his family, to the point that his family barely knows his face. That's *Funny Money.* An accomplished, as yet unmarried female cannot figure out why her budget keeps coming up short, just as she hears keys jingling in the front door. It's her part-time boyfriend, full-time, non-tax deductible dependent. That's *Funny Money.* But why isn't anyone laughing?

Here's the reality. We are living or reliving a *Tale of Two Cities*, the story that Charles Dickens used to describe the years up to and including the French Revolution.

> *"It was the best of times, it was the worst of times, it was the age of wisdom, it was the age of foolishness, it was the epoch of belief, it was the epoch of incredulity, it was the season of Light, it was the season of Darkness, it was the spring of hope, it was the winter of despair, we had everything before us, we had nothing*

before us, we were all going direct to Heaven, we were all going direct the other way – in short, the period was so far like the present period, that some of its noisiest authorities insisted on its being received, for good or for evil, in the superlative degree of comparison only."

Make no mistake; we are in the middle of a financial revolution. If you do not have some sort of financial plan for your family's future or have some control over how you earn a living, or if you do not know how to make better financial decisions than you did yesterday, then you should be seriously concerned.

The writing is on the wall (Daniel 5:1-31).

Whether we believe it or not, sometime in the near future Social Security is going to change, Medicare and Medicaid are going to decrease their rolls, and so too will food stamps and other welfare programs. This means that those who used to depend on the government for their survival are not going to be in that position much longer. And all of these changes are going to have untold rippling effects throughout the U. S. economy! That's *Funny Money.*

Funny Money is not just an idea that I had ten years ago. It is an idea that has withstood the test of time.

It was first seen in the Bible. Cain tried to offer a less than honorable gift to The Lord; Abram and Sarai in Egypt; Joseph; Israel's departure from Egypt; David; Solomon; the Prophets; and, Ananias and Sapphira in the *New Testament.*

More recent history includes Thomas Jefferson who abhorred debt, but always had debt. President Jefferson died bankrupt and owing $107,000, $2 million in today's value. But it did not stop him from authoring the Declaration of Independence, expanding the country through the Louisiana Purchase, and launching the Lewis and Clark Expedition.

During World War II, former President Nixon won $6,000 in a poker game during his first two months in the U. S. Navy. He used these winnings to finance his first successful bid for Congress and then onto the presidency. Then he fleeced the country.

In March 2007, no one was counting foreclosures – not the federal government, not state governments, and certainly not cities or counties. Now there are so many foreclosures no one wants to count them, cannot get an accurate account of exactly how many foreclosures there are in our communities, and do not have accurate documentation to do either.

We live in conflict, no matter whom you are or where you are, and not just monetary conflict, although that is more than enough conflict. But, if you are reading this and you have ever experienced any of the feelings or events I am describing, or ever dreamed a dream that has been deferred, or simply desire a real solution to a financial problem, then I am talking to you. If you are one of those 42 million people, then I am talking to you because I used to be barely surviving also. That means that I know what it means to live a mediocre life, barely getting by, forever frustrated and all that comes with that frustration.

Jesus said in Mark 2:17, "They that are whole have no need of the physician, but they that are sick." (KJV) If your finances are sick, and your life is not on track for happiness, then this black, white, unconventional, corny, poor, street, losing, and rejected idea may just help you find the solution to the *Funny Money* in your life.

I can assure you of its existence, if you would but only look...

Appendices

Acceptance of Offer

Once you have established and agreed upon a debt repayment plan with a collection agency or a creditor, you need to have a copy of the accepted terms and settlement issues documented with a company representative's signature on it. This document is a must for your records before you start with any monetary transactions. This letter will be sent in conjunction with one of the letters in this appendix.

Your Name:
Complete Address (including any apartment numbers)
City, State, Zip Code
Home Telephone Number or Best Contact Number
Email Address (if you have one, preferred but not required)

Name of Credit Reporting Agency or Name of Company
Mailing Address
City, State, Zip Code
RE: Account number

Date:

Dear Creditor,

In response to the mutual settlement between myself and <your customer service representative's name>, <phone number>, made on <date>, this is a letter of confirmation regarding the acceptance of my offer and the agreed upon terms.

I am very pleased we were able to come to mutual terms to settle this matter and help me to pay this debt.

The CREDITOR and the DEBTOR have agreed that the present debt due is <$ amount balance>. The parties have agreed that the Creditor shall accept the sum of <$___ > as full payment on the debt. The payment will be made in cash and will result in a complete discharge of the debt.

Both the parties have agreed on the date for payment as <date>, which includes enough time for the company to mail this receipt back to the DEBTOR as agreed upon prior to final payment being made. If the DEBTOR fails to pay the agreed amount on <date>, the original amount owed by the DEBTOR will stand to be immediately due. <Credit Agency> is hereby authorized to act as the agent of the <creditor>.

The parties, their successors and the assignees are bound to abide by this agreement and the resulting benefits.

Company Representative Signature ____

Yours truly,

Your signature
Your name
Enclosed attachments (if any)

Date:

Your Name:
Complete Address (including any apartment numbers)
City, State, Zip Code
Home Telephone Number or Best Contact Number
Email Address (if you have one, preferred but not required)

Name of Credit Reporting Agency or Name of Company
Mailing Address
City, State, Zip Code
Ref: SSN – Your full Social Security Number

To Whom It May Concern:

I am writing this letter to dispute some errors found in my recent credit report received from your office. I have circled the items in dispute in red on the attached copy of my report.

(Note to the readers: Depending on how many errors you find, you will list each error that has been circled in red in a separate paragraph and explain why it is an error [inaccurate, incomplete, or outdated]. Enclosed are copies of [name the specific documents enclosed with this letter and listed in your enclosure list] documents that substantiate your dispute.

Each error along with the requested response from your office is listed in a separate paragraph. Number the paragraphs so that the company knows exactly how many errors you are disputing. (Two example paragraphs are listed below.)

First, you have my name and my social number listed incorrectly. The full and complete spelling of my name is______________________and my correct Social Security Number is __-__-__. Enclosed you will find a copy of my mortgage agreement that shows my full name and current address, a copy of my driver's license, and a copy of my Social Security card.

Second, each paragraph will nicely state the problem, provide proof that the item is incorrect, and then ask the agency to do a specific act to rectify the problem. I am requesting that the item be removed, corrected, or updated.

Please reinvestigate this (these) item(s) with all diligence, and (delete or correct) the disputed item(s) as soon as possible.

Sincerely,

//Sign//

YOUR NAME

Enclosure: (List and number all of the enclosures included with your dispute.)

Note: Regardless of the type of letter you choose to send, do not forget to sign your letter.

Sample verbiage for body of letter of acceptance of a verbal offer for debt settlement

Date:

Your Name:
Complete Address (including any apartment numbers)
City, State, Zip Code
Home Telephone Number or Best Contact Number
Email Address (if you have one, preferred but not required)

Name of Credit Reporting Agency or Name of Company
Mailing Address
City, State, Zip Code
Ref: SSN – Your full Social Security Number

To Whom It May Concern:

This is to confirm the settlement offer agreed upon by me and your customer service representative <name>, <phone no.> on <date.>

The amount we agreed to settle this debt in full is $_____. We also agreed all late payments or charge off references on this account will be removed from my credit file held at all three major credit bureaus.

If the above terms are acceptable to your company, please sign the attached letter of agreement and return the copy to me. Upon the receipt of the signed agreement, I will send you a money order or certified funds in the amount stated above.

Sincerely,

Encl: <list of attachments>

Sample verbiage for body of letter making a written offer without any discussions / or counter offer

Date:

Your Name:
Complete Address (including any apartment numbers)
City, State, Zip Code
Home Telephone Number or Best Contact Number
Email Address (if you have one, preferred but not required)

Name of Credit Reporting Agency or Name of Company
Mailing Address
City, State, Zip Code

To Whom It May Concern:

Re: <Account number>

Dear Sir/Madam,

It has taken me a long time to settle my financial problems. I am now in a position to take care of the debt held by your company.

I have the ability to settle this debt in the amount of $_____. If this is a counter offer, use this sentence in place of the previous one...I am able to counter your offer with $_____. However, any references to late payments or charge offs on this account must be deleted from my credit files held at the three major credit bureaus.

I hope we can resolve this matter quickly. I have several other companies I am currently conducting debt negotiations with and have limited funds at my disposal. I will be able to pay only those companies who are willing to meet my terms first. I have reached a settlement with a few creditors and am undergoing the process with the others. I doubt if I will have enough funds to pay any additional creditors if these negotiations continue past the end of this month.

If your company accepts the above terms, please sign the attached letter of agreement and send a copy to me. Only upon the receipt of the signed agreement, will I send you a money order in the amount stated above.

Sincerely,

<Your Signature>
<Your Name>

Second sample verbiage for body of letter making a written offer without any discussions (unsolicited offer)

Date:

Your Name:
Complete Address (including any apartment numbers)
City, State, Zip Code
Home Telephone Number or Best Contact Number
Email Address (if you have one, preferred but not required)

Name of Credit Reporting Agency or Name of Company
Mailing Address
City, State, Zip Code

Dear Creditor,

Re: Account Number

This is to notify you that I have sincerely wanted to settle this debt for a while, but due to a poor financial situation it was not possible until now. My present financial situation has allowed me to take some steps to take care of the debt referenced above. Thank you in advance for your willingness to work with me to resolve this debt.

I am able to pay your firm the total of $.......... to resolve this debt. I also request you remove all derogatory entries on my credit report held at the three major credit reporting agencies.

Incidentally, I am already in negotiations with several other companies to clear up other delinquent debts, and I have a moderate amount of funds to accomplish these goals. In all probability I can only come to business terms with you if you agree on my proposal outlined above. Fortunately, I have already attained agreeable settlements with a couple of my creditors and will not have any funds leftover if our negotiations continue past the end of this month.

I hope that the above terms and conditions are acceptable to your company. If you accept my proposal, please sign the attached letter to confirm our agreement and forward me a copy of the same. Upon receipt of your signed approval letter I will send you a money order in the agreed upon amount stated above.

Thank you in advance for your assistance.

Sincerely,

Your signature
Your name
<Enclosed attachments>

Letter to the credit card companies asking for alternate payment plan

Date:

Your Name:
Complete Address (including any apartment numbers)
City, State, Zip Code
Home Telephone Number or Best Contact Number
Email Address (if you have one, preferred but not required)

Name of Credit Reporting Agency or Name of Company
Mailing Address
City, State, Zip Code
RE: Account number

To Whom It May Concern,

I am presently going through some difficult financial times and fear that I will not be able to meet my monthly obligations to your firm. I do not want to declare bankruptcy and want to try and work out an alternate payment plan so that I will not default on this debt.

I would like to suggest that you close my account, waive any additional interest payments, and accept a new balance of <50% or whatever you propose> of what I currently owe. I can afford to make a monthly payment of $__________ for <however many months you calculate is necessary to pay the debt in full, the shorter the better.>

(Relate your financial trouble, only as much as is required for official purposes)

If you are unwilling to adjust the payment plan, I will have no other choice but to default on this account and possibly file for bankruptcy.

Thank you in advance for you assistance.

Sincerely,

Your Name

Your Address

Credit Bureau Error Report			
Type of Error Found	**Equifax** P.O. Box 740241 Atlanta, GA 30374-0241	**TransUnion** P.O. Box 390 Springfield, PA 19064-0390	**Experian** P.O. Box 2104 Allen, TX 75013- 2014
Example: John Doe Credit Corp.		**Action:** Reported incorrect account history on charge card, mailed dispute form on 3/10/08	

House Checklist			
Square Footage		Number of Bedrooms	
Number of Baths		Overall Condition	
Closet and Storage Space		Basement	
Fireplace		Yard/Outdoor Space	
Patio or Deck		Garage	
Age/Quality of Windows		Age/Condition of Roof/Gutters	
Energy Efficiency (Make sure you find out the energy cost of your new home in the summer and winter from the service provider, in addition to power outage history for the area. You do not want be in an area where the power goes out once or twice every week or month.)			

Neighborhood Checklist			
Condition of Nearby Properties		Traffic	
Noise Level		Safety	
Quality of Schools		Age/Mix of Residents	
Children		Parking	
Zoning Regulations		Fire Protection	
Police		Snow Removal	
Garbage Service			

Proximity to Services Checklist			
Supermarket		Schools	
Work		Shopping	
Child Care		Hospitals	
Doctor/Dentist		Parks and Recreation	
Restaurants and Entertainment		Place of Religious Worship	
Public Transportation		Airport	
Highways			

Program	Max Amount	Percent of Guaranty	Use of Proceeds	Maturity	Max Interest Rate	Fees	Eligibility	Benefits
7(a) Loans	$2m	85% for loans ≤ $150K 75% for loans ≥ $150K	Working capital, expansion, construction, equipment, refinancing, line of credit, inventory, etc.	Depends on the ability to repay. Generally working capital & equipment is 5-10 yrs.	Loans < 7 yrs: Prime + 2.25% Loans ≥ 7 yrs: Prime + 2.75% Rates can be up to 2% higher for loans < $50K	2% guaranty for loans ≤ $150K; 3% for loans ≤ $700K; 3.5% for loans > $700K; 3.75% for loans > $1m.	For-profit small business; must show good character, credit and ability to repay	Long-term financing; fixed maturity; no ballons; no prepayment penalty (under 15yrs.)
SBA Express	$350K	50%	Revolving lines of credit or a term loan	See 7(a)	Loans ≤ $50K; Prime + 6.5% Loans > $50K: Prime + 4.5%	See 7(a)	See 7(a)	Faster turn-around, streamlined process; easy-to-use line of credit
Community Express	$250K	Same as 7(a)	Revolving lines of credit or a term loan	See 7(a)	See 7(a)	See 7(a)	Businesses in HUBZone or LMI areal; all loans ≤ $25K	Faster turn-around, streamlined process; easy-to-use line of credit; technical assistance provided
Patriot Express	$500K	Same as 7(a)	Same as SBAExpress	See 7(a)	See 7(a)	See 7(a)	Veteran, active duty military, reservist, Nat'l Guard member, spouse of any of the above, or a widowed spouse of a service member who died during service	Faster turn-around, lower rate maximums than other Express programs; electronic application

Program	Max Amount	Percent of Guaranty	Use of Proceeds	Maturity	Max Interest Rate	Fees	Eligibility	Benefits
CAPLines	$2m	Same as 7(a)	Seasonal working capital needs; advances against existing inventory & receivables; consolida-tion of short-term debt	Up to 5 yrs.	Same as 7(a) except the Standard Asset-Based no fee restric-tion. (Fee disclosure to be SBA required.)	See 7(a)	Existing Businesses	Short-term working capital; lines of credit allows business to get con-tracts; can be used to create or finance current assets
Interna-tional Trade	$2m	Same as 7(a)	Only for acquisition of long-term fixed assets	Up to 25 yrs.	See 7(a)	See 7(a)	Small businesses engaged/ about to engage in internat'l trade or adversely affected by competi-tion from imports	Long-term financing for land and build-ing where assets are used to produce exports
Export Working Capital	$2m	90% for loans up to $1.5m	Short-term working capital loans for exporters	Matched single trans-action cycle or about 1yr. line of credit	No cap	See 7(a)	Exporters who need short-term working capital	Allows for financ-ing for exporting without disrupting domestic financing; inexpen-sive min. guaranty fee

Program	Max Amount	Percent of Guaranty	Use of Proceeds	Maturity	Max Interest Rate	Fees	Eligibility	Benefits
Micro-loans	$35K	N/A	Same as 7(a) except cannot be used to repay existing debt	Not to exceed 6 yrs.	Negotiable	No guaranty fee	Only businesses in greater Charleston area	Direct loans from nonprofit intermediary; fixed rate financing
504 Loans	$1.5 -$4m, depending on type of business	Project costs financed by: Up to 40% from SBA 100% guarantied debenture; 50% from Lender 10-20% from Equity	Long-term fixed assets such as land, buildings and equipment	10-20 yrs.	Fixed rate on 504 loan established when debenture backing is sold	Under 3%	For-profit businesses that do not exceed $7.5m in tangible net worth and do not have average income over $2.5m for past 2 yrs.	Fees under 3%; long-term fixed rate; low down payment; no balloons

Type of Business	Costs	Management	Liability Protection	Income Tax Characteristics
Sole Proprietorship	Minimal	N/A	None	Reported on Schedule C of owner's tax form
1 Member LLC	Check with state for filing fee & annual report fee costs; may be attorney cost to form	N/A	Yes, but may be limited by owner actions	Can be reported on Schedule C of owner's tax form
LLC, multi-members	Check with state for filing fee & annual report fee costs; may be attorney costs to form & associated accounting costs for compliance	Flexible- many options for structure	Yes, but may be limited by owner's actions	Generally taxed as partnership; may choos taxation as corporation; considered best organization to hold real estate for liability protection and flexible taxation
General Partnership	Attorney costs for the formation; accounting costs for compliance; may be no or limited filing fees	<u>Must</u> have written partnership agreement; limited partners may not participate in day to day management	Limited partners protected; general partner has no protection	Complicated taxation - Subchapter K of IRS Code; but permits preferred returns and other earnings distributions - other tax benefits may apply
C Corporation	Fees may be significant; attorney costs for formation & accounting costs for compliance; annual taxes/other fees may be significant if earnings or assets are significant	Flexibility - set forth in corporation bylaws, articles, and shareholder agreements	Yes, except for shareholder's actions	Overall taxes may be low w/great planning to avoid double taxation potential; may have some positive small business impacts
S Corporation	Fees may be significant; attorney costs for formation & accounting costs for compliance; annual taxes/other fees may be significant if earnings or assets are significant	Flexibility - set forth in corporation bylaws, articles, and shareholder agreements	Yes, except for shareholder's actions	Not as flexible as partnership, see IRS Code Subchapter S; other tax implications may apply

INDEX

Made in the USA
Monee, IL
05 November 2026

67811383R10286